Advances in Intelligent Information Processing
Tools and Applications

Statistical Science and Interdisciplinary Research

Series Editor: Sankar K. Pal *(Indian Statistical Institute)*

Description:

In conjunction with the Platinum Jubilee celebrations of the Indian Statistical Institute, a series of books will be produced to cover various topics, such as Statistics and Mathematics, Computer Science, Machine Intelligence, Econometrics, other Physical Sciences, and Social and Natural Sciences. This series of edited volumes in the mentioned disciplines culminate mostly out of significant events — conferences, workshops and lectures — held at the ten branches and centers of ISI to commemorate the long history of the institute.

Platinum Jubilee Series

Statistical Science and
Interdisciplinary Research — Vol. 2

Advances in Intelligent Information Processing

Tools and Applications

Editors

B. Chanda

C. A. Murthy

Indian Statistical Institute, India

Series Editor: **Sankar K. Pal**

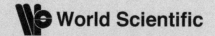

World Scientific

NEW JERSEY · LONDON · SINGAPORE · BEIJING · SHANGHAI · HONG KONG · TAIPEI · CHENNAI

Published by

World Scientific Publishing Co. Pte. Ltd.

5 Toh Tuck Link, Singapore 596224

USA office: 27 Warren Street, Suite 401-402, Hackensack, NJ 07601

UK office: 57 Shelton Street, Covent Garden, London WC2H 9HE

British Library Cataloguing-in-Publication Data
A catalogue record for this book is available from the British Library.

ADVANCES IN INTELLIGENT INFORMATION PROCESSING:
Tools and Applications
Statistical Science and Interdisciplinary Research — Vol. 2

Copyright © 2008 by World Scientific Publishing Co. Pte. Ltd.

ISBN-13 978-981-281-898-0
ISBN-10 981-281-898-7

Printed in Singapore.

Foreword

The Indian Statistical Institute (ISI) was established on 17th December, 1931 by a great visionary Professor Prasanta Chandra Mahalanobis to promote research in the theory and applications of statistics as a new scientific discipline in India. In 1959, Pandit Jawaharlal Nehru, the then Prime Minister of India introduced the ISI Act in parliament and designated it as an *Institution of National Importance* because of its remarkable achievements in statistical work as well as its contribution to economic planning.

Today, the Indian Statistical Institute occupies a prestigious position in the academic firmament. It has been a heaven for bright and talented academics working in a number of disciplines. Its research faculty has done India proud in the arenas of Statistics, Mathematics, Economics, Computer Science, among others. Over seventy-five years, it has grown into a massive banyan tree, like the institute emblem. The Institute now serves the nation as a unified and monolithic organization from different places, namely Kolkata, the Head Quarter, Delhi and Bangalore, two centers, a network of six SQC-OR Units located at Mumbai, Pune, Baroda, Hyderabad, Chennai and Coimbatore, and a branch (field station) at Giridih.

The platinum jubilee celebrations of ISI have been launched by Honorable Prime Minister Dr. Manmohan Singh on December 24, 2006, and the Government of India has declared 29th June as the "Statistics Day" to commemorate the birthday of Professor Mahalanobis nationally.

Professor Mahalanobis, was a great believer in interdisciplinary research, because he thought that this will promote the development of not only Statistics, but also the other natural and social sciences. To promote interdisciplinary research, major strides were made in the areas of computer science, statistical quality control, economics, biological and social sciences, physical and earth sciences.

The Institute's motto of 'unity in diversity' has been the guiding principle of all its activities since its inception. It highlights the unifying role of statistics in relation to various scientific activities.

v

In tune with this hallowed tradition, a comprehensive academic programme, involving Nobel Laureates, Fellows of the Royal Society, and other dignitaries, has been implemented throughout the Platinum Jubilee year, highlighting the emerging areas of ongoing frontline research in its various scientific divisions, centres, and outlying units. It includes international and national-level seminars, symposia, conferences and workshops, as well as series of special lectures. As an outcome of these events, the Institute is bringing out a series of comprehensive volumes in different subjects under the title *Statistical Science and Interdisciplinary Research*, published by World Scientific Publishing, Singapore.

The present volume titled *Advances in Intelligent Information Processing: Tools and Applications* is the second one in the series. It has thirteen chapters, written by eminent scientists from different parts of the world, dealing with different aspects, characteristics and methodologies of intelligent information processing with real life applications. Both classical and modern techniques are used. Chapters on image and video processing mainly deal with challenging problems like curve evolution for partially occluded patterns, contour tracking, region classification, object category identification in video sequence, facial expression recognition, duplicate image detection for efficient video retrieval, and hardware architecture for pixel classification. Besides, the issues of uncertainty handling in class definition by integrating fuzzy sets and rough sets with an application on bioinformatics data, and the reuse of domain knowledge in soft computing framework for efficient modeling of intelligent systems are described in two chapters. I believe the state-of-the-art studies presented in this book will be very useful to readers.

Thanks to the contributors for their excellent research contributions and to volume editors Professors Bhabatosh Chanda and C.A. Murthy for their sincere effort in bringing out the volume nicely in time. Thanks are also due to World Scientific for their initiative in publishing the series and being a part of the Platinum Jubilee endeavor of the Institute.

December 2007
Kolkata

Sankar K. Pal
Series Editor and
Director, ISI

Preface

Intelligent information processing methodologies adopt one of the two major approaches: model based or rule based. In the first approach a model is developed from the sufficient training data, the domain knowledge as well as the knowledge of the physical process giving out the data. All the subsequent analysis and decision making is based on the model itself. Hence, though does not cover much wide spectrum, the method developed by this approach is very robust. Second approach develops a rule-base based on extensive and meticulous observation of the system and its outcome as well as reasoning. This approach covers a wide spectrum of situation, but may not be as reliable as the first one.

In the first paper, Joshi and Brady have developed a novel non-parametric mixture model for the histogram of image intensities. This leads to the evolution of level sets in a Bayesian framework, which are applied to region classification and image segmentation problem. The experimental results on medical images demonstrate the effectiveness of the method. The next paper by Chattopadhyay and Mukherjee, describes the level set based curve evolution method for pattern generation in 2D space. The reaction-diffusion and shape optimization models are used to derive constraints for curve evolution. The proposed model is extended successfully to the reconstruction of partially occluded patterns, which is a problem in Computer vision. The problem of instability in curve evolution, while using active contours for object segmentation and tracking, is tackled by Srikrishnan and Chaudhuri in the third paper. They propose the use of an additional tangential component for stability while the shape of the curve remains intact. The next article deals with object tracking, object recognition and object reconstruction using a completely different approach, i.e., general state modeling and estimation. In this work, the method proposed by Derichs, Deutsch, Wenhardt, Niemann and Denzlery here is based on determining the next best view in active state estimation using the concept of mutual information. The problem of 3D object recognition is tackled by Zografos and Buxton in the fifth article. Their method combines linearly a few 2-dimensional intensity images of the same 3d object taken from vicinity but arbitrary viewpoints to obtain an overall idea about the object. They finally used an evolutionary algorithm for obtaining the 'optimal parameters for linear combination of views. Harit and Bharatia and Chaudhury present an approach for object category identification in video sequences. The proposed approach integrates object model knowledge with the perceptual organization process in human beings. The methods we have presented so far are for object segmentation, tracking and recognition in image or video. Emotion and expression recognition from an image is also an active research area nowadays. The article of Buciu and Pitas is on recognition of six basic facial expressions. The authors have developed a novel way of extracting features using discriminant non-negative matrix factorization algorithm. They successfully demonstrated the superior performance of their methodology over the competing strategies. Another active research area is retrieval of image and video from a large database. Search can be made more efficient and recall can be improved if the duplicate images can be trimmed off. Ghosh, Gelasca, Ramakrishnany and Manjunath tackled the problem of duplicate image detection in very large databases in the next article. They used a 12 dimensional descriptor based on Fourier Mellin transform. The detection of duplicate images is dependant o the dissimilarity measure. Another application of dissimilarity analysis may be found in the change detection problem in satellite images. Patra, Ghosh and Ghosh exploited the properties of self-organized feature map to reach a satisfactory solution to this problem. Another two important aspects of dealing with image and video data are compression and processing time. Liu, Zhu, Bosch and Delp provide an excellent review article describing the recent advances in video compression techniques. They additionally described the latest video coding standard. Compression is an essential tool for efficient storage and transmission of data. Another essential consideration is the processing time required for a given task. Hardware implementation of an algorithm always improves its efficiency in terms of speed. In the next article by Bishnu, Bhowmick, Bhattacharya, Kundu, Murthy and Acharya, a combinatorial approach is described for designing a hardware architecture for the classification each pixel into one of the three classes, namely, crest, valley and slope. The proposed pipeline design can be used to build a fast coprocessor for online finger print analysis. Intelligent information processing system should be able to handle uncertainties. Almost all the methods presented so far have some means of satisfying this criterion. For example, self-organized feature map, which is used in change detection in satellite image, has inherent capability to handle uncertainties to some extent. Rough set and fuzzy set based tools also have similar capabilities.

Maji and Pal propose a roughfuzzy C-medoids algorithm to select most informative bio-bases for amino acid sequence analysis in bioinformatics. The superior performance of the proposed method is demonstrated on different protein datasets. As indicated in the beginning the success of an intelligent information processing system greatly depends on the proper exploitation of domain and process knowledge. In the final article, Pedrycz describes the concept of knowledge reuse in the computational intelligence models. New performance index is defined whose minimization helps in the most effective level of knowledge reuse. The utility of the proposed methodology is demonstrated on fuzzy rule based systems.

First of all we express our heart-felt gratitude towards the contributors of this volume. This volume contains extended version of some articles presented at ICCTA. So we are grateful to Organizing Committee and Programme Committee of ICCTA to allow us to use the review reports of the articles. We also like to thank the reviewers of the articles processed for this volume. We also express our gratitude to the Indian Statistical Institute Platinum Jubilee Core Committee and the Series Editor for giving us opportunity to edit this volume. Finally, the help of Mr. Dilip Gayen and Mr. Indranil Dutta to prepare the camera-ready version is gratefully acknowledged.

Bhabatosh Chanda
C. A. Murthy
Editors

Contents

Chapter 1

Non-parametric Mixture Model Based Evolution of Level Sets

Niranjan Joshi and Michael Brady

Wolfson Medical Vision Laboratory,
University of Oxford,
Parks Road, Oxford OX1 3PJ, UK.
njoshi@robots.ox.ac.uk

We present a novel region-based level set algorithm. We first model the image histogram with a mixture of non-parametric probability density functions (PDFs), whose use we justify. The individual densities in the mixture are estimated using a recently proposed PDF estimation method which relies on a continuous representation of discrete signals. A Bayesian framework is then formulated in which likelihood probabilities are given by the non-parametric PDFs and prior probabilities are calculated using an inequality constrained least squares method. The segmentation solution is spatially regularised using a level sets framework. The log ratio of the posterior probabilities is used to drive the level set evolution. We also take into account the partial volume effect, which is important in medical image analysis. Results are presented on natural, as well as medical, two-dimensional images. Visual inspection of results on a range of images show the effectiveness of the proposed algorithm.

1.1 Introduction

Segmentation is a fundamental image analysis technique and has found application in many fields, ranging from satellite imagery to medical imaging. Design of a typical image segmentation method involves modelling of the data and spatial regularisation of the segmentation solution. Here, we present a method in which we model the histogram of image intensities using a mixture model and regularise the segmentation solution using level set methods. Although the method presented in the rest of this paper is sufficiently general to be applied to any kind of image, indeed we provide such an example, we are mainly interested in medical applications, particularly colorectal cancer image analysis.

Finite mixture model(FMM) methods are widely used in image segmentation. They assume that the image is comprised of a finite number of classes and that the intensities of each class follow a certain distribution. Gaussian mixture models(GMMs) are a popular instance of FMM methods[Zhu and Yuille (1996); Paragios (2000)]. They have the advantage of simplifying analytical treatment of the problem. While the assumption of class Gaussianity works well in many situations, a more generalised approach is to use non-parametric probability density/mass functions (PDFs/PMFs) to model the individual classes. We adopt the latter approach for the reasons discussed in Sec. 1.2. We refer to our mixture model as a non-parametric mixture model(NPMM)[Joshi and Brady (2005); Joshi (2005)]. Several methods are available to estimate the class non-parametric distributions, such as: histograms and kernel density estimates[Izenman (1991)]. However, histograms need a large number of samples to give smooth estimates and the kernel density estimates need proper selection of the bandwidth parameter of the kernel. The NP-window method[Kadir and Brady (2005); Joshi (2005)] used here attempts to overcome both these drawbacks. This method is briefly explained in Sec. 1.3.

Level set methods have been used successfully for curve evolution. Typically, these curves coincide with the boundaries of the segmentation classes. Because of the implicit nature of level set curve evolution, they can accommodate changes in topology of the curve, for example, across successive slices of a medical image volume. Available level set methods can be broadly divided into three categories: boundary-based methods[Caselles *et al.* (1997)], region-based methods[Zhu and Yuille (1996); Kim *et al.* (2005)], and combination of both[Paragios (2000)]. In our method, we use region-based forces to evolve the level sets. The region based forces are calculated using knowledge of the NPMM of the image. Brief introduction to level set terminology and how we use them in our segmentation method are given in Secs. 1.5 and 1.6 respectively.

As we mentioned earlier, our work is motivated by application to medical images. Therefore, we also consider certain issues that are particularly important to this field, for instance, the partial volume effect (PVE). Due to the limited resolution of a medical image acquisition system, any single pixel/voxel in the image may contain more than one kind of physical tissues[Leemput *et al.* (2003); Joshi (2005)]. As a result the intensity value at this pixel is a linear (or nonlinear) function of the individual tissue intensities depending upon the acquisition modality. In certain medical images as many as 40% of the total pixels may be affected by the PVE. Hence it is important to take this effect into account while designing any of the analysis methods for such images. In Secs. 1.4 and 1.6, we describe how we take the PVE into account.

1.2 Need for Modelling Class Distributions Non-parametrically

Most of the statistical mixture model methods in the current medical image analysis literature assume Gaussianity for individual class PDFs. This leads to straightforward analytical treatment of the problem. While, theoretically, the noise distribution in a magnetic resonance (MR) image is a Rician distribution, towards high signal to noise ratio (SNR) this tends to be a Gaussian distribution [Sijbers (1998)]. A few methods are also reported to have performed special transformation of intensity values in order to increase the Gaussianity of the data, where the individual class PDFs do not follow Gaussian distribution [Zeydabadi *et al.* (2004)]. This is how generally the use of the Gaussian distribution assumption is justified in MR image segmentation. This holds better for brain MR images where field coil technology is sufficiently advanced to give better quality images and the images are intrinsically more or less piecewise smooth. However such assumptions may not hold true for MR images of the other body parts, e.g. the colorectum, in which we are particularly interested. Due to magnetic field inhomogeneities in the MR scanner, some parts of the image appear 'brighter' or 'darker' than other parts. This is referred to as the bias field distortion. The bias field distortion due to body coils in the case of colorectal MR images is of such magnitude that a significant residue remains even after applying available preprocessing methods. The segmentation of colorectal MR images involves dividing the image into the colorectum, tumour, and mesorectum. While the tumour tend to be a heterogeneous mass, the mesorectum is chiefly made up of layers of fat, blood vessels, and lymph nodes. Due to these anatomical properties the colorectal MR image is not piecewise smooth. See Fig. 1.1 for a visual illustration. As a result, the shapes of the distributions of the individual classes are distorted, usually in a way that is unpredictable. Figure 1.2 shows one such example of the class PDFs. Primarily, to take all these effects into account we model the class PDFs using non-parametric distributions. However at the same time the use of non-parametric distributions has the potential of making the segmentation method more generally applicable and this is further illustrated in Sec. 6.5.

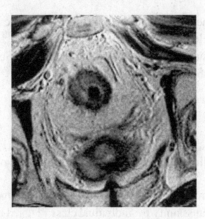

Fig. 1.1   One slice of a 3-dimensional (3D) colorectal MR image after preprocessing done to remove bias field. Notice the residual bias field in the upper part of the image and a complex heterogeneous nature of the central part of the image.

1.3   NP-windows Method for Non-parametric Estimation of PDFs

Recently Kadir and Brady proposed[Kadir and Brady (2005)], and we further developed [Joshi (2005)], a method to estimate the PDF of a discrete signal using a continuous representation. The method is based on the observation that a critically sampled or oversampled discrete signal can be reconstructed to the original continuous signal if an appropriate interpolation procedure is employed. Additional information, modelled in the interpolation method, helps to improve PDF estimation. For reasons of space, we limit the discussion here to 2-dimensional (2D) signals and to bilinear interpolation, though neither of these restrictions are intrinsic to the method.

Consider a 2-dimensional(2D) image. Let Y_1 denotes the intensity variable (in this section, all variables will be denoted by upper case letters and their particular values will be denoted by lower case letters). Continuous random variables X_1 and X_2 denote positional variables in 2D. We divide the image into several piecewise sections. The intensity variable Y_1 is deterministically related to the positional variables over these piecewise sections. Typically this relationship is polynomial. Our objective is to find out the PDF of the intensity values, given the nature of randomness in the positional variables and the deterministic relationship. In this paper it is assumed that Y_1 is related to the positional variables by bilinear interpolation over a piecewise section by joining the centres of four neighbouring pixels. This case was originally proposed in [Kadir and Brady (2005)]. Next, it is assumed that the positional variables are uniformly distributed over this piecewise

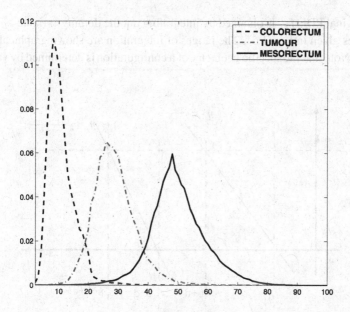

Fig. 1.2 Histograms of three different tissue classes in a 3D colorectal MR image. Notice the asymmetric nature of the probability distributions. This is mainly because of the residual artifacts such as bias field that remain after preprocessing, and also due to nonconformity to piecewise smooth image assumption.

bilinear region i.e. $f_{X_1,X_2}(x_1, x_2) = 1$ for $0 \leq x_1, x_2 \leq 1$, where $f(.)$ denotes a PDF. Hence the following equations, in which Y_2 is a dummy variable, can be written:

$$y_1(x_1, x_2) = ax_1x_2 + bx_1 + cx_2 + d \ , \ y_2(x_1, x_2) = x_1 \tag{1.1}$$

$$x_2(y_1, y_2) = \frac{y_1 - by_2 - d}{ay_2 + c} \ , \ x_1(y_1, y_2) = y_2 \tag{1.2}$$

The joint PDF f_{Y_1,Y_2} can be calculated by using the transformation formula for functions of random variables [Papoulis and Pillai (2002)]. In particular,

$$f_{Y_1,Y_2}(y_1, y_2) = f_{X_1,X_2}(y_2, \frac{y_1 - by_2 - d}{ay_2 + c})|J| \tag{1.3}$$

where, $|J|$ is the Jacobian and is equal to $|1/(ay_2 + c)|$ in this case. Therefore,

$$f_{Y_1,Y_2}(y_1, y_2) = \frac{1}{ay_2 + c} \tag{1.4}$$

subject to,

$$0 \leq y_2 \leq 1 \quad \text{and} \quad 0 \leq \frac{y_1 - by_2 - d}{ay_2 + c} \leq 1 \tag{1.5}$$

The marginal PDF f_{Y_1} is obtained by integrating out the dummy variable Y_2 over the ranges given in Eq. (1.5). The ranges of integration are shown graphically in Fig. 1.3. Note that the specific geometry of a configuration is determined by values

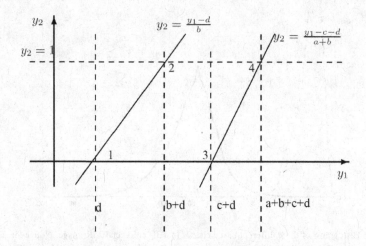

Fig. 1.3   Shown here is the particular configuration for $\{b, c, d\} > 0$, $a < 0$ and $a + b > 0$, which results into three different integration ranges marked by dashed lines.

of the coefficients in Eq. (1.1). In their original proposition [Kadir and Brady (2005)], the authors point out that there are 24 such configurations are possible, corresponding to 4! ways of arranging the values of the four corner pixels of the piecewise bilinear section. We have reduced the number of configurations in our implementation, which makes it simpler and faster than the original one. However due to space limitations we omit all the details related with implementation. The PDF obtained over each piecewise bilinear section is added and normalised to get the PDF of the given image.

A few comments are in order before we proceed further to look into applications of the NP windows method. The NP windows method converts the given discrete signal to its continuous counterpart based on the chosen interpolation method. Therefore the PDF estimate thus obtained is also the continuous one. In most applications in image processing we need the PMF of the discrete intensity values and this can be obtained by binning the PDF estimate. The bin width is dependent on the application and in most cases can be set naturally. The NP window estimate tends to be much smoother than the histogram estimate even for a small number of samples. This is because the NP windows estimate takes into account the information not only at the discrete locations but also the information at the in between locations. Such interpolated information is appropriate as long as the signals are smooth enough or in other words band limited. Comparing with the kernel estimators, we notice that in the case of the NP windows method there is absolutely no need to set up any parameters at all once we assume an interpolation model. The NP windows method is data driven, which can be seen from the fact that the coefficients in Eqs. 1.4 and 1.5 are all calculated from the input samples. Thus for smooth signals the NP windows method overcomes the drawbacks of both the histogram and the kernel estimators. Figure 1.4 shows various estimates of PMF for the given test image. The above statements can be visually assessed by looking at the estimates.

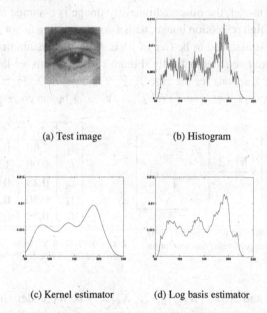

(a) Test image   (b) Histogram

(c) Kernel estimator   (d) Log basis estimator

Fig. 1.4 Graphical plots of the various PMF estimates. While the histogram estimate appears very spiky, the kernel estimate tends to be oversmooth for a given kernel bandwidth setting. The NP windows estimate provides a balance between the two.

1.4 NPMM-ICLS Framework

We have presented a detailed account of this method in [Joshi (2005); Joshi and Brady (2005)]. Let $\mathcal{S} = \{1, 2, \ldots, S\}$ be the set of indices for pixels of the image under consideration, where S is the number of pixels in the image. Let $Y = \{Y_1, Y_2, \ldots, Y_S\}$ be the observed intensity image, and y_i be a particular instance of the random variable Y_i. $y_i \in \mathcal{I} = \{0, 1, \ldots, I_{max}\}$, where I_{max} depends upon the number of possible intensity levels in the image; for example in an 8-bit grey scale image $I_{max} = 255$. Let $X = \{X_1, X_2, \ldots, X_S\}$ be the underlying partial volume(PV) segmentation for the image and x_i be a particular instance of the random variable X_i; such that $x_i \in \mathcal{L} = \{l_1, \ldots, l_K, \ldots, l_T\}$ where, $\mathcal{L}$ is the set of all possible tissue class labels, K is the number of *pure* tissue classes, and T is the total number of tissue classes including *partial* tissue classes. Note that each l_j corresponds to a K-dimensional tuple $\mathbf{t_j} = [t_{j1} \ldots t_{jK}]^T$ of the contributing tissue fractions of each pure tissue, such that $\sum_k t_{jk} = 1$.

The value of K is chosen after taking account of anatomical knowledge. To choose the value of T, we assume the image model mentioned in [Leemput *et al.* (2003)]. In their model, the observed intensity image is assumed to result from downsampling a high resolution image, with a downsampling factor M. The high resolution image is assumed to be free of PVE. With this assumption, the values that $\mathbf{t_j}$ can take are fixed automatically. Figure 1.6 lists the tissue labels and corresponding tissue fractions for the case $K = 2$ and $M = 2$. Figure 1.5 further illustrates this concept. Let $\tilde{Y} = \{\tilde{Y}_1, \tilde{Y}_2, \ldots, \tilde{Y}_q, \ldots\}$ be the corresponding high

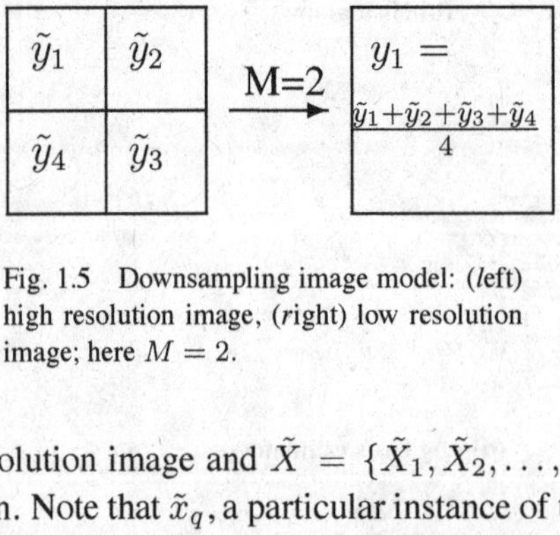

$\tilde{y}_1$	$\tilde{y}_2$
$\tilde{y}_4$	$\tilde{y}_3$

$\xrightarrow{M=2}$

$y_1 = \dfrac{\tilde{y}_1 + \tilde{y}_2 + \tilde{y}_3 + \tilde{y}_4}{4}$

Fig. 1.5   Downsampling image model: (*left*) high resolution image, (*right*) low resolution image; here $M = 2$.

	t_{j1}	t_{j2}
l_1	1.00	0.00
l_2	0.00	1.00
l_3	0.25	0.75
l_4	0.50	0.50
l_5	0.75	0.25

Fig. 1.6   List of all tissue class labels and corresponding tissue fractions; $K = 2$ and $M = 2$.

resolution image and $\tilde{X} = \{\tilde{X}_1, \tilde{X}_2, \ldots, \tilde{X}_q, \ldots\}$ be the underlying segmentation. Note that $\tilde{x}_q$, a particular instance of the random variable $\tilde{X}_q$, is drawn from $\mathcal{L}' = \{l_1, \ldots, l_K\}$, the set of only pure tissue class labels. We further assume that the random variables $\tilde{Y}_q$ are conditionally independent, i.e.

$$P(\tilde{Y}|\tilde{X}) = \prod_q P(\tilde{Y}_q|\tilde{X}_q) \qquad (1.6)$$

As shown in fig. 1.5, random variable Y_1 in the observed image is obtained by averaging four corresponding random variables $\tilde{Y}_1, \tilde{Y}_2, \tilde{Y}_3,$ and $\tilde{Y}_4$. Applying the conditional independence assumption and downsampling model for the image, it can be shown that the PMF

$$P(Y_1 = y_1|X_1 = x_1) = 4f(4y_1) \qquad (1.7)$$

where, $\quad f(.) = P(\tilde{Y}_1|\tilde{X}_1) * P(\tilde{Y}_2|\tilde{X}_2) * P(\tilde{Y}_3|\tilde{X}_3) * P(\tilde{Y}_4|\tilde{X}_4)$ (1.8)

and $*$ indicates convolution. Therefore, given an estimate of the PMFs for the pure tissue classes in the high resolution image, we can readily calculate the estimates of the basis PMFs of all tissues in the low resolution image.

In the following discussion, for notational convenience, we omit the suffices of the random variables Y_is and X_is. This should not lead to confusion because here we do not assume any spatial correlation, so the position of a pixel in the image does not affect the decision process of estimation of its class label. We now note that,

$$P(Y) = \sum P(Y|X)P(X) \tag{1.9}$$

where, $P(Y)$ is the overall intensity distribution, $P(Y|X)$ are the basis PMFs corresponding to each pure and partial class, and $P(X)$ is the prior PMF of all the classes. $P(Y)$ and $P(Y|X)$ are estimated using the NP-windows method described in the previous subsection. To estimate $P(X)$, we arrange the system of linear equations given in Eq.(1.9) in vector form: $\mathbf{p_y} = \mathbf{P_{y,x}} \, \mathbf{p_x}$ where, $\mathbf{p_y}$ and $\mathbf{p_x}$ are vectors, and $\mathbf{P_{y,x}}$ is a matrix whose columns represent the basis PMFs. In order to estimate $\mathbf{p_x}$, we seek a least squares solution of this equation. However we note that since $\mathbf{p_x}$ represents a PMF; its elements must follow the positivity and summability constraints of a PMF. Hence we formulate the problem as follows:

$$\hat{\mathbf{p}}_{\mathbf{x}} = arg \min_{\mathbf{p_x}} \quad \frac{1}{2}(\mathbf{P_{y,x}} \, \mathbf{p_x} - \mathbf{p_y})^T \, (\mathbf{P_{y,x}} \, \mathbf{p_x} - \mathbf{p_y})$$

$$\text{subject to,} \quad \mathbf{I} \, \mathbf{p_x} \geq \mathbf{0} \quad \text{and} \quad \mathbf{u}^T \, \mathbf{p_x} = 1 \tag{1.10}$$

where, $\mathbf{I}$ is the identity matrix, $\mathbf{u}$ is a vector with all its elements equal to 1, and $\hat{\mathbf{p}}_{\mathbf{x}}$ is the inequality constrained least square(ICLS) estimate of prior PMF of tissue classes. We adopt a Bayesian framework to obtain the following *maximum a posteriori* (MAP) estimate,

$$P(X|Y) = \frac{P(Y|X)P(X)}{P(Y)} \tag{1.11}$$

where, $P(X|Y)$ is posterior PMF of the pure and partial classes. The given pixel belongs to the class for which $P(X|Y)$ is maximum. We refer to this new algorithm as a non-parametric mixture model and inequality constrained least squares (NPMM-ICLS) algorithm.

1.5 Level Sets Method

Level set methods are used to evolve curves using partial differential equations. Consider a curve which is, for example, a boundary separating one image region from another. It is assumed that the curve is moving along the normal direction at each point. The speed at which it moves depends upon local geometric properties such as the curvature κ at the point, as well as global properties such as integral of the image gradients along the curve. In order to accommodate arbitrary speed functions for evolution, instead of one curve a higher dimensional function ϕ is evolved. The function ϕ can be seen as a set of curves or levels, each of which evolves when ϕ evolves. The curve that interests us is typically chosen as $\phi = 0$ or the zero level set. In our case, we consider region-based level set methods. A typical level set evolution equation for this case can be written as follows,

$$\frac{\partial \phi}{\partial t} = [\kappa + \alpha F]|\nabla \phi|, \tag{1.12}$$

where the curvature $\kappa = \nabla.(\nabla\phi/|\nabla\phi|)$, α is a constant, and F is a region based force term. The κ term provides geometric regularisation to the solution, whereas the region based term drives the solution towards a desired location in the image. So it now remains to choose this regional force term. That is the topic of discussion in the following subsection.

1.6   NPMM-ICLS Level Sets Method

Recall that our image model consists of a finite number of pure and partial classes. We presented earlier a NPMM based solution to segment an image. However our model did not consider any spatial regularisation and hence it was possible to get spatially disconnected solutions. We now propose to incorporate this NPMM-ICLS solution into the region-based level set framework. In particular, the curvature term will provide the spatial regularisation to our solution whereas NPMM will provide the regional force term. Suppose we have $x_1, x_2, \ldots, x_n$ pure classes. We consider n separate level set functions $\phi_1, \phi_2, \ldots, \phi_n$, one for each pure class. For small n, it makes sense to use separate level sets functions for each class. We evolve each level sets function separately. So for each evolution equation we consider the following region based force.

$$F_{1n} = \log\left[\frac{P(Y|x_n)P(x_n)}{\sum_{i,i\neq n} P(Y|x_i)P(x_i)}\right] \tag{1.13}$$

Because the numerator of the log(.) term denotes *a posteriori* probability, we refer to this term as log *a posteriori* ratio force. The likelihood probabilities $P(Y|x_i)$ are the basis functions of our NPMM, and are estimated using the NP windows method described earlier. The mixture weights or the *a priori* probabilities are calculated using the NPMM-ICLS algorithm. While this regional force term could be sufficient for many image analysis problems, in medical imaging applications we frequently need to take care of the PVE. We do this in the following manner. We formulate a second regional force term which inhibits the level sets to enter into the region which NPMM deems as a partial volume region. Let $f_{x_1}, f_{x_2}, \ldots, f_{x_n}$ be the fractions of pure classes present in a pixel. Then the inhibition force term is given as,

$$F_{2n} = \sum_{i, i \neq n} f_{x_i} \qquad (1.14)$$

Therefore the overall evolution equation of the nth level set function is given as follows,

$$\frac{\partial \phi_n}{\partial t} = [\kappa + \alpha F_{1n} - \beta F_{2n}] |\nabla \phi_n| \qquad (1.15)$$

We now summarise various steps of this new NPMM-ICLS level set formulation.

(1) Initialisation: Draw initial curves manually. Calculate initial level set functions using the fast marching method. Calculate initial PMF estimates of pure and partial classes. Set initial mixture weights.
(2) Estimate PMFs corresponding to pure classes using the NP windows method.
(3) Calculate the log *a posteriori* ratio force.
(4) Set the inhibition force term.
(5) Evolve the the level set functions.
(6) Calculate the mixture weights and partial volume fractions using NPMM-ICLS algorithm.
(7) Repeat the steps (2) to (6) for a fixed number of iterations.

1.7 Results and Discussion

We have implemented this algorithm using a freely available level set method toolbox[Sumengen] in Matlab. We tested our algorithm on a set of medical images. The images used were colorectal magnetic resonance(MR) images. The image acquisition protocol comprised axial small field of view T2 weighted MR images (TE = 90ms, TR =3500-5000ms, α = 90deg, slice thickness = 3mm) acquired using a 1.5T MRI machine. We assumed three pure tissue classes namely, colorectum, tumour, and mesorectum. The original images contained whole abdominal section, which were then manually cropped to contain only region of interest.

Figure 1.7 shows the results of our new level set algorithm on four consecutive slices of a 3D colorectum MR image. We notice that all three solutions (corresponding to each level set function) are spatially continuous. This is due to the

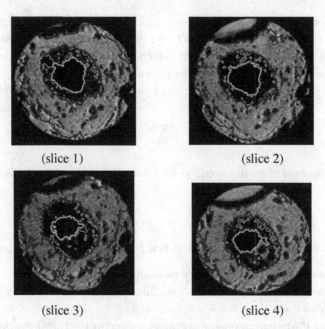

(slice 1)   (slice 2)

(slice 3)   (slice 4)

Fig. 1.7   Level set segmentation of four colorectal MR image slices using NPMM-ICLS algorithm.
Colour code: green - colorectum, red - tumour, blue - mesorectum.

curvature based regularisation. At the same time there are certain regions which
do not lie inside any of the zero level sets. This happens because the NPMM
deems those regions to be partial volumed regions, and therefore the inhibition
force stops the zero level sets entering into these regions. These regions can be
further studied using more accurate pixel-by-pixel image analysis methods such as
NPMM-ICLS algorithm. We also observe that there are small "holes" in the outer-
most segmentation class (mesorectum). Some of them are present in the consecutive slices whereas some of them disappear. Based on their pattern of appearance,
one can either classify them as tubular(blood vessels) or ellipsoidal(lymph nodes)
structures. This classification can potentially help deciding the stage to which colorectal caner has grown. Not many reliable methods have been proposed so far to
detect lymph nodes, and we believe our new method could be helpful for that task
[Bond *et al.* (2007)].

Figure 1.8 shows various distributions involved in driving the level set solu-
tion. The NPMM-ICLS fitted PMF matches very closely with the overall intensity
PMF, which shows better modelling of the intensity values. The individual class
PMFs are also shown and have non-Gaussian shapes. To further verify the de-

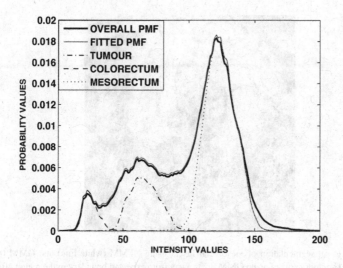

Fig. 1.8 Various distributions for the fi rst slice of the colorectal MR images.

pendance of the segmentation procedure on Gaussian distribution assumption we performed the following experiment. We constrained the individual pure tissue class distributions to be Gaussian. The rest of the segmentation procedure was kept same. The results are shown in Fig. 1.9. Only the boundary of the mesorectum area (called as mesorectal fascia) is shown. The segmentation contour derived from GMM assumption drifts away from expected boundary location in the upper part of the image which is affected by the bias field. This clearly points out the need for modelling the intensity histogram with NPMM assumption.

Figure 1.10 shows a typical result for a natural image. Here we use only two pure classes namely, zebra and background, and no partial classes. The zero level set of the class "zebra" has also been shown. Figure 1.11 shows various PMFs involved in the experiment. Careful examination of the zebra image reveals that the class "zebra" has a bimodal PMF while the background has unimodal PMF. Although the zero level set of the zebra class segments it out quite satisfactorily, it is not a perfect segmentation. See, for example, the front leg and the region near its tail. This is because the characteristic striped texture is absent in these regions and the intensity values are very similar to that of the background. Therefore, the only distinguishing information is the edge between the two classes. Since we have not considered any edge or boundary information here, the zero level set is not "trapped" at the boundary of these two regions. The shapes of the individual

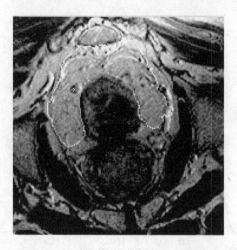

Fig. 1.9   Level set segmentation of mesorectal fascia using NPMM (white line) and GMM (green line). Level set contour evolved using GMM drifts away from expected boundary in the region affected by residual bias field.

Fig. 1.10   Level set segmentation of zebra image with green coloured zero level set laid on the zebra class.

class PMFs demonstrate the non-Gaussian nature of the distributions involved and hence justify our use of the non-parametric estimation method of PMFs.

Finally, our method resembles the region competition method [Zhu and Yuille (1996)] and the method of Ref. [Paragios (2000)] in the sense that both these methods model the image histogram with mixture models. While they make use of Gaussian mixture models and likelihood probabilities, for the reasons stated earlier we use non-parametric distributions and their mixtures along with *a pos-*

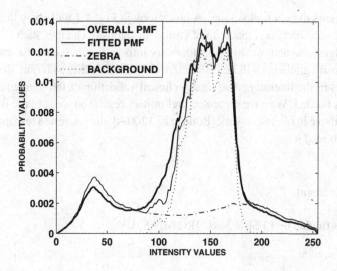

Fig. 1.11   Various distributions for the zebra image.

teriori probabilities. Also we take into account the partial volume effect which is particularly important in medical image analysis applications.

1.8 Conclusions

We presented a novel level set evolution method. The novelty of our algorithm stems out from the three contributions: non-parametric estimation of probability distributions using a recently proposed method, NPMM-ICLS modelling of the image histogram, and accommodation of the partial volume effect. While the utility of each of the individual method has been shown already in various image analysis applications, we show here that they can be used for curve evolution purposes. A number of extensions to this method are in order. The most straightforward one is to work directly on 3D datasets. The colorectal MR datasets are acquired as a series of 2D images with a considerably lower resolution along the third dimension. Additional information along the third dimension is expected to improve the segmentation considerably, but the lower resolution along the third direction must be tackled. Another direction of improvement will be to incorporate the boundary information. Although the level set framework itself allows such incorporation very easily, set of features to be considered for the detection of boundary seems to be a tricky issue. A quick look at Fig. 1.1 will show that the boundary of mesorectum is made up of variety of intensity changes such as step changes, ridges, and texture changes. Boundary information based on the magnitude of intensity gradients will be insufficient for such purposes as it only detects step changes in the intensity. And finally clinical validation of the segmentation procedure is needed. We have presented preliminary results on some of the issues mentioned above in our latest work [Bond *et al.* (2007)], the interested researchers are invited to read it.

Acknowledgement

This work is funded by EPSRC/MRC IRC MIAS, UK.

Bibliography

Bond, S., Joshi, N. B., Petroudi, S. and Brady, M. (2007). Estimating the mesorectal fascia in mri, in *the proceedings of Information Processing in Medical Imaging - IPMI (to appear)*.

Caselles, V., Kimmel, R. and Sapiro, G. (1997). Geodesic active contours, *International journal of computer vision* **22**, 1, pp. 61–79.

Izenman, A. J. (1991). Recent developments in non-parametric density estimation, *Journal of the Americal Statistical Association* **86**, 413, pp. 205–224.

Joshi, N. B. (2005). Non-parametric mixture model based segmentation of medical images, First year report, University of Oxford.

Joshi, N. B. and Brady, M. (2005). A non-parametric mixture model for partial volume segmentation of MR images, in *the proceedings of British Machine Vision Conference - BMVC*.

Kadir, T. and Brady, M. (2005). Non-parametric estimation of probability distributions from sampled signals, Tech. rep., OUEL No: 2283/05, (available at http://www.robots.ox.ac.uk/~timork/PDFEstimation/TR-2283-05.pdf).

Kim, J., Fisher, J. W., Yezzi, A., Cetin, M. and Willsky, A. S. (2005). A nonparametric statistical method for image segmentation using information theory and curve evolution, *IEEE trans. on image processing* **14**, 10, pp. 1486–1502.

Leemput, K. V., Maes, F., Vandermuelen, D. and Suetens, P. (2003). A unifying framework for partial volume segmentation of brain MR images, *IEEE Trans. on Medical Imaging* **22**, 1, pp. 105–119.

Papoulis, A. and Pillai, S. U. (2002). *Probability, random variables and stochastic processes* (McGraw-Hill).

Paragios, N. (2000). *Geodesic active regions and level set methods: contributions and applications in artificial vision*, Ph.D. thesis, University of Nice Sophia Antipolis/INRIA, France.

Sijbers, J. (1998). *Signal and noise estimation from magnetic resonance images*, Ph.D. thesis, University of Antwerp, Belgium.

Sumengen, B. (). A matlab toolbox implementing level set methods, Tech. rep., Vision research lab, UC Santa Barbara, (available at `http://barissumengen.com/level_set_methods/index.html`).

Zeydabadi, M., Zoroofi, R. A. and Soltanian-Zadeh, H. (2004). Multiresolution automatic segmentation of T1-weighted brain MR images, in *proceedings of IEEE international symposium on Biomedical imaging conference*, pp. 165–168.

Zhu, S. C. and Yuille, A. (1996). Region competition: unifying snakes, region growing, and bayes/mdl for multiband image segmentation, *IEEE trans. on pattern analysis and machine intelligence* **18**, 9, pp. 884–900.

Chapter 2

Pattern Generation Using Level Set Based Curve Evolution

Amit Chattopadhyay[1] and Dipti Prasad Mukherjee[2]

[1]*RuG, University of Groningen, Groningen, The Netherlands*
amit@cs.rug.nl
[2]*Indian Statistical Institute, Kolkata, India*
dipti@isical.ac.in

Patterns are being generated in nature through biological and chemical processes. In this paper we are proposing artificial pattern generation technique using curve evolution model. Given a closed curve in 2D space the curve is deformed under a set of constraints derived from biological and physical pattern generation models. In the proposed approach the reaction-diffusion and shape optimization models are used to derive the constraints for curve evolution. The evolution of curve is implemented in level set framework as the level set based curve evolution supports change in topology of the closed contour. The proposed model is used to generate number of patterns and also successfully tested for reconstructing partially occluded patterns.

2.1 Introduction

Patterns generated in nature often enchant us. However reproduction of such patterns for realistic rendering of a physical object or for animation is a major research challenge in image processing and computer graphics. Natural patterns are so diverse that it is impossible to describe and generate them in a single mathematical framework. This motivates researchers to propose different pattern generation models. There are many pattern generation models in literature. [Meinhardt (1982); Murray (2002); Turing (1952)] In this work we utilize reaction-diffusion model of Turing [Turing (1952)] and shape optimization model typically used for analyzing strength of materials [Beendsoe (1989)].

The reaction-diffusion model, proposed by Turing [Turing (1952)] and which is based on reaction and diffusion of chemicals, can be used to explain biological patterns, for example the spots of Cheetah or Leopard, patterns on the skin of Giraffe etc. Meinherdt [Meinhardt (1982)] has extended Turing's reaction-diffusion model to generate patterns like stripes of Zebra. Recently, Murray has used net-like structure generation model [Murray (2002)], which can as well be used for pattern generation. In a related context reaction-diffusion model is also extended for fingerprint and natural texture generation and for solving pattern disocclusion (when part of the pattern is missing) problem. [Acton *et al.* (2001)]

The motivation behind our work is to design an alternative model of pattern generation using level set framework. [Sapiro (2001)] Level set based curve evolution is a well-researched topic and has wide application ranging from image restoration to image segmentation, tracking etc. [Aubert and Kornprobst (2002); Mukherjee *et al.* (2004); Sapiro (2001)] Since a topology adaptive closed curve can be evolved in the level set paradigm, and can be converged to a desired shape depending on the constraint to the curve evolution, level set based curve evolution is adapted in this paper as the framework for pattern generation. In this approach we have used constraints from reaction-diffusion model to evolve the level set function for curve evolution. Similar to reaction-diffusion model, shape optimization technique can also be used to drive the evolving curve or level set function for pattern generation. Optimization of shape (that is the distribution of the material density within the shape) under different physical conditions, for example, a rectangular piece of material subjected to a pre-designed stress, also generates patterns. [Beendsoe (1989)] The boundary of the shape expressed in level set function is deformed to generate a particular pattern. The contribution of this paper is in demonstrating the use of level set paradigm in generating patterns utilizing both these biological (reaction-diffusion) and physical (shape optimization) models.

In Section 2.2, we briefly review the level set model of curve evolution followed by the description of reaction-diffusion and shape optimization models that eventually drives the curve for pattern generation. The proposed level set based curve evolution scheme for pattern generation is described in Section 2.3. The results and applications related to pattern disocclusion are presented in Section 2.4 followed by conclusions.

2.2 Background

The understanding of level set based curve evolution is the prerequisite for under-standing our proposed pattern generation model. Level set based curve evolution is briefly introduced in the next section. As explained in the last section the con-straints for curve evolution come from the traditional model of biological pattern generation using reaction-diffusion and shape optimization schemes. These topics are introduced in Sections 2.2.2 and 2.2.3 respectively.

2.2.1 *Level set model of curve evolution*

A closed curve $c(s)$ embedded in a 2D image matrix $I \subset Z^2$, can be evolved with respect to time t along any direction vector decomposed into normal and tangen-tial components. However, since curve evolution along tangential component is essentially a re-parameterization of the curve [Sapiro (2001)] and since we are in-terested only in the deformation of curve shape and not in parameterization of the curve, the equation of curve evolution (with respect to time t) can be expressed as,

$$\frac{\partial \vec{c}(s)}{\partial t} \approx \beta \vec{N}(t), \tag{2.1}$$

where β is the speed of deformation of $\vec{c}(s)$ along $\vec{N}(t)$, the normal to the curve $\vec{c}(s)$. The problem of generating a pattern can be posed as detecting the position of $\vec{c}(s)$ at specific time steps when $\vec{c}(s)$ is continuously being deformed along $\vec{N}(t)$. In the proposed approach, reaction-diffusion and shape optimization based mod-els supply the requisite constraint to monitor β. The initial curve is specified by $\vec{c}(s)$ at $t = 0$ and the iterative evolution of the curve terminates when $\vec{c}(s)$ evolves into a desired pattern. We now define the curve evolution in level set domain.

It is a common practice to define the level set function φ as the signed distance function [Sapiro (2001); Sethian (1999)] such that $\varphi(x, y) > 0$ if (x, y) is outside $c(s)$, $\varphi(x, y) < 0$ if (x, y) is inside $c(s)$ and $\varphi(x, y) = 0$ if (x, y) is on $c(s)$. The element of the image matrix I having m and n numbers of rows and columns respectively, is $(x, y), 0 \leq x < m, 0 \leq y < n$. Therefore, by definition $c(s)$ is embedded in the *zero level set* of φ at any time instant t;

$$\varphi(c(s), t) = 0. \tag{2.2}$$

The zero level set is the intersection of the level set function (assuming the signed distance values of φ are plotted along z-axis) and the plane at $z = 0$. Differ-entiating (2.2) with respect to t and using (9.1), the evolution of signed distance function φ is given by[8,9]:

$$\frac{\partial \varphi}{\partial t} = -\beta \vec{N} \nabla \phi = -\beta \left\| \nabla \phi \right\| . \tag{2.3}$$

The equivalent numerical approximation is given by $\varphi_{ij}^{n+1} = \varphi_{ij}^{n} - \Delta t \beta \left| \nabla \varphi_{ij}^{n} \right| = 0$ where φ_{ij}^{n} and φ_{ij}^{n+1} are level set functions at (i,j) location at iteration n and $(n+1)$ respectively and Δt is the time step. Since, β is the speed of deformation of $c(s)$ along $\vec{N}(t)$ and $c(s)$ is embedded in φ, we design β to deform φ and the modified shape of $c(s)$ is obtained from the zero level set of the deformed φ. In context of pattern generation, β controls the deformation of φ such that after certain time $c(s)$ takes the shape of a desired pattern. So the art of pattern generation using level set method is the art of constructing suitable velocity field, which evolves the level set function to give a particular pattern. Throughout this paper our objective is to design β based on the reaction-diffusion and shape optimization based pattern generating process. In the next section we introduce reaction-diffusion model.

2.2.2 *Reaction-diffusion model*

Observing patterns generated through biological process, for example, patterns of Zebra, Jaguar, Leopards etc, Alan Turing is the first to articulate an explanation of how these patterns are generated in nature. [Turing (1952)] Turing observed that patterns could arise as a result of instabilities in the diffusion of morphogenetic chemicals in the animals' skins during the embryonic stage of development. The basic form of a simple reaction-diffusion system is to have two chemicals (call them a and b) that diffuse through the embryo at different rates and then react with each other to either build up or break down the chemicals a and b. Following are the equations showing the general form of a two chemical reaction-diffusion system in 1D. [Turing (1952)]

$$\frac{\partial a}{\partial t} = F(a,b) + D_a \nabla^2 a, \text{ and} \tag{2.4}$$

$$\frac{\partial b}{\partial t} = G(a,b) + D_b \nabla^2 b. \tag{2.5}$$

The equation (2.4) conveys that the change of concentration of a at a given time depends on the sum of the local concentrations of a and b, $F(a,b)$ and the diffusion of a from places nearby. The constant D_a defines how fast a is diffusing, and the Laplacian $\nabla^2 a$ is a measure of how high the concentration of a is at one location with respect to the concentration of a nearby in a local spatial neighbourhood. If nearby places have a higher concentration of a, then $\nabla^2 a$ is positive and *a* diffuses towards the center position of the local region. If nearby places have lower concentrations, then $\nabla^2 a$ is negative and *a* diffuses away from the center of the local region. The same analogy holds for the chemical *b* as given in (2.5).

The key to pattern formation based on reaction-diffusion is that an initial small amount of variation in the concentrations of chemicals can cause the system to be unstable initially and then to be driven to a stable state in which the concentrations of *a* and *b* vary across a boundary. A typical numerical implementation of (2.4), (2.5) due to [Witkin and Michael (1991)] is given as:

$$\Delta a_i = s(16 - a_i b_i) + D_a(a_{i+1} + a_{i-1} - 2a_i), \quad \text{and} \qquad (2.6)$$

$$\Delta b_i = s(a_i b_i - b_i - \xi_i) + D_b(b_{i+1} + b_{i-1} - 2b_i). \qquad (2.7)$$

In an array of cells the concentration of chemical *a* (*b*) in *i*, (*i*+1) and (*i*-1) locations are given by a_i (b_i), a_{i+1} (b_{i+1}) and a_{i-1} (b_{i-1}) respectively. The value of ξ_i is the source of slight irregularities in chemical concentrations at *i*th location. Fig. 2.1 illustrates the progress of concentration of chemical *b* across an array of 60 cells as its concentration varies over time. Initially the values of a_i and b_i are set to 4 for all the cells in the array. The value of ξ_i is perturbed around 12 ± 0.05. The diffusion constants are set to $D_a = 0.25$ and $D_b = 0.0625$, which means *a* diffuses more rapidly than *b* and we take reaction constant s as 0.03125.

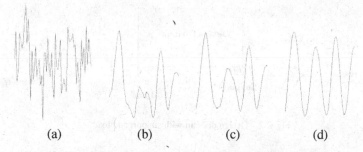

(a)   (b)   (c)   (d)

Fig. 2.1   1D example of reaction-diffusion. (a): Initial concentration of chemical *b*. (b) – (d): Concentrations of *b* after every 4000 iterations.

The numerical scheme of (2.6) and (2.7) can easily be extended for 2D grid where a matrix of cells are defined in terms of 4 or 8 neighbourhood connectivity. The two-chemical model of Turing is extended to five chemical systems by Meinherdt [Meinhardt (1982)] for periodic stripe generation.

As discussed in the introduction, attractive pattern can also be generated through shape optimization when the shape is subjected to certain physical constraints. We present this concept in the next section.

2.2.3 Shape optimization

The problem of shape optimization is often referred as structural shape optimization where an optimized structure is obtained as the original shape is subjected to certain pre-defined load. Through shape optimization process, the mass of the shape is redistributed within the shape boundary (also referred as design domain) optimally to counter the effect of load and support to the shape. This optimal mass distribution is what we perceive as a pattern. In one sense it is a user defined pattern as the extent and position of load and support to the shape or structure is user selectable. Consider a design domain or a shape as shown in Fig. 2.2. Under a given load and support, the mass of the shape is redistributed as shown in Fig. 2.3. The optimized shape boundary is always constrained within the initial design domain. The pattern generated in Fig. 2.3 is what interests us and we show in subsequent section that it is possible to pose this problem as curve evolution problem.

It is a standard practice to assume that the shape under consideration is a collection of finite elements to find stresses and displacements of individual elements and consequently the entire shape. [Zeinkiewicz (1979)] Utilizing the displacement information of individual element, the method of moving asymptotes (MMA) finds the optimal mass distribution within the design domain.

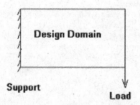

Fig. 2.2   Design domain with support and load.

Fig. 2.3   Optimized shape as the desired pattern.

Considering the top left corner of the design domain as origin and the displacements of ith element u_i due to load F_i at the ith element of the design domain, the work done or compliance C is expressed as force *times* displacement $C = F^T U$ after arranging displacement and forces of all elements in vectors U and F respectively. Given K as the global stiffness matrix of the discretized design domain $F = KU$, compliance can be written as, $C = F^T U = U^T K U$.

Considering that the design domain consists of N number of unit elements each having material densities x, the mass m of the shape is given by,

$$m = x_1 v_1 + x_2 v_2 + \ldots + x_N v_N, \tag{2.8}$$

where v is the element volume. The distribution of this material density x due to different load and support arrangements to the design domain is what we perceive as desired pattern. Therefore, the objective of this derivation is to find the solution of x under different load and support conditions.

The total stiffness of the shape using finite element method is given by,

$$K = x_1 k_0 + x_2 k_0 + \ldots + x_N k_0, \tag{2.9}$$

where k_0 is the stiffness of individual element. The above model suggests that the stiffness of each element is proportional to the density of the material the element contains. The effect of material density on the stiffness value can be penalized by introducing penalization power p as:

$$K = x_1^p k_0 + x_2^p k_0 + \ldots + x_N^p k_0. \tag{2.10}$$

The objective of the topology optimization problem is to minimize the compliance $\min_{x} : C(x) = U^T K U = \sum_{i=1}^{N} (x_i)^p u_i^T k_0 u_i$ subject to constraints $(V(x)/V_0) = f, F = KU, 0 < x_{\min} \leq x \leq 1$. The index i stands for the ith element and x_{min} is a vector of minimum material densities (non-zero to avoid singularity). The predefined volume fraction f is defined as the ratio of volume $V(x)$ at a given instant (that is, $V(x)$ is the volume at a particular material density x which is changing with time) and the initial volume V_0. This optimization problem can be solved using different approaches such as optimality criteria (OC) method or using the Method of Moving Asymptotes (MMA). [Beendsoe (1989)] Following [Beendsoe (1989)] the heuristic updating scheme for the design variable can be formulated as

$$x_i^{new} = \begin{cases} \max(x_{\min}, x_i - \theta) & \text{if } x_i B_i^\eta \leq \max(x_{\min}, x_i - \theta) \\ x_i B_i^\eta & \text{if } \max(x_{\min}, x_i - \theta) < x_i B_i^\eta < \min(1, x_i + \theta) \\ \min(1, x_i + \theta) & \text{if } \min(1, x_i + \theta) \leq x_i B_i^\eta \end{cases} \tag{2.11}$$

where x_i^{new} is the updated design vector, θ is a positive constant which is the limit of change of the design vector. The parameter η is a numerical damping coefficient and B_i is found from the optimality condition $B_i =$

$(-\left(\partial C/\partial x_i\right)/\lambda\left(\partial V/\partial x_i\right))$ where λ is a Lagrangian multiplier evaluated from well-known bi-sectioning algorithm. The element sensitivity (i.e. the change in compliance with respect to the change in design variable) of the objective function is found as $(\partial C/\partial x_i) = -p\left(x_i\right)^{p-1} u_i^T k_0 u_i$. In order to ensure existence of solutions to the topology optimization problem some restrictions on the resulting design are usually introduced.[10]

For Fig. 2.2, the design space is discretized into 32x20 elements whose left side is fixed (as support) and unit force is applied at the position (30,20). The initial volume fraction and penalization power are taken as 0.5 and 3 respectively. The optimized shape following (2.11) is shown in Fig. 2.3.

From the pattern generation point of view we investigate how patterns as in Fig. 2.3 can be generated using level set curve evolution method. As discussed earlier, the reaction diffusion based approach or optimized shape boundary technique should be implemented to guide the evolution of level set function. This is explained next.

2.3   Proposed Methodology

So far we have investigated reaction-diffusion and shape optimization based pattern generation. The point is whether these techniques can be unified in the level set framework. Alternately, the challenge is to develop β of (9.2) which is to be motivated from either reaction-diffusion approach or shape optimization approach. This is taken up next.

2.3.1   *Reaction-diffusion influenced curve evolution*

In reaction-diffusion system, two unstable chemicals have different levels of density distribution. A stable pattern is formed when two chemicals and the interface between them describe stable configurations. For implementation using level set function, the interface between the chemicals at stable state should be given by the zero level set. The proposed model should evolve the level set function with a velocity such that the chemicals or the resulting interface between the chemicals goes to a stable state. One of the preconditions to generate stable state is that the energy corresponding to the system should be minimum. The energy term corresponding to a reaction-diffusion system of two chemicals with densities a and b can be expressed as [Murray (2002)],

$$E(t) = \frac{1}{2}\int_{\Pi} \|\nabla w\|^2 \, dx, \qquad (2.12)$$

where the norm $\|\nabla w\|^2 = |\nabla a|^2 + |\nabla b|^2$ and Π is the domain of reference. The variable w can be visualized as the surface of average concentrations of the chemicals a and b put together. The domain of reference represents the surface plane of chemicals at $z = 0$ where the chemical concentrations are being varied as the deformation of zero level set.

The initial boundary condition is given as $(n.\nabla)w = 0$ on $\partial\Pi$. The normal unit vector n is defined on the boundary $\partial\Pi$ of reference domain Π. The initial boundary condition $(n.\nabla)w = 0$ implies that the rate of variation of concentration w along the normal to the boundary $\partial\Pi$ of reference domain is zero. The initial condition $w(x, 0) = w_0(x)$ on Π gives the concentration of the chemical w in Π at time t=0. To find the gradient descent direction so that energy defined in (2.12) is minimized, we get

$$\frac{\partial E}{\partial t} = \frac{1}{2}\frac{\partial}{\partial t}\int_\Pi (|\nabla a|^2 + |\nabla b|^2)dx. \tag{2.13}$$

From the derivation in Appendix I and applying the boundary conditions, (2.13) can be simplified as

$$\frac{\partial E}{\partial t} = \int_\Pi \langle -div(\nabla a),\ a_t \rangle\ dx + \int_\Pi \langle -div(\nabla b),\ b_t \rangle\ dx. \tag{2.14}$$

Using Cauchy-Schwartz inequality the field for which $E(t)$ decreases most rapidly is given by,

$$\frac{\partial a}{\partial t} = div(\nabla a), \tag{2.15}$$

$$\frac{\partial b}{\partial t} = div(\nabla b). \tag{2.16}$$

We can take either of the above fields along normal to the boundary of concentration as our required velocity field of level set evolution. So we write the curve evolution based pattern generation algorithm using reaction-diffusion model as follows:

Algorithm 1
Step 1: Initialize the embedding level set function $\varphi(x, y, 0)$ at $t = 0$ by the distance function of any closed curve in the domain Π. So $\varphi(x, y, 0) = 0$ on $\partial\Pi$, $\varphi(x, y, 0) > 0$ inside $\partial\Pi$ and $\varphi(x, y, 0) < 0$ outside $\partial\Pi$.

Step 2: Initiate minor (random) perturbation of a or b in the desired locations of Π.

Step 3: Calculate the speed function $\beta = div(\nabla b)$ following (2.16). This defines the speed of propagation of level set function $\varphi(x, y, t)$. Similarly, speed for chemical a can also be evaluated.

<u>Step 4</u>: Update the level set function $\varphi(x, y, t)$ following (9.2). Stop update $\varphi(x, y, t)$ when we get a stable pattern or there are *insignificant* changes in pattern in two consecutive iterations.

Next we show how shape optimization can be expressed as level set based curve evolution technique.

2.3.2 *Shape optimization based curve evolution*

In this case the challenge is to express the compliance minimization problem of Section 2.2.3 as curve boundary evolution problem. The velocity field for curve evolution is derived utilizing shape derivative technique. [Murat and Simon (1976)]

In linear elasticity setting (i.e. stress strain relation of the material is linear), let $\Omega \subset R^2$ be a bounded open set occupied by a linear isotropic elastic material (i.e. elastic properties are independent of the orientation of the axes of coordinates) with elasticity coefficient A. For simplicity we assume that there is no volume force but only surface loadings g. The boundary of Ω is made of three disjoint parts $\partial\Omega \equiv \Gamma \bigcup \Gamma_N \bigcup \Gamma_D$ with Dirichlet boundary conditions on Γ_D and Neumann boundary conditions on $\Gamma \bigcup \Gamma_N$ as shown in Fig. 2.4. The portion of the boundary where load is being applied is Γ_N whereas the portion of the boundary that is fixed is Γ_D. Remaining part of the boundary is Γ, which is allowed to vary in the optimization process.

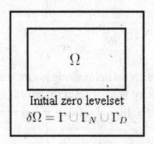

Fig. 2.4   Boundary defined on design domain for shape optimization.

The displacement field u of Ω is the unique solution of the linearized elasticity system $-div\,(A\,e\,(u)) = 0$ in Ω with boundary conditions $u = u_0$ on Γ_D and $(A\,e(u))\,n = g$ on $\Gamma \bigcup \Gamma_N$ [Murat and Simon (1976)]. The solution involving displacement field u interprets that the variation in stress tensor is zero once the solution is reached. The solution of displacement field u is the desired pattern.

The strain tensor $e(u)$ is given as, $e(u) = 0.5(\nabla u + \nabla^t u)$ with t denotes the transpose operator. $A\,e(u)$ is the stress tensor. The prescribed initial value of u on Γ_D is u_0. The unit normal direction to boundary $\partial\Omega$ is n. The objective function for minimization is denoted by,

$$J(\Omega) = \int_{\Gamma \cup \Gamma_N} gu\,ds = \int_\Omega A\,e(u)\,e(u)\,dx. \tag{2.17}$$

To take into account the weight of the structure, we rewrite (2.17) as minimization of $\inf_\Omega J(\Omega) + l\int_\Omega dx$ where l is the positive Lagrange multiplier l. In general this minimization is well posed only if some geometrical and topological restrictions on the shape are enforced. [Aubert and Kornprobst (2002)] Using shape derivative method [Murat and Simon (1976)] and following the derivation in Appendix II, we find a gradient descent field, which minimizes the objective function, as

$$\theta = -v_0 n, \tag{2.18}$$

where $v_0 = 2[\frac{\partial(gu)}{\partial n} + H\,(gu)] - Ae(u)e(u)$ and n is the normal to Ω. Assuming a displacement from reference domain Ω_0 to $\Omega = (Id + \theta)\,\Omega_0$, θ is the displacement field of Ω_0 and Id is the identity mapping in $W^{1,\infty}\,(R^2, R^2)$. To implement numerically, the design domain Ω_t is updated at every iteration with time step $\Delta t > 0$ as,

$$\Omega_t = (Id + \Delta t\theta)\Omega_{t-1}. \tag{2.19}$$

From (2.18), we observe that the gradient descent field acts in the normal direction of the boundary as stipulated in level set based curve evolution. Controlling the boundary conditions, for example, nature and location of surface loading and support (g, e), various patterns are generated. The corresponding pattern generation algorithm is given as follows:

Algorithm 2

Step 1: Initialize the level set function similar to step 1 of Algorithm 1. Specify loading and support conditions for the shape.

Step 2: The boundary conditions are solved to find the displacement u.

Step 3: Calculate the speed function v_0 of (2.18) that defines the speed of propagation of $\varphi\,(x, y, t)$ and then update the level set function following (9.2).

Step 4: Stop update of $\varphi\,(x, y, t)$ when a stable pattern is obtained. The stability condition is also achieved when there are marginal changes in volume fraction of the shape (that is insignificant change of u) in two consecutive iterations.

In the next section, we show how these methods can be used to generate fascinating patterns.

2.4 Results

We first present the results obtained using Algorithm 1. The spot and stripes
patterns after 8000 and 1000 iterations are shown in Fig. 2.5 respectively. For spot
pattern, perturbation to the tune of 12 ± 0.5 is given in every alternate coordinate
of 80x80 matrix. For the stripe pattern, the same perturbation is given at the centre
of the 80x80 matrix.

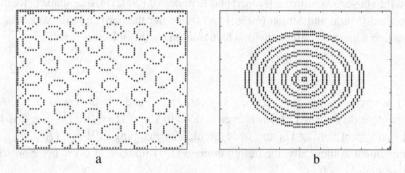

a   b

Fig. 2.5   (a) Spot pattern (8000 iterations). (b) Stripe pattern (1000 iterations)

The application of Algorithm 2 is shown in Fig. 2.6. Several patterns are
shown and in each case the input is a rectangular design domain from which the
patterns are carved out. The size of the rectangular design domain, the load applied to the shape including its coordinate and the support to the design domain
are given in the Table 2.1.

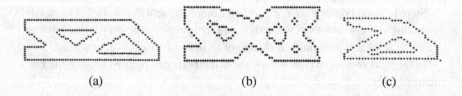

(a)   (b)   (c)

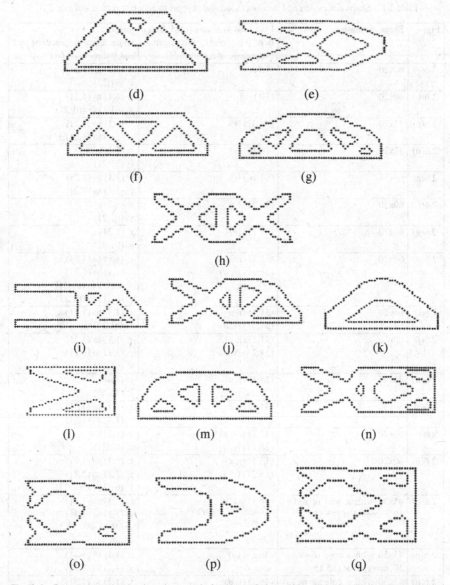

Fig. 2.6 Patterns generated using shape optimization technique (Algorithm 2). The original shape dimension, load distribution on the shape and fixed supports for the shape for these patterns are given in Table 2.1.

An important use of pattern generation scheme is to regenerate a part of the missing pattern or reconstruct a noise-corrupted pattern given the database of

Table 2.1   Shape dimension and details of load and support to generate patterns of Fig. 2.6.

Fig.	Shape dimension	Unit load at nodes (load direction - v-vertical, h-horizontal, u-upwards, d-downwards)	Support nodes along x-directions (x:) and y-directions (y:)
2.6(a)	60x20	(1,1) (v)	x: (1,1) to (1,21) y: (61,21)
2.6(b)	60x20	(1,1) (v)	x: (1,1) to (1,21) y: (61,1) to (61,21)
2.6(c)	32x20	(33,21) (v)	x: (1,1) to (1,21) y: (1,1) to (1,21)
2.6(d)	32x20	(16,10) (v)	x: (1,21) y: (33,21)
2.6(e)	61x31	(62,16) (v)	x: (1,1) to (1,21) y: (1,1) to (1,21)
2.6(f)	60x20	(30,21) (v)	x: (1,21) y: (61,21)
2.6(g)	60x20	(31,11) (v)	x: (1,21) y: (61,21)
2.6(h)	60x20	(31,1) (v, u) (31,21) (v, d)	x: (1,1) to (1,21) y: (1,1) to (1,21) x: (61,1) to (61,21) y: (61,1) to (61,21)
2.6(i)	60x20	(31,1) (v, u) (31,21) (v, d)	x: (1,1) to (1,21) y: (61,21)
2.6(j)	60x20	(31,1) (v, u) (31,21) (v, d)	x: (1,1) to (1,21) y: (1,1) to (1,21) y: (61,21)
2.6(k)	45x45	(23,1) (v, u) (23,46) (v, d)	y: (1,46) y: (46,46)
2.6(l)	30x30	(31,1) (v, u) (31,31) (v, d)	x: (1,1) to (1,31) y: (1,1) to (1,31)
5(m)	60x20	(32,21) (v, u) (28,21) (v, d)	y: (1,21) y: (61,21)
2.6(n)	60x20	(15,1) (v, u) (15,21) (v, d)	x: (1,1) to (1,21) y: (1,1) to (1,21) y: (61,1) to (61,21)
2.6(o)	45x30 with a hole of radius 10, centered at (15,15).	(46,31) (v, u)	x: (1,1) to (1,31) y: (1,1) to (1,31) y: (46,1) y: (46,31)
2.6(p)	45x30 with a hole of radius 10, centered at (15,15).	(46,15) (h)	x: (1,1) to (1,31) y: (1,1) to (1,31)
2.6(q)	45x30 with a hole of radius 10, centered at (15,15).	(46,1) (v, d) (46,31) (v, u)	x: (1,1) to (1,31) y: (1,1) to (1,31)

model parameters for pattern generation. This problem is often referred as pattern disocclusion problem as discussed next.

2.4.1 *Pattern disocclusion*

The problem of pattern disocclusion is addressed using a pattern database, which contains different pattern generation models, and the range of parameters required for the respective model (for example, perturbation amount and location, load and support for the models discussed in this paper). Note that there is no need of explicitly storing the patterns in the pattern database. Given a partially occluded pattern where part of the pattern is missing as shown in Fig. 2.7(a), patterns created from the pattern database are point-wise matched to the pattern of Fig. 2.7(a) to calculate the mean square error (MSE). MSE is calculated using point-wise multiplication of occluded pattern and the reconstructed pattern matrices followed by summation of non-zero elements of the product matrix. For the model and model parameters for which the generated pattern gives minimum MSE with respect to the occluded pattern is selected as the model for reconstructed pattern. The reconstructed pattern for Fig. 2.7(a) is shown in Fig. 2.7(b). The MSE plot against iterations is shown in Fig. 2.7(c). Note that the MSE increases initially and then stabilizes approximately around 630. This stabilized value is minimum compared to all other stabilized MSEs using other reconstructed patterns derived from pattern database.

The same experiment is repeated where the occluded region of the pattern of Fig. 2.7(a) is filled with random dots. This is shown in Fig. 2.7(d). The corresponding reconstructed pattern is the same as that of Fig. 2.7(b) and is shown in Fig. 2.7(e). The MSE plot shown in Fig. 2.7(f) shows that the stabilized MSE is slightly increased, as expected due to noise in the occluded region, at around 645. In both cases the correct pattern could be identified from the occluded and noise-corrupted patterns.

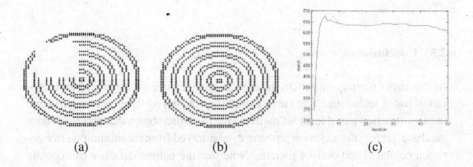

(a)   (b)   (c)

This is further extended for patterns developed using shape optimization model. The noise-corrupted pattern of Fig. 2.8(a) is successfully reconstructed

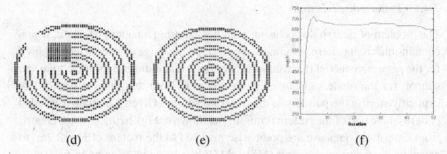

(d)   (e)   (f)

Fig. 2.7   Pattern disocclusion using reaction-diffusion model based curve evolution.

as shown in Fig. 2.8(b) where MSE is stabilized at around 60 (Fig. 2.8(c)), which is minimum when the MSE of the noisy pattern is compared with the other reconstructed patterns of Fig. 2.6.

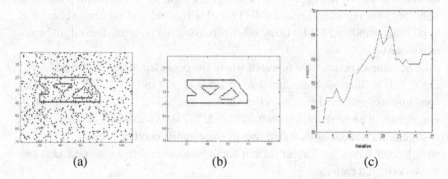

(a)   (b)   (c)

Fig. 2.8   Pattern disocclusion using shape optimization model.

2.5   Conclusions

In this paper a group of pattern generation methods is established as curve evolution based technique. The curve evolution is achieved through geometric and implicit function based level set method. We have also shown that given a pattern database, pattern disocclusion problem can be solved from the minimum error between occluded and derived pattern. Note that the pattern database can contain model parameters and there is no need to store the pattern itself. The extension of this technique for generating textured images and quasi-periodic patterns like human fingerprint etc. is what we are investigating now. At the same time suitable intensity interpolation scheme can be integrated with curve evolution to generate realistic rendering.

Appendix I

Given $\|\nabla w\|^2 = |\nabla a|^2 + |\nabla b|^2$, the gradient descent direction for minimizing (2.12) is given by,

$\frac{\partial E}{\partial t} = \frac{1}{2} \frac{\partial}{\partial t} \int_\Pi (|\nabla a|^2 + |\nabla b|^2) dx$

$\Rightarrow \frac{\partial E}{\partial t} = \int_\Pi |\nabla a| \frac{\nabla a . \nabla a_t}{|\nabla a|} dx + \int_\Pi |\nabla b| \frac{\nabla b . \nabla b_t}{|\nabla b|} dx$

$\Rightarrow \quad \frac{\partial E}{\partial t} = \int_{\partial \Pi} \nabla a . a_t \, \vec{n} \, ds - \int_\Pi div(\nabla a) \, a_t dx + \int_{\partial \Pi} \nabla b . b_t \, \vec{n} \, ds - \int_{\partial \Pi} div(\nabla b) \, b_t dx$

$\Rightarrow \frac{\partial E}{\partial t} = - \int_\Pi div(\nabla a) \, a_t dx - \int_\Pi div(\nabla b) \, b_t dx$

$\Rightarrow \frac{\partial E}{\partial t} = \int_\Pi \langle -div(\nabla a), \, a_t \rangle \, dx + \int_\Pi \langle -div(\nabla b), \, b_t \rangle \, dx$ (using boundary conditions specified in Section 2.3.1).

Appendix II

For the reference domain Ω_0 consider its variation $\Omega = (Id + \theta)\Omega_0$ with $\theta \in W^{1,\infty}(R^2; R^2)$. $W^{1,\infty}(R^2; R^2)$ is the space of all mappings from R^2 to R^2 which are differentiable infinitely many times and Id is the identity mapping in $W^{1,\infty}(R^2; R^2)$. The set $\Omega = (Id + \theta)\Omega_0$ is defined by $\Omega = \{ x + \theta(x) \mid x \in \Omega_0 \}$ where the vector field $\theta(x)$ is the displacement of Ω_0. We consider the following definition of shape derivative as the Frechet derivative.

Definition A: Let T be an operator on a normed space X into another normed space Y. Given $x \in X$, if a linear operator $dT(x) \in \chi[X, Y]$ exists such that $\lim_{\|h\| \to 0} \frac{\|T(x+h) - T(x) - dT(x)h\|}{\|h\|} = 0$ then $dT(x)$ is said to be the Frechet derivative of T at x, and T is said to be Frechet differentiable at x. $\chi[X, Y]$ is the space of bounded linear operators on a normed space X into another normed space Y. The operator $dT : X \to \chi[X, Y]$, which assigns $dT(x)$ to x is called the Frechet derivative of T.

Definition B: The shape derivative of $J(\Omega)$ at Ω_0 is the Frechet derivative in $W^{1,\infty}(R^2; R^2)$ of $\theta \rightarrow J((Id + \theta)\Omega_0)$ at 0. Then, $\lim_{\|\theta\| \to 0} \frac{\|J((Id + \theta)(\Omega_0)) - J(\Omega_0) - J'(\Omega_0)\|}{\|\theta\|} = 0$. We apply the following results of shape derivative [Murat and Simon (1976)].

Result (B.1): If $J_1(\Omega) = \int_\Omega f(x) \, dx$, then shape derivative of $J_1(\Omega)$ at Ω_0 is given by, $J_1'(\Omega_0)(\theta) = \int_{\Omega_0} div(\theta(x) f(x)) dx = \int_{\partial \Omega_0} \theta(x) . n(x) f(x) ds,$

where $n(x)$ is the unit normal vector to $\partial\Omega_0$(boundary of Ω_0) and for any $\theta \in W^{1,\infty}(R^2; R^2)$.

Result (B.2): If $J_2(\Omega) = \int_{\partial\Omega} f(x)\, ds$, then shape derivative of $J_1(\Omega)$ at Ω_0 is given by,

$J_2'(\Omega_0)\,(\theta) = \int_{\partial\Omega_0} \theta(x).n(x)(\frac{\partial f}{\partial n} + H\,f)\,ds$, where H is the mean curvature of $\partial\Omega_0$ which is defined by, $H = div\,(n\,(x))$. Applying results (B.1) and (B.2), we get shape derivative of compliance as $J'(\Omega_0)\,(\theta) = \int_\Gamma \theta(x).n(x)(2[\frac{\partial(g.u)}{\partial n} + H\,(g.u)] - Ae(u)e(u))\,ds$, where Γ is the variable part of the boundary of the reference domain Ω_0, $n(x)$ is the normal unit vector to Γ, H is the curvature of Γ and u is the displacement field solution space of $-div\,(A\,e\,(u)) = 0$ in Ω_0. By Cauchy-Schwartz inequality we find a gradient descent field, which minimizes the objective function as, $\theta = -v_0\,n$ and then update the shape as $\Omega_t = (Id + \Delta t\theta)\Omega_{t-1}$ with $\Delta t > 0$ is the time step.

Bibliography

Acton, S. Mukherjee, D.P., Havelichek, J., and Bovik, A., *IEEE Transactions on Image Processing*, **10**(6), pp. 885-896.

Aubert, G. and Kornprobst, P., *Applied Mathematical Sciences Series*, Springer–Verlag, p. 147.

Bendsoe, M., *Structural Optimization*, **1**, pp. 193-202.

Meinhardt, M., *Models of Biological Pattern Formation*, Academic Press, NY.

Mukherjee, D. P., Ray, N. and Acton, S. T., *IEEE Transactions on Image Processing*, **134**, pp. 562-572.

Murat, F. and Simon, S., *Lecture notes in computer Science*, **41** pp. 54-62.

Murray, J., *Mathematical Biology*, Springer-Verlag, Heidelberg.

Sapiro, G., *Geometrical Partial Differential Equations and Image Analysis*, Cambridge University Press, MA.

Sethian, J., *Fluid Mechanics, Computer Vision and Material Sciences*, Cambridge University Press, MA.

O. Sigmund, *Mechanics of structures and machines*, **254**, pp. 495-526.

Turing, A., *Phil. Trans. of Roy Soc. B*, **237**, pp. 37-72.

Witkin, A. and Michael, K., *ACM SIGGRAPH Computer Graphics*, **4**, 25.

Zeinkiewicz, C., *Finite Element Method*, 3rd Edition., Tata McGraw Hill.

Chapter 3

Stable Contour Tracking Through Tangential Evolution

V. Srikrishnan and Subhasis Chaudhuri

Vision and Image Processing Laboratory, Electrical Engineering Department.,
Indian Institute of Technology, Bombay, Mumbai-400076, India,
krishnan@ee.iitb.ac.in

Active contours are very widely used in computer vision problems. Their usage has a typical problem: bunching together of curve points. This becomes apparent especially when we use active contours for object tracking leading to instability in curve evolution. In this paper, we propose an additional tangential component to stabilise the evolution while at the same time ensuring that the curve shape is not changed. The proposed method is simple and the computational overhead is minimal, while the results are very good.

3.1 Active Contours: Introduction

Active contours are very widely used in computer vision tasks like tracking[Paragios and Deriche (1998); Freedman and Zhang (2004)] and segmentation[Cremers *et al*. (2001)]. A flurry of research was sparked off by the original paper of Kass and Witkin[Kass *et al*. (1988)] and the area continues to remain active, with some recent interesting works being those of Charpiat et al.[G.Charpiat *et al*. (2007)] and Rochery et al.[Rochery *et al*. (2005)]. Active contours are simply connected closed curves which move so as to minimise some energy functionals. The minimisation yields the curve evolution equations and depending on the numerical implementation, contours have been classified as parametric active contour or geometric active contour. As their name suggests, parametric active contours are implemented using parametric curves like splines[Menet *et al*. (1990)] or finite element method[Cohen and Cohen (1993)] in a Lagrangian framework

37

and these were the initial choices for implementation. On the other hand, geometric active contours are implemented in an Eulerian framework using the level set methods[Sethian (1999); S.Osher and R.Fedkiw (2003)]. An interesting paper[Xu *et al.* (2001)] links these two approaches.

The review of the entire active contour literature is not possible here, however we do mention a few of the important works. Active contour energy functionals are based both on gradient and region based strategies. The initial energy functional defined by Kass et al.[Kass *et al.* (1988)] was based on image gradients. A very interesting extension of this work, called the gradient vector force (GVF),was done by Prince[C.Xu and J.L.Prince (1998)]. The region based approach was proposed by Ronfard[Ronfard (1994)]. Some other region based approaches are the region competition model[Zhu and Yuille (1996)] and the work by Chan and Vese[Chan and Vese (2001)]. All these authors have used parametric contours for implementation.

Malladi et al.[Malladi *et al.* (1995)] introduced the level set method into the computer vision community. Theirs was a gradient based approach which used a velocity function to control the movement of the level sets. Another landmark paper in the active contour literature is the work by Sapiro et al. [Caselles *et al.* (1997)] which converted the gradient problem, initially proposed by Kass[Kass *et al.* (1988)], into that of finding a geodesic path in a Riemannian space defined by the image. They have used the level set method for implementation. Delingette[Delingette (2001)] has listed and analysed a number of smoothness measures for regularising active contours. Siddiqi et al.[Siddiqi *et al.* (1997)] introduced an area based energy functional which is shown to have a better convergence to the final target. Li et al.[Li *et al.* (2005)] have proposed a method for automatic initialisation of multiple snakes and also a solution for edge based segmentation which alleviated the problem faced by the GVF method.

The advantages and disadvantages of both these methods are well documented in the work by Delingette[Delingette and Montagnat (2001)]. The level set based method allows topological change but has the disadvantage of being slow; converse is the case with parametric representation. In applications like tracking, which is our primary interest, topological changes seldom occur. Therefore we concentrate on parametric active contours only in this paper. We use a spline based implementation similar to the one used by Medioni et al.[Menet *et al.* (1990)]

In the next section, we describe the problem and discuss a few solutions which have been proposed in literature. After that, we describe our solution and finally we present results and conclusions.

3.2 Curve Evolution

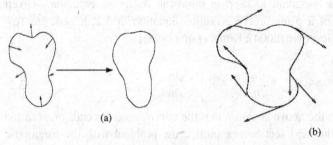

Fig. 3.1 Illustration of curve force components. (a) Normal component shrinks, expands or distorts the shape of curve, (b) Tangential component reparameterises the curve, shape remains unchanged.

We first describe the notation used in this article. A curve is denoted by $C(p, t)$, where p is the curve parameter and t is the artificial time parameter. Thus t parameterises a family of curves while p parameterises a single member of this family. The initial curve is $C(p, 0)$ and the family of curves is obtained by evolving $C(p, 0)$ as per some curve evolution equation. The local tangent and *inward* normal are denoted by $\mathbf{T}$ and $\mathbf{N}$, respectively. The curvature is denoted by κ and the arc length parameter by s. The quantity $g = |C_p|$, is interpreted as the speed of a particle on the curve. This quantity is a measure of the parameterisation of the contour.

The force at each point on the curve can be resolved into two orthogonal components: one along the local tangent and one along the normal denoted by α and β, respectively. This is written as:

$$\frac{\partial C}{\partial t} = \alpha(p, t)\mathbf{T} + \beta(p, t)\mathbf{N}. \qquad (3.1)$$

The significance of tangential and normal components is explained briefly below. This will help us in understanding the problem of curve degeneracy later. It has been shown by researchers[Kimia *et al.* (1992)] that only the normal component of the force, i.e. β, influences the shape of the curve. This is illustrated in Figure 3.1. The tangential component α reparameterises the curve. Based on this fact, most researchers have concentrated on constructing energy functions and paid attention to the normal term to speed up the convergence, increase the capture range, etc. No specific efforts were made to give some shape to the tangential term or at best it got constructed as a side effect. This did not pose any problems as many researchers have used level sets to evolve the curves or adopted some special techniques to solve the problems faced with parametric contours, which is discussed next.

However, it is important to keep in mind the following equation. Given the general form of a planar curve evolution equation in 3.1, g varies as follows[Mikula and Sevcovic (2004); Kimia *et al.* (1992)]

$$\frac{\partial g}{\partial t} = -g\kappa\beta + \frac{\partial \alpha}{\partial p}. \tag{3.2}$$

It is seen from the above equation that the curve speed depends on both the components. In the next section, we outline the problem with the parametric curves, explain the significance of the curve speed parameter g and show how it affects the curve stability. In fact, the key to our approach for maintaining the curve stability is the realisation that the curve speed parameter g should be controlled very carefully.

3.3 Difficulties with Parametric Curves

A well known problem with the parametric representation of curves is that during evolution the points on the curve bunch close together at some regions and they space out elsewhere. The problem with this phenomenon is that this increases error in numerical approximation of curve measures like tangent and curvature. Moreover, this leads to a poor segmentation. In a spline implementation, the curve quantities like tangent, curvature and normal are computed analytically and non uniform spacing of points is not a problem. However, in regions where the points come close together the control points also bunch together. This may lead to formation of discontinuities in the curve. Subsequently the normal gets highly ill-defined. Also, with splines, small local loops form when the distance between the control points decreases. These loops blow up in size and ultimately the curve degenerates. In regions where the points space out, the segmentation will, of course, be much poorer. This problem which is disturbing in segmentation problems, becomes intolerable while tracking. Therefore our aim in this work is to maintain a uniform spacing of points during curve evolution.

As an example of curve degeneracy, we show two frames from a tracking of a hand sequence. We use the final curve of the previous frame as the initialisation for the current frame. Figure 3.2(a) shows the curve just after initialisation. The points on the curve are nearly equidistant. We use a minor modification of the region competition model[Zhu and Yuille (1996)] for tracking and segmentation (this is explained in detail later). After four frames, as marked in figure 3.2(b),

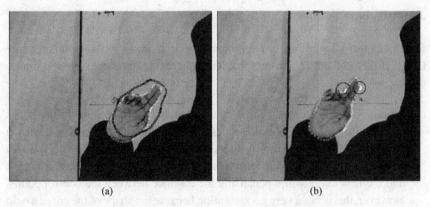

(a)   (b)

Fig. 3.2   Illustration of curve evolution. (a) Initial curve marked in black and convergence of curve to target in white, (b) Illustration of loop formation (in black) due to target motion.

Fig. 3.3   Illustration of curve degeneration. The curve blows up near the regions marked in black in Figure3.2(b).

the points accumulated in two regions are marked by circles. In the very next frame, in figure(3.3), we notice that small loops have formed in these regions. These loops keep blowing up and the curve becomes unstable. The occurrence of degeneracy depends partly on the motion direction. In the example shown, as the hand moves from the right to left, the points accumulate to the right and vice versa for the hand movement to the left. Of course, the exact number of frames between initialisation and loop formation depends on the nature of the object shape and the amount of motion.

3.4   Existing Solutions

In this section, we present a few approaches very commonly used in the literature to tackle the problem of non-uniform point distribution and discuss their limitations.

(1) Reinitialisation of curve can be done either after a fixed number of frames or when the distance between successive control points falls below a certain threshold. As proposed in by Menet et al. [Menet *et al*. (1990)], this can be done by minimising the least squared distance between the current curve and the new curve while penalising the distance between the control points. However, this is not a very good solution because the shape of the curve would change during the re-positioning of the control points. The computation is also increased in checking the distances in each frame after every iteration.

(2) Another ad-hoc solution is inserting or deleting points from the curve when the distance between them exceeds or falls below a certain threshold. This again is not a very good solution; the thresholds have to be set manually and, in general, it is a naive procedure.

(3) In a spline based implémentation; we could also control the curve by deleting or inserting control points. Although algorithms exist for such a procedure; this solution is not natural, is specific to splines and is computationally expensive. Also, if we were to use the control points to represent the shape space, these operations would change the dimensions of the feature space.

All of the methods mentioned here work more or less well in practice. The problem is that the above methods are rather ad-hoc in the sense that they are methods to adjust Euclidean distance between points after they space out and do not actually try to prevent this phenomenon from occurring. There is always the matter of setting thresholds while using any of the methods mentioned. Some better methods to obtain a more uniform point spacing have been proposed in literature[Delingette and Montagnat (2001); Jacob *et al*. (2004); Mikula and Sevcovic (2004)]. We however postpone the discussion of these methods to the next section. This would enable us to compare immediately our method with these approaches.

3.5   Proposed Method

We first qualitatively describe the cause for the bunching of the points on the curve and the control points. As mentioned previously, β controls the shape while

α controls the parameterisation. It might be thought that if we set the tangential component α to zero, the curve would retain its parameterisation and be well behaved. It is now important to realise that g determines the sparsity or density of points while discretisation. This is so because g determines the length traversed along the curve for change in the curve parameter. It is seen from equation (3.2) that g depends on both components of the motion force. Therefore, while reconstructing the curve with a discrete set of points, the spacing between the points varies in an unpredictable manner. This leads to uneven spacing of points at certain portions of the curve and the consequent problems described in the earlier section.

In our approach we ensure curve stability by using a very simple equation to control g. It is a well known fact that the arc length is the desired parameterisation to describe the curve. This is an intrinsic description of the curve. Also, we note that when the curve is parameterised by its arc length, the curve speed function quantity g becomes equal to 1. We make use of this simple fact to control the curve. Though arc length parameterisation is most desirable, it cannot always be achieved in practice. This is because of the representation used. For example, when we use closed periodic B-Splines to represent a curve, the parameter range is N_b, the number of basis functions. Obviously, it cannot be guaranteed that the length of the curve would always be equal to this or even close to this. Therefore, the next practical compromise would be to have g to be a constant K.

It is then natural to use equation(3.2) to force the curve to-wards the parameterisation which would make $g = K$. The left hand side of this equation predicts how g changes given β and α. We know the normal component β; this is obtained from minimising the energy function defined on the curve. Equation 3.2 can be rewritten as:

$$\frac{\partial \alpha}{\partial p} = \frac{\partial g}{\partial t} + g\kappa\beta. \tag{3.3}$$

Let us set

$$\frac{\partial g}{\partial t} = K - g. \tag{3.4}$$

Qualitatively, at each point we try to find α by pushing g at that point to the constant K. For a constant value of K, the steady state solution reaches the value of K. We obtain α by substituting equation(3.4) in equation(3.3) and then numerically solving the resulting PDE

$$\frac{\partial \alpha}{\partial p} = K - g + g\kappa\beta. \tag{3.5}$$

After solving for $\alpha(p, t)$, we use the values in equation(3.1). This simple term gives very good stabilisation of the curve as we shall see in the next section on results.

A question remains as to the selection of the constant K. Intuitively, one would set K to be simply the average of g over the curve. Moreover, instead of traversing the curve twice, once for averaging g and once for computing α, one could use the approximation calculated in the previous iteration. We shall discuss the choice of K in a subsequent subsection and its practical approximation in the section on implementation.

3.5.1 *Comparison with other works*

As we had mentioned earlier, we will now compare the proposed stabilising ODE in equation(3.5) with related work in literature. Specifically, it is interesting to compare the proposed energy term with those in references[Delingette and Montagnat (2001); Jacob *et al.* (2004); Mikula and Sevcovic (2004)].

Delingette et al. [Delingette and Montagnat (2001)] have set the tangential energy term (for maintaining uniform parameterisation) to be

$$\alpha = \frac{\partial g}{\partial p}. \tag{3.6}$$

Their argument is that when the normal force component β has a smaller magnitude compared to the tangential part, the above force is equivalent to the diffusion of g along the curve as time progresses. The above assumption may not be strictly valid in regions of high curvature. The term proposed in this article is better because it directly addresses the issue at hand. We do not make any assumptions on the curvature in our work. In fact, we use β while computing α at each point.

Mikula and Sevcovic[Mikula and Sevcovic (2004)] have proposed two terms for calculating α. In the first term, which is a non local term, α is obtained by solving the following ODE

$$\frac{\partial \alpha}{\partial s} = \kappa\beta - <\kappa\beta> + (\frac{L}{g} - 1)\omega, \tag{3.7}$$

where $< . >$ denotes averaging over the curve and $\omega = k_1 + k_2 <\kappa\beta>$, k_1 and k_2 are two non-negative constants. The authors have shown that this term leads asymptotically to a uniform parameterisation. Note that there are two unknown parameters k_1 and k_2 to be fixed here in an ad-hoc basis.

In the second method, α is obtained by letting $\alpha = \partial_s\theta$, where $\theta = ln(\frac{g}{L})$. The rationale behind this term is that it is obtained as the tangential component of the solution of the intrinsic heat equation. The normal component of the solution is the mean curvature motion. However, it is well known that mean curvature motion is too slow in practice for convergence [Siddiqi *et al.* (1997)]. Therefore researchers speed up convergence by adding a normal term. Hence, we feel that the term might not perform so well in practice. One drawback of both these methods is that stable numerical implementation requires updating of g, curvature and tangent angle after α is calculated; only then are the curve points updated. In our method we can directly apply the calculated α in equation(3.1). Finally, Matthews et al.[Jacob *et al.* (2004)] obtain the internal energy term by minimising the following

$$E = \int_0^M (g^2 - F)^2 dp, \qquad (3.8)$$

where M depends on the representation used and F is proportional to the length of the curve. The above energy term minimises the difference between g^2 and quantity F, which is proportional to the curve length, over the entire curve. Conceptually, this work is similar to our work. However, the above term will also cause a shrinkage of the curve. Therefore, although there may be a stabilisation of the curve, there is also a change in the shape of the curve because of the normal component. This is not at all a desirable side effect. Also, there is no justification for the choice of F. In our method, there is no feedback term like this because we deal with each energy component directly and hence we expect better results.

3.5.2 Choice of the ideal constant K

The goal of this section is to determine an appropriate value for K in the constitutive equation

$$\frac{\partial g}{\partial t} = K - g,$$

yielding asymptotically uniform redistribution of numerically computed grid points. In what follows, we denote the curve $C(p,t)$ by C^t in a slight abuse of notation. Recall that K is independent of the spatial parameter p. Without loss of generality we assume that the fixed domain parameter p belongs to the interval $[0,1]$. We note that K depends on the artificial time parameter t because the curve parameterisation changes every iteration of the evolution.

Recalling equation(3.5), if we take into account periodic boundary conditions imposed on tangential velocity term α then the term $K = K^t$ has to satisfy

$$0 = \alpha(1,t) - \alpha(0,t) = \int_0^1 (\partial_p \alpha(p,t))\, dp$$

$$= \int_0^1 (K - g + \kappa\beta g)\, dp$$

$$= K - L^t + \int_{C^t} \kappa \beta \, ds$$

and therefore $K = K^t$ is given by

$$K = L^t - \int_{C^t} \kappa \beta \, ds \tag{3.9}$$

where L^t is the length of the curve at time t, i.e. $L^t = \int_{C^t} ds = \int_0^1 g \, dp$. The value of the control parameter K defined in equation(3.9) should be used in equation(3.5) for proper evolution of the curve. This gives us the exact value of K to be derived *per time step*. Thus there is no need to select the curve controlling parameter heuristically as has been done in equation(3.7).

3.5.3 *Proof of conditional boundedness*

In this section, we show that the ODE proposed in equation(3.5) is bounded with respect to that proposed in Mikula et al.[Mikula and Sevcovic (2004)] or in other words, the proposed curve evolution will be asymptotically at a finite distance from that of the evolved curve of Mikula et al. Mikula and Sevcovic[Mikula and Sevcovic (2004)] have shown in their work that using their proposed tangential component, the 4-tuple (C, κ, ν, L) remains bounded, under the condition that the normal force is bounded. To prove this, we need the form of Gronwall's inequality[Gronwall (1919)] stated below. This inequality is well known in the area of adaptive control.

The Gronwall inequality as stated here is adapted closely from Howard[Howard]. We include the statement for the sake of completeness, the proof can be found in the same reference The inequality relates the solutions of two ODEs. The theorem is stated below.

Gronwall's Inequality

Theorem 3.1. *Let* $\mathbf{X}$ *be a Banach space. Let* $U \subset \mathbf{X}$ *and* U *be an open subset. Let* $f, g : [a, b] \times U \to \mathbf{X}$. *We assume that* f, g *are continuous functions. Let* $y, z : [a, b] \to U$ *satisfy the initial value problem*

$$\dot{y}(t) = f(t, y(t)), \; y(a) = y_0 \tag{3.10}$$

$$\dot{z}(t) = g(t, y(t)), \; z(a) = z_0 \tag{3.11}$$

Let us assume that there is a constant H *such that*

$$\| \, g(t, x_2) - g(t, x_1) \, \| \leq H \, \| \, x_2 - x_1 \, \| \tag{3.12}$$

and a continuous function $\psi : [a, b] \to [0, \infty)$, such that

$$\|f(t, g(t)) - g(t, y(t))\| \leq \psi(t). \tag{3.13}$$

Then, for $t \in [a, b]$

$$\|y(t) - z(t)\| \leq e^{H|t-a|} \|y_0 - z_0\| + e^{H|t-a|} \int_a^t e^{-H|s-a|} \psi(s) ds. \tag{3.14}$$

The above inequality gives a bound on how different two temporally evolving functions are. In order to prove the conditional boundedness of the proposed solution, let us denote by α_1 and α_2 the proposed ODE in equation(3.5) and the ODE proposed in [Mikula and Sevcovic (2004)], respectively. Following Gronwall's inequality in the stated form, we can write equations(3.5) and (3.7) as:

$$\frac{\partial \alpha_1}{\partial s} = h_1(p, \alpha_1) = \frac{K}{g} - 1 + \kappa\beta \tag{3.15}$$

$$\frac{\partial \alpha_2}{\partial p} = h_2(p, \alpha_2) = \kappa\beta - \frac{1}{L} < g\kappa\beta > +(\frac{L}{g} - 1)\omega \tag{3.16}$$

in place of equations(3.10) and (3.11). Note that here the derivatives are with respect to the arc length parameter s. We note that in both the equations(3.15) and (3.16), the RHS is independent of variables α_1 and α_2, respectively.

First, we show that there exists such a constant H, so that $\|h_2(p, x_2) - h_2(p, x_1)\| \leq H$. Since h_2 is independent of α_2, we set $H = 0$. Any finite non-negative choice can be used here.

Next, we show that there exists such a ψ such that $\|h_2(p, x_2) - h_1(p, x_1)\| \leq \psi(p) \, \forall p \in [p_i, p_f]$, where p_i and p_f denote the limits of the curve parameterisation, for any x_1 and x_2. This expression after substitution of the right hand sides of equations(1.15) and (1.16) can be written as,

$$\|\frac{L}{g}\omega - \omega - \frac{1}{L} < g\kappa\beta > -\frac{K}{g} + 1\| \leq \|\frac{L\omega - K}{g}\| + \|1 - < \kappa\beta > -\omega\|, \tag{3.17}$$

where the inequality follows from the triangular inequality property of norms. The second term of the inequality is essentially constant, as $< . >$ denotes averaging over the curve. Let us denote this by C_1, i.e, $C_1 = 1 - < \kappa\beta > -\omega$. Therefore, we set,

$$\psi = \|\frac{L\omega - K}{g}\| + \|1 - < \kappa\beta > -\omega\|. \tag{3.18}$$

Finally, we use the above results to prove that $\|\alpha_1 - \alpha_2\|$ is bounded over the curve. We use H and ψ as obtained earlier. Using Gronwall's inequality as given in equation(3.14) and keeping in mind that $H = 0$, we have:

$$\|\alpha_2(p) - \alpha_1(p)\| \leq \|\alpha_2(0) - \alpha_1(0)\| + \int_{p_i}^p \left(\|\frac{L\omega - K}{g}\| + \|C_1\| \right) ds.$$

The above expression can be easily shown to be bounded since g is finite and greater than zero, $||C_1||$ is finite and the first term in the RHS is bounded as curve initializations are usually done very close to each other for both the methods. If one uses the same initialization, then the first term also becomes zero. This proves that the tangential evolution is always bounded.

3.6 Applications in Image Segmentation and Tracking

Active contours have been typically used in segmentation and tracking tasks in the vision community. For segmentation using contours, there are two common approaches based on edge and region information, respectively. For edge based segmentation, we have implemented the gradient vector force(GVF) method to segment out objects based on edge strength. For further details regarding the GVF approach, the reader is referred to the paper by Prince et al.[C.Xu and J.L.Prince (1998)]. For the region based approach, we have used the region competition method[Zhu and Yuille (1996)]. We describe the tracking algorithm next.

This model was proposed for segmentation of an object in an image I using the statistical properties of the object. The idea is to move a point on the curve C along either inward or outward normal direction depending on the image properties of the point lying on the curve $I(C)$. We build histograms of the target and the background. These are denoted by p_T and p_B, respectively. Therefore, the probability of this pixel belonging to the target and the background is $p_T(I(C))$ and $p_B(I(C))$, respectively.

The curve evolution equation then is as follows[Zhu and Yuille (1996)]

$$\frac{\partial C}{\partial t} = \mu \kappa \mathbf{N} + \log\left[\frac{p_B(I(C))}{p_T(I(C))}\right]\mathbf{N}, \qquad (3.19)$$

where μ is the weight of the regularising term. The interpretation of the above equation is as follows: if the probability that the curve point belongs to the background is higher than the probability that it is a part of the target then the point moves in the inward direction and vice versa. This means that the initialisation is such that the curve should at least partially cover the target. This is a very common assumption in tracking. We have used histograms because they are simple and fast. We ignore the specific bins of the histogram where the probability values are too low.

We extend the same model for tracking. We use the converged contour in the previous frame as the initialisation of the contour in the next image. We use histograms to model the target and background feature distributions in the RGB colour space. We generate the target histogram offline manually and generate the background dynamically. The B-Spline curve lies entirely within the convex hull of its control points and we assume that the target lies mostly within the region enclosed by the spline curve. Computing the convex hull is computationally expensive. We therefore find the biggest rectangular bounding box enclosing the curve and sample the image randomly outside this box.

3.7 Implementation Details

In this work, we use B-Splines[Rogers and Adams (1990); Bartels *et al*. (1987)] for implementation. The advantages of cubic splines and especially cubic B-Splines is well documented in literature[Brigger *et al*. (2000)]. Briefly, we use them for their simplicity of implementation, locality of control and in-built smoothness depending on the order of the B-Spline. Of course, other representations can also be used as the method proposed is quite independent of the choice of representation. For implementing the curve evolution equation, we have used the technique outlined by Cremers[Cremers (2002)].

We discretised equation(3.5) simply by using backward differences as follows.

$$\alpha(i) = \alpha(i-1) + K - g(i-1) + g(i-1)\kappa(i-1)\beta(i-1).$$

We assume an initial condition of $\alpha(0) = 0$.

In subsection(3.5.2), we had derived an exact expression for the choice of K in equation(3.9) assuming periodic boundary conditions. We had also stated that intuitively, one would choose K to be the average for g over the curve from the previous iterations. The validity of such an approximation depends on the magnitude of the normal force. This can be seen by considering the second term in equation(3.9) which is the integral of the product of curvature with normal force. Therefore, if the normal force can be considered to be negligible, the approximation holds valid. Experimental validation confirms the above statement.

3.8 Results

We observed that an initial smooth contour degenerates when there is a rapid motion of the target or there is a rapid shape change or a combination of both. We first implemented the proposed method on the same sequence as shown in figure(3.2) for the purpose of comparison. In this sequence the shape change is slow but the object moves fast. Not only at frame 31, in figure(3.4(a)) is the curve stabilised but also remains so during the entire sequence. To illustrate the result of tracking at frame 40, see the figure shown in figure(3.4(b)).

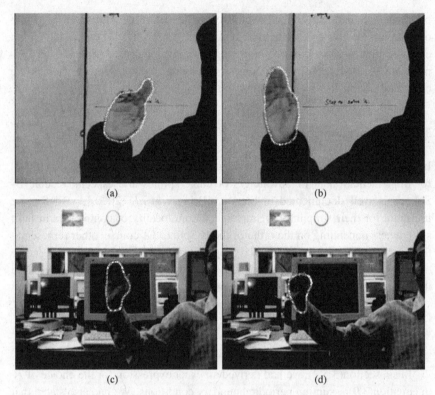

Fig. 3.4 Results of curve stabilisation for HAND-1 and HAND-2 sequences. (a,c) Convergence of curve to target in white in an initial frame, (b,d) stable convergence at later frames.

We next take a more difficult sequence where there is a combination of shape change and motion. Figures 3.4(c) and 3.4(d) shows one such sequence. Here, the open palm shrinks rapidly to a closed fist within 6 frames. We again note that the curve remains stable despite this combination of motion and shape change.

Figure(3.5) shows four frames from a tracking of a balloon sequence. For this sequence, we have used a combination of the kernel based tracker[Comaniciu *et al.* (2003)] along with the contour tracker as explained above. The aim of such a combination is to reduce the number of iterations required for the contour tracker to converge to the final target. Also, as has been reported in literature, the mean shift tracker as proposed in the original work of Meer et al., suffers from the problem of determining the bandwidth or scale, especially when the size and orientation of target changes[Comaniciu (2003); Wang *et al.* (2004)]. We then use the final converged contour to determine the bandwidth matrix. We fit an ellipse around the contour points using the approach by Fitzgibbon et al.[Fitzgibbon *et al.* (1999)]. For our experiments using the combined tracker , we found that the number of iterations required for the contour reduces to about one-fifth.

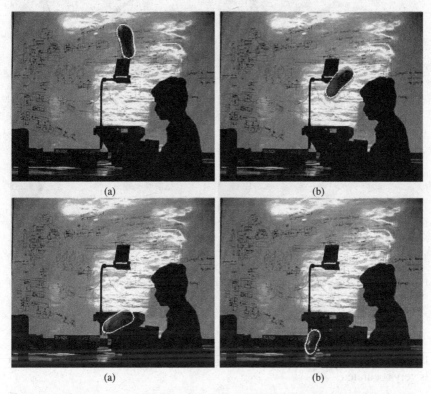

Fig. 3.5 Stable curve tracking. (a) Frame 246, (b) Frame 252, (c) Frame 260, and (d) Frame 268.

In figure(3.6), we show two more examples of the curve stabilisation using the proposed ODE. We have used active contours for image segmentation in these examples. For the top row, we have used the GVF method for segmentation while for the bottom row images we use the region based approach. In both the images, we note that the target has some sharp corners. This requires a higher number of control points for getting an accurate segmentation. Therefore, the possibility of loop formation during evolution increases. Figures 3.6(a) and (c) show the results of static segmentation without the stabilisation term. As can be seen, there are small loops at different points on the curve. Therefore, one may want to reduce the number of control points which results in a poor segmentation. However, using

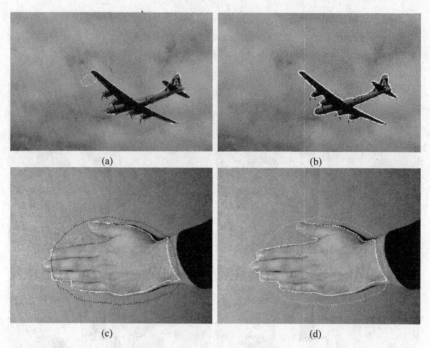

(a)   (b)

(c)   (d)

Fig. 3.6   Results of region segmentation. (a,c) without the stabilisation term, (b,d) with the proposed stabilisation term.

the proposed stabilising term, we see in figures 3.6(c) and (d) that the segmentation is very accurate.

3.9   Conclusions and Future Work

Parametric active contours are simple to implement and much faster than level set based methods; however their stability is always suspect. In this work, we have presented a simple method to stabilise parametric active contours. We have derived an ODE for controlling the curve parameterisation and also proved conditional convergence of the ODE. In our future work, we intend to present stronger theoretical results regarding the unconditional stability of the curve during evolution. We also intend to address two aspects of curve evolution, viz., speeding up of convergence in tracking by combining with a region based tracker, and explore the applications in open curve evolution problems.

Acknowledgment

We would like to thank Prof. Harish Pillai, I.I.T Bombay, Prof. Sumantra Dutta Roy at I.I.T Delhi and Prof. Daniel Sevcovic at Comenius University, Bratislava for their insightful comments and suggestions. Research funding from DST in form of a *Swarnajayanti Fellowship* is gratefully acknowledged.

Bibliography

Bartels, R. H., Beatty, J. C. and Barsky, B. A. (1987). *An introduction to splines for use in computer graphics & geometric modeling* (Morgan Kaufmann Publishers Inc., San Francisco, CA, USA), ISBN 0-934613-27-3.

Brigger, P., Hoeg, J. and Unser, M. (2000). B-spline snakes: A flexible tool for parametric contour detection. *IEEE Trans. on Image Proc.* **9**, 9, pp. 1484–1496.

Caselles, V., Kimmel, R. and Sapiro, G. (1997). Geodesic active contours, *IJCV* **22**, 1, pp. 61–79.

Chan, T. F. and Vese, L. A. (2001). Active contours without edges, *IEEE Trans. on Image Proc.* **10**, 2, pp. 266–277.

Cohen, L. and Cohen, I. (1993). Finite-element methods for active contour models and balloons for 2-d and 3-d images, *PAMI* **15**, 11, pp. 1131–1147.

Comaniciu, D. (2003). An algorithm for data-driven bandwidth selection, *IEEE Trans. Pattern Anal. Mach. Intell.* **25**, 2, pp. 281–288.

Comaniciu, D., Ramesh, V. and Meer, P. (2003). Kernel-based object tracking, *IEEE Trans. Pattern Anal. Mach. Intell.* **25**, 5, pp. 564–575.

Cremers, D. (2002). *Statistical shape knowledge in variational image segmentation*, Ph.D. thesis, Deptt. of Mathematics and Computer Science, University of Mannheim, Germany.

Cremers, D., Schnorr and J.Weickert (2001). Diffusion snakes: Combining statistical shape knowledge and image information in a variational framework, in *Proc. IEEE VLSM* (Vancouver).

C.Xu and J.L.Prince (1998). Snakes, shapes, and gradient vector flow, *IEEE Trans. on Image Proc.* **7**, 3, pp. 359–369.

Delingette, H. (2001). On smoothness measures of active contours and surfaces, in *IEEE Workshop on VLSM* (Vancouver, Canada), pp. 43–50.

Delingette, H. and Montagnat, J. (2001). Shape and topology constraints on parametric active contours, *Computer Vision and Image Understanding* **83**, 2, pp. 140–171.

Fitzgibbon, A., Pilu, M. and Fisher, R. B. (1999). Direct least square fitting of ellipses, *IEEE Trans. Pattern Anal. Mach. Intell.* **21**, 5, pp. 476–480.

Freedman and Zhang (2004). Active contours for tracking distributions, *IEEE Trans. Image Proc.* **13**, 4, pp. 518–527.

G.Charpiat, P.Maurel, J.P.Pons, R. and Faugeras, O. (2007). Generalized gradients: Priors on minimization flows, *IJCV* **73**, 3, pp. 325–344.

Gronwall, T. (1919). Note on the derivatives with respect to a parameter of the solutions of a system of differential equations, *Ann. of Math* **20**, 4, pp. 292–296.

Howard, R. (????). The Gronwall Inequality, Note available at the following URL
    `http://www.math.sc.edu/~howard/Notes/gronwall.pdf`.

Jacob, M., Blu, T. and Unser, M. (2004). Effi cient energies and algorithms for parametric
    snakes, *IEEE Trans. on Image Proc.* **13**, 9, pp. 1231–1244.

Kass, M., Witkin, A. and Terzopoulos, D. (1988). Snakes: Active contour models, *IJCV* ,
    pp. 321–331.

Kimia, B. B., Tannenbaum, A. R. and Zucker, S. W. (1992). On the evolution of curves via
    a function of curvature, I: The classical case, *JMAA* **163**, 2, pp. 438–458.

Li, C., Liu, J. and Fox, M. (2005). Segmentation of edge-preserving gradient vector fbw:an
    approach towards automatic initialization and splitting of snakes, in *Proc. IEEE
    CVPR* (San Diego).

Malladi, R., A.Sethian, J. and C.Vemuri, B. (1995). Shape modeling with front propagation:
    A level set approach, *IEEE Trans. PAMI* **17**, 2, pp. 158–175.

Menet, Saint-Marc and Medioni (1990). Active contour models: Overview, implementation
    and application, in *IEEE Conf. on SMC*, pp. 194–199.

Mikula, K. and Sevcovic, D. (2004). Computational and qualitative aspects of evolution of
    curves driven by curvature and external force, *Computing and Vis. in Science* **6**, 4,
    pp. 211–225.

Paragios, N. and Deriche, R. (1998). A PDE-based level-set approach for detection and
    tracking of moving objects, in *ICCV*, pp. 1139–1145.

Rochery, M., Jermyn, I. and Zerubia, J. (2005). Phase fi eld models and higher-order active
    contours, in *ICCV*.

Rogers, D. F. and Adams, J. A. (1990). *Mathematical elements for computer graphics (2nd
    ed.)* (McGraw-Hill, Inc., New York, NY, USA), ISBN 0-07-053529-9.

Ronfard, R. (1994). Region based strategies for active contour models. *Intl Journal of
    Comp. Vis.* **13**, 2, pp. 229–251.

Sethian, J. A. (1999). *Level Set Methods and Fast Marching Methods* (Cambridge Univer-
    sity Press).

Siddiqi, K., Zucker, S. W., Lauzière, Y. B. and Tannenbaum, A. (1997). Area and length
    minimizing fbws for shape segmentation. in *IEEE CVPR*, pp. 621–627.

S.Osher and R.Fedkiw (2003). *Level Set Method and Dynamic Implicit Surfaces* (Springer).

Wang, J., Thiesson, B., Xu, Y. and Cohen, M. (2004). Image and video segmentation by
    anisotropic kernel mean shift. in *ECCV (2)*, pp. 238–249.

Xu, C., Anthony Yezzi, J. and L.Prince, J. (2001). A summary of geometric level-set ana-
    logues for a general class ofparametric active contour and surface models, in *IEEE
    VLSM* (Vancouver, Canada), pp. 104–111.

Zhu, S. C. and Yuille, A. L. (1996). Region competition: Unifying snakes, region growing,
    and bayes/mdl for multiband image segmentation. *IEEE Trans. PAMI* **18**, 9, pp.
    884–900.

Chapter 4

Information Theoretic Approaches for Next Best View Planning in Active Computer Vision

C. Derichs[1], B. Deutsch[1], S. Wenhardt, H. Niemann and J. Denzler[2]

Chair for Pattern Recognition, University of Erlangen-Nuremberg,
Martensstr. 3, 91058 Erlangen,
{derichs,deutsch,wenhardt,niemann}@informatik.uni-erlangen.de

[2] *Chair for Computer Vision, Friedrich-Schiller-University Jena*
Ernst-Abbe-Platz 2, 07743 Jena, denzler@informatik.uni-jena.de

This paper describes an information theoretic approach for next best view planning in active state estimation, and its application to three computer vision tasks. In active state estimation, the state estimation process contains sensor actions which affect the state observation, and therefore the final state estimate. We use the information theoretic measure of mutual information to quantify the information content in this estimate. The optimal sensor actions are those that are expected to maximally increase the information content of the estimate.

This action selection process is then applied to three seperate computer vision tasks: object recognition, object tracking and object reconstruction. Each task is formulated as an active state estimation problem. In these tasks, a given sensor action describes a camera position, or view. The information theoretic framework allows us to determine the next best view, i.e. the view that best supports the computer vision task.

We show the benefits of next best view planning in several experiments, in which we compare the estimation error produced by planned views with the error produced by regularly sampled or unchanging views.

[01] This work was partly funded by the German Research Foundation (DFG) under grant SFB 603/TP B2. Only the authors are responsible for the content.

4.1 Introduction

We present a general framework for determining the next best view in active state estimation problems. In active state estimation, the state observation process is additionally parameterized with a sensor action which is freely selectable and adaptable at run-time. The observation taken with the action which most supports the state estimation is referred to as the next best view. This framework is adapted to three computer vision tasks: object recognition, object tracking, and object reconstruction. We formulate each task as a state estimation problem and use the framework to determine the next best view.

This work is based primarily on the work of Denzler and Brown [Denzler and Brown (2002)], who introduce a formalism for sensor parameter optimalization in general state estimation problems and demonstrated its validity with a simple object classification task (which, unlike the approach outlined later in this work, does not use Reinforcement Learning, but evaluates the mutual information directly). Such a state estimation problem produces not only an estimate of the state, but also a measure of the reliability of this estimate, in that the *a posteriori* estimate is of the form of a probability density function (pdf). The information theoretic method of maximal mutual information is used to optimize the information content of this *a posteriori* pdf by finding the optimal action, or view, *in advance*. This corresponds to minimizing the expected entropy of the pdf. We define the next best view as the one that maximizes the mutual information, and adapt this framework to our computer vision tasks.

The notion of a "next best view" depends strongly on the goals of the system. The following is a short overview of related work in active next best view selection for the three computer vision tasks:

In object recognition, a common approach for viewpoint selection is the exploitation of a few distinctive object views computed offline, as in Sipe and Casasent [Sipe and Casasent (2002)] or Dickinson [Dickinson (1997)]. Others, similar to this work, apply more complex training phases, e. g. performing a cluster analysis like Kovačič [Kovačič *et al.* (1998)]. Similar to our approach, which will be shown to utilize Reinforcement Learning training, Arbel and Ferrie [Arbel and Ferrie (2001)] also combine an information theoretic measure with a training stage by setting up entropy maps. However, they do not consider inaccuracies in the sensor movement. Thirdly, the works of Zhou and Comaniciu [Zhou *et al.* (2003)] and of Laporte [Laporte *et al.* (2004)] omit any training, but concentrate on passing the most supporting features to information theoretic approaches, an approach which is convenient but naturally less reliable.

In object tracking, views have typically been changed reactively. Tordoff and

Murray[Tordoff and Murray (2004)] use zoom control to keep the scale of an object of interest fixed over time. Micheloni and Foresti[Micheloni and Foresti (2005)] adapt this approach with a feature clustering technique to detect moving objects, and zoom on an object if required. Both approaches do not adapt the zoom based on any predicted information gain, unlike the methods shown here. Recently, Tordoff and Murray[Tordoff and Murray (2007)] have considered the uncertainty of the estimate for zoom planning; however their approach considers the innovation covariance as an indicator to adapt the process noise, not the expected gain in information. Davison [Davison (2005)] also uses mutual information to guide the search of features on an image for 2-D object tracking. In contrast, the tracking discussed here optimizes the continuous parameterization of several cameras, tracking in 3-D.

In view planning for 3-D reconstruction, several authors use range scanners, e. g. Banta [Banta *et al.* (2000)], Pito [Pito (1999)], or Scott[Scott *et al.* (2003)]. However, these works are not comparable to 3-D reconstruction from intensity images, since the reconstruction process is completely different. Works which optimize 3-D reconstruction results by next best view planning are quite rare in literature[Kutulakos and Dyer (1994); Marchand and Chaumette (1999); Niem (1999)]. Furthermore, those algorithms use geometrical considerations in contrast to the information theoretical approach introduced in this work and adopted to this special task.

This paper is organized as follows: The next section describes the general problem of state estimation, and shows how optimal views can be determined using the information theoretic measures of mutual information and entropy. Section 4.3 then applies and adapts this view planning process to three basic computer vision tasks. Section 4.4 contains experiments for each of the three tasks, showing the validity of the next best view planning process. The last section contains a summary of this work.

4.2 Information Theoretical Approaches for Next Best View Planning

In the following we treat computer vision algorithms as probabilistic state estimation problems. The unknown state is estimated by one or more observations from the environment. The probabilistic formulation of the problem makes it possible to explicitly model uncertainty, arising from using real sensors, and to use *a priori* information, which is sometimes available and can improve the quality or robustness of the results. As mentioned before, prominent examples from computer vision tackled in this article are object recognition (discrete state space with the class label being the state), object reconstruction (continuous state space with the object's points in 3-D being the state) and object tracking (continuous, time varying state space with the position, velocity and acceleration being the state).

Next best view planning is understood as acquiring those observations that are most valuable for the subsequent state estimation process. The term view is used to indicate that the focus in this work is on cameras, whose parameters (internal or external parameters) are optimized during the planning approach. Optimization is done by modeling the benefit of each new view with respect to the state estimation problem.

Strong relations can be drawn to sequential decision making. Aside from the decision (planning), which next view is taken, fusion of the information is also an important aspect. In the next two sections, we present a very general model for sequential decision making and fusion for state estimation. In the later sections, this very general model is applied to problems in computer vision.

4.2.1 *General state modeling and estimation*

The term state, or state vector q_t, of a system at time step t comprises all the relevant parameters of that system to be determined from observations $o_0 \ldots o_t$ taken by sensors. For static systems, the state does not change over time and we can omit the parameter t. For an estimation of the true state usually the *a posteriori* probability

$$p(q_t|o_0,\ldots,o_t) = \frac{p(o_t|q_t)p(q_t|o_0,\ldots,o_{t-1})}{p(o_t)} \tag{4.1}$$

of the state given the observations needs to be computed using the well known Bayes formula. In (4.1), the usual Markovian assumption is made, i.e. the current observation o_t only depends on the current state q_t. The *a posteriori* density can then be the basis for a maximum a posteriori estimation (MAP) or a minimum mean square error estimator (MMSE). Again, for static systems the parameter t can be omitted. For dynamic systems, the computation of the so called *temporal prior* $p(q_t|o_0,\ldots,o_{t-1})$ involves the *a posteriori* probability from the previous time step $t-1$ as well as the state transition probability $p(q_t|q_{t-1})$ of the system, i.e.

$$p(q_t|o_0,\ldots,o_{t-1}) = \int p(q_{t-1}|o_0,\ldots,o_{t-1})p(q_t|q_{t-1})dq_{t-1} \tag{4.2}$$

It is worth noting that for static systems, although the true state remains constant over time, the estimated *a posteriori* density will change due to the collection of observations o_k. This situation will be discussed in section 4.3.1. For dynamic systems, the estimation and tracking of an evolving density is one of the main ideas behind the Kalman filter.

If the assumptions are met, the Kalman filter is sometimes more intuitive to apply due to its algebraic formulation. The basic model of the linear Kalman filter consists of two equations for state transition and observation. The state transition is given by

$$q_{t+1} = F_t q_t + w_t \qquad (4.3)$$

with W_t being the covariance matrix of the Gaussian noise process w_t. This equation describes the dynamics of the system and is in general equivalent to the density $p(q_{t+1}|q_t)$. The relation between state and observation is modeled by

$$o_t = G_t q_t + r_t \qquad (4.4)$$

with R_t being the covariance matrix of the Gaussian noise process r_t. Again, we can relate this equation to the density $p(o_t|q_t)$ in the probabilistic formulation of the problem. In the extended Kalman filter the linear relationships in (4.3) and (4.4) are substituted by in general non-linear functions $f(q_t)$ and $g(q_t)$ for state transition and observation, respectively.

The basic assumption behind the Kalman filter are Gaussian noise processes during state transition and observation, which gives us Gaussian densities for $p(q_{t+1}|q_t)$ and $p(o_t|q_t)$. As a consequence, the resulting *a priori* and *a posteriori* densities in (4.1) are also Gaussian, with the notation

$$p(q_t|o_0, \ldots, o_{t-1}) \sim \mathcal{N}(\widehat{q}_t^-, P_t^-) \quad \text{and} \quad p(q_t|o_0, \ldots, o_t) \sim \mathcal{N}(\widehat{q}_t^+, P_t^+)$$
$$(4.5)$$

and the Kalman update step (not detailed here) containing

$$P_t^+ = (I - K_t G_t) P_t^- \qquad (4.6)$$

where K_t is the *Kalman gain matrix* and I the identity matrix.

Thus, both the MAP and the MMSE estimate are the mean of (4.1). In case, that the involved densities cannot be modeled as Gaussian densities, the solution to MAP and MMSE can be achieved using particle filters. A short introduction to particle filters in practice is given in section 4.3.1.

4.2.2 *Optimality criteria for active view planning*

Having in mind that the *a posteriori* density from (4.1) is the basis of the state estimate in probabilistic estimation theory, it is quite natural to search for such observations that make (4.1) most suited for the following steps. One simple example is a MAP estimation. Having a density that consists of local maxima makes

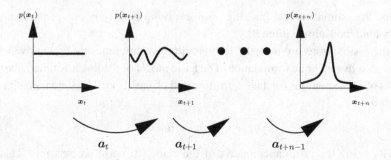

Fig. 4.1   General principle of active view planning in state estimation.

the estimation process ambiguous. A second example is a very flat density that makes the estimation process uncertain. Thus, the key aspect of an optimal state estimation is the collection of those observations from the data that the resulting density in (4.1) is at the best unimodal and with small variance. This situation is indicated in Fig. 4.1. Starting with a uniform density over the state space (i.e. knowing nothing at all), we choose so called actions a_t at each time t step to influence the subsequent observations, such that the observation will lead to a more suited density. In our case, an action is any change in the internal or external parameters of a camera. However, the whole formulation is not restricted to actions for cameras. Arbitrary actions are possible, for example, one that might influence the environment (for example, the illumination of the scene) or those which select algorithms for further processing of the data.

The problem formulation directly points to the solution. To find the best action at each time step, we have to define a criterion that favors unambiguous densities with small variance. The entropy

$$H(q_t) = \int p(q_t) \log p(q_t) dq_t \qquad (4.7)$$

could serve as a criterion, as done by other researchers before

$$I(q_t; o_t | a_t) = \int_{q_t} \int_{o_t} p(q_t | a_t) p(o_t | q_t, a_t) \log \left(\frac{p(o_t | q_t, a_t)}{p(o_t | a_t)} \right) do_t dq_t \qquad (4.8)$$

and depends in our case on the chosen action, which influences the observation at time step t. Another information theoretic quantity is the conditional entropy[Papoulis (2002)]

$$H(q_t | o_t, a_t) = -\int p(o_t | a_t) \int p(q_t | o_t, a_t) \log p(q_t | o_t, a_t) dq_t do_t \qquad (4.9)$$

There is a nice relationship between the mutual information in (4.8) and the conditional entropy:

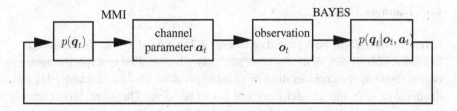

Fig. 4.2 Sequential decision process of maximum mutual information (MMI) for camera parameter selection and Bayesian update of $p(q_t|o_t, a_t)$ based on the observed feature o_t. Taken from Denzler and Brown[Denzler and Brown (2002)].

$$I(q_t; o_t|a_t) = H(q_t|a_t) - H(q_t|o_t, a_t) \qquad (4.10)$$

The reader should note that the entropy $H(q_t|a_t)$ of the *a priori* probability (which lacks the current observation o_t) usually does not depend on the chosen action a_t. Thus, it is also possible to minimize the conditional entropy $H(q_t|o_t, a_t)$, i.e. the entropy of the *a posteriori* probability (which includes the current observation o_t), averaged over all possible observations.

The optimal action a_t^* with respect to the following state estimation process is now given either by the maximum of mutual information (MMI)

$$a_t^* = \underset{a_t}{\operatorname{argmax}} I(q_t; o_t|a_t). \qquad (4.11)$$

or equivalently by the minimum of the conditional entropy.

To complete the discussion of state estimation from Section 4.2.1, we have to add the dependency on the chosen action a_t to all densities. More precisely, the *likelihood* $p(o_t|q_t)$ from (4.1) will become $p(o_t|q_t, a_t)$ considering that the current observation now depends not just on the state but also on the chosen action.

The optimal action a_t^* is now used to adjust the camera parameters to acquire the next best view. The observation taken by that view is fed into the estimation process (4.1) (BAYES). By definition the *a posteriori* density from (4.1) will have minimum expected entropy, i.e. *on average* minimum ambiguity and variance. Finally, this *a posteriori* density can be input directly to the whole planning process at the next time step (for time invariant systems) or by means of the temporal prior (4.2) (for dynamic systems). More details can be found in Denzler and Brown[Denzler and Brown (2002)]. The next sections will demonstrate how this information theoretic concept can be applied to three different state estimation problems in computer vision.

4.3   Planning Tasks

Given the theoretical background of chapter 4.2, we need to specify parameters like *state*, *observation* or *action* more precisely when applied to a specific application. Next to the consideration of possible problem based constraints, this is the decisive scientific transfer work one has to perform. Therefore, this chapter introduces the adaption of the theory explained above to three applications in the research fields of computer vision. It will be shown that in all these topics, active view planning is of distinct advantage.

4.3.1   *Active object recognition*

Taking a look at the majority of research work in the field of object recognition, problems deal with single image processing and the assumption that the object can actually be distinguished from all others by that single view. In opposite, active object recognition searches for a selectively chosen series of different images of one object in order to combine their information for gaining the optimal improvement of certainty. So active object recognition permits the handling of more difficult classification problems, e.g. when objects show ambiguities (see Fig. 4.5) or single image quality prohibits a reliable discrimination at all.

4.3.1.1   *State representation and information fusion*

With reference to section 4.2.1, we first need to define a meaningful state q_t in the process of object recognition. In the first instance, the state has to contain the attributes we are finally interested in. Basically, always assuming a probabilistic representation of class certainties, in the most simple case this would just be a group of κ probabilities regarding all classes $\Omega_{l=1,\cdots,\kappa}$ under consideration. For each test image and object class, such a value definitely has to be calculated by the summation over a theoretically continuous set of poses $\phi = (\phi_1, \ldots, \phi_J)^T$ which represent the camera position relative to the object in the various dimensions:

$$p(\Omega_l) = \int_\phi p(\Omega_l|\phi)d\phi \ . \tag{4.12}$$

So, for gaining a more distinguishing and less ambiguous state representation, it is only meaningful and free of additional effort to augment it with the pose ϕ, yielding $q_t = (\Omega_\kappa, \phi_1, \ldots, \phi_J)^T$. Given this state representation we can establish (4.1) with the recognition specific parameters. Consequently, (4.1) can be considered to be a combined discrete-continuous density, i.e. discrete regarding the class assumption and continuous in ϕ.

When performing a camera action

$$a_t = (\Delta\phi_1^t, \ldots, \Delta\phi_J^t) \quad \text{with} \quad \Delta\phi^t = \phi^{t+1} - \phi^t \tag{4.13}$$

relative to the object, we gather a new image whose pixel intensity value vector v provides the information to be fused to the current density representation, thus the observation $o_t = v_t$. This fusion is a task which is generally tackled using the Kalman filter in various state estimation problems, like in section 4.3.2. But mainly due to ambiguities in the recognition process, we cannot generally assume the required normal distribution form for $p(o_t|q_t)$, thus making the Kalman filter unemployable here. Instead, we apply the so called *particle filters*. The basic idea is to approximate the multi-modal probability distribution by a set of M weighted samples $y^i = \{x^i, p^i\}$. Each sample y consists of the point $x = (\Omega_l, \phi_1, \ldots, \phi_J)$ within the state space and the weight p for that sample, with the condition that $\sum_i p^i = 1$.

Now, each time step t a new image of the object is received—no matter if randomly or purposefully—we initiate the fusion process. In the case of the particle representation, this can be simple done by applying the Condensation algorithm [Isard and Blake (1998)], which adapts the given samples of the a priori density to an adequate representation of the a posteriori density, using the observation o_t. Additionally, the camera action a_{t-1} between the image acquisition positions is considered in the sample transition:

$$\underbrace{p(q_{t-1}|\langle o \rangle_{t-1}, \langle a \rangle_{t-2})}_{\text{a posteriori } (t-1)} \longrightarrow \underbrace{p(q_t|\langle o \rangle_{t-1}, \langle a \rangle_{t-1})}_{\text{a priori } (t)} \longrightarrow \underbrace{p(q_t|\langle o \rangle_t, \langle a \rangle_{t-1})}_{\text{a posteriori } (t)} \tag{4.14}$$

where $\langle o \rangle_k$ is the sequence of observations $o_0 \ldots o_k$ and $\langle a \rangle_k$ the sequence of actions $a_0 \ldots a_k$.

4.3.1.2 *Optimal action selection*

So far, all discussions of section 4.3.1.1 have been so general that it does not matter whether we acquire views randomly or purposefully, since the state representation and propagation is identical. To meet the focus of this paper we now describe the optimality criteria for view planning in object recognition. Unlike the data driven solutions for object tracking and reconstruction, which will be presented in section 4.3.2 and section 4.3.3 respectively, object recognition must be approached quite differently. For recognition, we must always be aware of at least a probabilistic assumption of the properties of *all* our objects under consideration, since we need to know whether a view is discriminative or not. Obviously this information cannot be provided by an image sequence of just one object, which is all we would have in a data driven setup.

Thus, a model-based method was created, representing the features of equidistantly taken images from a circle around all possible objects. Appropriate feature vectors c are calculated by applying the well known PCA values of these input images, represented in vector form v. At this point, please note that our objective is not the improvement of an individual classifier but the determination of an optimal image acquisition strategy for an *arbitrary classifier*. Accordingly, the measure of quality is not so much the absolute classification ratio, but its increase within the the process of active image acquisition compared to a random proceeding. Thus, while omitting further details in this work, we will just mention that for experimental results, an eigenspace classifier [Murase and Nayar (1995)] was used.

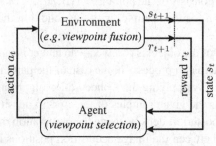

Fig. 4.3   Reinforcement learning loop.

Regarding the optimization we decided for a Reinforcement Learning (RL) [Sutton and Barto (1998)] approach utilizing a training phase, consisting of ϵ episodes with maximally $\tilde{\epsilon}$ steps each. In every single step, a closed loop between sensing s_t and acting a_t is performed (Fig. 4.3). The generally randomly chosen *action* a_t corresponds to the executed camera movement. Accordingly, the *RL-state*

$$s_t := p(\boldsymbol{q}_t|\langle \boldsymbol{o} \rangle_t, \langle \boldsymbol{a} \rangle_{t-1}) \tag{4.15}$$

is the density as given in (4.1). Additionally, the classification module returns a so called *reward* r_t, which measures the quality of the chosen action. Clearly, the definition of the reward is an important aspect as this reward should model the goal that has to be reached. Section 4.2 named the entropy to be a suitable measure of a distribution's information content, i.e. the discriminability potential in classification tasks. So setting

$$r_t = -H(s_t) = -H\left(p(\boldsymbol{q}_t|\langle \boldsymbol{o} \rangle_t, \langle \boldsymbol{a} \rangle_{t-1})\right) \tag{4.16}$$

we highly reward views that increase the information observed so far in a training episode and thus supports the goal of maximally improving the classification at every time step.

In order to optimize the viewpoint planning in an anticipatory manner, Reinforcement Learning provides the so called *return*:

$$R_t = \sum_{n=0}^{\infty} \gamma^n r_{t+n+1} \quad \text{with } \gamma \in [0; 1] . \tag{4.17}$$

Instead of the immediate reward r_t, a γ-weighted combination of all rewards arising in later steps n of the episode is applied. During training, this is done subsequently after having finished the episode. Consequently, all acquired combinations of current state s_{t-1}, ensuing action a_{t-1} and resulting return R_t are stored in a training database.

Switching from the training phase to the later evaluation phase, naturally the future rewards cannot be observed at time step t. Thus, the following function, called the *action-value function*

$$Q(s, a) = E\{R_t | s_t = s, a_t = a\} \tag{4.18}$$

is defined. It describes the expected return when starting at time step t in presumption state s with action a. Please note that by calculating the expectation value of the γ-weighted and added up entropy in (4.18), $Q(s, a)$ is nothing but the conditional entropy which we postulated to be a meaningful optimization criterion in (4.9).

Trying to optimize the camera action in the evaluation phase, the first task is to extract those entries from the database that are relevant for the current state. So, for determining the similarity between the current state and each one in the database, the *extended Kullback-Leibler* **distance function** $d_{\text{EKL}}(s_n, s'_m) = d_{\text{KL}}(s_n, s'_m) + d_{\text{KL}}(s'_m, s_n,)$ with

$$d_{\text{KL}}(s_n, s'_m) = \int p(q| \langle o \rangle_n, \langle a \rangle_{n-1}) \log \frac{p(q| \langle o \rangle_n, \langle a \rangle_{n-1})}{p(q| \langle o' \rangle_m, \langle a' \rangle_{m-1})} dq \tag{4.19}$$

is used. Please note that in general there is no analytic solution for d_{EKL}, but as we represent our densities as sample sets anyway (see section 4.3.1.1) there are well-known ways to approximate d_{EKL} by Monte Carlo techniques [Deinzer *et al.* (2006)].

In order to provide a continuous search space to the optimization problem, we calculate a weighted sum of the action-values $Q(s', a')$ of all previously collected state/action pairs (s', a') :

$$\widehat{Q}(s, a) = \frac{\sum_{(s',a')} K(d_{EKL}(\theta(s, a), \theta(s', a'))) \cdot Q(s', a')}{\sum_{(s',a')} K(d_{EKL}(\theta(s, a), \theta(s', a')))} . \tag{4.20}$$

Thereby, the **transformation function** $\theta(s, a)$ transforms a presumption state s with a known action a with the intention of bringing a state to a "reference point" (required for the distance function in the next item). Actually, it simply performs a shift of the density according to the action a. The **kernel function** $K(\cdot)$ finally weights the calculated distances. A suitable kernel function is, for example, the Gaussian $K(x) = \exp(-x^2/D^2)$ where D denotes the width of the kernel.

Using (4.20), the viewpoint selection problem of finding the optimal action a^* can now be written as a continuous optimization problem

$$a^* = \operatorname{argmax}_a \widehat{Q}(s, a) \quad . \tag{4.21}$$

4.3.2   *Active object tracking*

For the task of visual object tracking, one is interested in the *motion* of a given object, often called the "target" and treated as a point-sized entity. To acquire this motion, the target is observed by several cameras. Using object tracking on the camera images, each camera effectively generates a two-dimensional observation from the target position. These observations are then used to recover the 3-D position of the target, as well as other indirectly observable motion parameters, such as the velocity and the acceleration. The dimensionality of the observations and the position alone require that more than one camera be used for tracking. In practice, two cameras are sufficient, though more may be used.

4.3.2.1   *State and observation representation*

The relatively low-dimensional, single-target nature of object tracking makes it an ideal candidate for the Kalman filter. In our object tracking tasks, we use a Newtonian position-velocity-acceleration motion model. The state vector $q_t \in \mathbb{R}^9$ at time step t, which is part of the discrete-time dynamic system being observed by the Kalman filter, is defined as

$$q_t = (x, y, z, \dot{x}, \dot{y}, \dot{z}, \ddot{x}, \ddot{y}, \ddot{z})^{\mathrm{T}} \tag{4.22}$$

where the component triplets correspond to the position, velocity and acceleration of the target, in world coordinates, respectively. The state transition function function $f(\cdot)$, described in (4.3), transforms one state to the next according to

$$
\begin{aligned}
x_{t+1} &= x_t + \Delta t \cdot \dot{x}_t + \tfrac{1}{2}(\Delta t^2) \cdot \ddot{x}_t & \dot{x}_{t+1} &= \dot{x}_t + \Delta t \cdot \ddot{x}_t & \ddot{x}_{t+1} &= \ddot{x}_t \\
y_{t+1} &= y_t + \Delta t \cdot \dot{y}_t + \tfrac{1}{2}(\Delta t^2) \cdot \ddot{y}_t & \dot{y}_{t+1} &= \dot{y}_t + \Delta t \cdot \ddot{y}_t & \ddot{y}_{t+1} &= \ddot{y}_t \\
z_{t+1} &= z_t + \Delta t \cdot \dot{z}_t + \tfrac{1}{2}(\Delta t^2) \cdot \ddot{z}_t & \dot{z}_{t+1} &= \dot{z}_t + \Delta t \cdot \ddot{z}_t & \ddot{z}_{t+1} &= \ddot{z}_t
\end{aligned} \tag{4.23}
$$

plus an additive white Gaussian noise. In time-discrete systems, such as discussed here, Δt is a unitless factor with value 1. Note that this state and state transition system observes the Markov property, in that the next state only depends on the current state, and not on past states. This property is necessary for applying the Kalman filter.

Since the state transition function is linear and time-invariant, we can express it as the state transition matrix $F_t \in \mathbb{R}^{9 \times 9}$. This matrix is defined as

$$
F_t = \begin{pmatrix}
1 & 0 & 0 & \Delta t & 0 & 0 & \frac{1}{2}(\Delta t^2) & 0 & 0 \\
0 & 1 & 0 & 0 & \Delta t & 0 & 0 & \frac{1}{2}(\Delta t^2) & 0 \\
0 & 0 & 1 & 0 & 0 & \Delta t & 0 & 0 & \frac{1}{2}(\Delta t^2) \\
0 & 0 & 0 & 1 & 0 & 0 & \Delta t & 0 & 0 \\
0 & 0 & 0 & 0 & 1 & 0 & 0 & \Delta t & 0 \\
0 & 0 & 0 & 0 & 0 & 1 & 0 & 0 & \Delta t \\
0 & 0 & 0 & 0 & 0 & 0 & 1 & 0 & 0 \\
0 & 0 & 0 & 0 & 0 & 0 & 0 & 1 & 0 \\
0 & 0 & 0 & 0 & 0 & 0 & 0 & 0 & 1
\end{pmatrix}
\tag{4.24}
$$

with, again, Δt being equal to 1 in our time-discrete system. The process noise covariance $W_t \in \mathbb{R}^{9 \times 9}$ is set to a diagonal matrix for simplicity, see section section 4.4.2 for an example.

The target is observed by m cameras, each of which produce a 2-D observation: the projection of the point-sized target on each camera image. The observation $o_t \in \mathbb{R}^{2m}$ is defined as the concatenation of all individual 2-D observations at time t:

$$
o_t = (o_{x1}, o_{y1}, \ldots, o_{xm}, o_{ym})^\mathrm{T}
\tag{4.25}
$$

with o_{xj} and o_{yj} being the horizontal and vertical coordinates reported by the jth camera and typically measured in pixels. The observation o_t is derived from the state q_t by the observation function (4.4), which is based on the perspective projection in the cameras.

For perspective projection, each camera is parameterized with its *internal* and *external* parameters. The internal parameters are the *focal lengths* ξ_u, ξ_v, the *principal point* σ_u, σ_v and possible skew or distortion parameters (not included here). The external parameters define the affine transformation between the camera coordinates and the world coordinates, given as a rotation matrix $\Phi = (\Phi_{i,j}) \in \mathbb{R}^{3 \times 3}$ and a translation vector $(\tau_x, \tau_y, \tau_z)^\mathrm{T}$. The actual projection of a 3-D point in world coordinates $(x, y, z)^\mathrm{T}$ to 2-D screen coordinates is typically modeled as a matrix multiplication in homogeneous coordinates:

$$
\begin{pmatrix} u \\ v \\ w \end{pmatrix} = \begin{pmatrix} \xi_u & 0 & \sigma_u \\ 0 & \xi_v & \sigma_v \\ 0 & 0 & 1 \end{pmatrix} \begin{pmatrix} \Phi_{0,0} & \Phi_{0,1} & \Phi_{0,2} & \tau_x \\ \Phi_{1,0} & \Phi_{1,1} & \Phi_{1,2} & \tau_y \\ \Phi_{2,0} & \Phi_{2,1} & \Phi_{2,2} & \tau_z \end{pmatrix} \begin{pmatrix} x \\ y \\ z \\ 1 \end{pmatrix}
\tag{4.26}
$$

where the final observation is derived by

$$\begin{pmatrix} o_x \\ o_y \end{pmatrix} = \begin{pmatrix} \frac{u}{w} \\ \frac{v}{w} \end{pmatrix} \tag{4.27}$$

Since this function is not linear (due to the division), we use the extended Kalman filter and obtain the observation matrix $G_t \in \mathbb{R}^{2m \times 9}$ as the derivative of the observation function about the estimated state $\widehat{q}_t^-$, shown here for $m = 1$:

$$G_t = \begin{pmatrix} \frac{\xi_u \cdot (\eta_z \cdot \Phi_{0,0} - \eta_x \cdot \Phi_{2,0})}{\eta_z^2} & \frac{\xi_u \cdot (\eta_z \cdot \Phi_{0,1} - \eta_x \cdot \Phi_{2,1})}{\eta_z^2} & \frac{\xi_u \cdot (\eta_z \cdot \Phi_{0,2} - \eta_x \cdot \Phi_{2,1})}{\eta_z^2} & 0 \cdots 0 \\ \frac{\xi_v \cdot (\eta_z \cdot \Phi_{1,0} - \eta_x \cdot \Phi_{2,0})}{\eta_z^2} & \frac{\xi_v \cdot (\eta_z \cdot \Phi_{1,2} - \eta_x \cdot \Phi_{2,1})}{\eta_z^2} & \frac{\xi_v \cdot (\eta_z \cdot \Phi_{1,2} - \eta_x \cdot \Phi_{2,2})}{\eta_z^2} & 0 \cdots 0 \end{pmatrix} \tag{4.28}$$

where $\eta = (\eta_x, \eta_y, \eta_z)^T$ are the target world coordinates rotated and translated into the camera coordinate system, i.e. $\eta = \Phi \widehat{q}_t^- + \tau$. The zeroes to the right of the matrix correspond to the non-observable parts of the state.

Active object tracking parameterizes the observation function with an action vector a_t for each time t. This action directly affects the internal parameters, such as changing the focal length, or the external parameters, such as panning and tilting of the camera. For example, for a purely zooming camera, $a_t = (a_1)$ is a one-dimensional factor for the focal lengths, i.e.

$$\xi_u = a_1 \cdot \xi_{u0} \tag{4.29}$$

$$\xi_v = a_1 \cdot \xi_{v0} \tag{4.30}$$

for starting focal lengths ξ_{u0} and ξ_{v0}. For a camera on a pan-tilt unit, $a_t = (a_{\text{pan}}, a_{\text{tilt}})$ would describe the pan and tilt angles a_{pan} and a_{tilt}, respectively. These angles change the rotation matrix Φ and possibly the translation vector τ. The observation matrix G_t is changed equivalently.

For systems with more than one camera, as is usually the case, the corresponding observation matrix is achieved by vertical concatenation of the single-camera observation matrix shown above.

4.3.2.2 *Optimal action selection*

Given the above definitions of F_t and G_t, the motion of the target can be reconstructed for any action a_t by use of the Kalman filter. More specifically, this allows us to *predict* the effect any given action will have on the uncertainty of the estimate, measured by the *a posteriori* state covariance matrix P_t^+ after observation o_t has been integrated into the estimate, since P_t^+ does not depend on o_t, seen in (4.6).

As mentioned before, we find the optimal action a_t^* by minimizing the expected entropy of the state estimate. Since the state estimate is in the form of a normal distribution, $q_t \sim \mathcal{N}(\hat{q}_t, P_t^+)$, its conditional entropy has the closed form

$$H(q_t|a_t) = \frac{n}{2} + \frac{1}{2}\log(2\pi^n|P_t^+|), \tag{4.31}$$

where $|\cdot|$ denotes the determinant of a matrix. Since the covariance matrix P_t^+ as calculated in eq. (4.6) depends on a_t but *not* on o_t, we can simplify eq. (4.9) by pulling $H(q_t|a_t)$ out of the integral. The remaining integral now integrates a probability density function and is therefore 1. If we further disregard constant terms and factors, the optimality criterion is

$$a^* = \operatorname*{argmin}_{a_t} \log|P_t^+|. \tag{4.32}$$

The logarithm could even be dropped due to its monotony. Due to the independence of P_t^+ from o_t, we can find the optimal action *before* the associated observation is made.

4.3.2.3 *Visibility*

However, even though the actual value of o_t is not relevant, the *presence* of an observation is. If no complete observation can be made at a certain time step, the Kalman update step cannot be performed. In this case, the *a posteriori* state estimate uncertainty is unchanged from the *a priori* state estimate uncertainty. In other words, $P_t^+ = P_t^-$.

In many cases, this availability of an observation depends on the camera action. Consider the classic focal length dilemma. Using a large focal length (zooming in) gives the best view of an object, but the object risks moving outside the field of view of the camera. Using a small focal length (zooming out) reduces the risk of losing the object, but the object is now very small in the image, and a tracking error of one pixel translates to a much larger world coordinate distance. So the optimal focal length is most likely in between: small enough not to lose the object, but large enough to gain the most information.

In object tracking, each observation is a point on the image plane of a camera (or concatenation of several such points). Since the camera sensor is finite, there are points on this plane which do not lie on the sensor. We will call observations on the camera sensor *visible* observations, and those outside the sensor *non-visible* observations. The impact of this classification is that states that the observation function maps to non-visible observations would not generate any observation at all, i.e. the update step would be skipped.

Assume that we could partition the set of observations into the sets of *visible* observations $\mathcal{O}_v$ and *non-visible* observations $\mathcal{O}_{\neg v}$, and revisit equation (4.9):

$$H(q_t|o_t, a_t) = \int p(o_t|a_t) H(q_t|a_t) \mathrm{d}o_t \tag{4.33}$$

$$= \int_{o_t \in \mathcal{O}_v} p(o_t|a_t) H(q_t|a_t) \mathrm{d}o_t + \int_{o_t \in \mathcal{O}_{\neg v}} p(o_t|a_t) H(q_t|a_t) \mathrm{d}o_t \tag{4.34}$$

due to the summation rule of integers. Given that $H(q_t|a_t)$ is independent of o_t in the Kalman filter case, *except* for the membership of o_t in $\mathcal{O}_v$ or $\mathcal{O}_{\neg v}$, the entropy $H(q_t|a_t)$ can only have (or rather, be proportional to) one of two values:

$$H(q_t|a_t) \propto \begin{cases} \log|P_t^+| & \text{if a visible observation occurs,} \\ \log|P_t^-| & \text{otherwise.} \end{cases} \tag{4.35}$$

This simplifies equation (4.34) to

$$H(q_t|o_t, a_t) \propto \int_{o_t \in \mathcal{O}_v} p(o_t|a_t) \log|P_t^+| \mathrm{d}o_t + \int_{o_t \in \mathcal{O}_{\neg v}} p(o_t|a_t) \log|P_t^-| \mathrm{d}o_t \tag{4.36}$$

$$= \log|P_t^+| \cdot \int_{o_t \in \mathcal{O}_v} p(o_t|a_t) \mathrm{d}o_t + \log|P_t^-| \cdot \int_{o_t \in \mathcal{O}_{\neg v}} p(o_t|a_t) \mathrm{d}o_t \tag{4.37}$$

$$= w \cdot \log|P_t^+| + (1 - w) \cdot \log|P_t^-| \tag{4.38}$$

with w being the probability that the to-be-acquired observation will be visible.

Obviously, w depends on a_t. The probability w can be calculated for each a_t by regarding the observation estimate. In the Kalman filter case, the observation follows a normal distribution, with $o_t \sim \mathcal{N}(g(\widehat{q}_t^-, a_t), S_t)$. The probability w is then the integral over the area of visible observations:

$$w = \int_{o_t \in \mathcal{O}_v} p(o_t|a_t) \mathrm{d}o_t = \int_{o_t \in \mathcal{O}_v} \mathcal{N}(g(\widehat{q}_t^-, a_t), S_t) \mathrm{d}o_t \tag{4.39}$$

In object tracking, $\mathcal{O}_v$ is a rectangular area in the observation space (for each camera). A closed solution exists for this problem. For more than one camera, we will assume that the Kalman update step can only be performed if all cameras produce a visible observation. In this case, w is the product of all individual visibility probabilities.

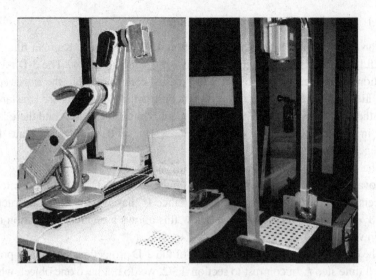

Fig. 4.4   SCORBOT (left) and turn table (right).

4.3.2.4   *Multi-step action selection*

The above method selects the optimal view if all sensor actions are equally valid
and reachable. However, in real world systems, the range of actions available
for the next camera image may be considerably reduced. For example, in zoom
planning, the speed of the zoom motor in the camera determines how far the zoom
settings can be changed in the time between two camera images.

Generally, we associate a *cost* with each action. If the costs of different actions
are not equal, and depend on the previous action (available zoom settings depend
on the current motor position, for example), the above method may not yield the
optimal settings. Instead, we must evaluate a *sequence* of future views. Planning
a sequence of actions, especially given computation time constraints, is discussed
in more detail in Deutsch et al.[Deutsch *et al.* (2006)]

4.3.3   *Active object reconstruction*

We study the problem of finding the next best view in 3-D reconstruction from
intensity images, using the above introduced information theoretical algorithm.
We show how the general algorithm can be adopted to the special task and discuss
some boundary conditions.

4.3.3.1   *State and observation representation*

Similar to active object tracking (cf. section 4.3.2), we use a Kalman filter approach [Kalman (1960)]. Therefore, we use the same notations. The 3-D reconstruction is represented by a list of i 3-D points, concatenated to the *state vector* $q_t \in \mathbb{R}^{3i}$. Since the coordinates of the reconstructed 3-D points are constant in time, the state transition matrix F_t is the identity matrix $I \in \mathbb{R}^{3i}$ and there is no noise in this process, i.e. the noise covariance $W_t = 0$. Further, the state does not depend on time: $q = q_t$.

The state estimate is represented by the state vector, as defined above, and the covariance P_t. We assume each estimate of the 3-D point coordinates is independent of the other ones, so the covariance P_t has a block diagonal structure with 3×3 blocks. As we will see below this allows a efficient evaluation of a certain view.

The observation o_t is a concatenation of the 2-D projections of the 3-D points in each time step t. In contrast to section 4.3.2, we do not have one object, which is observed by m cameras, but we have i points, which are observed by one camera. So the dimension of o_t is $\mathbb{R}^{2i}$. The observation is assumed to be noisy, with an additive Gaussian Noise with zero mean and covariance R_t. The observation function $g(q_t, a_t)$ depends on the modifiable camera parameters a_t (focal length, rotation and translation of the camera), non modifiable ones (principal point, skew and distortion parameters), which are not denoted explicitly, and projects the vector of the 3-D points q_t to the 2-D image plane by the perspective projection model. Therefore, we can use equations (4.26) and (4.27) to evaluate $g(\cdot, \cdot)$.

Since $g(\cdot, \cdot)$ is a nonlinear function, we have to use the extended Kalman filter, which uses a first order Taylor approximation to linearize $g(\cdot, \cdot)$. Thus, we need the Jacobian G of $g(\cdot, \cdot)$, which is derived analytically from equations (4.26) and (4.27). Incidently, it is easy to show that the first order Taylor approximation and the paraperspective projection model, well known in computer vision, are equivalent.

4.3.3.2   *Optimal action selection*

The goal of next best view selection is to find the optimal next view point a_t^* to improve the reconstruction accuracy. One optimality criterion is to reduce the uncertainty in the state estimation, which is measured in information theory by its entropy $H(q|a_t)$. This entropy, however, has to be calculated *a priori* to optimize the view before obtaining a new image.

Therefore, we need to determine the expected entropy $H(q|o_t, a_t)$. The expected entropy is the mean of the entropy of q over all observations and was introduced in equation (4.9). The optimality criterion is the determination of the view a_t^* which maximizes the mutual information (cf. eq. (4.11)), which is equivalent to minimizing the conditional entropy. As in (4.32), this corresponds to minimizing the logarithm of the determinant of P_t. Since P_t is a block diagonal matrix with blocks $P_t^{(k)}$, $k = 1, \ldots i$ the calculation can be simplified to

$$a^* = \underset{a_t}{\operatorname{argmin}} \log \prod_{k=1}^{i} |P_t^{(k)}| = \underset{a_t}{\operatorname{argmin}} \sum_{k=1}^{i} \log |P_t^{(k)}|. \qquad (4.40)$$

So the high computational complexity of calculation of the determinant of a $3i \times 3i$ covariance can be reduced to i calculations of the determinant of 3×3 matrices.

Some constraints on the modifiable camera parameters a_t must be considered. Not every optimal view point, in the sense of (4.32), results in a usable image. Some examples of effects that can make a view point completely or partly unusable are:

- Field of view: all 3-D points to be reconstructed have to be visible in the image, otherwise they cannot observed by the camera. We can ensure this by backprojecting the mean of 3-D estimate of the points to the image plane. If this projection is in the image, we assume that this point is visible.
- Occlusion: again, the 3-D points must be visible in the image. But this constraint may fail for a point, because the point is occluded by parts of the object itself or by the robot arm. This condition is independent of the upper one, since the projection of one point can be in the image, but it is not visible if it lies behind another surface. This constraint is not modeled for the experiments, because we analyze only flat objects. So self occlusions do not occur in this case.
- Reachability: the view point must be reachable by the robot. To ensure this, we use the 4 by 4 *Denavit-Hartenberg* matrix [Craig (2004)], which depends on the angles of the rotation axes and the distances between the joints, to calculate the transformation to a fixed world coordinate system. Since the lengths are fixed, only the angles are relevant.

These constraints determine the search space for our optimization. We are able now to search for the optimal view point a_t^* with an exhaustive search over the discretely sampled action space. The action space in our case is the space with all reachable angles of the joints of the robot. If the expected observation contains image points outside the field of view, we discard this sample. The best-rated undiscarded sample is the next best view.

4.4   Experiments

4.4.1   *Evaluation for active object recognition*

In order to show the benefit of active object recognition we should be able to point out that—compared to an unplanned proceeding—we gain an enhancement in classification results after the same number of views. To satisfy the demands of arbitrary applications for our approach, non-synthetic objects with ambiguities are favorable to be evaluated. So we decided on the toy manikins shown in Fig. 4.5, provided with a quiver, a lamp, a bib, or any of the eight possible combinations of these equipments, consequently arranging a classification problem with eight classes. Image acquisition was done by fixing the manikins on a turntable while getting images from a camera located at a fixed position. Moving the turntable, we cover a circular action space with $J = 1$, as mentioned in section 4.3.1.1. To occasionaly provide perfect ambiguities to our algorithm, we work on fixed croppings of the original images, which can be regarded as zoomed-in image acquisition. This way, decisive equipments can just drop out of the scope, thus from time to time even the best classifier cannot decide reliably on the object class when given a single image.

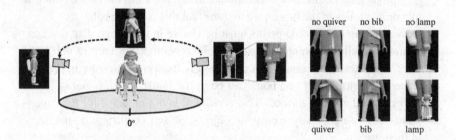

Fig. 4.5   Views of the toy manikin object classes.

For our purpose, we chose steps of 1.0 degree in the horizontal direction to gain a fundamental image set of 360 entries per class. Taking every other image and calculating its features (see 4.3.1.2), we can construct the underlying model.

Given the classifier model, we now take the other half of all taken images for the purpose of the Reinforcement Learning based training phase as well as for the ensuing evaluation phase. This way we avoid getting wrongly conditioned results by working on images that already appear in the model representation.

During the Reinforcement Learning training phase, for each class in the database we now provide ν episodes of randomly chosen sensor actions and resulting images to the algorithm. Each episode contains at most eight steps of image retrieval and consecutive information fusion. Following the intent of this paper, we consequently applied the entropy reward (4.16) during Reinforcement Learning for rating positions, i.e. camera actions. Handling the two-dimensional space, the density representation depends on $M = 2880$ particles altogether, that is 360 particles per class.

Concerning the influence of variable parameters, in a first instance we chose two different values for the number of training episodes $\nu \in \{3, 50\}$ which provides us with two differently reliable databases. Additionally we tested two variations of the weighting $\gamma \in \{0, 0.5\}$ and two kernel parameters $D \in \{2, 5\}$. Fig. 4.6 shows the corresponding classification results in each step, compared to those generated by unplanned sensor action. Results of the planned and random sequences were computed relying on 250 episodes with a maximum of eight steps for each parameter combination and object class.

Taking a look at the results, our choice of reward as well as the complete view planning approach is justified since we almost universally get higher classification rates when not performing arbitrary sensor movements. Especially early steps within an episode ($t = 2, 3$) partially gain a benefit of more then 10% in classification rate.

Furthermore, it is observable that the kernel parameter D and the step influence parameter γ can be altered within an adequate range of values without loosing the view planning benefit compared to the random proceeding. Additionally, a quite small database with only $\nu = 3$ training episodes per class already causes a significant advantage of the planned proceeding. Thus, a possibly desired adaption of training time because of computation time constraints appears to be feasible within a very wide range.

4.4.2   *Evaluation for active object tracking*

The next best view planning for active object tracking is evaluated in a simulation. Object tracking is a relatively easy task to simulate, and ground truth and repeatability are also present. The experimental setup is visible in figure 4.7(a). Two cameras, at right angles, observe a point-shaped tracking target moving in an ellipsis in the center of the scene. The target is tracked by a Kalman filter using a polynomial motion model, as described in section 4.3.2.1. The axes have lengths 400mm and 800mm, respectively. The state transition noise matrix $W_t \in \mathbb{R}^{9 \times 9}$ is a constant diagonal matrix, corresponding to a standard deviation in the position of 100mm, in the velocity of $100mm/\Delta t$ and in the accelleration of $10mm/(\Delta t)^2$.

The generated observations are perturbed by white Gaussian noise with zero mean and a known covariance matrix $R_t \in \mathbb{R}^{4 \times 4}$, corresponding to a standard

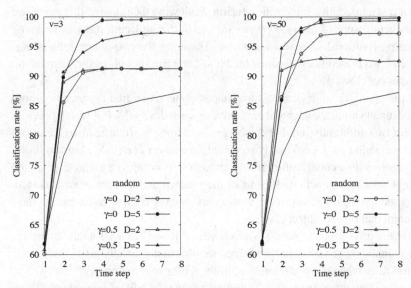

Fig. 4.6   Classifi cation rate after t time steps of planned and unplanned viewpoint selection. For the planned variation combinations of the free parameters ν, γ and D are evaluated. Ratios at the fi rst time step differ, because initial viewpoints were selected randomly.

deviation of 1% of the image width and height for both cameras. If a perturbed observation lies outside the simulated camera field-of-view, it is discarded and is not used to update the Kalman filter. A time step without update results in the *a posteriori* state probability being the same as the *a priori* state probability, with a much larger state entropy $H(q_t|a_t)$ and a larger expected estimation error. This reflects the fact that we have lost information about the target due to the noisy state transition, but not regained it with up-to-date observations. This forces the view optimization system to incorporate the expected visibility in order to avoid such information loss. The target is (potentially) reacquired in the next time step.

Each camera can change its focal length within a certain range, i.e. $a_t = (a_1, a_2)^T$ with a_j the focal length factor for camera j. For comparison, we also run the experiment with a fixed focal length, chosen in such a way that the object is always visible.

Figure 4.7(b) shows the ground truth path of the target and the estimated positions with and without zoom planning. It can be seen that the estimation is error-prone due to the observation noise. The average error was 15.11mm without planning vs. 6.93mm with planning. This is a reduction to 45.9% of the original error.

Figure 4.8(a) shows the zoom levels each camera assumes at each of 200 time

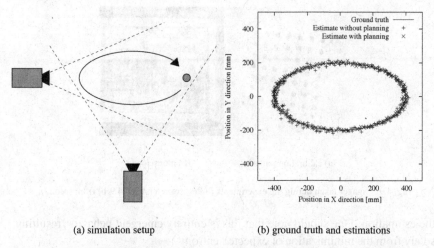

(a) simulation setup   (b) ground truth and estimations

Fig. 4.7   Overview of the object tracking simulation (4.7(a)). Two cameras with variable focal lengths observe an object moving on an elliptical path. Fig. 4.7(b) shows the ground truth object path for two full cycles and the estimated positions without and with view planning.

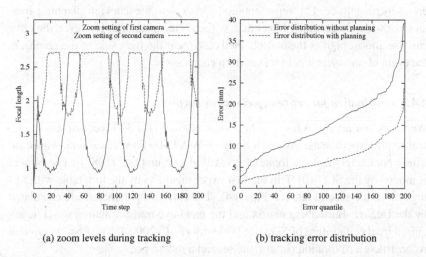

(a) zoom levels during tracking   (b) tracking error distribution

Fig. 4.8   The zoom levels assumed assumed by the two cameras during zoom planning. (4.8(a)) and the distribution of the Euclidian estimation error for simulations with planned and non-planned views, sorted by error value (4.8(b)).

steps (two full object cycles) during zoom planning. Higher focal length values correspond to a narrower field of view. Each camera follows the object, keeping the expected projection close to its image borders. This allows the maximal focal length to be used at all times, minimizing the effect of the observation noise on

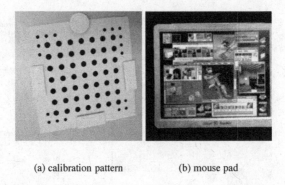

(a) calibration pattern   (b) mouse pad

Fig. 4.9   Images taken during the experiments (4.9(a) from fi rst and 4.9(b) from second).

the estimation. One should note that this is entirely emergent behavior, resulting solely from the minimization of expected entropy.

Figure 4.8(b) shows the distribution of the Euclidian distance between the estimated position and the ground truth position, the estimation error. These distributions were obtained by acquiring the error at each time step, and then sorting all errors by magnitude. This representation allows us to see that view planning gives an error which is generally lower than without view planning. However, the error can rise almost high as the non-planned case (near the right side of the graph), in the event of an object loss in one or both cameras.

4.4.3 *Evaluation for active object reconstruction*

We verify our approach for next best view planning for 3-D reconstruction with real world experiments. We use a Sony DFW-VL500 firewire camera, whose intrinsic parameters were calibrated by Tsai's algorithm [Tsai (1987)]. The camera is moved by the SCORBOT in the first experiment and by the turn table with tilting arm in the second one (cf. Fig. 4.4). The extrinsic parameters are calculated by the Denavit-Hartenberg matrix and the hand-eye transformation, which is acquired by the algorithm of Schmidt [Schmidt *et al.* (2004)]. The first experiment reconstructs a calibration pattern, the second a mouse pad.

In both experiments, we start with an initial estimation, obtained by triangulation from an image pair from two view points. This gives us an initial estimate of q. The initial covariance matrix P_0 is set to a diagonal matrix $\text{diag}(10, \ldots, 10)$, as we assume that the uncertainty is equal in each direction.

To evaluate the expected uncertainty, we calculate the determinant of P_t (eq. (4.32)). The Jacobian $G_t(a_t)$ of the observation function depends on the axis values of the robot and must be calculated for each candidate view point. The

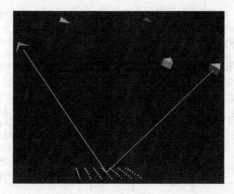

Fig. 4.10 View points for reconstruction of the calibration pattern, with two lines of sight for one point from different view points. We can observe, the angle between the lines of sight is approximately 90 degrees.

computation time for the next best view for the SCORBOT (5 degrees of freedom, due to its 5 axes, 384000 view points analyzed, 49 3-D points) is about 9 minutes on a system with an Pentium IV processor with 3 GHz, and 1 GB RAM, and about 45 seconds for the turntable (2 degrees of freedom, 2000 view points analyzed, 50 3-D points). The computation time is linear in the number of points.

4.4.3.1 *Reconstructing a calibration pattern*

A calibration pattern (cf. Fig. 4.9(a)) is viewed from the top of the SCORBOT. The pattern simplifies the acquisition of 2-D points, and allows us to compare our results with ground truth data. After the initialization, we start the optimization process to take new images from the optimal view point.

Table 4.1 shows the results for the first 5 iterations in the optimized case and a non-optimized one. The images for the non-optimized view points were taken by alternating between the two initial positions.

By construction, the determinant of P_t is reduced faster in the optimized case than in the non-optimized case. Additionally, the mean of the errors of all points decreases after each time step, except for some outliers. This rise in error is not a contradiction to the decrease in uncertainty, since the Kalman filter cannot judge the quality of an observation.

The view points are shown in Fig. 4.10. After the initialization steps (middle top) the optimized view points lie as expected: the cameras are opposite each other and the angle between each line of sight is approx. 90 degrees.

Table 4.1   First experiment: μ_t is the mean of the difference between reconstructed points and the ground truth data in mm, σ_t is the standard deviation of this error, $|P_t|$ is the determinant of the covariance matrix. We display the values for the optimized and a non-optimized view point sequence, which is taken by the SCORBOT.

t	optimized			non-optimized		
	μ_t	σ_t	$|P_t|$	μ_t	σ_t	$|P_t|$
1	0.132	0.080	7.281	0.132	0.080	7.281
2	0.128	0.079	1.762	0.125	0.072	3.338
3	0.115	0.062	0.705	0.128	0.073	1.468
4	0.108	0.062	0.385	0.129	0.074	0.905
5	0.107	0.061	0.244	0.127	0.074	0.531

4.4.3.2   *Reconstructing a mouse pad*

In this experiment we use a mouse pad (cf. Fig. 4.9(b)), requiring us to track feature points during movement, using the algorithm of Zinsser [Zinßer *et al.* (2004)]. However, only the tracked points from the optimal positions are used to update the state estimation. Integration of the points tracked *en route* to the optimal positions is possible, but this would prevent a comparison of two view point sequences due to a diverging number of integrated observations.

Table 4.2 shows the root mean square error between the reconstructed 3-D points and their regression plane, as well as the trend of the covariance matrix P_t, for the first 5 iterations. We compare the values from the optimized view points to an experiment with view points uniformly distributed on a circle perpendicular to the rotation axis of the turn table, and to one completely random view point sequence on the half sphere. The error decreases fastest in the optimized case, signifying a measurable benefit from view point optimization.

Table 4.2   Second experiment: μ_t is the mean of the root mean square error of the points to their regression plane in mm, $|P_t|$ the determinant of the covariance matrix after each iteration. The optimized, one uniform and one random view point sequence are shown.

t	optimized		circle		random	
	μ_t	$|P_t|$	μ_t	$|P_t|$	μ_t	$|P_t|$
1	0.073	8.62	0.073	8.62	0.073	8.65
2	0.050	1.75	0.041	1.98	0.054	2.76
3	0.033	0.636	0.038	0.845	0.043	1.20
4	0.030	0.315	0.038	0.428	0.041	0.479
5	0.026	0.175	0.041	0.235	0.041	0.329

4.5 Summary

We have described an information theoretic framework for selecting the next best view in a computer vision task, based on mutual information. We have applied this framework to three typical computer vision tasks: object recognition, tracking and reconstruction.

State representation in object recognition consists of assumptions about class and pose of the object under consideration. While setting up probability densities of a state, it emerged to be suitable to calculate information theoretic values of those densities, like the conditional entropy, for measuring the impact of a current state. That is, the reduction of ambiguities and favouring of small variances is exactly what is needed in recognition tasks. Thus, utilizing the conditional entropy for planning next best views, we were able to enhance the classification rate from less than 85% to more than 95% for certain parameter settings within the very first step of active data selection.

In object tracking, the state is the position, velocity and acceleration of an object. This object is observed by several cameras, whose internal or external parameters can change. Next best view planning selects the optimal parameters for the estimation of the object state. We have shown the benefit of next best view planning for object tracking in a simulation with cameras with a changeable focal length. Using next best view planning, the tracking error is noticably lower than the same task with fixed focal lengths. In our case, we were able to reduce the estimation error to 45.9% of the error in the fixed focal length setup.

In 3-D reconstruction, the state consists of the 3-D coordinates of the reconstructed points and the observation consists of tracked feature points. Additional constraints, field of view, occlusions, and reachability have to be considered to get a feasible next best view. In two real world experiments, we have shown that optimal selected view points reduce the reconstruction error significantly. In one experiment the error was reduced to 63.4% of the error of unplanned views.

Bibliography

Arbel, T. and Ferrie, F. (2001). Entropy-based gaze planning, *Image and Vision Computing* **19**, 11, pp. 779–786.

Banta, J. E., Wong, L. R., Dumont, C. and Abidi, M. A. (2000). A next-best-view system for autonomous 3-d object reconstruction. *IEEE Transactions on Systems, Man, and Cybernetics, Part A* **30**, 5, pp. 589–598.

Craig, J. J. (2004). *Introduction to Robotics: Mechanics and Control*, 3rd edn. (Prentice Hall, Upper Saddle River, USA).

Davison, A. (2005). Active search for real-time vision, in *Proceedings of the International Conference on Computer Vision (ICCV)*, Vol. 1 (Beijing, China), pp. 66–73.

Deinzer, F., Denzler, J., Derichs, C. and Niemann, H. (2006). Aspects of optimal viewpoint selection and viewpoint fusion, in *Computer Vision – ACCV 2006* (Hyderabad, India), pp. 902–912.

Denzler, J. and Brown, C. (2002). An information theoretic approach to optimal sensor data selection for state estimation, *IEEE Transactions on Pattern Analysis and Machine Intelligence* **24**, 2, pp. 145–157.

Deutsch, B., Wenhardt, S. and Niemann, H. (2006). Multi-Step Multi-Camera View Planning for Real-Time Visual Object Tracking , in *Pattern Recognition - 28th DAGM Symposium* (Berlin), pp. 536–545.

Dickinson, S. J. (1997). Active object recognition integrating attention and viewpoint control, *Computer Vision and Image Understanding* **67**, 3, pp. 239–260.

Isard, M. and Blake, A. (1998). CONDENSATION — Conditional Density Propagation for Visual Tracking, *International Journal of Computer Vision* **29**, 1, pp. 5–28.

Kalman, R. (1960). A new approach to linear filtering and prediction problems, *Journal of Basis Engineering* **82**, pp. 35–44.

Kovačič, S., Leonardis, A. and Pernuš, F. (1998). Planning sequences of views for 3-D object recognition and pose determination, *Pattern Recognition* **31**, 10, pp. 1407–1417.

Kutulakos, K. N. and Dyer, C. R. (1994). Recovering shape by purposive viewpoint adjustment, *International Journal of Computer Vision* **12**, 2, pp. 113–136.

Laporte, C., Brooks, R. and Arbel, T. (2004). A fast discriminant approach to active object recognition and pose estimation, in *Proceedings of the 17th International Conference on Pattern Recognition* (Cambridge), pp. 91–94.

Marchand, E. and Chaumette, F. (1999). Active vision for complete scene reconstruction and exploration, *IEEE Transactions on Pattern Analysis and Machine Intelligence* **21**, 1, pp. 65–72.

Micheloni, C. and Foresti, G. L. (2005). Zoom On Target While Tracking , in *International Conference on Image Processing - ICIP'05* (Genua, Italy), pp. 117–120.

Murase, H. and Nayar, S. (1995). Visual learning and recognition of 3-D objectsfrom appearance, *International Journal of Computer Vision* **14**, pp. 5–24.

Niem, W. (1999). *Automatische Rekonstruktion starrer dreidimensionaler Objekte aus Kamerabildern* (VDI Verlag GmbH).

Papoulis, A. (2002). *Probability, Random Variables, and Stochastic Processes*, 4th edn. (McGraw-Hill, Inc, Singapore).

Pito, R. (1999). A solution to the next best view problem for automated surface acquisition, *IEEE Transactions on Pattern Analysis and Machine Intelligence* **21**, 10, pp. 1016–1030.

Schmidt, J., Vogt, F. and Niemann, H. (2004). Vector Quantization Based Data Selection for Hand-Eye Calibration, in *Vision, Modeling, and Visualization 2004* (Stanford, USA), pp. 21–28.

Scott, W., Roth, G. and Rivest, J.-F. (2003). View planning for automated three-dimensional object reconstruction and inspection, *ACM Computing Surveys* **35**, 1, pp. 64–96.

Sipe, M. A. and Casasent, D. (2002). Feature space trajectory methods for active computer vision, *IEEE Transactions on Pattern Analysis and Machine Intelligence* **24**, 12, pp. 1634–1643.

Sutton, R. S. and Barto, A. G. (1998). *Reinforcement Learning* (A Bradford Book, Cambridge, London).

Tordoff, B. J. and Murray, D. W. (2004). Reactive Control of Zoom while Fixating Using Perspective and Affi ne Cameras, *IEEE Transactions on Pattern Analysis and Machine Intelligence* **26**, 1, pp. 98–112.

Tordoff, B. J. and Murray, D. W. (2007). A method of reactive zoom control from uncertainty in tracking, *Computer Vision and Image Understanding* **105**, 2, pp. 131–144.

Tsai, R. Y. (1987). A Versatile Camera Calibration Technique for High–Accuracy3D Machine Vision Metrology Using Off–the–ShelfTV Cameras and Lenses, *IEEE Journal of Robotics and Automation* **RA–3**, 4, pp. 323–344.

Zhou, X. S., Comaniciu, D. and Krishnan, A. (2003). Conditional feature sensitivity: A unifying view on active recognition and feature selection, in *Proceedings of the 9th International Conference on Computer Vision* (Nice, France), pp. 1502–1509.

Zinßer, T., Gräßl, C. and Niemann, H. (2004). Effi cient Feature Tracking for Long Video Sequences, in *Pattern Recognition, 26th DAGM Symposium* (Tübingen, Germany), pp. 326–333.

Chapter 5

Evaluation of Linear Combination of Views for Object Recognition on Real and Synthetic Datasets

Vasileios Zografos and Bernard F. Buxton

Department of computer science,
University College London,
Malet Place, London, WC1E 6BT
{v.zografos,b.buxton}@cs.ucl.ac.uk

In this work, we present a method for model-based recognition of 3d objects from a small number of 2d intensity images taken from nearby, but otherwise arbitrary viewpoints. Our method works by linearly combining images from two (or more) viewpoints of a 3d object to synthesise novel views of the object. The object is recognised in a target image by matching to such a synthesised, novel view. All that is required is the recovery of the linear combination parameters, and since we are working directly with pixel intensities, we suggest searching the parameter space using a global, evolutionary optimisation algorithm combined with a local search method in order efficiently to recover the optimal parameters and thus recognise the object in the scene. We have experimented with both synthetic data and real-image, public databases.

5.1 Introduction

Object recognition is one of the most important and basic problems in computer vision and, for this reason, it has been studied extensively resulting in a plethora of publications and a variety of different approaches[1] aiming to solve this problem. Nevertheless accurate, robust and efficient solutions remain elusive because of the inherent difficulties when dealing in particular with 3d objects that may be seen

---

[1]For a comprehensive review of object recognition methods and deformable templates in particular, see Refs. [Jain *et al.* (1998); Pope (1994); Yang *et al.* (2002); Besl and Jain (1985)].

from a variety of viewpoints. Variations in geometry, photometry and viewing angle, noise, occlusions and incomplete data are some of the problems with which object recognition systems are faced.

In this paper, we will address a particular kind of extrinsic variations: variations of the image due to changes in the viewpoint from which the object is seen. Traditionally, methods that aimed to solve the recognition problem for objects with varying pose relied on an explicit 3d model of the object, generating 2d projections from that model and comparing them with the scene image. Such was the work by Lee and Ragnarath.[Lee and Ranganath (2003)] Although 3d methods can be quite accurate when dealing with pose variations, generating a 3d model can be a complex process and require the use of specialised hardware. Other methods[Lamdan *et al.* (1988); Beymer (1994)] have thus tried to capture the viewpoint variability by using multiple views of the object from different angles, covering a portion of, or the entirety of, the view sphere. If the coverage is dense these methods require capture and storage of a vast number of views for each object of interest. Quite recently, new methods have been introduced that try to alleviate the need for many views while still working directly with 2d images.They are called *view-based* methods and represent an object as a collection of a small number of 2d views. Their advantage is that they do not require construction of a 3d model while keeping the number of required stored views to a minimum. Prime examples are the works by Bebis et al.[Bebis *et al.* (2002)] and Turk and Pentland.[Turk and Pentland (1991)]

Our proposed method is a view-based approach working directly with pixel values and thus avoids the need for low-level feature extraction and solution of the correspondence problem such as in Ref. [Bebis *et al.* (2002)]. As a result, our model is easy to construct and use, and is general enough to be applied across a variety of recognition problems. The disadvantage is that it may also be sensitive to illumination changes, occlusions and intrinsic shape variations.[Dias and Buxton (2005)] We adopt a "generate and test" approach using an optimisation algorithm to recover the optimal linear combination of views (LCV) coefficients that synthesise a novel image which is as similar as possible to the target image. If the similarity (usually the cross-correlation coefficient) between the synthesised and the target images is above some threshold then an object is determined to be present in the scene and its location and pose are defined (at least in part) by the LCV coefficients.

In the next section we introduce the LCV and explain how it is possible to use it to synthesise realistic images from a range of viewpoints. In section 5.3 we present our 3d object recognition paradigm which incorporates the LCV and the optimisation solution, and in section 5.4 we show some experimental results of our approach on synthetic and real imagery. Finally, we conclude in section 5.5 with a critical evaluation of our method and suggest how it could be further improved in the future.

5.2 Linear Combination of Views

LCV is a technique which belongs in the general theory of the tri- and multi-focal tensors , or Algebraic Function of View (AFoV)[Shashua (1995)] and provides a way of dealing with variations in an object's pose due to viewpoint changes. This theory is based on the observation that the set of possible images of a set of landmarks points on an object undergoing 3d rigid transformations and scaling is, under most (i.e. affine) imaging conditions, to a good approximation embedded in a linear space spanned by a small number of 2d images of the landmark points. With the aid of an additional assumption as to how to combine the pixel intensities in the 2d images, it follows that the variety of 2d views depicting an object can be represented by a combination of a small number of 2d *basis views* of the object.

Ullman and Basri[Ullman and Basri (1991)] were the first to show how line drawings or edge map images of novel views of a 3d object could be generated via a linear combination of similar 2d basis views. More specifically, they showed that under the assumption of orthographic projection and 3d rigid transformations, 2 views are sufficient to represent any novel view of a polygonal object from the same aspect. The proof may easily be extended to any affine imaging condition. Thus, to a good approximation, given two images of an object from different (basis) views I' and I'' with corresponding image coordinates (x', y') and (x'', y''), we can represent any point (x, y) in a novel, target view I_T according to, for example:

$$\begin{aligned} x &= a_0 + a_1 x' + a_2 y' + a_3 x'' \\ y &= b_0 + b_1 x' + b_2 y' + b_3 x'' \end{aligned} \quad (5.1)$$

The target view is reconstructed from the above two equations given a set of valid coefficients (a_i, b_j). Provided we have at least 4 corresponding landmark points in all three images (I_T, I', I'') we can estimate the coefficients (a_i, b_j) by using a standard least squares approach. Based on a method for weighting the combination of the intensities (or colours) of corresponding points in the basis views I' and I'', several others have taken this concept further from its initial application to line images and edge maps to the representation of real images I_T.[Koufakis and Buxton (1998); Hansard and Buxton (2000); Peters and von der Malsburg (2001); Bebis *et al.* (2002)]

Such results suggest that it is possible to use LCV for object recognition in that target views of an object can be recognised by matching them to a combination of stored, basis views of the object. The main difficulty in applying this idea within a pixel-based approach is the selection of the LCV coefficients (a_i, b_j). In particular, as described in the next section, synthesis of an image of a novel view from the images of the basis views, although straightforward, is a non-linear and non-invertible process.

5.2.1 *Image synthesis*

To synthesise a single, target image using LCV and two views we first need to determine its geometry from the landmark points. In principle we can do so by using (5.1) and n corresponding landmark points (where $n \geqslant 4$), and solving the resulting system of linear equations in a least squares sense. This is straightforward if we know, can detect, or predict the landmark points in image I_T. Such methods may therefore be useful for image coding and for synthesis of target views of a known object.[Koufakis and Buxton (1998); Hansard and Buxton (2000)] For pixel-based object recognition in which we wish to avoid feature detection a direct solution is not possible, but we instead use a powerful optimisation algorithm to search for and recover the LCV coefficients for the synthesis.

Given the geometry of the target image I_T, in a pixel-based approach we need to synthesise its appearance (colour, texture and so on) in terms of the basis images I' and I''. Since we are not concerned here with creation of a database of basis views of the objects of interest, we may suppose that a sparse set of corresponding landmark points $(x'(j), y'(j))$ and $(x''(j), y''(j))$ may be chosen manually and offline in images I' and I'' respectively and used to triangulate the images in a consistent manner. An illustration of the above can be seen in Fig. 5.1.

Given a set of hypothesised landmark points $(x(j), y(j))$ in the target image we can, to a good approximation, synthesise the target image I_T as described in Refs. [Buxton *et al.* (1998); Dias and Buxton (2005); Koufakis and Buxton (1998)] from a weighted linear combination:

$$I_T(x,y) = w'I'(x',y') + w''I''(x'',y'') + \epsilon(x,y) = I_S(x,y) + \epsilon(x,y), \quad (5.2)$$

in which the weights w' and w'' my be calculated from the LCV coefficients to form the synthesised image I_S. Essentially this relies on the fact that, in addition to the multi-view image geometry being to a good approximation affine, the photometry is to a good approximation affine or linear.[Shashua (1992)] The synthesis essentially warps and blends images I' and I'' to produce I_S. It is important to note therefore that (5.2) applies at all points (pixels) (x,y), (x',y') and

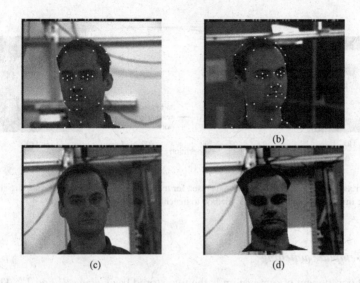

Fig. 5.1   Example of real data from the CMU PIE database. The two basis views (a) and (b) and the target image (c). The synthesised image (d) is at the correct pose identified by our algorithm. Note that in (d) the face is missing some information (around the ears for example). This is because these areas do not appear in both basis views due to self-occlusion and cannot be modelled by the two images alone.

(x'', y'') in images I_S, I' and I'' with the dense correspondence defined by means of the LCV equations (5.1) and a series of piecewise linear mappings[Goshtasby (1986)] within each triangle of the basis images. If (x', y') and (x'', y'') do not correspond precisely to pixel values, bilinear interpolation is used.[Hansard and Buxton (2000); Koufakis and Buxton (1998)] The same idea may be extended to colour images by treating each spectral band as a luminance component (e.g. I_R, I_G, I_B).

5.3   The Recognition System

In principle using the LCV for object recognition is easy. All we have to do is find the LCV coefficients in an equation such as (5.1) which will optimise the sum of squared errors ϵ from (5.2) and check if it small enough, or our synthesised and target images I_S and I_T are sufficiently similar, to enable us to say that they match.

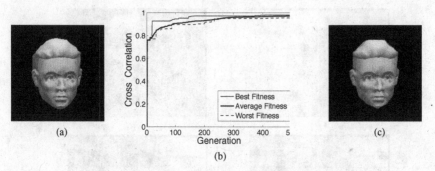

Fig. 5.2   Example of a synthetic target image used for testing (a). The average test results are shown in (b). The image produced by the LCV method to match the target (a) is shown in (c).

5.3.1   *Template matching*

The first component of our system is the two stored basis views I' and I''. These are rectangular bitmap images that contain gray-scale (or colour), pixel information of the object without any additional background data. The images are obtained from basis views chosen, as indicated earlier, so that the viewpoint from which the target image I_T is taken lies on the view sphere between or almost between the basis views from which I' and I'' are taken. It is important not to choose a very wide angle between the basis views since this can lead to I' and I'' belonging to different aspects of the object and thus to landmark points being occluded[2]. Having selected the two basis views, we pick a number of corresponding landmark points in particular lying on discontinuity boundaries, edges and other prominent features. When the appropriate number of landmarks have been selected we use constrained Delaunay triangulation to produce consistent and corresponding triangular meshes of all the images. The above processes may be carried out during an offline training stage and are not examined here. The recognition system involves choosing the appropriate LCV coefficients (a_i, b_j), synthesising an image I_S and comparing it with the target image I_T, using some similarity or dissimilarity metric. The synthetic image of the object is compared from (5.1) and (5.2) only over the region covered by the object. However, in order to make a probabilistic interpretation of the match, the synthesised image must be superimposed on the background as shown in Fig. 5.1(d) and all the pixels compared, such as in Ref. [Sullivan *et al.* (2001)]. The background must therefore be known as it is in the CMU PIE database[Sim *et al.* (2002)], or very simple (e.g. a uniform black

---

[2]It is still quite possible to synthesise novel images at wider angles and remove any self-occluded triangles, although we do not address this problem here, see Ref. [Hansard and Buxton (2000)].

background as in the COIL-20 database[Nene *et al.* (1996)]) or itself calculated from an appropriate model. Making the comparison over all pixels belonging to both the foreground and background in this way means that either a dissimilarity metric such as the sum of squared differences (SSD) or a similarity measure such as the cross-correlation coefficient $c(I_T, I_S)$ may be used, without generating spurious solutions for example, when the area of the foreground region covered by the object shrinks to zero.[Buxton and Zografos (2005)] We have used the latter because when applied to the whole image it is invariant to affine photometric transformations.[Buxton and Zografos (2005)] The choice of LCV coefficients is thus determined by maximising the cross-correlation coefficient:

$$\min_{a_i, b_j}(1 - c(I_T, I_S)). \qquad (5.3)$$

Essentially we are proposing a flexible template matching system, in which the template is allowed to deform in the LCV space until it matches the target image.

5.3.2 *Optimisation*

To find the LCV coefficients (a_i, b_j) we need to search a high-dimensional parameter space using an efficient optimisation algorithm. For this purpose, we have chosen a hybrid method, which combines a global (albeit slower) stochastic algorithm with a local, direct search approach. The idea is that when we find a good-enough solution with the stochastic method (usually after a pre-determined number of function evaluations) and we are inside the basin of attraction of the optimal solution, we can switch over to the local method to refine the results and quickly reach the optimum.

The stochastic method used is a recent evolutionary, population-based optimisation algorithm that works on real-valued coded individuals and is capable of handling non-differentiable, nonlinear and multi-modal objective functions. It is called Differential Evolution (DE) and was introduced by Storn and Price.[Storn and Price (1997)] Briefly, DE works by adding the weighted difference between two randomly chosen population vectors to a third vector, and the fitness of the solution represented by the resultant is compared with that of another individual from the current population. In this way, in DE we can deduce from the distances between the population vectors where a better solution might lie, thereby making the optimisation self-organising. In addition, it is efficient in searching high-dimensional spaces and is capable of finding promising basins of attraction[Buxton and Zografos (2005)] early in the optimisation process without the need for good initialisation.

For the local method, we have selected the algorithm[3] by Nelder and Mead,[Nelder and Mead (1965)] since it is very simple to implement and its use does not require calculation (or approximation) of first or second order derivatives. A simplex is a polytope of N+1 vertices in N dimensions with each vertex corresponding to a single matching function evaluation. In its basic form (as described by Nelder and Mead) the simplex is allowed to take a series of steps, the most common of which is the *reflection* of the vertex having the poorest value of the objective. It may also change shape (*expansion* and *contraction*) to take larger steps when inside a valley or flat areas, or to squeeze through narrow cols. It can also change direction (*rotate*) when no more improvement can be made in a current path. Since the simplex is a local, direct search method, it can become stuck in local optima and therefore some modifications of its basic behaviour are necessary. The first modification we introduced was the ability of the simplex to *restart* whenever it stalled inside a local optimum. The restart works as follows. After a specific number of function evaluations where there has been no change in the value of the tracked optimum, we keep the best vertex P_0 and we generate n new vertices P_i using the formula:

$$P_i = P_0 + \lambda e_i, \tag{5.4}$$

where e_i are n random unit vectors, $i = 1, .., n$ and λ is a constant that represents the step-size. The idea is that by restarting the simplex close to the best point P_0 we can escape a local optimum but without jumping too far away from the last good solution that we have found. We soon discovered that any fixed step λ will eventually become too big as the algorithm progresses, and the simplex will keep jumping in and out of a good optimum without making any significant improvement for the remaining function evaluations. We therefore allowed λ to reduce as the algorithm progressed using the reduction schedule (typically met in Simulated Annealing):

$$\lambda = \lambda_0 C^{(k-1)} \tag{5.5}$$

where k is the current function evaluation, and C is the "cooling rate". In this way, when the algorithm first stalls, it makes big jumps to attempt to escape from the local optimum and as it progresses the jumps become smaller and smaller, so that the algorithm tries to "burrow" deeper into the basin of attraction. As a result, the algorithm keeps on improving the location of the optimum unlike the fixed-step version which stalls early in the optimisation process. We can see both these two methods illustrated in Fig. 5.3.

[3]Also known as the downhill simplex method or simplex method. It is not to be confused with the simplex algorithm for the solution of the linear programming problem.

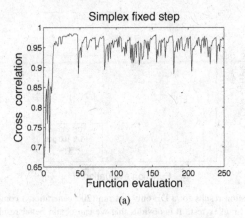

(a)

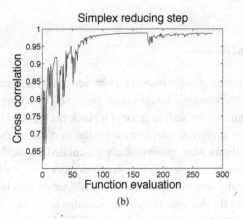

(b)

Fig. 5.3   Comparison between a fixed step simplex method (a) and a reducing step variant (b). In the latter, the algorithm keeps on improving the object recognition.

As mentioned above, the reason for using a hybrid approach as opposed to the global, stochastic method alone, is that we can get very close to the optimum solution in many fewer iterations. This is because evolutionary methods, although they find a "fairly-good" solution early in the optimisation process, they spend the remainder of the function evaluation "budget" carrying out small improvements in the recovered optimum. If we therefore switch to the local, deterministic method once a fairly good solution is recovered by the stochastic method, we can get to a near-globally optimal solution much earlier. The comparison between a stochastic-only and hybrid optimisation methods can be seen in Fig. 5.4.

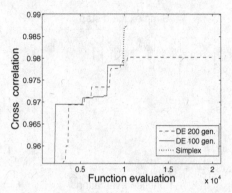

Fig. 5.4 The optimisation results for a DE-only test run (200 generations) compared with that of a DE (100 generations)+Simplex test. It is obvious that we can obtain better results in the latter case with many fewer iterations.

5.4 Experimental Results

We performed a number of experiments on synthetic and real images under varying camera angle. The synthetic images were generated by taking 2d snapshots of a 3d object (a human head model) in front of a black background (see Fig. 5.2(a)). Landmarks where manually selected amongst the vertices of the 3d object and their projected positions were automatically calculated in the 2d images. This way we could eliminate the approximation errors associated with manual placement of corresponding landmarks in the two basis views and have control over the projection model (in this case orthographic projection). Our synthetic dataset consisted of a number of pose angles between $\pm 14^o$ about the vertical and $\pm 10^o$ about the horizontal axes. The majority of the target views lay on the portion of the view-sphere between the basis views, but in a few examples the system had to extrapolate away from the great circle on the viewsphere between the basis views, in order to recover the optimal coefficients. In terms of optimisation complexity, these synthetic examples are considered quite simple since we are dealing with an object with diffuse (Lambertian) reflectivity, which is fairly convex (i.e. not self-occluding, at least over the range of angles we are testing), under constant lighting and distance from the camera, and there is no approximation error on the landmarks of the two basis views. In addition, the object is imaged against a constant background, which produces a convex error surface with a wide basin of attraction. The optimum solution in such cases can be easily and efficiently recovered. Therefore, we only needed to carry out a few experiments on this dataset in order to determine whether the method works in principle or not. In total, we ran 10 synthetic experiments and the results are illustrated in Fig. 5.2(b). These results are very encouraging with the majority of the experiments converging to the correct solution with a cross-correlation of > 0.97. The only cases which failed to converge to the correct optimal solution occurred when the target viewpoint was far from the great circle in view space between the basis views. In such cases, the LCV could not synthesise the target view accurately indicating the need to use more than two basis views in order to better represent that portion of the view-sphere.

5.4.1 *Experiments on the CMU PIE database*

For the real image experiments, we used two publicly available datasets: the CMU PIE database[Sim *et al.* (2002)] and the COIL-20 database.[Nene *et al.* (1996)] The CMU PIE contains examples of facial images from various individuals across different pose, illumination and expression conditions. In our tests, we used pose variation subsets, making sure the manually chosen landmarks were visible in both basis views (see Fig. 5.1). We constructed LCV models from 10 individuals using as basis views the left and right images ($c29, c05$) of each individual with a natural expression (see Fig. 5.8(a)). The face, once synthesised, was then superimposed onto the background which is given separately in the database, and the resulting image was compared with a test, target view. Comparisons were carried out against the images of the 10 individuals in the database, while attempting to detect poses from $-45^o, -22.5^o, 0^o, 22.5^0, 45^o$ about the vertical and a limited range about the horizontal axes (images $c09$ and $c07$).

In total we carried out 700 experiments across pose and constructed a $10 \times 10 \times 7$ "confusion array" of model$\times$image$\times$pose. Each 10×10 pose-slice of this array contains information about the recognition responses (cross-correlation) of our tests, the highest being along the main diagonal, where each individual's model is correctly matched to that individual's image. The recognition response should be less when comparing a specific model with images of other individuals. This behaviour, averaged over pose can be seen as a "heatmap" in Fig. 5.5(a) whilst the pose-dependent recognition rate and recognition response (averaged over the 10 models) are shown in Fig. 5.5(b) and (c) respectively. We can see from the high values (white) along the leading diagonal of the averaged "heatmap" Fig. 5.5(a) that for all 10 experiments, the calculated cross-correlation $c(I_S(i), I_T(j))$, where $I_S(i)$ is the image synthesised from the model of the ith object (i.e. its basis views) and $I_T(j)$ a target image of the jth object, is generally greatest when $i = j$. The response usually falls off for $i \neq j$, with some individuals being more similar than others (grey areas in the heatmap). For the average recognition rate, we checked

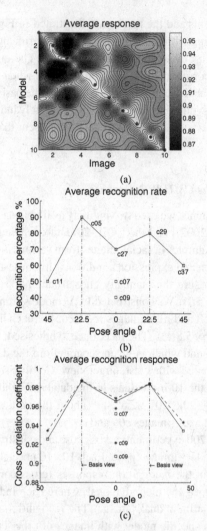

Fig. 5.5   A heatmap (a) showing the entries in the confusion array averaged over pose. (b) shows the recognition rate as a function of pose angle averaged over all models and (c) the recognition response at the same angles as in (b). Solid symbols are used for the best match and open squares for the correct match with i=j.

to see if the highest response corresponded to a correct match between the model and an image of that individual at every pose. As expected, we had the highest recognition rates at the basis views ($\pm 22.5^o$) when no interpolation is necessary, slightly lower rates when we had to interpolate to find the frontal view (0°) and

(a)   (b)

Fig. 5.6   This figure shows the ghosting effects that might occur from warping the intensities of the two basis views. (a) is the target view that we are trying to reconstruct and (b) is the synthesised image. As we can see the geometry is correct but there are some ghosting effects in (b) from one of the basis views, in particular just behind the eye and behind the wing of the image of the toy duck. This usually occurs when a few triangles cover large, detailed areas of the image. This problem can be usually remedied by using more landmark points, and thus triangles, in those areas.

still lower rates when extrapolation was required to synthesise the correct view at ($\pm 45^{o}$). The same reduction in recognition rate also applies to pose variation about the vertical axis ($c07, c09$). Examination of the average recognition response in Fig. 5.5(c) shows the expected "M-Shaped" curve, with the highest response being at the basis views, slightly lower for the frontal image (interpolation) and still lower for images taken from "outside" the basis views (extrapolation). The solid line shows the response for the tests in the leading diagonal of the confusion array (i.e. where the correct solutions lie) and the dashed line shows the maximum response in each column of the image$\times$pose slice of the confusion array. Where there are large discrepancies between the solid line and the dashed-line, the recognition rate will be low, whilst there will be no difference if the recognition rate is 100%. Thus, at the two basis views where we have a high recognition rate, there is little difference between the solid and dashed lines, there is a slight difference for the frontal image and a bigger difference for the target images where we need to extrapolate beyond the basis views.

In general, the results are quite pleasing with the correct person identified the vast majority of times when the target view was between the basis views and no extrapolation was required. It is important to note that the recognition rate is not 100% at the two basis views as we might have expected it to be. There are many reasons for this, mainly the fact that we have carried out only 10 experiments per individual per pose, and therefore a single failure reduces the recognition rate to 90%. Also, the landmarking of the face images (and other objects to be discussed later in the COIL-20 database) is quite sparse (Fig. 5.1), resulting in particular errors around the extremal boundaries of the face images. Additionaly, the cho-

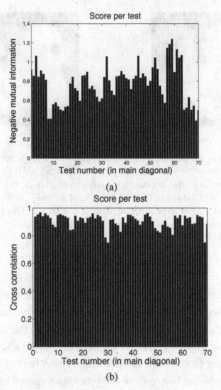

Fig. 5.7 Barplots showing the scores per test in the main diagonal, arranged by pose, both for the mutual information (a) and the cross-correlation (b). A "good" measure should exhibit an almost constant value, such as the cross-correlation in (b).

sen objects (facial images) are quite similar to each other (facial features, skin tone, hair colour and so on) and in this case, unlike for the synthetic examples, we are dealing with a much more complex optimisation problem, partially caused by the cluttered background.[Buxton and Zografos (2005)] The lower than expeced recognition rates thus are a combination of the sparse landmarking, the limited number of experiments and the occassional failure of the optimisation algorithm to converge to the correct solution. It should be possible to increase the recognition rates by using more landmark points and views during the modelling stage, constructing models for a larger set of objects and thus making additional tests against more target images, possibly taken from a greater number of viewpoints, and also initialising the optimisation algorithm closer to the basin of attraction of the optimal solution.

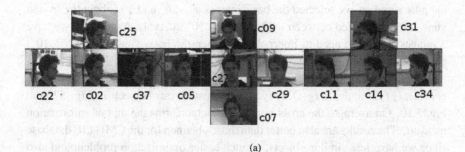

(a)

(b)

Fig. 5.8   Image samples from the CMU PIE (a) and COIL-20 (b) databases.

5.4.2   Experiments on the COIL-20 database

The COIL-20 database contains examples of 20 objects imaged under varying pose (horizontal rotation around the view-sphere at 5° intervals) against a constant background, with the camera position and lighting conditions kept constant (see Fig. 5.8(b)). In this case, we created two "confusion arrays", one using the cross-correlation coefficient and the other using the negative of the mutual information:

$$M(I_S, I_T) = - \sum p(I_S, I_T) \log \frac{p(I_S, I_T)}{p(I_S)p(I_T)}, \tag{5.6}$$

where $p(I_S, I_T)$ is the joint p.d.f. and $p(I_S), p(I_T)$ the marginal p.d.f.s of the synthesised and target images I_S and I_T respectively. In these calculations, the probability distributions were approximated by histograms computed from the images, akin to Ref [Maes *et al.* (1997)]. Mutual information was used to see if there was any advantage in using a matching measure that is known not to be dependent on a simple, direct mapping between the pixel attributes. For the mutual information measure, a low score (i.e. a negative number of larger magnitude) indicates a better match. In these experiments, we selected two basis views from images of half of the objects and tested the matching across all objects both those modelled (here labeled 1-10) and unmodelled (here labeled 11-20) and across 7 poses. The image confusion array was thus of dimensions $10 \times 20 \times 7$ (model$\times$image$\times$pose). For the pose samples, we selected the basis images at -20° and 20° about the frontal view at 0°, and tested between -30° to 30° at 10° intervals. As a result, we have 3 images where we need to interpolate between the basis views $(-10^o, 0^o, 10^o)$ and two where extrapolation is required $(-30^o, 30^o)$.

In total, we carried out 2800 experiments, 1400 for each of the error measures $c(I_S(i), I_T(j))$ and $M(I_S(i), I_T(j))$. The results can be seen in Fig. 5.9 and Fig. 5.10. On average, the cross-correlation outperforms the mutual information measure. The results are also better than those obtained for the CMU PIE database since we have less similar objects, a much easier optimisation problem and also we have carried out more experiments. What is interesting to note from Fig. 5.9 is how much more distinctive the leading diagonal is in the heatmaps for the cross-correlation (b) than that for the mutual information (a). This indicates that the true positive responses are quite distinct from those of the true negatives and that there is less chance for miss-recognitions. The same conclusion may be drawn from the second half of the heatmap showing the scores obtained for matching the models (1-10) to images of the other objects (11-20). In this case, there are no very good matches to any of the models and all of the images are likely to be rejected as unrecognised. The point that miss-recognition is unlikely is also reinforced by (c),(d),(e) and (f) in Fig. 5.10 which show the matching scores and recognition rates at different pose angles, averaged over the modelled objects as in Fig. 5.5(b) and (c).

Furthermore, the heatmaps (a) and (b) in Fig. 5.10 show the average response over all the modelled objects at different pose angles. In the case of mutual information, we would expect lower scores (i.e. valley) at a pose of 0°, which actually occurs, and minima at the basis views at $\pm 20^o$ which do not occur. This is perhaps because when reconstructing at one basis view, there are some "ghosting" (Fig. 5.6) effects from the other basis view that affect pixel intensities even though the geometry is correct. It seems that mutual information is more sensitive to this effect than cross-correlation. Also we notice in Fig. 5.10(a) and (b) some spreading of high and low response values across pose. This spreading is very significant and explains how well a model matches to other objects (including itself) at different poses. For example, a generic looking object (e.g. a box) that can easily "morph" under the LCV mapping (5.1) to match the shape of the images of many objects from the database, will show a spread of high values (for mutual information) across pose angles. On the other hand, a complex object with unique geometry and intensity will show a spread of low values (again for mutual information).

We finally include two bar plots comparing the cross-correlation and mutual information measures (Fig. 5.7). These show the response values per test arranged

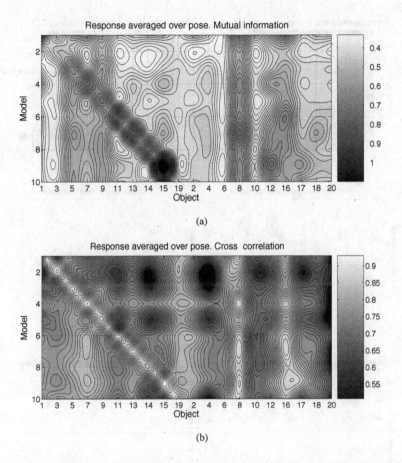

Fig. 5.9   Analysis of the results obtained from experiments on the COIL-20 database using cross-correlation and mutual information error measures. (a) shows the 10x20 matrix of responses averaged over the pose for the mutual information measure and (b) shows similar results for the cross-correlation. It is obvious that in the case of the cross-correlation (b) the resulting leading diagonal in the first half of the heatmap is more distinctive than that of the mutual information.

by pose and model, where the model is chosen to be the correct one for the target image, i.e. along the leading diagonal of the confusion array. What we must note here is that an "appropriate" matching measure should give consistently good responses throughout all the tests, both as the viewing angle of the target images for a given object changes and as we change from object to object, resulting in a uniform distribution of the response values. This is in fact the case for the cross-correlation (b) for which the distribution of the matching scores appears quite

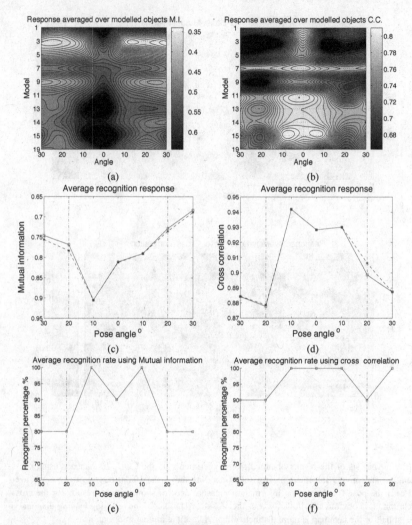

Fig. 5.10   Some additional results from the COIL-20 database. Plots (a) and (b) show the 10x10 matrix of responses averaged over the modelled objects for the mutual information and cross-correlation measures respectively. (c) and (d) show the average recognition response for the two error measures and (e) and (f) the similarly averaged recognition rates.

uniform, but not so for the mutual information (a), a further indication that cross-correlation is the appropriate matching metric for object recognition by image-based template matching.

5.5   Conclusion

We have shown how the linear combination of views (LCV) method may be used in view-based object recognition. Our approach involves synthesising intensity images using LCV and comparing them to the target, scene image. The LCV coefficients for the synthesis are recovered by a hybrid optimisation algorithm, comprised of differential evolution[Storn and Price (1997)] combined with the simplex method.[Nelder and Mead (1965)] Experiments on both synthetic and real data from the CMU PIE and COIL-20 databases, demonstrate that the method works well for pose variations especially those where the target view lies between, or almost between the basis views. DE plays an important role in our method, by searching efficiently the high-dimensional, LCV space. Such an algorithm can narrow the search space to a promising area within the basin of attraction of a good solution, in which a local optimisation method can be used for finding an accurate solution. For objects from the COIL database, we also compared the use of cross-correlation and mutual information for intensity-based template matching. We have seen from our experiments on real data that the cross-correlation slightly outperforms the mutual information measure. This is possibly because of the type of error surfaces it produces especially around the basin of attraction.

Additional work is required, however. In particular, we would like to reformulate (5.1) by using the affine tri-focal tensor and introducing the appropriate constraints in the LCV mapping process. Formulating (5.1) in term of individual 3d transforms might also help bound the range of the LCV coefficients and make initialisation of the optimisation algorithm more intuitive. Furthermore, we would like to introduce probabilistic weights on the coefficients as prior information about the range of likely views and formulate a Bayesian inference mechanism. This, we believe, will greatly aid the recognition process. At this stage we have only addressed extrinsic, viewpoint variations, but we have indicated how it should be possible to include intrinsic, shape variations (see for example Ref. [Dias and Buxton (2005)].) and lighting variations on the image pixels.

Bibliography

Bebis, G., Louis, S., Varol, T. and Yfantis, A. (2002). Genetic object recognition using combinations of views, *IEEE Transactions on Evolutionary Computation* **6**, 2, pp. 132–146.

Besl, P. J. and Jain, R. C. (1985). Three-dimensional object recognition, *ACM Computing Surveys (CSUR)* **17**, pp. 75–145.

Beymer, D. J. (1994). Face recognition under varying pose, in *Proc. IEEE Conf. CVPR*, pp. 756–761.

Buxton, B. and Zografos, V. (2005). Flexible template and model matching using image intensity, in *Proceedings Digital Image Computing: Techniques and Applications (DICTA)*.

Buxton, B. F., Shafi , Z. and Gilby, J. (1998). Evaluation of the construction of novel views by a combination of basis views. in *Proc. IX European Signal Processing Conference (EUSIPCO-98)* (Rhodes, Greece).

Dias, M. B. and Buxton, B. F. (2005). Implicit, view invariant, linear flexible shape modelling, *Pattern Recognition Letters* **26**, 4, pp. 433–447.

Goshtasby, A. (1986). Piecewise linear mapping functions for image registration, **19**, 6, pp. 459–466.

Hansard, M. E. and Buxton, B. F. (2000). Parametric view-synthesis, *In Proc. 6th ECCV* **1**, pp. 191–202.

Jain, A. K., Zhong, Y. and Dubuisson-Jolly, M.-P. (1998). Deformable template models: A review, *Signal Processing* **71**, 2, pp. 109–129.

Koufakis, I. and Buxton, B. F. (1998). Very low bit-rate face video compression using linear combination of 2dfaceviews and principal components analysis, *Image and Vision Computing* **17**, pp. 1031–1051.

Lamdan, Y., Schwartz, J. and Wolfson, H. (1988). On recognition of 3d objects from 2d images, *Proceedings of the IEEE International Conference on Robotics and Automation* , pp. 1407–1413.

Lee, M. W. and Ranganath, S. (2003). Pose-invariant face recognition using a 3d deformable model, *Pattern Recognition* **36**, pp. 1835–1846.

Maes, F., Collignon, A., Vandermeulen, D., Marchal, G. and Suetens, P. (1997). Multimodality image registration by maximization of mutual information, *IEEE Transactions on Medical Imaging* **16**, 2, pp. 187–198.

Nelder, J. A. and Mead, R. (1965). A simplex method for function minimization, *Computer Journal* **7**, pp. 308–313.

Nene, S. A., Nayar, S. K. and Murase, H. (1996). Columbia Object Image Library (COIL-20), Tech. Rep. CUCS-006-96, Department of computer science, Columbia University, New York, N.Y. 10027.

Peters, G. and von der Malsburg, C. (2001). View reconstruction by linear combination of sample views, *In Proc. British Machine Vision Conference BMVC 2001* **1**, pp. 223–232.

Pope, A. R. (1994). Model-based object recognition. a survey of recent research, Tech. Rep. 94-04.

Shashua, A. (1992). *Geometry and Photometry in 3D Visual Recognition*, Ph.D. thesis, Massachusetts Institute of Technology.

Shashua, A. (1995). Algebraic functions for recognition, *IEEE Transactions on Pattern Analysis and Machine Intelligence* **17**, 8, pp. 779–789.

Sim, T., Baker, S. and Bsat, M. (2002). The CMU pose, illumination and expression (PIE) database, in *Proc. of the 5th IEEE international conference on automatic face and gesture recognition*.

Storn, R. and Price, K. V. (1997). Differential evolution - a simple and effi cient heuristic for global optimization overcontinuous spaces, *Journal of Global Optimization* **11**, 4, pp. 341–359.

Sullivan, J., Blake, A., M.Isard and J.MacCormick (2001). Bayesian object localisation in images, *Int. J. Computer Vision* **44**, 2, pp. 111–136.

Turk, M. and Pentland, A. (1991). Eigenfaces for recognition, *Journal of Cognitive Neuroscience* **3**, 1, pp. 71–86.

Ullman, S. and Basri, R. (1991). Recognition by linear combinations of models, *IEEE Transactions on Pattern Analysis and Machine Intelligence* **13**, 10, pp. 992–1006.

Yang, M.-H., Kriegman, D. J. and Ahuja, N. (2002). Detecting faces in images: A survey, *IEEE Pattern Analysis and Machine Intelligence* **24**, 1, pp. 34–58.

Chapter 6

Using Object Models as Domain Knowledge in Perceptual Organization: An Approach for Object Category Identification in Video Sequences

Gaurav Harit and Rajesh Bharatia and Santanu Chaudhury

Electrical Engineering Department,
IIT Delhi, Hauz Khas, New Delhi 110016,
gharit@gmail.com, rajesh.bharatia@gmail.com, schaudhury@gmail.com

In this paper we present a framework which integrates object-model knowledge with the perceptual organization process. We demonstrate the advantages of the add-on grouping evidences as contributed by the object models for a more robust perceptual organization in the spatio-temporal domain. Our system performs detection of foreground objects along with recognition in video.

6.1 Introduction

Perceptual grouping has been used to identify meaningful structures in images [Sarkar and Boyer (1993a)] and videos [Sarkar *et al.* (2002); Harit and Chaudhury (2006b)]. Such structures correspond to the inherent organizations of simpler primitives in the scene. Perceptual grouping work has mostly made use of Gestalt relationships like continuation of boundaries, proximity, enclosures, and similarity of shape, size, intensity, and directionality, which play a key role in the formation of "good" structures in the spatial domain. However, it has been suggested [Sarkar and Boyer (1993b)] that higher level knowledge also plays a crucial role in the perceptual grouping process. The Gestalt psychology has indicated that interest, intention, past-experience, etc. have an important role to play in the perception processes. The contribution of this work lies in providing a framework and demonstrating the advantages of the explicit use of the object model knowledge in conjunction with the perceptual grouping process. Using perceptual grouping in spatio-temporal domain avoids the need of bootstrapping, i.e. having a correct recognition of the object in the first frame. Further, it gathers grouping evidences from all the frames of a video, and is thus more reliable in detecting specific (with known models) objects as well as general objects. The object model knowledge used by our grouping framework takes the form of a learned pictorial structure [Felzenszwalb and Huttenlocher (2004); Kumar *et al.* (2004)] model for the object.

We review some related works which attempt grouping based on some kind of object model. Deva et al [Ramanan and Forsyth (2003b)] build models for animals as an assembly of rectangular segments. They use temporal coherence to identify tracks of segments, much in the same way as we identify blob tracks. The foreground tracks are identified as those for which the segments follow a bounded velocity model from frame to frame. However, they assume that all the segment tracks identified in a sequence belong to the body model, and thus do not make use of any perceptual characteristics (like adjacency) for grouping. Ramanan and Forsyth [Ramanan and Forsyth (2003a)] manually construct the body model as a fully deformable connected kinematic model. The body region is composed of nine segments which are connected up using kinematic constraints. Forsyth et al [Forsyth *et al.* (1999)] introduce a grouping model called as *body plan*, which is a sequence of grouping stages, each assembles image components that could correspond to appropriate body segments. Kinematic plausibility is used to train projected classifiers for assembling the segments. Mikolazczyk et al [Mikolazczyk *et al.* (2004)] assemble body parts with a joint probabilistic model which computes the likelihood score for the assembly using appearance and relative configuration. They build robust part detectors which work on a single image, and do not use temporal coherence.

We see that the existing approaches have used spatial grouping models, or have used temporal coherence without a formal grouping model. The approach proposed in this paper integrates temporal coherence in a formal spatio-temporal grouping model. Integration of perceptual grouping with object models allows the system to recognize objects that follow the object model, as well as to detect general objects which exhibit distinct perceptual characteristics from the background.

The organization of this chapter is as follows. In the next section we give an overview of the perceptual grouping process and describe how the domain knowledge is incorporated into the grouping framework. In section 6.3 we describe our object model formulated as Pictorial Structures. The perceptual grouping algorithm which uses the domain knowledge is discussed in section 6.4. Finally section 6.5 presents the experimental results and section 6.6 gives the conclusions for this chapter.

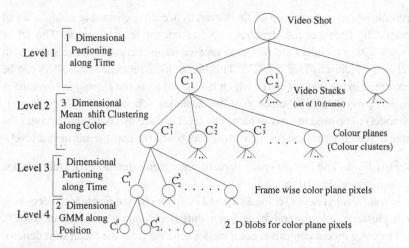

Fig. 6.1 Shows the decoupled semantics clustering tree for video. The DSCT methodology yields 2-D blobs at the 4th level. Tracks of 2-D blobs across frames describe homogeneous color patches in space and time.

6.2 Perceptual Grouping in Video

A grouping process requires extraction of primitive visual patterns which can be organized into perceptual clusters by making use of perceptual grouping principles. The visual patterns used in this work are space-time regions homogeneous in color. We identify such patterns using the Decoupled Semantics Clustering Tree (DSCT) [Harit and Chaudhury (2006a)] algorithm which models them as tracks of 2-D blobs. A brief description of the algorithm is given in the following subsection.

6.2.1 *Video data clustering*

The objects in a real world scene are generally complex in structure and may constitute of several parts each homogeneous in some visual properties. Segmentation of a video scene, using low level descriptors like color, texture, or motion, decomposes an object into several component space-time regions, each depicting homogeneity in some property. The feature space of video data is 6-D (3 for color, 2 for position and 1 for time coordinates), and is a semantically heterogeneous feature space since color, position, and time are features with different semantics. Instead of doing a clustering using all the 6 feature dimensions taken together, the scheme [Harit and Chaudhury (2006a)] uses a decoupled clustering along different feature dimensions. It is a hierarchical clustering methodology with a divisive approach where in each step of the hierarchy we do a clustering along a set of semantically homogeneous features chosen from the feature vector. The set of samples within a cluster are further organized into subclusters in the subsequent level of the hierarchy (see Fig 6.1). This hierarchical sequence of clusters can be represented in the form of a tree which is referred to as the *Decoupled Semantics Clustering tree* (DSCT). Selection of the clustering scheme (and thus the clustering model) to be used at a given hierarchy level is done by taking into account the nature of data distribution for the feature set chosen for partitioning at that level.

- *First level:* The feature space is partitioned along time to give video stacks, each comprising 10 frames.
- *Second level:* The 3-D color data (in LUV space) for the pixels in a video stack is clustered using hierarchical mean shift [DeMenthon and Megret (2002)]. The color model comprises color modes selected from the mean shift dendrogram. The algorithm takes into account the color modes of the previous stack to derive the color model of a given stack and ensures that the inter-mode color distance for the modes selected for the color model is greater than a threshold τ_c.
- *Third level:* Each color cluster is partitioned along time to yield frame wise subsets for the color cluster pixels, which depict regions homogeneous in that color in a frame.
- *Fourth level:* We apply Gaussian Mixture Modeling (GMM) clustering on the (x,y) spatial position of a frame subset of the pixels of a color cluster, to model them as 2-D blobs.

As a final step, we generate tracks of these 2-D blobs. The tracks are generated using criteria of spatial overlap, color similarity, and size compatibility of the 2-D blobs. The blob tracks get linked across occlusion.

Fig 6.2 shows some such tracks of 2-D blobs. The first row shows a foreground pattern and the second row shows a background pattern.

In the next section we discuss how we apply perceptual grouping to group the blob tracks into meaningful components in the video scene.

6.2.2   *The perceptual grouping model.*

The grouping process [Harit and Chaudhury (2006b)] works on the premise that the patterns which belong to the same object would strongly exhibit certain associations. The grouping paradigm follows the Gestalt principle of common fate, and the association measures evaluate the temporal coherence of spatial properties. The observed inter-pattern associations contribute an evidence for a putative

Fig. 6.2   Blob tracks of two patterns. The top row shows a foreground pattern and bottom row shows a background pattern

grouping i.e. a set of patterns, say c_j. All such evidences are incorporated as virtual evidence nodes in a belief network (Fig 6.3) which provides the grouping probability (i.e. a measure of grouping saliency) for a set of patterns. The propositional variable S takes on two states [*groupingIsSalient,groupingIsNonSalient*]. Likewise the nodes A, B, C, D, E also take on two discrete states for saliency given the observation of their respective grouping criterion. The explanations for these nodes are as follows:

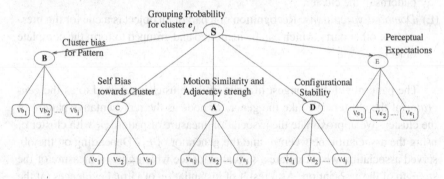

Fig. 6.3   Grouping model belief network. The nodes shown in dotted rectangles are the virtual evidences.

(A) *Motion Similarity and Adjacency:* This association plays the important role of grouping the foreground blobs having a distinct motion relative to the background blobs. We compute the frame to frame motion vector for a blob track as the displacement between the blob centroids. The evidence is proportional to the average difference in the motion vectors of the two patterns computed over all the frames in which the patterns exist simultaneously. Adjacency evidence is formulated as proportional to the number of frames for which the pattern has an overlapping boundary with the cluster.

(B) *Cluster bias for a Pattern:* The cluster bias signifies the affinity of the cluster towards the pattern. A pattern may be important for the cluster if it could facilitate the adjacency of other patterns towards the cluster. For example, removing a pattern p_i may cause a set of patterns q to get disconnected from the cluster. The cluster bias for p_i is formulated as proportional to $\sum_{\forall q_k \in q} d_k$, where d_k is the period for which the pattern $q_k \in q$ gets disconnected from the cluster

(C) *Self bias of a Pattern:* It signifies the pattern's affinity towards a cluster. A pattern will have a self bias to a cluster if it happens to share an adjacency to the cluster for a temporal period which is a large fraction of its own lifespan. These are the patterns which remain mostly occluded during the cluster lifespan and appear for only short durations. The self bias is proportional to the fraction of the pattern's lifespan relative to the cluster lifespan.

(D) *Configuration Stability:* There are situations when it is desirable that the relative geometrical configuration of the patterns in a cluster be stable for the grouping to be valid. Our formulation for configuration stability quantifies the relative change in the configuration of the pattern with respect to other patterns in the cluster.

(E) *Domain Expectations:* Recognition of a part of an object is a cue for the presence of other parts, which can be identified and grouped to form the complete object.

The pattern with the longest lifespan in the cluster is referred to as the *generator* of the cluster. We take the generator node as the representative pattern of the cluster. We approximate the association measure of pattern p_i with cluster c_j using the association between p_i and the generator of c_j. Depending on the observed association we formulate a virtual evidence which gives a measure of the strength of the association. As a result of instantiation of virtual evidences (at the leaf nodes Va_i, Vb_i, Vc_i, etc), belief propagation takes place and the marginal probability for the positive state at node S is taken as the grouping probability for the putative cluster c_j.

The node E in the network corresponds to the domain knowledge. The identification of any of a part of an object would lead to a strong grouping probability with other parts of the object, provided the identified part conforms to the object model. We shall demonstrate that this kind of an add-on grouping evidence benefits the grouping process in terms of grouping speed-up and accuracy. In the next section we describe the object model we have used in our work. Specifically, we have used pictorial structures [Felzenszwalb and Huttenlocher (2004)] since this kind of representation involves modeling an object as a composition of parts. It offers a probabilistic model which allows us to compute the likelihood of a part or the whole object in the process of grouping. This in turn provides a scheme for object recognition through a grouping process in a video sequence.

6.3   Object Model as a Pictorial Structure

Given an object with parts v_1, v_2,..., v_n, where each part v_i has a configuration-label specified as l_i on a common coordinate frame. $l_i = (x_i, y_i, \theta_i, \sigma_i)$ where (x_i, y_i) is the location, θ_i is the orientation, σ_i is the scale at which the object part occurs in the image plane. An instance of the pictorial structure model for an object can be defined using its part-configuration parameters $\mathbf{l} = \{l_1, l_2, .., l_n\}$ and the part-appearance parameters $\mathbf{a} = \{a_1, a_2, .., a_n\}$, where the subscript indicates the part index. Pictorial structures are characterized by pairwise only dependencies between sites which can be modeled as a prior on the labels $\mathbf{l}$:

$$P(\mathbf{l}) \propto exp\left(-\sum_{i=1}^{i=n_P}\sum_{j=1}^{j=n_P} \psi(l_i, l_j) \right)$$

We have adopted the Bayesian formulation for pictorial structures as given by Kumar et al [Kumar *et al.* (2004)]. Let n_P be the set of parts which together comprise the object model. Let D_i denote the image region of the ith part. We can compute the likelihood ratio of the object being present in the image D to the object being absent as

$$\frac{P(D|a, l)}{P(D|a_{bg}, l)} = \prod_{i=1}^{i=n_P} \frac{P(D_i|a_i)}{P(D_i|a_{bg})}$$

The posterior distribution for the model parameters given an image D can be defined as:

$$P(\mathbf{a}, \mathbf{l}|D) \propto \prod_{i=1}^{i=n_P} \frac{P(D_i|a_i)}{P(D_i|a_{bg})} \exp\left(-\sum_{j\neq i} \Psi(l_i, l_j) \right) \tag{6.1}$$

where $\Psi(l_i, l_j)$ is the potential between parts v_i and v_j, a_i and a_{bg} are appearance parameters for part v_i and background respectively. The labels which maximize the above probability are taken as the best fit for the pictorial structure model.

6.3.1 *Formulation of the potential between object parts*

Considering analogy with a Markov Random Field model where each object-part can be considered to be a site, the potential between two parts captures the configuration compatibility of the two parts. Kumar et al [Kumar *et al*. (2004)] have formulated the pair-wise potential $\Psi(l_i, l_j)$ between two object parts using a Potts model, which is defined as 0 for a valid configuration and a *const* if the configuration is not valid. In our work, instead of simply saying that the configuration of two parts is valid or not, we attempt to compute a *continuous* measure of conformance of an observed configuration with the expected (true) configuration. For this purpose, we model the relative configuration of two parts using the parameters $h_{ij} = \{length, orientation\}$ of a hypothetical line joining the centroid of the parts v_i, v_j. Next we model the distribution of the two parameters as a mixture of Gaussians. We formulated the potential $\Psi(l_i, l_j)$ between 2 parts as:

$$\sum_{x=0}^{g} w_x \frac{|\Sigma_{x_{ij}}^{-1}|^{1/2}}{2\pi} exp(-\frac{1}{2}(h_{ij} - \boldsymbol{\mu}_{x_{ij}})^t \Sigma_{x_{ij}}^{-1}(h_{ij} - \boldsymbol{\mu}_{x_{ij}}))$$

where g is the number of Gaussians, w_x is the weight given to the xth Gaussian parametrized with covariance matrix $\Sigma_{x_{ij}}$ and mean $\boldsymbol{\mu}_{x_{ij}}$. The proposed formulation of potential gives a more accurate measure of part-configuration validity rather than simply giving binary values.

6.3.2 *Formulation of appearance parameters for object parts*

An object part may have fine distinguishing image features and may also contain important information in lower frequencies. It is desirable that the visual attributes provide a representation of appearance that is jointly localized in space, frequency and orientation. We perform a wavelet transform to decompose the image into various sub-bands localized in orientation and frequency. The sub-bands represent different frequencies in horizontal, vertical and diagonal orientations, and also in multiple resolutions. The coefficients within a sub-band are spatially localized. We perform a 3-level wavelet decomposition using Haar filter as shown in Fig 6.4. Level-1 describes the lowest octave of frequency. Each subsequent level represents the next higher octave of frequencies.

We represent the statistics of both object appearance and "non-object" appearance using a set of histograms. A histogram offers a compact representation and a statistically optimal measure to represent the appearance statistics. However, as the appearance attributes can assume a large number of discrete values, the histogram size may become very large if it jointly models a large number of co-

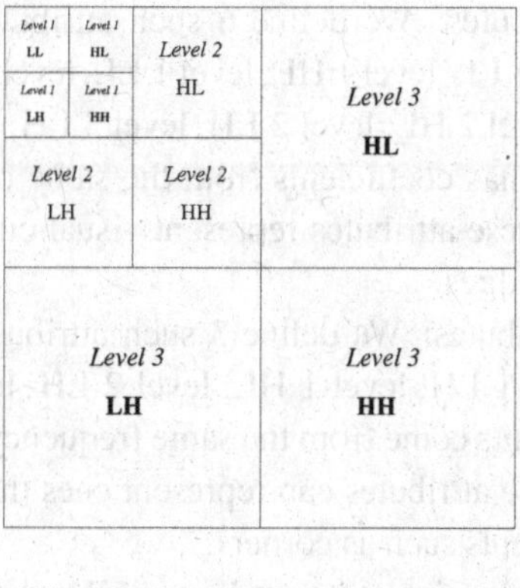

Level 1 LL	Level 1 HL	Level 2 HL	Level 3 HL
Level 1 LH	Level 1 HH		
Level 2 LH	Level 2 HH		
Level 3 LH		Level 3 HH	

Fig. 6.4 · Wavelet representation of an image.

efficients. To limit the size of the histogram, we use multiple histograms where each histogram, $H_k(\text{attribute}_k|\text{object})$, represents the probability of appearance over some specified visual attribute$_k$; that is, attribute$_k$ is a random variable describing some chosen visual characteristic such as low frequency content. Each histogram represents the joint statistics of a subset of wavelet coefficients and their position on the object.

We assume that the statistical distribution of different attributes of an image is independent of each other. Hence the likelihood of observing an image given the object is the product of the likelihood of observing the different appearance attributes taken as:

$$P(\text{image}|\text{object}) \simeq \prod_k H_k(\text{attribute}_k|\text{object})$$

$$P(\text{image}|\text{non-object}) \simeq \prod_k H_k(\text{attribute}_k|\text{non-object})$$

As given in [Schneiderman and Kanade (2000); Cosman *et al.* (1996)], we use 17 attributes that sample the wavelet transform in groups of 8 coefficients. Such attributes are grouped into 4 major categories.

(1) Intra-Subband attributes: There are 7 of these attributes which sample coefficients from the following sub-bands: level 1 LL; level 1 LH; level 1 HL; level 2 LH; level 2 HL; level 3 LH; level 3 HL. All coefficients included in an attribute come from the same sub-band. These attributes are the most localized in frequency and orientation.

(2) Inter-frequency attributes: We define 6 such attributes using the following subband pairs: level 1 LL, level 1 HL; level 1 LL, level 1 LH; level 1 LH, level 2 LH; level 1 HL, level 2 HL; level 2 LH, level 3 LH; level 2 HL, level 3 HL. Thus, each attribute has coefficients from the same orientation but multiple frequency bands. These attributes represent visual cues that span a range of frequencies such as edges.

(3) Inter-orientation attributes: We define 3 such attributes using the following subband pairs: level 1 LH, level 1 HL; level 2 LH, level 2 HL; level 3 LH, level 3 HL. Coefficients come from the same frequency band but multiple orientation bands. These attributes can represent cues that have both horizontal and vertical components such as corners.

(4) Inter-frequency / inter-orientation attributes: We define one such attribute combining coefficients from the following subbands: level 1 LL; level 1 LH; level 1 HL; level 2 LH; level 2 HL. This combination of coefficients is designed to represent cues that span a range of frequencies and orientations.

In terms of spatial-frequency decomposition, attributes that use level 1 coefficients describe large spatial extents over a small range of low frequencies. Attributes that use level 2 coefficients describe mid-sized spatial extents over a midrange of frequencies, and attributes that use level 3 coefficients describe small spatial extents over a large range of high frequencies.

The steps in formulating the object-part detector using the appearance attributes formulated on wavelet coefficients are as follows:

(1) Decompose the known object region (rectangular) into sub-windows.

(2) Within each sub-window (w_x, w_y), model the joint statistics of a set of quantized wavelet coefficients using a histogram. Several such histograms are computed, each capturing the joint distribution of a different set of quantized wavelet coefficients. In all, we formulate 17 such histograms using different sets of coefficients, as explained before.

(3) The set of histograms is a non-parametric statistical model for the wavelet coefficients evaluated on the sub-window. Hence they can be used to compute the likelihood for an object being present and the object not being present. The detector makes its decision using the likelihood ratio test:

$$\frac{\prod\limits_{w_x, w_y} \prod\limits_{k=1}^{17} H_k\left(\text{attribute}_k(w_x, w_y), w_x, w_y \mid \text{object}\right)}{\prod\limits_{w_x, w_y} \prod\limits_{k=1}^{17} H_k\left(\text{attribute}_k(w_x, w_y), w_x, w_y \mid \text{non-object}\right)} > \lambda \quad (6.2)$$

where the outer product is taken over all the sub-windows (w_x, w_y) in the image region of the object. The threshold λ is taken as $\frac{P(non-object)}{P(object)}$ as given in [Schneiderman and Kanade (2000)] . The likelihood ratio test is equivalent to the Bayes decision rule and is optimal if the representations for $P(\text{image}|\text{object})$ and $P(\text{image}|\text{non-object})$ are accurate.

Having defined the pictorial structure model for an object in terms of statistics of appearance attributes and part-configuration parameters, we next discuss how the spatio-temporal grouping model can make use of the pictorial structure based object model as domain knowledge to aid formation and recognition of meaningful perceptual clusters.

6.4 Spatio-Temporal Grouping

The spatio-temporal grouping framework relies on making use of grouping evidences formulated on the observed associations amongst the patterns. Typically an association measure is computed in the range [0,1] in a way that higher values signify a stronger grouping. In the Bayesian network for spatio-temporal grouping (Fig 6.3), an evidence contributed by a pattern signifies its association strength with the *rest of the grouping* as per a grouping criteria. We now explain the computation of probability at the virtual evidence nodes $v_{e1}, v_{e2}, ... v_{en}$ of the network in Fig 6.3. These nodes contribute evidences corresponding to the conformance of the blob-patterns (in a putative grouping) to a known object model as a pictorial structure.

6.4.1 *Formulation of object model evidence*

We now present the formulation of the grouping probability of a pattern p_i with the rest of the patterns in the grouping given the knowledge of the object model. A pattern p_i may exhibit only a partial overlap with an object. Given an object O_m comprising $v_1^m, v_2^m, .., v_n^m$ parts, first we need to find whether p_i overlaps with any of the object parts. The steps followed for this purpose are as follows:

(1) Define a search window (around the pattern) which is larger than the size of the pattern.
(2) We do a search for each as yet undetected object-part, at all locations (w_x, w_y) within that window, and at 3 different scales. An object-part is taken to be detected correctly if its posterior (Eq 6.1) is above a threshold. Note that when using Eq 6.1 the product index i is taken over the n_D parts which have been already detected up to this step.
(3) The overlap of p_i with object-part(s) is an indicator of the degree to which the

pattern *belongs* to the object grouping. If the overlap (in number of pixels) of p_i with the object-part(s) is found to be more than 30% of the area of p_i, the pattern is said to have a *qualified* overlap with the object O_m.

(4) To establish consistency of overlap of pattern p_i with object O_m, we repeat step-3 for all the frames for which pattern p_i exists. The association strength of the pattern p_i with the object O_m is formulated as: $\frac{\sum_{\forall f \in F_{p_i}} \alpha_{p_i}^f}{N_{p_i}}$ where $\alpha_{p_i}^f = 1$ if p_i has a qualified part match in the frame f, and $\alpha_{p_i}^f = 0$ otherwise. We have F_{p_i} as the set of all frames in which pattern p_i exists and N_{p_i} is the number of frames in the set F_{p_i}. This association measure gets computed in the range [0 to 1]. It is taken as the probabilistic evidence contributed at nodes $v_{e1}, v_{e2}, ...v_{en}$, in favour of the putative cluster.

6.4.2   *The grouping algorithm*

In this section we discuss our algorithm for identifying the clusters from a given set of perceptual units (spatio-temporal patterns). The grouping saliency of a cluster c_j is formulated as $S_{c_j} = P(c_j)$ where $P(c_j)$ is the grouping probability of the cluster c_j. For a cluster comprising a single pattern, the grouping probability is 0.5 since none of the grouping evidence nodes gets instantiated. The grouping saliency for the entire scene is formulated as:

$$S_{scene} = \sum_{\forall c_j \in C} S_{c_j} \qquad (6.3)$$

where C is the set of all perceptual clusters identified in the scene.

The spatio-temporal grouping problem is to identify the set C of perceptual clusters in the scene so as to maximize S_{scene} such that the final set of clusters have:

$$P(c_i) \geq 0.5, \;\; P(c_i \cup c_j) < 0.5, \text{ and } c_i \cap c_j = \phi \qquad \forall \; c_i, c_j \in C, \;\; i \neq j \;\; (6.4)$$

The first condition in (6.4) mandates that each cluster in the set of groupings be valid. The second condition constrains the set of valid groupings so that no two clusters can be further grouped together to form a valid cluster as per the specified grouping model. The third condition specifies that a pattern can be a member of only one cluster.

We have thus formulated the perceptual grouping problem as an optimization problem. A naive perceptual grouping algorithm would explore all possible sets of clusters and output the one that has the maximum scene's grouping saliency and all the clusters valid as per the conditions (6.4). However to our advantage, the conditions (6.4) restrict the set of groupings which need to be explored.

Having formulated the grouping evidence for a pattern using the object-model knowledge, we now list the steps of the grouping algorithm [Harit and Chaudhury (2006b)]. Given a set of object models $\mathcal{O} = \{O_1, O_2, ...O_s\}$ and a set of patterns $P = \{p_1, p_2, ...p_n\}$, our algorithm outputs the set of perceptual clusters $C = \{c_1, c_2, ...c_r\}$. The algorithm maximizes the scene saliency measure $\mathcal{S}_{scene}$ which is formulated as $\mathcal{S}_{scene} = \sum_{\forall c_j \in C} \mathcal{S}_{c_j}$ where $\mathcal{S}_{c_j} = \mathrm{P}(c_j)$ is the grouping saliency of a cluster c_j computed using the belief network in Fig 6.3.

1   Initialize the set of clusters $C = \{\}$. Hence $\mathcal{S}_{scene} = 0$. Instantiate a queue, *clusterQ*, to be used for storing the clusters. Initially none of the patterns have any cluster label.

2   If all the patterns have cluster labels and the *clusterQ* is empty, then exit. Otherwise, instantiate a new cluster if there are patterns in set C that do not have any cluster label. From amongst the unlabeled patterns, pick up the one that has the maximum lifespan. This pattern is taken as the generator pattern for the new cluster c_{new}.

3   The generator may be or may not be a part of any of the objects in set $\mathcal{O}$. We define a search region around the generator and look for possible parts of any of the objects. The object-part(s) which compute (by virtue of their appearance) the a posteriori probability in Eq 6.1 to be greater than a threshold are considered as *present* in the search region. The generator pattern is labelled as belonging to the object with which it shares the maximum overlap (in terms of number of pixels). We further verify the correctness of the object label by checking its consistency in 5 other frames in which the generator blob exists. With the generator associated with object label O_m, the node E is used to provide the probability of a pattern being a part of the object O_m. If the generator pattern cannot be associated with any object label from set $\mathcal{O}$, the node E is not used in the grouping model to compute the saliency of the putative cluster for this generator. The cluster formed by such a generator corresponds to a general grouping without any specific object tag. Such a grouping would use only the general associations [Harit and Chaudhury (2006b)] for grouping.

4a Compute associations of the generator pattern of c_{new} with the unlabeled patterns. An unlabeled pattern p_i is added to the cluster c_{new} if $\mathrm{P}(p_i \cup c_{new}) > 0.5$. Repeat this step till no more unlabeled patterns get added to c_{new}. Any unlabeled patterns that exist now are the ones which do not form a valid grouping with any of the existing clusters.

4b Compute associations of the generator pattern of c_{new} with the labelled patterns of other clusters. If there are patterns, say p_k (with a cluster label c_j) which form a valid grouping with c_{new}, i.e. $\mathrm{P}(p_k \cup c_{new}) > 0.5$, then put c_{new}

and c_j into the *clusterQ* if they are not already there inside it.

5 If the *clusterQ* is empty, go to step 2. Otherwise, take the cluster at the front of the *clusterQ*. Let this cluster be c_f.

6 Pick a pattern, say p_i, of the cluster c_f. We consider the pattern p_i to be a part of, one by one, every cluster c_j which is currently in the set C. The association measures between p_i and a cluster c_j need to be recomputed if c_j has been updated. For each cluster c_j in C, we compute the grouping probability for the putative grouping $\{p_i \cup c_j\}$. If the grouping $\{p_i \cup c_j\}$ is valid (i.e. $P(p_i \cup c_j) > 0.5$), we note the change in the scene grouping saliency, $\delta_S = P(p_i \cup c_j) - P(c_j)$. The pattern p_i is labelled with the cluster (say c_m) for which δ_S computes to the highest value. Put c_m into the *clusterQ* if it is not already inside it. Repeat step 4 for all the patterns in c_f.

7 If any pattern in c_f changes its label as a result of step 5, then go to step 4. If none of the patterns changes its label, remove the front element of the *clusterQ* and go to step 4.

The iterative process terminates when the pattern labels have stabilized. It attempts to hypothesize new clusters and organizes them such that $\mathcal{S}_{scene}$ reaches a local maximum. Convergence to a local maximum is guaranteed since we ensure that at every step of the algorithm, $\triangle\mathcal{S}_{scene} \geq 0$. A grouping formed out of a single pattern always leads to an increase in $\mathcal{S}_{scene}$. A pattern would change its cluster label only when the increase in saliency of the cluster to which it is joined is larger compared to the decrease in saliency of the cluster from which it is defected. Thus, instantiation of clusters as well as relabeling of patterns always leads to an increase in the $\mathcal{S}_{scene}$.

6.5 Results

We have trained models for two object categories: cows and horses. For the purpose of learning the appearance attribute histograms for the object parts and the non-object regions we computed the appearance features for each object part for about 650 images, sampled from cow/horse videos. We needed a large training set since the skin texture/color has substantial variations within certain animal categories. The attribute histograms should incorporate all such variations. We also learned the features for the mirror images of the object regions. To minimize the classification error, we have used different weights for the different attributes [Schneiderman and Kanade (2000)]. The GMM distribution of configuration for each pair of object parts was also learned. The appearance attribute histograms for non-object regions were learned from about 1200 random images which did not have the object.

We have demonstrated two advantages to the perceptual grouping process through an effective use of the object model knowledge. Firstly, once an object-part has been reliably detected (with high probability), other (computationally costly) evidences like adjacency, cluster-bias, etc., need not be gathered for all the frames since an object model is a very strong grouping evidence which would allow grouping of only those blobs which overlap with some part of the same object. Secondly, there are scenes in which the foreground subjects do not show a distinct motion w.r.t. the background. For such a case, the general grouping criteria would group all the blobs in the scene to output a single cluster having both the background and the foreground. Such failure cases are shown to be successfully handled by use of object models which provide a stronger grouping evidence to override the (non-exhibited) general grouping criteria. Searching an object part around a blob-pattern is a costly operation, however, it needs to be done only once, and not in every iteration of the grouping algorithm. Moreover, it can be computed on a few frames (around 5) and *not* on all the frames of the blob-track, since a consistent overlap of the blob with an object part on a few frames can be taken as an indicator that the blob belongs to the object region. We have observed that certain object parts get missed by the detectors when a large object motion causes blur in the object appearance, since the appearance gets confused with the background. For such cases, the generic grouping evidences play the major role in the grouping process. Fig 6.5 shows the results of grouping with learned object models. Rows 1 and 2 show the result of applying the grouping algorithm on a test videos of a horse galloping in a barn. The camera is panning and the background remains almost constant. Thus blob-patterns belonging to both the object and the background have almost no motion. Hence simple generic grouping (using motion similarity, adjacency, etc.) when applied to such a video fails to successfully cluster the patterns into meaningful organizations and clusters all patterns into one large cluster. This situation is resolved in our model guided perceptual grouping scheme where the evidence from the object model knowledge correctly groups the object region blobs into a separate cluster. We show the blobs (in red) belonging to the horse region and the recognized object part rectangles are overlayed in white.

Fig 6.5 rows 3,4,5 show results on various test videos with cows of very different texture and appearance. The algorithm is successfully able to cluster all the blob-patterns belonging to the cows (shown in red) and detect and recognize parts around the patterns (shown in blue).

As part of our ongoing work, we have done initial experiments on using human models in conjunction with the perceptual grouping process. We defined a

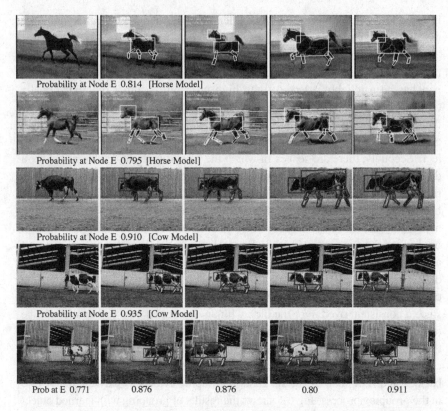

Fig. 6.5   Results on horse and cow videos (test cases).

Fig. 6.6   Experiment with human model (Training case). Probability at node E: 0.69, 0.69, 0.74 for the 3 clusters left to right.

simple human model as a composition of 4 parts — head, torso, and two legs. The part appearance parameters and part configuration parameters were learned using a test video shown in Fig 6.6. We then used the trained human model for perceptual grouping on the same video. Use of object model successfully identifies the 3 persons as distinct, as shown in the second row of Fig 6.6. Without the use of object model, the two persons on the left side would get clubbed as a single perceptual cluster due to the adjacency of the blobs belonginng to the two persons. The trained human model is definitely not exhaustive, but our experiment demonstrates the advantage of using object models for multiple object tracking.

6.6   Conclusions

In this paper we have demonstrated the benefits of using object models as domain knowledge to assist (in both computational speed-up and detection accuracy) in the perceptual organization process applied to videos. We have demonstrated results on two object classes; and as future work, we shall demonstrate use of object models for correctly grouping multiple foreground-objects which could be sharing similar motion and adjacency in the video frames.

Bibliography

Cosman, P. C., Gray, R. M. and Vetterli, M. (1996). Vector Quantization of Image Subbands: A Survey, *IEEE Transactions on Image Processing* **5**, 2, pp. 202 – 225.
DeMenthon, D. and Megret, R. (2002). Spatio-temporal segmentation of video by hierarchical mean shift analysis, Tech. Rep. LAMP-TR-090, University of Maryland, College Park, MD 20742, USA.
Felzenszwalb, P. and Huttenlocher, D. (2004). Effi cient belief propagation for early vision, in *CVPR*, pp. 261 – 268.
Forsyth, D. A., Ioffe, S. and Haddon, J. (1999). Finding Objects by Grouping Primitives, in *Shape, Contour and Grouping in Computer Vision, Springer-Verlag*, Vol. 1681, LNCS, pp. 302 – 318.
Harit, G. and Chaudhury, S. (2006a). Clustering in video data: Dealing with heterogeneous semantics of features. *Pattern Recognition* **39**, 5, pp. 789 – 811.
Harit, G. and Chaudhury, S. (2006b). Video Scene Interpretation using perceptual prominence and mise-en-scène features, in *(Asian Conference on Computer Vision) ACCV*, Vol. LNCS 3852, pp. 571 – 580.
Kumar, M. P., Torr, P. H. S. and Zisserman., A. (2004). Extending pictorial structures for object recognition, in *BMCV*, Vol. 2.
Mikolazczyk, K., Schmid, C. and Zisserman, A. (2004). Human Detection based on Probabilistic Assembly of robust Part Detectors, in *European Conference on Computer Vision*, Vol. 1, pp. 69 – 82.
Ramanan, D. and Forsyth, D. A. (2003a). Finding and Tracking people from the Bottom

Up, in *Proc. IEEE International Conference on Computer Vision and Pattern Recognition (CVPR)*, Vol. 2, pp. 467 – 474.

Ramanan, D. and Forsyth, D. A. (2003b). Using Temporal Coherence to Build Models of Animals, in *Proc. IEEE International Conference on Computer Vision (ICCV)*, pp. 338 – 345.

Sarkar, S. and Boyer, K. L. (1993a). Integration, Inference, and Management of Spatial Information Using Bayesian Networks: Perceptual Organization, *IEEE Transactions on Pattern Analysis and Machine Intelligence* **15**, 3, pp. 256 – 274.

Sarkar, S. and Boyer, K. L. (1993b). Perceptual Organization in Computer Vision: A Review and a Proposal for a Classificatory Structure, *IEEE Transactions on Systems, Man, and Cybernetics* **23**, 2, pp. 382 – 399.

Sarkar, S., Majchrzak, D. and Korimilli, K. (2002). Perceptual Organization Based Computational Model for Robust Segmentation of Moving Objects, *Computer Vision and Image Understanding* **86**, pp. 141 – 170.

Schneiderman, H. and Kanade, T. (2000). A Statistical Method for 3D Object Detection Applied to Faces and Cars, in *Proc. Conf. Computer Vision and Pattern Recognition*, Vol. 1, pp. 746 – 751.

Chapter 7

Image Representations Based on Discriminant Non-negative Matrix Factorization with Application to Facial Expression Recognition

Ioan Buciu [1,2] and Ioannis Pitas [1]

[1] *Department of Informatics, Aristotle University of Thessaloniki*
GR-541 24, Thessaloniki, Box 451, Greece
pitas@aiia.csd.auth.gr
[2] *Electronics Department*
Faculty of Electrical Engineering and Information Technology
University of Oradea
410087, Universitatii 1, Romania
ibuciu@uoradea.ro

In this chapter, we present a novel algorithm for extracting features in a supervised manner. This algorithm is derived from the local non-negative matrix factorization (LNMF) algorithm, which is an extension of non-negative matrix factorization (NMF) method. We call this newly proposed algorithm Discriminant Non-negative Matrix Factorization (DNMF). Given an image database, all these three algorithms decompose the image database into basis images and their corresponding coefficients. This decomposition is computed differently for each method. The decomposition results are applied on facial images for the recognition of the six basic facial expressions. We found that our algorithm shows superior performance by achieving a higher recognition rate, when compared to NMF and LNMF. Moreover, we compared DNMF classification performance with principal component analysis (PCA), Fisher Linear Discriminant (FLD), independent component analysis (ICA) and Gabor approaches. We found they are outperformed by DNMF. The experiments were conducted for a varying number of basis images (subspaces). The recognition rate of the proposed algorithm seems to be more robust than that of other methods with respect to the choice of the number of basis images.

7.1   Introduction

Human facial expression analysis has recently captured an increased attention from psychologists, anthropologists and computer scientists. Classifying facial expressions is a difficult task due to many factors such as face orientation, scale, head pose or illumination variations. Different methods that rely on either holistic or sparse image representation have been proposed to deal with facial expression classification. While holistic representation treats an image as a whole (global feature), where each pixel has a major contribution to representation, sparse representation is characterized by a highly kurtotic distribution, where a large number of pixels have zero value, and, small number of pixels have positive or negative values (local features). In its extreme, sparse representation provides a local image representation having only just a few contributing pixels. Image representation is closely related to feature selection. For example, Principal Component Analysis (PCA) models the second order statistics of the data by keeping those eigenvectors that correspond to the largest eigenvalues, while discarding those components that have insignificant contribution for data representation. Human facial image representations based on principal components give us a dense representation and whose basis images have holistic ("ghost" - like) appearance. PCA has been successfully applied to recognize facial expressions [Cottrell and Metcalfe (1991); Padgett and Cottrell (1997); Calder *et al.* (2001)].

Another image representation approach is based on Independent Component Analysis (ICA) that looks for components that are as independent as possible and produces image features whose properties are related to the ones of V1 receptive fields and have orientation selectivity, bandpass nature and scaling ability. ICA produces either a sparse or a holistic image representation, depending on the architecture used (i.e. the independence is either assumed over images or pixels). This approach has been successfully applied to recognize facial actions by Donato et al. [Donato *et al.* (1999)]. ICA outperforms PCA for facial expression recognition [Draper *et al.* (2003)].

A third approach implies a convolution of each image with Gabor filters, whose sparse responses, extracted from the face images at fiducial points, form vectors that are further used for classification. The fiducial points of the face are selected either manually [Zhang *et al.* (1998)] or automatically [Wiskott *et al.* (1997)]. Alternatively, the Gabor filters can be applied to the entire face image instead to specific face regions [Buciu *et al.* (2003)].

A geometric-based method, where the positions of a set of fiducial points in a face form a feature vector that represents facial geometry has also been combined with Gabor wavelets [Zhang *et al.* (1998); Tian *et al.* (2002)]. Although

Gabor wavelets seem to yield a reasonable recognition rate, the highest recognition rate is obtained when these two main approaches are combined. The work of Donato et al. shows that the extraction of local features from the entire face space by convolving each image with a set of Gabor filters having different frequencies and orientations can outperform other methods that invoke the holistic representation of the face, when it comes to classify facial actions. They achieved the best recognition results by using ICA and Gabor filters. However, they also found that other local spatial approaches, like local PCA and PCA jets provide worse accuracy than, for example, Fisher Linear Discriminant (FLD), which is a holistic approach. A survey on automatic facial expression analysis can be found in [Fasel and Luettin (2003)].

Two more recent methods, Non-negative Matrix Factorization (NMF) [Lee and Seung (1999)] and Local Non-negative Matrix Factorization (LNMF) [Li *et al*. (2001)] have been applied for face representation and recognition. Li et al. found that, while NMF representation yields low recognition accuracy (actually lower than the one that can be obtained by using the PCA method), LNMF leads to a better classification performance [Li *et al*. (2001)]. Chen et al. [Chen *et al*. (2001)] successfully applied LNMF for face detection. LNMF has also been found to give higher facial expression recognition rate than NMF, when applied to recognize facial expressions [Buciu and Pitas (2004)].

A fully automatic framework to analyze facial action units is investigated by Kapoor et al. [Kapoor *et al*. (2003)]. However, classifying facial action is quite a different task from classifying facial expressions and the results are different and not necessarily comparable, as noted in [Donato *et al*. (1999)].

A more recent paper [Littlewort *et al*. (2004)] dealt with facial expression, where Gabor features were extracted from samples that belong to the Cohn-Kanade database. The Gabor features were then selected by AdaBoost and the combination of AdaBoost and SVMs (called AdaSVMs system) yielded the best classification performance of 93.3%. We must note here that the selected subset of samples from the database is likely to be different of ours. Moreover, in the case of Gabor approach we did not select any features subset from the original Gabor feature vector. The preprocessing steps may have a great influence of the classifier accuracy. A survey on facial expression recognition can be found in [Pantic and Rothkrantz (2003)].

In this paper, we further extend LNMF technique in order to enhance its performance regarding the recognition of the six basic expressions. All the previously mentioned representation methods (except FLD) are unsupervised. On the contrary, we propose here a novel supervised technique called Discriminant Non-negative Matrix Factorization (DNMF) that takes into account facial expression class information, which is not used in NMF and LNMF methods. This paper presents an extension of our previous work [Buciu and Pitas (2004)]. Our approach uses class information in a discriminant way in order to improve the discrimination between classes and, hence, classification accuracy. Furthermore, the proposed approach is consistent with the image representation paradigms of neuroscience that involve representation such as sparseness, non-negative constraints and minimization of redundant information. Our technique is proven to perform better than either NMF or LNMF by achieving a higher facial expression recognition rate. Besides, it shows superior performance with respect to PCA, ICA, FLD, Gabor or SVMs approaches. A highly related work has recently been conducted by Y. Wang et al. [Wang *et al.* (2005)], where their method, called Fisher non-negative matrix factorization (FNMF), gave better recognition rate than NMF and LNMF for face recognition. However, contrary to our method, they modified the NMF rather then the LNMF cost function, leading to a different expression for factor updating. As we shall see, our proposed method outperforms FNMF approach.

The rest of the chapter is organized as follows. Starting from the definition of Bregman distance, Section 7.2 continues with the presentation of the cost function used to define the NMF decomposition. The underlying mathematical tool of LNMF is briefly shown in Section 7.3. LNMF is extended in the Section 7.4, leading to our DNMF method. The data description and the setup of our experiment is presented in Section 7.5. The result achieved by our algorithm are further compared with the results given by NMF, LNMF, FNMF, ICA, PCA, FLD and Gabor approaches in a facial expression recognition task in Section 7.6. The conclusions are drawn in Section 7.7.

7.2 Bregman Distance, Kullback-Leibler Divergence and Non-negative Matrix Factorization

In this Section we shall briefly present the connection between Bregman distance, Kullback-Leibler divergence and non-negative matrix factorization. Firstly, let $\phi : \Delta \rightarrow \mathbb{R}$ be a convex function defined on a closed convex set $\Delta \subseteq \mathbb{R}_+^m$. Given two positive vectors $\mathbf{x}, \mathbf{h} \in \mathbb{R}_+^m$, their Bregman distance associated with ϕ is defined by [Bregman (1967)]:

$$B_\phi(\mathbf{x} \parallel \mathbf{h}) \triangleq \phi(\mathbf{x}) - \phi(\mathbf{h}) - \nabla\phi(\mathbf{x})(\mathbf{x} - \mathbf{h}) \tag{7.1}$$

where $\nabla\phi(\mathbf{x})$ is the gradient of ϕ at $\mathbf{x}$. When $\phi(\mathbf{x})$ takes the form of $\phi(\mathbf{x}) = \sum_i x_i \ln x_i$, where $i = 1, \ldots, m$, then, the Bregman distance recasts into Kullback-

Leibler (KL) divergence between x and h as [Kullback and Leibler (1951)]:

$$KL(\mathbf{x} \parallel \mathbf{h}) = \sum_i \left(x_i \ln\left(\frac{x_i}{h_i}\right) + h_i - x_i \right). \tag{7.2}$$

Now, let us consider that the vector x can be approximated by a linear combination of the elements of h such as $\mathbf{x} \approx \mathbf{Zh}$, where $\mathbf{Z} \in \mathbb{R}^{m \times m}$ is a non-negative matrix, whose columns sum to one. KL divergence is written as:

$$D(\mathbf{x} \parallel \mathbf{Zh}) \triangleq KL(\mathbf{x} \parallel \mathbf{Zh}) = \sum_i \left(x_i \ln\frac{x_i}{\sum_k z_{ik} h_k} + \sum_k z_{ik} h_k - x_i \right) \tag{7.3}$$

where $k = 1, \ldots, m$. It is obvious that, in order to have a good estimate of x by approximating it with the factorization Zh (and finding a proper Z), it is necessary to minimize $D(\mathbf{x} \parallel \mathbf{Zh})$.

Non-negative matrix factorization has been proposed by Lee and Seung as a method that decomposes a given $m \times n$ non-negative matrix X into non-negative factors Z and H such as $\mathbf{X} \approx \mathbf{ZH}$, where Z and H are matrices of size $m \times p$ and $p \times n$, respectively [Lee and Seung (1999)]. Suppose that $j = 1, \ldots, n$ and $k = 1, \ldots, p$. Then, each element x_{ij} of the matrix X can be written as $x_{ij} \approx \sum_k z_{ik} h_{kj}$. The quality of approximation depends on the cost function used. Two cost functions were proposed by Lee and Seung [Lee and Seung (2001)]: the Euclidean distance between X and ZH and KL divergence. In this case, KL has a expression similar to that in (7.3):

$$D_{NMF}(\mathbf{X} \parallel \mathbf{ZH}) \triangleq \sum_{i,j} \left(x_{ij} \ln\frac{x_{ij}}{\sum_k z_{ik} h_{kj}} + \sum_k z_{ik} h_{kj} - x_{ij} \right), \tag{7.4}$$

where x is now replaced by the matrix X and the summation is over the two indices i and j. This expression can be minimized by applying multiplicative update rules subject to $\mathbf{Z}, \mathbf{H} \geq 0$. Since both matrices Z and H are unknown, we need an algorithm which is able to find these matrices by minimizing the divergence (7.4). By using an auxiliary function and the Expectation Maximization (EM) algorithm [Dempster (1977)], the following update rule for computing h_{kj} is found to minimize the KL divergence at each iteration t [Lee and Seung (2001)]:

$$h_{kj}^{(t)} = h_{kj}^{(t-1)} \frac{\sum_i z_{ki}^{(t)} \frac{x_{ij}}{\sum_k z_{ik}^{(t)} h_{kj}^{(t-1)}}}{\sum_i z_{ik}^{(t)}}. \tag{7.5}$$

By reversing the roles of Z and H in (7.5), a similar update rule for each element z_{ik} of Z is obtained:

$$z_{ik}^{(t)} = z_{ik}^{(t-1)} \frac{\sum_j \frac{x_{ij}}{\sum_k z_{ik}^{(t-1)} h_{kj}^{(t)}} h_{jk}^{(t)}}{\sum_j h_{kj}^{(t)}}. \tag{7.6}$$

Both updating rules are applied alternatively in an EM manner and they guarantee a nonincreasing behavior of the KL divergence. A disadvantage of this algorithm is the fact that it may converge towards a local minima and, hence, that there is no guarantee that it reaches a global minimum. Therefore, the procedure is usually applied many times with different starting points.

The positivity constraints arise in many real image processing applications. For example, the pixels in a grayscale image have non-negative intensities. In the NMF approach, its proposers impose non-negative constraints, partly motivated by the biological aspect that the firing rates of neurons are non-negative. It has been shown that, if the matrix $\mathbf{X}$ contains images from an image database (one in each matrix column), then the method decomposes them into basis images (columns of $\mathbf{Z}$) and the corresponding coefficients (or hidden components) (rows of $\mathbf{H}$) [Lee and Seung (1999)]. The resulting basis images contain parts of the original images, parts that are learned thorough the iterative process in the attempt of approximating $\mathbf{X}$ by the product $\mathbf{ZH}$. In this context, m represents the number of pixels in the image, n is the total number of images and p is the number of basis images.

7.3 Local Non-negative Matrix Factorization

Local non-negative matrix factorization has been developed by Li et al [Li *et al.* (2001)]. This technique is a version of NMF which imposes more constraints on the cost function that are related to spatial localization. Therefore, the localization of the learned image features is improved. If we use the notations $[\mathbf{u}_{ij}] = \mathbf{U} = \mathbf{Z}^T\mathbf{Z}$ and $[\mathbf{v}_{ij}] = \mathbf{V} = \mathbf{HH}^T$, the following three additional constraints can be imposed on the NMF basis images and decomposition coefficients:

1. $\sum_i u_{ii} \longrightarrow$ min. This guarantees the generation of more localized features on the basis images $\mathbf{Z}$, than those resulting from NMF, since we impose the constraint that basis image elements are as small as possible.

2. $\sum_{i \neq j} u_{ij} \longrightarrow$ min. This enforces basis orthogonality, in order to minimize the redundancy between image bases. It must be noted that, while LNMF enforces basis orthogonality, NMF does not necessarily do so.

3. $\sum_i v_{ii} \longrightarrow$ max. By means of this constraint, the total "activity" on each retained component (total squared projection coefficients summed over all training images) is maximized.

Therefore, the new cost function takes the form of the following divergence:

$$D_{LNMF}(\mathbf{X}||\mathbf{ZH}) \triangleq D_{NMF}(\mathbf{X}||\mathbf{ZH}) + \alpha \sum_{ij} u_{ij} - \beta \sum_i v_{ii}, \qquad (7.7)$$

where α, $\beta > 0$ are constants. A solution for the minimization of relation (7.7) can be found in [Li *et al.* (2001)]. Accordingly, if we use the following update rules for image basis and coefficients:

$$h_{kj}^{(t)} = \sqrt{h_{kj}^{(t-1)} \sum_i z_{ki}^{(t)} \frac{x_{ij}}{\sum_k z_{ik}^{(t)} h_{kj}^{(t-1)}}}. \tag{7.8}$$

$$z_{ik}^{(t)} = \frac{z_{ik}^{(t-1)} \sum_j \frac{x_{ij}}{\sum_k z_{ik}^{(t-1)} h_{kj}^{(t)}} h_{jk}^{(t)}}{\sum_j h_{kj}^{(t)}}. \tag{7.9}$$

$$z_{ik}^{(t)} = \frac{z_{ik}^{(t)}}{\sum_i z_{ik}^{(t)}}, \quad \text{for all } k \tag{7.10}$$

the KL divergence is nonincreasing.

7.4 Discriminant Non-negative Matrix Factorization

Let us suppose now that we have $\mathcal{Q}$ distinctive image classes and let n_c be the number of training samples in class $\mathcal{Q}$, $c = 1, \ldots, \mathcal{Q}$. Each image from the image database corresponding to one column of matrix $\mathbf{X}$, belongs to one of these classes. Therefore, each column of the $p \times n$ matrix $\mathbf{H}$ can be expressed as image representation coefficients vector $\mathbf{h}_{cl}$, where $c = 1, \ldots, \mathcal{Q}$ and $l = 1, \ldots, n_c$. The total number of coefficient vectors is $n = \sum_{c=1}^{\mathcal{Q}} n_c$. We denote the mean coefficient vector of class c by $\boldsymbol{\mu}_c = \frac{1}{n_c} \sum_{l=1}^{n_c} \mathbf{h}_{cl}$ and the global mean coefficient vector by $\boldsymbol{\mu} = \frac{1}{n} \sum_{c=1}^{\mathcal{Q}} \sum_{l=1}^{n_c} \mathbf{h}_{cl}$. Both NMF and LNMF consider the database as a whole and treat each image in the same way. There is no class information integrated into the cost function. Here, we extend the cost function given by the LNMF technique by proposing a class-dependent approach called *Discriminant Non-negative Matrix Factorization* (DNMF). The decomposition coefficients encode the image representation in the same way for each image. Therefore, by modifying the expression for the coefficients in a such a way that the basis images incorporate class characteristics, we obtain a class-dependent image representation. We preserve the same constraints on basis as for LNMF and we only introduce two more constraints on the coefficients:

1. $\mathbf{S}_w = \sum_{c=1}^{\mathcal{Q}} \sum_{l=1}^{n_c} (\mathbf{h}_{cl} - \boldsymbol{\mu}_c)(\mathbf{h}_{cl} - \boldsymbol{\mu}_c)^T \longrightarrow$ min. $\mathbf{S}_w$ represents the within-class scatter matrix and defines the scatter of the coefficient vector samples corresponding to the class around their mean. The dispersion of samples that belong to the same class around their corresponding mean should be as small as possible.

2. $\mathbf{S}_b = \sum_{c=1}^{Q}(\boldsymbol{\mu}_c - \boldsymbol{\mu})(\boldsymbol{\mu}_c - \boldsymbol{\mu})^T \longrightarrow$ max. $\mathbf{S}_b$ denotes the between-class scatter matrix and defines the scatter of the class mean around the global mean $\boldsymbol{\mu}$. Each cluster formed by the samples that belong to the same class must be as far as possible from the other clusters. Therefore, $\mathbf{S}_b$ should be as large as possible.

We modify the divergence by adding these two more constraints. The new cost function is expressed as:

$$D_{DNMF}(\mathbf{X}||\mathbf{ZH}) \triangleq D_{LNMF}(\mathbf{X}||\mathbf{ZH}) + \gamma \sum_{c=1}^{Q}\sum_{l=1}^{n_c}(\mathbf{h}_{cl} - \boldsymbol{\mu}_c)(\mathbf{h}_{cl} - \boldsymbol{\mu}_c)^T$$

$$-\delta\sum_{c=1}^{Q}(\boldsymbol{\mu}_c - \boldsymbol{\mu})(\boldsymbol{\mu}_c - \boldsymbol{\mu})^T, \qquad (7.11)$$

where γ and δ are constants. Since DNMF is based on LNMF formulation according to (7.11), the orthogonality of the basis images is enforced. Following the same EM approach used by NMF and LNMF techniques, we come up with the following update expression for each element h_{kl} of coefficients from class c:

$$h_{kl(c)}^{(t)} = \frac{2\mu_c - 1 + \sqrt{(1 - 2\mu_c)^2 + 8\xi h_{kl(c)}^{(t-1)} \sum_i z_{ki}^{(t)} \frac{x_{ij}}{\sum_k z_{ik}^{(t)} h_{kl(c)}^{(t-1)}}}}{4\xi}. \qquad (7.12)$$

The elements h_{kl} are then concatenated for all Q classes as:

$$h_{kj}^{(t)} = [h_{kl(1)}^{(t)} \mid h_{kl(2)}^{(t)} \mid \cdots \mid h_{kl(Q)}^{(t)}] \qquad (7.13)$$

where "$\mid$" denotes concatenation. The expression (7.14) and (7.15) for updating the image basis remains unchanged from LNMF:

$$z_{ik}^{(t)} = \frac{z_{ik}^{(t-1)} \sum_j \frac{x_{ij}}{\sum_k z_{ik}^{(t-1)} h_{kj}^{(t)}} h_{jk}^{(t)}}{\sum_j h_{kj}^{(t)}} \qquad (7.14)$$

$$z_{ik}^{(t)} = \frac{z_{ik}^{(t)}}{\sum_i z_{ik}^{(t)}}, \quad \text{for all } k \qquad (7.15)$$

The derivation of (7.12) is given in the Appendix. The method proposed here is a supervised method that preserves the sparseness of basis images through (7.14), while enhancing the class separability by the minimization of $\mathbf{S}_w$ and the maximization of $\mathbf{S}_b$. Note that this idea is similar with the FLD method. However, the difference is fundamental: whilst FLD preserves the class discriminatory information on the original images, DNMF performs on the decomposition coefficients.

7.5 Facial Expression Recognition Experiment

7.5.1 *Data description*

We have tested our method along with PCA, FLD [Belhumeur *et al.* (1996)], NMF, LNMF, FNMF, ICA, Gabor and SVMs [Vapnik (1995)] approaches for recognizing the six basic facial expressions namely, anger, disgust, fear, happiness, sadness and surprise from face images. The facial images used come from Cohn-Kanade AU-coded facial expression database [Kanade *et al.* (2000)]. The database was originally created for Action Units (AU) representation appearing in the FACS coding system and not for explicit facial expression recognition. The facial action (action units) that are described in the image annotations have been converted into emotion class labels according to [Pantic and Rothkrantz (2000)]. Despite the fact that 100 posers were available, we were only able to identify thirteen of them who displayed all the six facial expressions. These thirteen persons have been chosen to create the image database that has been used in our experiments. Each subject from Cohn-Kanade database expresses an expression over time starting from a neutral pose and ending with a very intense expression, thus having several frames with different expression intensities. However, the number of frames is not constant for each subject. We picked up three poses with low (close to neutral), medium and high (close to the maximum) facial expression intensity, respectively. This newly formed database was used in our experiments. We must notice that the samples that are necessary for facial expression recognition training do not vary in their appearance as much as they vary, for example, in the face recognition task, where much more samples are needed to "extract" a representative identity from the training samples. The registration of each original image **x** was performed by mouse clicking on the eyes, thus retrieving the eyes coordinates, followed by an image shift step for centering the eyes. Furthermore, the images are rotated to horizontally align the face according to eyes. In the next step, the face region is cropped in order to remove the image borders, while keeping the main facial fiducial points (as eyebrows, eyes, nose and chin). Finally, each image of a resulting size 80×60 pixels was downsampled to a final size of 40×30 pixels for computational purposes (except for the Gabor case). The face image pixels were stored into a $m = 1200$ - dimensional vector for each image. These vectors form the columns of matrix **X** for PCA, FLD, DNMF, LNMF, NMF, FNMF and ICA approaches. In the case of the Gabor feature method, each 80×60 image was convolved with 12 Gabor filters, corresponding to the low frequency range for three frequencies $\nu = 2,3,4$ and four orientations $\mu = 0, \frac{\pi}{4}, \frac{\pi}{2}, \frac{3\pi}{4}$. Each resulting image was further downsampled by a factor of 3 to an image of 20×15

pixels, which was scanned row-wise to form a final feature vector of dimension 300 for each Gabor filter output. The 12 outputs have been concatenated to form a new longer feature vector of dimension 3600. Hence, in the case of Gabor filter approach, the final matrix $\mathbf{X}$ is of size $3600 \times n$, where n is the number of facial images [Buciu *et al.* (2003)]. The resulting feature vectors have been stored in the columns of $\mathbf{X}$ and were directly used for classification. We used only the magnitude of Gabor filter output, because it varies slowly with the pixel position, while the phase is very sensitive with respect to position. In the case of the SVM method, there are two approaches that can be taken into account. In the first one, the SVM is applied on the gray level values, i.e. directly on the face images, without extracting any feature. In the second approach, the SVM is applied on the features extracted by the aforementioned image representation methods. We employed here both approaches for SVMs. The sequential minimal optimization technique developed by Platt [Platt (1999)] was used to train SVMs having the original images as input. Since classical SVM theory was intended to solve a two class classification problem, we chose the Decision Directed Acyclic Graph (DDAG) learning architecture proposed by Platt et al. to cope with the multi-class classification [Platt *et al.* (2000)].

7.5.2   *Training procedure*

In the classical facial expression classification context, the n face images are split into a training set containing $n_{(tr)}$ images and a disjoint test set containing $n_{(te)}$ ones, with the corresponding matrices denoted by $\mathbf{X}_{(tr)}$ and $\mathbf{X}_{(te)}$, respectively. The training images $\mathbf{X}_{(tr)}$ are used in the expression for updating $\mathbf{Z}$ and $\mathbf{H}$. To form the training set, $n_{(tr)} = 164$ face images were randomly chosen from the Cohn-Kanade derived database, while the remaining $n_{(te)} = 70$ images were used for testing, thus forming the test face image set. Both the training and the test set contains all expressions. This has been checked before we proceeded further to processing. Out of the training images we formed the basis images corresponding to NMF, LNMF, FNMF, DNMF (by executing the algorithms described in this paper) and to ICA (by using the so-called architecture I approach described in [Barlett et al. (1998)]). The training procedure was applied eleven times for various numbers of basis images.

7.5.3   *Feature extraction and image representation*

By imposing only non-negativity constraints, the features extracted by NMF have a rather holistic appearance. To enhance the sparsity of NMF decomposition,

Hoyer has proposed a combination of sparse coding and NMF in [Hoyer (2002)]. LNMF greatly improves the sparseness and minimizes redundant information by imposing other constraints. DNMF also minimizes redundant information, but the degree of sparseness is limited by those retrieved features that are crucial for maximizing class separability. Figure 7.1 shows the creation of a sample basis image after a number of iterations. The features are automatically selected according to their discriminative power. For comparison, a number of 25 basis images out

Fig. 7.1   Creation of a sample basis image by DNMF algorithm after 0 (random initialization of basis images matrix **Z**), 300, 600, 900, 1200, 1500 and 1800 iterations, respectively.

of 144 for NMF, LNMF, FNMF and DNMF, respectively, are depicted in Figure 7.2. It can be noticed by visual inspection that the basis images retrieved by DNMF are not as sparse as those extracted by LNMF but are sparser than the basis images found by NMF. The basis images extracted by FNMF are almost as sparse as those corresponding to LNMF. To quantify the degree of sparseness, we measured the normalized kurtosis of a base image **z** (one column of **Z**) defined as $k(\mathbf{z}) = \frac{\sum_i (z_i - \overline{z})^4}{(\sum_i (z_i - \overline{z})^2)^2} - 3$, where z_i are the elements of **z** (pixels of the basis image) and $\overline{z}$ denotes the sample mean of **z**. It was found experimentally that the average kurtosis over the maximum number of 144 basis images is: $\overline{k}_{NMF} = 7.51$, $\overline{k}_{LNMF} = 152.89, \overline{k}_{FNMF} = 151.46, \overline{k}_{DNMF} = 22.57$. Therefore, in terms of basis image sparseness, DNMF is a compromise between NMF and LNMF. We have noticed in our experiments that the degree of sparseness corresponding to basis images extracted by DNMF did not increase after a number of iterations. We believe this is caused by those patterns in the basis images that encode meaningful class information and they cannot be disregarded as the iterations proceed further. Probably, the most important issue concerning DNMF algorithm is the fact that almost all features found by its basis images are represented by the salient face features such as eyes, eyebrows or mouth, features that are of great relevance for facial expressions. While discarding less important information, conveyed by nose and cheek (which is not the case for NMF), or putting less stress on it, DNMF preserves spatial topology of salient features (which are mostly absent in the case of LNMF or FNMF) by emphasizing them. The features retrieved by LNMF and FNMF have rather random positions.

For PCA, FLD, NMF, LNMF, FNMF and DNMF, the image data are then pro-

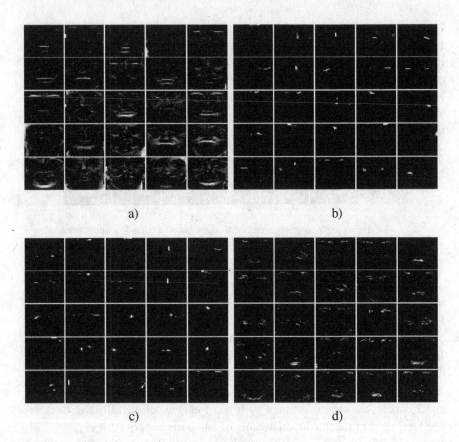

Fig. 7.2   A set of 25 basis images out of 144 for a) NMF, b) LNMF, c) FNMF and d) DNMF. They were ordered according to their decreasing degree of sparseness.

jected onto the image basis in an approach similar to the one used in classical PCA, yielding a feature vector $\mathbf{F}_{(tr)} = \mathbf{Z}^T(\mathbf{X}_{(tr)} - \mathbf{\Psi})$, where $\mathbf{\Psi}$ is a matrix whose columns store the average face $\mathbf{\Psi} = \frac{1}{n_{(tr)}} \sum_{j=1}^{n_{(tr)}} \mathbf{X}_{j(tr)}$. Since $\mathbf{X}_{(tr)} = \mathbf{ZH}$, a more natural way to compute $\mathbf{F}_{(tr)}$ would be $\mathbf{F}_{(tr)} = \mathbf{Z}^{-1}(\mathbf{X}_{(tr)} - \mathbf{\Psi})$. However, in our previous experiments we found that, by projecting the face images into the basis images instead of working directly with the coefficients $\mathbf{F}_{(tr)}$ given by the above expression, we can have slightly better results. Moreover, due to the fact that $\mathbf{Z}$ is not a square matrix, we would be forced to use its pseudoinverse, which may suffer from numerical instability. In any case, we can not use the coefficient matrix $\mathbf{H}$ computed directly by (7.12) in the training phase, since we do not have any expression for calculating a representation of test images. Let us enumerate the six facial expressions so that "1" is anger, "2" is disgust, "3" is fear, "4" is happiness, "5" is sadness and "6" is surprise. To have a first visualization on how efficient is to project the facial images onto the basis images, Figure 7.3 displays the projection of images coming from three expression classes (anger, disgust, surprise) on the first two basis images shown in Figure 7.2. Let us denote by $M1$, $M2$ and $M6$ the mean of the three clusters formed by these projections and the distance between the means by d_{12}, d_{16} and d_{26}, respectively. Then, for this metric space we have $d_{12} = 5.9$, $d_{16} = 6.1$, and $d_{26} = 3.4$ in the case of NMF, $d_{12} = 9, d_{16} = 21.8$ and $d_{26} = 20.4$ for LNMF, $d_{12} = 11.1, d_{16} = 26.2$ and $d_{26} = 21.7$ for FNMF and $d_{12} = 12.5$, $d_{16} = 27.9$ and $d_{26} = 28$ for DNMF approaches, respectively. For simplicity, Figure 7.3 shows only M2 and M6. The distance between them is depicted by a line segment. It can be noted that the classes do not overlap in the case of DNMF as much as they do in the case of NMF, LNMF or FNMF methods. The distance between the means corresponding to the four NMF derived algorithms for all expressions are tabulated in Table 7.1. For all expressions, the best between-class separability is obtained by DNMF, followed by FNMF, LNMF and NMF.

Table 7.1 Distance between the means of the database projection onto the first two basis images corresponding to the four NMF derived algorithms for all six facial expressions.

	NMF	LNMF	FNMF	DNMF
d_{12}	5.9	9	11.1	12.5
d_{13}	8.9	9.2	16.0	17.4
d_{14}	9.5	14.0	30.3	40.8
d_{15}	5.9	10.3	16.9	18.6
d_{16}	6.1	21.8	26.2	27.9
d_{23}	6	7.6	9.5	25.6
d_{24}	6.8	12.3	23.3	46.5
d_{25}	3.6	8.8	10.9	26.1
d_{26}	3.4	20.4	21.7	28
d_{34}	9.5	12.9	29.4	53.6
d_{35}	5.9	8.9	15.7	34
d_{36}	6.3	20.2	24.4	35.2
d_{45}	6.8	13.6	29.9	57
d_{46}	6.9	24.6	37.2	62
d_{56}	3.4	21.7	26	38.6

For the ICA approach, we used the first architecture described in [Barlett et al. (1998)] that gives us the coefficients to be applied for classification. The coefficients of each image form essentially a row of the matrix $\mathbf{F}_{(tr)} = (\mathbf{X}_{(tr)} - $

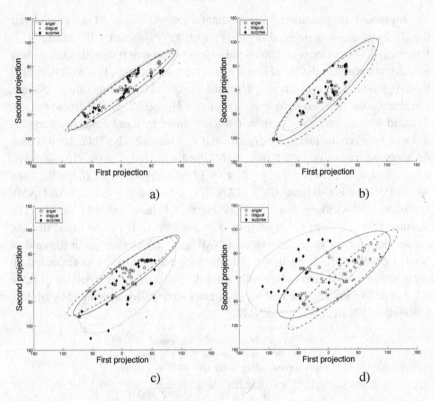

Fig. 7.3 Scatter plot of the clusters formed by the projection of three expression classes (anger, disgust, surprise) on the first two basis images shown in Figure 7.2 for a) NMF, b) LNMF, c) FNMF, and d) DNMF. $M2$ and $M6$ represent the mean of the clusters corresponding to "disgust" and "surprise" classes and the distance between they is depicted by a line segment. The ellipse encompasses the distribution with a confidence factor of 90 %.

$\Psi)\mathbf{P}_p\mathbf{A}^{-1}$. Here $\mathbf{P}_p$ is the projection matrix resulting from PCA procedure applied a priori to ICA and $\mathbf{A}$ is the unmixing matrix found by ICA algorithm. The number of independent components is controlled by the first p eigenvectors [Barlett et al. (1998)]. Note that the training phase is related to the process of finding $\mathbf{W}$, $\mathbf{H}$ and $\mathbf{A}$, in order to form the new feature vector, which is further used in the classification procedure. In the case of the Gabor approach, there is no training step and the feature vectors $\mathbf{f}_{(tr)}$ used for classification comprise in the columns of $\mathbf{X}$, as described in the Subsection 7.5.1.

7.5.4   Test procedure

In the test phase, for PCA, FLD, DNMF, LNMF, FNMF and NMF, for each test face image $\mathbf{x}_{(te)}$, a test feature vector $\mathbf{f}_{(te)}$ is then formed by $\mathbf{f}_{(te)} = \mathbf{Z}^T(\mathbf{x}_{(te)} - \psi)$. For the ICA approach, the test feature vector is formed by $\mathbf{f}_{(te)} = (\mathbf{x}_{(te)} - \psi)\mathbf{P}_p\mathbf{A}^{-1}$. In the case of Gabor approach, the classification procedure is applied directly to the columns of matrix $\mathbf{X}_{(te)}$ that contain Gabor features, obtained as described previously.

7.5.5   Classification procedure

The six basic facial expressions i. e. anger (*an*), disgust (*di*), fear (*fe*), happiness (*ha*), sadness (*sa*) and surprise (*su*), available for the facial image database form the six expression classes. If we construct a classifier whose class label output for a test sample $\mathbf{f}_{(te)}$ is $\tilde{l}$, the classifier accuracy is defined as the percentage of the correctly classified test images when $\{\tilde{l}(\mathbf{f}_{(te)}) = l(\mathbf{f}_{(te)})\}$, where $l(\mathbf{f}_{(te)})$ is the correct class label. Once we have formed $c = 6$ classes of new feature vectors (or prototype samples), a nearest neighbor classifier is employed to classify the new test sample by using the following similarity measures:

1. *Cosine similarity measure* (CSM). This approach is based on the nearest neighbor rule and uses as similarity the angle between a test feature vector and a prototype one. We choose $\tilde{l} = \mathrm{argmin}_{l=1,\ldots,c}\{d_l\}$, where $d_l = \frac{(\mathbf{f}_{(te)})^T \mathbf{f}_{l(tr)}}{\|\mathbf{f}_{(te)}\|\|\mathbf{f}_{l(tr)}\|}$ and d_l is the cosine of the angle between a test feature vector $\mathbf{f}_{(te)}$ and the prototype one $\mathbf{f}_{l(tr)}$.

2. *Maximum correlation classifier* (MCC). The second classifier is a minimum Euclidean distance classifier. The Euclidean distance from $\mathbf{f}_{(te)}$ to $\mathbf{f}_{l(tr)}$ is expressed as $\|\mathbf{f}_{(te)} - \mathbf{f}_{l(tr)}\|^2 = -2h_l(\mathbf{f}_{(te)}) + (\mathbf{f}_{(te)})^T\mathbf{f}_{(te)}$, where $h_l(\mathbf{f}_{(te)}) = (\mathbf{f}_{l(tr)})^T\mathbf{f}_{(te)} - \frac{1}{2}\|\mathbf{f}_{l(tr)}\|^2$ is a linear discriminant function of $\mathbf{f}_{(te)}$. A test image is classified by this classifier by computing c linear discriminant functions and choosing $MCC = \mathrm{argmax}_{l=1,\ldots,c}\{h_l(\mathbf{f}_{(te)})\}$.

Besides, as already mentioned, SVMs were used as classifiers where, either the original gray level values or the features extracted by the presented algorithms are considered as input.

7.6   Performance Evaluation and Discussions

We have tested the algorithms for several numbers of basis images (subspaces) and for all three classifiers. The results are shown in Figure 7.4. Unfortunately, the accuracy does not increase monotonically with the number of basis images

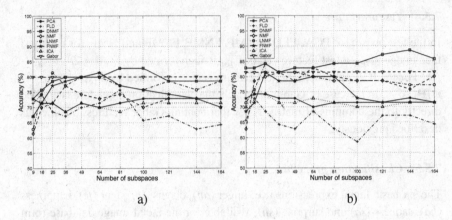

Fig. 7.4 Accuracy achieved in the case of a) CSM and b) MCC classifi er, respectively, for DNMF, NMF, LNMF, FNMF, ICA and Gabor methods versus number of basis images (subspaces).

(for any of the methods and classifiers). Table 7.2 depicts the maximum, mean classification accuracy and its standard deviation over the number of basis images for all methods involved in experiment and for the three classifiers (CSM, MCC and SVM). In this Table 7.2, SVM1 SVM2 denote the Support Vector Machine applied to the features extracted by the image representation methods involved in the experiment or to the downsampled original gray level images, respectively. For SVMs, the best accuracy was obtained with a polynomial kernel having degree 3 and setting up the penalizing term to 100 in the case of PCA, PDA, Gabor and LNMF image representations. When NMF and DNMF are combined with SVMs, the best accuracy is provided by an RBF kernel having parameter value $\sigma = 0.00005$ (width of RBF) and penalizing term value 500. Except for DNMF, the classifier accuracy is better for SVM1 than for CSM, MCC and SVM2. However, none of the image representations combined with the three classifiers reaches the maximum accuracy 88.57 % achieved by DNMF combined with the MCC classifier. The maximum classification accuracy obtained by DNMF is followed by DNMF plus SVM1 and LNMF plus SVM1, respectively. NMF extracts "noisy" features that can decrease its classiciation accuracy. Features that might be crucial for facial expression recognition are lost by LNMF in its attempt to obtain a local image representation. DNMF balances between NMF and LNMF. Despite the fact that FNMF is based on the same discriminant criteria as DNMF, the accuracy corresponding to this algorithm is comparable with the one yielded by LNMF but lower than the one obtained by DNMF. When combined with SVM, FNMF outperforms LNMF, but its performance does not reach the maximum accuracy

Table 7.2 Maximum, mean and standard deviation of the classification accuracy (%) calculated over the number of basis images.

		PCA	FLD	DNMF	NMF	LNMF	FNMF	ICA	Gabor	Downsampled images
CSM	max	72.85	75.71	82.85	77.14	81.42	81.42	71.42	80	x
	mean	71.68	68.96	79.04	71.58	76.34	75.06	70.15	x	x
	std	1.40	4.04	3.19	4.42	5.53	4.39	1.66	x	x
MCC	max	74.28	72.85	**88.57**	82.85	84.28	81.42	74.28	81.40	x
	mean	72.33	65.71	83.65	77.93	78.88	75.06	71.74	x	x
	std	1.32	3.77	1.61	5.85	3.69	4.62	1.71	x	x
SVM1	max	81.42	84.28	87.14	78.57	81.42	84.28	80.00	82.85	x
	mean	78.57	78.5	83.71	71.96	65	68.28	78.09	x	x
	std	3.84	6.55	5.18	5.06	24.55	22.11	1.74	x	x
SVM2	max	x	x	x	x	x	x	x	x	81.6
FLD	max	x	x	x	87.14	84.85	x	75.71	85.71	x

corresponding to DNMF. For this data set the poorest performance is achieved by FLD. This can be caused either due to an insufficient data size or to the highly non linear class separability.

Moreover, DNMF algorithm has larger mean accuracy and smaller standard deviation than NMF and LNMF for CSM, as can be seen in Table 7.2. The DNMF mean accuracy is greatly improved when MCC is applied, achieving the biggest average classification accuracy (83.65 %) and the smallest standard deviation (1.61 %).

To establish to what degree the performance benefit is due to adding class-specific information to NMF or LNMF and to what degree it is due to putting this information directly in the feature LNMF learning stage (as DNMF does), we performed FLD on top of either NMF (FLD+NMF) or LNMF (FLD+LNMF), respectively. Also, this approach has been used for ICA (FLD+ICA) and Gabor representations (FLD+Gabor). The last row of the Table 7.2 shows the comparison results. For all these image representations, the use of FLD on top of them seems to be a good idea, since the results show an increase in the accuracy compared with the case when MCC and CSM were applied directly to those image representations. The biggest gain was obtained for FLD+NMF, where the accuracy increased from 82.85% to 87.14%, a value that is still smaller by 1.43% then the best case (DNMF with 88.57%). As DNMF is built on LNMF by incorporating the discriminant information in the learning process, the comparison of the result of FLD+LNMF with that of LNMF and DNMF is of particular interest. In this case, FLD+LNMF improves the accuracy insignificantly, compared with LNMF (from 84.28% to 84.85%) and did not reach the maximum of 88.57% obtained by DNMF with MCC.

As far as the ICA approach is concerned, we should mention that a supervised ICA technique, called ICA - FX, has been developed [Kwak et al. (2002)] to obtain features that are not only independent from each other, but also convey class information, contrary to the classical ICA, which is an unsupervised approach and does not utilize class information. In order to establish to what extent the classification performance is affected by incorporating class information, we ran the ICA - FX approach and compared it with classical ICA in our experiments. Due to the fact that the first ICA architecture does not allow us to make a comparison against ICA - FX, since this architecture performs ICA on the PCA projection matrix (thus performing ICA on the reduced data size and loosing the class labels), we have chosen to run the experiments for comparison with the second ICA architecture [Barlett et al. (1998)]. In this case, ICA operates on the PCA coefficients where the data dimensionality is reduced and the class label is preserved. For 49 basis images we obtained an accuracy of 70% and 71.1% with CSM classifier corresponding to ICA and ICA - FX approach, respectively. When the MCC classifier is involved, we have yielded an accuracy of 61.5% and 72.9% corresponding to ICA and ICA - FX.

A very careful attention must be paid to ξ since it appears in (7.12), making its tuning a difficult task. Due to the fact that the cost function defined by DNMF is formed by several terms that are simultaneously optimized (minimized or maximized), its global optimization may suffer. Although the cost function is globally minimized, each term has its own rate of convergence. The parameter ξ governs the convergence speed for minimizing $\mathbf{S}_w$ while maximizing $\mathbf{S}_b$. However, it also interferes with the expression that minimizes the approximation $\mathbf{X} \approx \mathbf{ZH}$, i.e., the term $D_{NMF}(\mathbf{X} \| \mathbf{ZH})$. An overly small value of ξ will speed up the decrease of $\mathbf{S}_w$, the increase of $\mathbf{S}_b$ and the minimization of $D_{NMF}(\mathbf{X} \| \mathbf{ZH}))$. However, the algorithm may stop too early and the number of iterations might not be sufficient to reach a local minimum for $D_{DNMF}(\mathbf{X} \| \mathbf{ZH})$. A premature stop can affect the process of correctly learning the basis images that might not be sparse anymore. On the other hand, the algorithm may converge very slowly if an overly large value of ξ is chosen. By keeping γ and δ fixed at value one, experimentally, we have chosen a value of $\xi = 0.5$ in our experiments that gave us a good trade-off between sparseness and convergence speed. Besides, it keeps the value of $D_{NMF}(\mathbf{X} \| \mathbf{ZH})$ low.

It is worth noting that DNMF shares some common characteristics with the biological visual models proposed by neuroscience. In the light of the sparse image coding theory, the neural interpretation of this model is that the neural cell performs sparse coding on the visual input, having its receptive fields closely related to the sparse coding basis images while its firing rates are proportional to the representation coefficients. Compared to NMF (holistic) and LNMF or FNMF (local), the sparse representation given by DNMF is preferred, having some advantages over holistic and local representations [Foldiak (2002)]. Another important aspect is related to the nature of features extracted by these methods. Obviously, the human face has some salient features such as eyebrows, eyes, and mouth. DNMF emphasizes salient face features and diminishes other features, as opposite to NMF approach, which puts approximately the same weight on each image pixel. In contrary, the features discovered by LNMF or FNMF have rather random position and they do not always correspond to salient facial image features.

7.7   Conclusion

In this chapter, we have presented a novel image representation approach, namely, Discriminant Non-negative Matrix Factorization. A systematic analysis of the algorithm has been carried out in terms of its convergence and subspace image representation. Then the algorithm has been applied to facial expression recognition task and its performance has been compared to several existing state-of-the art techniques. Comprehensive experiments showed that the DNMF produced a higher recognition accuracy than any of the PCA, FLD, NMF, LNMF, FNMF, ICA or Gabor approaches. DNMF presents a sparse structure of the basis images. The basis image sparse "active" patterns (just a few pixel patterns have non-zero value) are selected by the representation coefficients that convey class information. The proposed approach is a supervised learning algorithm that keeps the original non-negative constraints on basis and coefficients borrowed from the original NMF approach, enhances the sparseness of basis images and eliminate redundant information (with respect to NMF) by adding the constraints taken from LNMF approach, and improves the classification accuracy by following a class discriminant approach. As far as the basis image sparseness is concerned, DNMF is a good trade-off between local image representation produced by LNMF and the holistic image representation produced by NMF. DNMF is proven to provide the best classification accuracy when used for facial expression recognition having the maximum accuracy 88.57 % and the best average accuracy 83.65 % on the Cohn-Kanade facial image database. Although DNMF has been applied to classify expressions, other applications can benefit from it, such as categorization of different objects into different classes, where the latent features that are relevant for this task can be discovered by this approach.

Aknowledgement

This work has been conducted in conjunction with the "SIMILAR" European Network of Excellence on Multimodal Interfaces of the IST Programme of the European Union (www.similar.cc).

Appendix

Derivation of the DNMF coefficients update

The expressions (7.12) and (7.14) can be proved by using an auxiliary function similar to those used in EM algorithm [Dempster (1977)]. G is said to be an auxiliary function for $Y(\mathbf{F})$ if $G(\mathbf{F}, \mathbf{F}^{(t-1)}) \geq Y(\mathbf{F})$ and $G(\mathbf{F}, \mathbf{F}) = Y(\mathbf{F})$. If G is an auxiliary function for Y, then Y is nonincreasing under the update $\mathbf{F}^{(t)} = \operatorname{argmin}_{\mathbf{F}} G(\mathbf{F}, \mathbf{F}^{(t-1)})$. With the help of G taking $\mathbf{Z}$ and $\mathbf{H}$ as argument, a learning algorithm that alternates between updating basis images and updating coefficients can be derived. Since we did not impose any other constraints on the basis than those required by LNMF the derivation of (7.14) can be found in [Li *et al.* (2001)]. We have modified the coefficient expression, therefore we only give the derivation of its formulae. By fixing $\mathbf{Z}$, $\mathbf{H}$ is updated by minimizing $Y(\mathbf{H}) = D_{DNMF}(\mathbf{X}||\mathbf{ZH})$. Let us define:

$$
\begin{aligned}
G(\mathbf{H}, & \mathbf{H}^{(t-1)}) \\
&= \sum_{i,j}(x_{ij}\ln x_{ij} - x_{ij}) + \sum_{i,j,k} x_{ij}\frac{z_{ik}h_{kj}^{(t-1)}}{\sum_k z_{ik}h_{kj}^{(t-1)}}\left(\ln(z_{ik}h_{kj}) - \ln\frac{z_{ik}h_{kj}^{(t-1)}}{\sum_k z_{ik}h_{kj}^{(t-1)}}\right) \\
&\quad + \sum_k z_{ik}h_{kj} + \alpha\sum_{i,j}u_{ij} - \beta\sum_i v_{ii} + \gamma\sum_{c=1}^{\mathcal{Q}}\sum_{l=1}^{n_c}(h_{cl} - \mu_c)(h_{cl} - \mu_c)^T \\
&\quad - \delta\sum_{c=1}^{\mathcal{Q}}(\mu_c - \mu)(\mu_c - \mu)^T,.
\end{aligned}
\tag{7.16}
$$

This function is an auxiliary function for $Y(\mathbf{H})$. It is straightforward to show that $G(\mathbf{H}, \mathbf{H}) = Y(\mathbf{H})$. In order to prove that $G(\mathbf{H}, \mathbf{H}^{(t-1)}) \geq Y(\mathbf{H})$, since $\ln(\sum_k z_{ik}h_{kj})$ is convex, the following inequality holds:

$$
-\ln\left(\sum_k z_{ik}h_{kj}\right) \leq -\sum_k a_{ijk}\ln\frac{z_{ik}h_{kj}}{a_{ijk}},
\tag{7.17}
$$

for all non-negative a_{ijk} that satisfy $\sum_k a_{ijk} = 1$. By denoting $a_{ijk} =$

$\frac{z_{ik}h_{kj}^{(t-1)}}{\sum_k z_{ik}h_{kj}^{(t-1)}}$ we obtain:

$$-\ln\left(\sum_k z_{ik}h_{kj}\right) \le -\sum_k \frac{z_{ik}h_{kj}^{(t-1)}}{\sum_k z_{ik}h_{kj}^{(t-1)}}\left(\ln z_{ik}h_{kj} - \ln\frac{z_{ik}h_{kj}^{(t-1)}}{\sum_k z_{ik}h_{kj}^{(t-1)}}\right).$$

(7.18)

From this inequality it follows that $G(\mathbf{H}, \mathbf{H}^{t-1}) \ge Y(\mathbf{H})$.

By setting $\frac{\partial G(\mathbf{H},\mathbf{H}^{(t-1)})}{\partial h_{kl}}$ to zero for all $kl, l = 1, \ldots, n_c$ the partial derivative of G with respect to h_{kl} gives us:

$$-\sum_i x_{il}\frac{z_{ik}h_{kl}^{(t-1)}}{\sum_k z_{ik}h_{kl}^{(t-1)}}\frac{1}{h_{kl}} + \sum_i z_{ik} - 2\beta h_{kl} + 2\gamma(h_{kl} - \mu_c) = 0. \quad (7.19)$$

The equation can be rearranged as:

$$2\xi h_{kl}^2 + \left(\sum_i z_{ik} - 2\mu_c\right)h_{kl} - \sum_i x_{il}\frac{z_{ik}h_{kl}^{(t-1)}}{\sum_k z_{ik}h_{kl}^{(t-1)}} = 0, \quad (7.20)$$

where $\xi = \gamma - \beta$.

This is a quadratic equation in h and it has the solution:

$$h_{kl} = \frac{2\mu_c - \sum_i z_{ik} + \sqrt{(\sum_i z_{ik} - 2\mu_c)^2 + 8\xi h_{kl}^{(t-1)}\sum_i z_{ki}\frac{x_{il}}{\sum_k z_{ik}h_{kl}^{(t-1)}}}}{4\xi}.$$

(7.21)

Taking into account that $\sum_i z_{ik} = 1$, we obtain (7.12).

Bibliography

Bartlett, M. S., Lades, H. M. and Sejnowski, T. K. (1998), Independent component representations for face recognition, *Proc. SPIE Conf. Human Vision and Electronic Imaging III*, **3299**, pp. 528–539.

Belhumeur, P. N., Hespanha, J. P. and Kriegman, D. J. (1996), Eigenfaces vs. Fisherfaces: Recognition using class specifi c linear projection, *ECCV*, **1**, pp. 45–58.

Bregman, L. M. (1967), The relaxation method of fi ndind the common point of convex sets and its application to the solution of problems in convex programming, *U.S.S.R. Computational Mathematics and Mathematical Physics*, **1**, no. 7, pp. 200–217.

Buciu, I., Kotropoulos, C. and Pitas, I. (2003), ICA and Gabor representation for facial expression recognition, in *Proc. 2003 IEEE Int. Conf. Image Processing*, pp. 855–858.

Buciu, I. and Pitas, I. (2004), Application of non-negative and local non-negative matrix factorization to facial expression recognition, *Int. Conf. on Pattern Recognition*, pp. 228–291.

Buciu, I. and Pitas, I. (2004), A new sparse image representation algorithm applied to facial expression recognition, in *Proc. IEEE Workshop on Machine Learning for Signal Processing*, pp. 539–548.

Calder, A. J., Burton, A. M., Miller, P., Young, A. W. and Akamatsu, S. (2001), A principal component analysis of facial expressions, *Vision Research* , **41**, pp. 1179–1208.

Chen, X., Gu, L., Li, S. Z. and Zhang, H-J. (2001), Learning representative local features for face detection, *Int. Conf. Computer Vision and Pattern Recognition*, pp. 1126–1131.

Cottrell, G. and Metcalfe, J. (1991), Face, gender and emotion recognition using holons, *Advances in Neural Information Processing Systems*, **3**, pp. 564–571.

Padgett, C. and Cottrell, G. (1997), Representing face images for emotion classifi cation , *Advances in Neural Information Processing Systems*, **9**, pp. 894–900.

Dempster, A. P., Laird, N. M. and Rubin, D. B. (1977), Maximum likelihood from incomplete data via the EM algorithm, *Journal of Royal Statistical Society*, **39**, no. 1, pp. 1–38.

Donato, G., Bartlett, M. S., Hager, J. C., Ekman, P. and Sejnowski, T. J. (1999), Classifying facial actions, *IEEE Trans. on Pattern Analysis and Machine Intelligence*, **21**, no. 10, pp. 974–989.

Draper, B. A., Baek, K., Bartlett, M. S. and Beveridge, J. R. (2003), Recognizing faces with PCA and ICA , in *Computer vision and image understanding*, **91**: Special issue on Face Recognition, pp. 115–137.

Fasel, B. and Luettin, J. (2003), Automatic Facial Expression Analysis: A Survey, *Pattern Recognition*, **1**, no. 30, pp. 259–275.

Foldiak, P. (2002), Sparse coding in the primate cortex, *The Handbook of Brain Theory and Neural Networks*, Second Edition, pp. 1064–1068, MIT Press.

Hoyer, P. O. (2002), Non-negative sparse coding, *Proc. IEEE Workshop on Neural Networks for Signal Processing*, pp. 557–565.

Kanade, T., Cohn, J. and Tian, Y. (2000), Comprehensive database for facial expression analysis, in *Proc. IEEE Inter. Conf. on Face and Gesture Recognition*, pp. 46–53.

Kapoor, A. Qi, Y. and Picard, R. (2003), Fully automatic upper facial actions recognition, *in IEEE Inter. Workshop. on Analysis and Modeling of Faces and Gestures*, pp. 195–202.

Kullback, S. and Leibler, R. (1951), On information and suffi ciency, *Annals of Mathematical Statistics*, no. 22, pp. 79–86.

Kwak, N., Choi, C. -H., and Ahuja, N. (2002), Face recognition using feature extraction based on independent component analysis, in *Proc. 2002 IEEE Int. Conf. Image Processing*, pp. 337–340.

Lee, D. D., and Seung, H. S. (1999), Learning the parts of the objects by non-negative matrix factorization, *Nature*, **401**, pp. 788–791.

Lee, D. D. and Seung, H. S. (2001), Algorithms for non-negative matrix factorization, *Advances Neural Information Processing Systems*, **13**, pp. 556–562.

Li, S. Z., Hou, X. W. and Zhang, H. J. (2001), Learning spatially localized, parts-based representation, *Int. Conf. Computer Vision and Pattern Recognition*, pp. 207–212.

Littlewort, G., Bartlett, M., Fasel, I., Chenu, J., Kanda, T., Ishiguro, H. and Movellan, J. (2004), Towards social robots: Automatic evaluation of human-robot interaction by face detection and expression classifi cation, *Advances in Neural Information Processing Systems*, **16**, pp. 1563–1570.

Pantic, M. and Rothkrantz, L. J. M. (2000), Expert system for automatic analysis of facial expressions, *Image and Vision Computing*, **18**, no. 11, pp. 881–905.

Pantic, M. and Rothkrantz, L. (2003), Toward an affect-sensitive multimodal human-computer interaction, *Proc. of the IEEE*, **91**, no. 9, pp. 1370–1390.

Platt, J. C. (1999), Fast training of support vector machines using sequential minimal optimization, *Advances in Kernel Methods - Support Vector Learning*, **12**, pp. 185–208.

Platt, J. C., Cristianini, N. and Taylor, J. S. (2000), Large margin DAGs for mutliclass classifi cation, *Advances in Neural Information Procesing Systems*, **12**, pp. 547–553.

Tian, Y.-Li, Kanade, T. and Cohn, J. (2002), Evaluation of Gabor-wavelet-based facial action unit recognition in image sequences of increasing complexity, in *Proc. of Fifth IEEE Int. Conf. on Automatic Face and Gesture Recognition*, May, pp. 229–234.

Vapnik, V. (1995), *The nature of statistical learning theory*, Springer-Verlag.

Wang, Y., Jia, Y. Hu, C. and Turk, M. (2005), Non-negative matrix factorization framework for face recognition, *Int. Journal of Pattern Recognition and Artificial Intelligence*, **19**, no. 4, pp. 1-17.

Wiskott, L., Fellous, J.-M., Kruger, N. and von der Malsburg, C. (1997), Face recognition by elastic bunch graph matching, *IEEE Trans. on Pattern Analysis and Machine Intelligence*, **19**, no. 7, pp. 775–779.

Zhang, Z., Lyons, M., Schuster, M. and Akamatsu, S. (1998), Comparison between geometry-based and Gabor-wavelets-based facial expression recognition using multi-layer perceptron, in *Proc. of Third IEEE Int. Conf. Automatic Face and Gesture Recognition*, April 14-16 1998, Nara Japan, pp 454-459.

Chapter 8

Duplicate Image Detection in Large Scale Databases

Pratim Ghosh, E. Drelie Gelasca, K.R. Ramakrishnan† and B. S. Manjunath

Vision Research Lab., Electrical and Computer Engineering Department,
University of California, Santa Barbara 93106-9560.
†Indian Institute of Science, Bangalore, 560 012,India.

We propose an image duplicate detection method for identifying modified copies of the same image in a very large database. Modifications that we consider include rotation, scaling and cropping. A compact 12 dimensional descriptor based on Fourier Mellin Transform is introduced. The compactness of this descriptor allows efficient indexing over the entire database. Results are presented on a 10 million image database that demonstrates the effectiveness and the efficiency of this descriptor. In addition, we also propose extension to arbitrary shape representations and similar scene detection and preliminary results are also included.

8.1 Introduction

Automated robust methods for duplicate detection of images/videos is getting more attention recently due to the exponential growth of multimedia content on the web. The large quantity of multimedia data makes it infeasible to monitor them manually. In addition, copyright violations and data piracy are significant issues in many areas including digital rights management and in the entertainment industry. In this chapter, our main aim is to propose a system that can detect *duplicate* images in very large image databases. We specifically focus on the scalability issue. Our proposed approach results in a very compact image signature that is robust to many image processing operations, can be indexed to efficiently search large databases (we show results on a 10 million image database), and is quite ef-

Table 8.1 Operations corresponding 4 bytes
signatures for images in Figure 8.1.

Operations performed	Compact Signature
Original Image	122 197 157 73
Gaussian Noise addition	122 197 156 73
Gaussian Blurring (2)	122 196 158 73
Rotation (90)	122 197 155 73
Rotation (180)	122 197 155 73
Rotation (270)	121 197 157 73
Scaling down (x1.3)	115 196 166 74
Scaling down (x2)	103 197 178 80
Scaling down (x4)	93 194 181 95
JPEG Compressed (90)	122 197 156 73
JPEG Compressed (70)	122 196 156 74
JPEG Compressed (50)	122 197 156 72
JPEG Compressed (30)	122 197 156 72
Cropping (by 10%)	129 201 146 72
Cropping (by 20%)	127 203 154 79
Cropping (by 30%)	126 205 165 86

fective (about 82% precision). Our method can also be extended for similar image detection and "region of interest" duplicate detection.

In many practical scenarios, the duplicates are not identical replicas of the images in the database, but are digitally processed versions of the original images in the database. In these cases, standard hashing methods will not work. Here, "duplicate" refer to digitally modified versions of the image after manipulations such as those shown in Figure 8.1. Duplicate detection of exact copy using hashing techniques has been already addressed in the literature [Lu *et al.* (2004); Venkatesan *et al.* (2000)]. Figure 8.1 (a) shows the original image and Figures 8.1 (b)-(p) are obtained after digital processing such as scaling, rotation and cropping. One can consider duplicate detection as a subset of similarity search and retrieval, see for example [Chang *et al.* (1998); Fridrich *et al.* (2003); Luo and Nascimento (2003); Meng *et al.* (2003)].

Real time retrieval from a large image archive such as the World Wide Web (WWW) necessarily demands robust systems in terms of

- *efficiency*, time performance;
- *accuracy*, precision and recall;
- *scalability*, the property of accommodating significant changes in data volume without affecting the system performance.

Many of the results reported in the literature are on small databases, ranging from a few thousand (e.g., [Ke and Suthankar (2004); Maret *et al.* (2005); Roy and

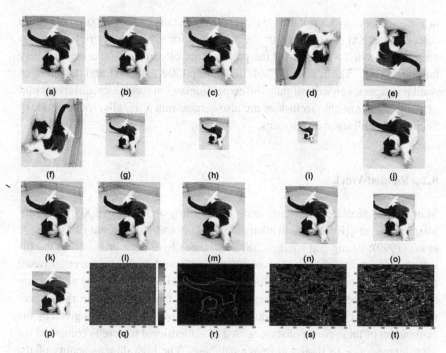

Fig. 8.1 (a) original image; (b) gaussian noise added image; (c) blurred image; (d)-(f) rotated images: $90^o, 180^o, 270^o$; (g)-(i) scaled images: $75\%, 50\%, 25\%$; (j)-(m) JPEG compressed images: 90, 70, 50, 30; (n)-(p) cropped images: $10\%, 20\%, 30\%$; (q)-(t) difference images with respect to the original one for (b),(c),(l) and (m). The compact signatures of all these images are summarized in the Table 8.1 sequentially.

Chang (2005)]) to 1.4 million images in the case of Wang *et al.* [Wang *et al.* (2006)].

The key steps in our duplicate detection includes the computation of the Fourier Mellin Transform (FMT) [Casasent and Psaltis (1976)] followed by a dimensionality reduction resulting in a 12 dimensional quantized vector. These quantized vectors are represented using unsigned characters (total of 96 bits). This compact representation allows us to build an efficient indexing tree, such as a k-d tree, that can search the database in 0.03 seconds on an Intel Xeon with CPU 2.33GHz. The accuracy is evaluated using a query data set of 100 images. We are also exploring the use of clustering methods for approximate search and retrieval and results are presented.

The rest of the chapter is organized as follows. Section 8.2 gives an overview of related work. In Section 8.3, we present the details of the proposed duplicate detection method. Extensions of the algorithm for sub image retrieval are also proposed. Section 8.4 discusses the performance of compact signature on a very large database. The results for sub image duplicate detection and detection of similar images taken with slightly different illumination conditions, different point of views, rotations and occlusions are also demonstrated. Finally, we conclude in Section 8.5 with some discussions.

8.2 Related Work

Many duplicate detection [Maret *et al.* (2005); Roy and Chang (2005)] and sub-image retrieval [Ke and Suthankar (2004); Luo and Nascimento (2003); Sebe *et al.* (1999); Zhang and Chang (2004)] schemes have been proposed in the literature. Maret *et. al* [Maret *et al.* (2005)] proposed duplicate detection based on support vector classifier. Different image features such as color and texture are first extracted from the image. Distances are then computed in the respective feature space and finally the dissimilarity between two images is given by the summation of these partial distances. A 138 dimensional feature is computed for each image, on a 18 thousand image database. The high dimensionality of the feature vector is a limiting factor in scaling this approach to large databases.

Another method, RAM (Resolving Ambiguity by Modification) [Roy and Chang (2005)], was proposed for duplicate detection using Analytical Fourier Mellin Transform (AFMT). First, in the pre-processing stage, the feature vectors are extracted from the database. A modified version of the original feature space is obtained by increasing the mutual distances among the features maintaining the semantic content of the image. Second, the algorithm searches through the modified database for a given query. A constrained optimization problem was solved in order to generate the modified feature space. This optimization problem has $d \times n$ variables and a minimum of n^2 constraints where d and n are the dimensions and number of points considered respectively (specifically, $d = 400$ was used in their case). This method also suffers from the scalability issue and some ad hoc post processing steps were suggested in the paper to address this.

There are also methods that deal with sub image retrieval [Ke and Suthankar (2004); Luo and Nascimento (2003); Sebe *et al.* (1999); Zhang and Chang (2004)]. The main idea of all these approaches is based on extracting a large number of local features and then using sophisticated algorithms for their efficient matching. These methods are computationally very expensive and require significant amount of storage/memory. In the above mentioned sub image retrieval methods, the database size ranges from few hundreds to thousands and their scalability is not demonstrated.

Few web image search engines for large scale duplicate detection have been also proposed [Chang *et al.* (1998); Wang *et al.* (2006)]. RIME (Replicated IMage dEtector) [Chang *et al.* (1998)] detects duplicate images by representing them with feature vectors (wavelet co-efficients) and employing an indexing scheme (multidimensional extensible hashing) to index the high dimensional feature vectors. Experimental results on a database of about 30000 images are provided. In [Wang *et al.* (2006)], each image was compactly represented (≤ 32 *bits*) by a hash code. These compact hash codes are then compared for duplicate image retrieval yielding a high precision recall ratio (more than 90%) on 1.4 million images considering only the simple manipulations such as minor scale changes, image storage format (PNG, JPEG, GIF) conversions and color/grayscale conversion.

Our proposed method makes the following contributions:

- a compact signature that can be used to detect duplicates when the original image is modified significantly is proposed;
- the compactness of the signature allows efficient indexing tree to be built;
- the scheme shows to be scalable for large image database containing over 10 million images;
- possible extensions to similar scene and region of interest identification are also shown.

In the following section, we discuss the system level issues in more detail.

8.3 System Overview

The overall block diagram of the web duplicate image retrieval system is depicted in Figure 8.2. The current version of our system contains about 10 million images. The database used in these experiments can be found at `http://cortina.ece.ucsb.edu/`. These images are downloaded from the web using a web crawler and stored into the image database along with the associated meta-data (text and keyword).

CFMT block. The CFMT (Compact Fourier Mellin Transform) is computed for each image in the database. It takes approximately 50 msec in our current C implementation to compute this descriptor. The details of the CFMT algorithm are discussed in details in Section 8.3.1.

K-d tree indexing. A *k*-d tree indexing scheme is also implemented to struc-

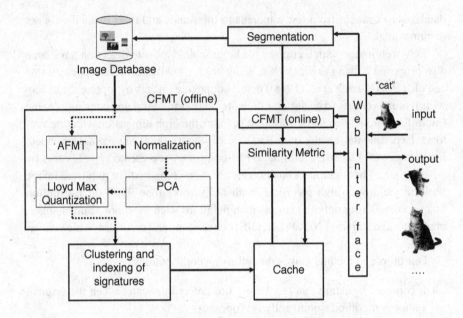

Fig. 8.2   System Architecture.

turally range the signatures for fast search and retrieval. It takes around 30 msec to retrieve the 20 nearest neighbors for a given query from the entire database. Indexing performance is discussed in Section 8.4.

Similarity metric. Both L_1 and L_2 distance measure have been implemented for comparing the feature vectors. The L_2 distance measure was found to improve the results marginally.

Arbitrarily shaped region based CFMT. On a smaller dataset (MM270K with about 18000 images) we have tested an adaptation of CFMT algorithm for arbitrarily shaped regions. Firstly, GPAC (Graph Partitioning Active contours), a recently proposed segmentation scheme [Sumengen and Manjunath (2006)] is applied to segment foreground regions within the image. The GPAC method was selected after exploring different foreground/background segmentation methods (e.g. active contour model by Chan and Vese [Chan and Vese (2001)] and Geodesic Active Contour [Casellas *et al.* (1997)]) since it gives better results overall. Then, the CFMT is extracted on the foreground region instead of the whole image. The adaptation of CFMT algorithm for arbitrarily shaped regions is presented in Section 8.3.2 and preliminary results in Section 8.4.4.

8.3.1 CFMT descriptor for images

Fourier-Mellin transform (FMT) has been studied extensively in the context of watermarking [Lin *et al.* (2001); Zheng and Zhao (2003)] and invariant object recognition [Derrode and Ghorbel (2001); Gotze *et al.* (2000); Raman and Desai (1995)]. All these methods exploit the fact that this transform generates a rotation, translation and scale invariant representation of the images. The FMT was first introduced in [Casasent and Psaltis (1976)] and our implementation is based on the fast approximation described in [Derrode and Ghorbel (2001)].

The classical FMT of a 2D function f, $T_f(k, v)$ is defined as:

$$T_f(k,v) = \frac{1}{2\pi} \int_0^\infty \int_0^{2\pi} f(r,\theta) r^{-iv} e^{-ik\theta} d\theta \frac{dr}{r} \qquad (8.1)$$

where (k, v) and (r, θ) are respectively the variables in Fourier Mellin and polar domain representation of the function f. Ghorbel [Ghorbel (1994)] suggested the AFMT, an important modification to the problem associated with the existence of standard FM integral (the presence of $\frac{1}{r}$ term in the definition necessarily requires f to be proportional to r around the origin such that when $r \to 0$ then $f \to 0$). The AFMT, $T_{f\sigma}(k, v)$, is defined as:

$$T_{f\sigma}(k,v) = \frac{1}{2\pi} \int_0^\infty \int_0^{2\pi} f(r,\theta) r^{\sigma-iv} e^{-ik\theta} d\theta \frac{dr}{r} \qquad (8.2)$$

where σ, a strictly positive parameter, determines the rate at which f tends toward zero near the origin.

Let $f_1(x, y)$ be an image and its rotated, scaled, translated version $f_2(x, y)$ be related by the equation:

$$f_2(x,y) = f_1(\alpha(x\cos\beta + y\sin\beta) - x_o, \alpha(-x\sin\beta + y\cos\beta) - y_o) \quad (8.3)$$

where the rotation and scale parameters are β and α respectively, and $[x_o, y_o]$ is the translation. It can be shown that for rotated and scaled images, the magnitudes of the AFM transforms, $|T_{f_1\sigma}|$ and $|T_{f_2\sigma}|$, (corresponding to f_1 and f_2) are related by the equation:

$$|T_{f_2\sigma}(k,v)| = \alpha^{-\sigma} |T_{f_1\sigma}(k,v)| \qquad (8.4)$$

Concisely, an AFMT leads to a scale and rotation invariant representation after proper normalization by $1/\alpha^{-\sigma}$. Finally, the CFMT representation can be made translation invariant by computing the AFMT on the Fourier transformed image (considering only the magnitude part).

Once the AFM coefficients are extracted, Principal Component Analysis (PCA) [Jolliffe (2002)] and Lloyd Max non uniform scalar quantization [Gonzales and Woods (1992)] are applied to obtain a compact representation, the CFMT descriptor. Each dimension of the CMFT descriptor is quantized to 256 levels. After extensive experimentation, we choose the 12 dimensional CFMT descriptor for our duplicate detection since it provided a good trade off between accuracy and efficiency.

8.3.2 *CFMT extraction for arbitrarily shaped regions*

Here we extend the CFMT computation for arbitrarily shaped regions (SA-CFMT, Shape Adaptive CFMT). This is useful in many applications where one is looking for specific objects or regions of interest within a larger image. A schematic of this region of interest CFMT computation is shown in Figure 8.3. We first applied

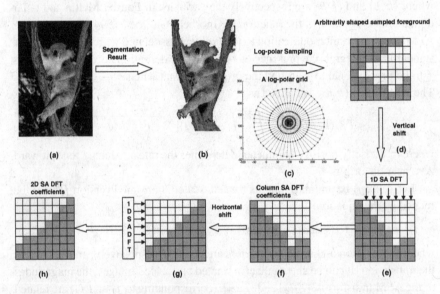

Fig. 8.3   A typical 2D SA DFT work fbw: (a) original image, (b) segmented Region of Interest(ROI), (c)-(d) sampled foreground using the log-polar grid, (e) up-shifting and 1D SA DFT on each column, (f) column SA DFT coeffi cients, (g) left-shifting and 1D SA DFT on each row, (h) fi nal 2D SA DFT coeffi cients. Darker and brighter regions correspond to background and foreground respectively in all these matrices.

the GPAC[Sumengen and Manjunath (2006)] segmentation on a given image to extract the foreground region. Then a log-polar transform is computed with the center of the coordinate system for the transformation being the centroid of the region of interest. The pixel values inside the foreground are mapped to a log-polar sampling grid and the rest of the positions in the grid are filled with zeroes. Since all the grid positions do not correspond to foreground, normal 2D FFT can not be employed on the sampled values directly. Instead, we use the Shape Adaptive Discrete Fourier Transform (SA-DFT) [Stasinski and Konrad (1999)]. SA-DFT was first proposed for coding of arbitrary shaped image segments in the MPEG-4 image compression standard.

The SA DFT coefficients of a vector $x[n]$ where $n = 0, 1, 2, ..., N - 1$ are computed in a two step approach:

(1) Let $x[n]$ has N_s samples belonging to the foreground and the rest to the background samples. Also consider a new sequence $x'[n]$ to be constructed using only the foreground samples of $x[n]$. Two cases can occur. In the first case, the foreground samples can form a contiguous cluster:
$$x[n] = \{0, 0., ., 0, a_1, a_2, a_3, .., a_{N_s}, 0, ..0, 0\}$$
where $\{a_i\}_{i=1,2,...,N_s}$ denotes the foreground and the zeros are the background samples. In this case, $x'[n]$ is obtained by taking the contiguous block from $x[n]$ e.g. $x'[n] = \{a_1, a_2, a_3, ..., a_{N_s}\}$. In the second case, the foreground samples in $x[n]$ can be separated by the background samples like:
$$x[n] = \{0, 0.., a_1, a_2, 0, 0, 0, a_3, a_4, a_5, 0, 0, .., a_{N_s}, 0, 0\}$$
Therefore, in this case, $x'[n]$ is constructed by replacing the background ones with following foreground samples e.g. $x'[n] = \{a_1, a_2, a_3, ..., a_{N_s}\}$ ($x'[n]$ is the condensed version of $x[n]$ without any background samples). Also the relative positions of the foreground samples in $x[n]$ are maintained in $x'[n]$.

(2) Then, a N_s point DFT is applied to $x'[n]$, followed by a scaling of $1/\sqrt{N_s}$ which preserves the orthogonality property of the DFT 2D transform. Let us define, $X'[k]$ where $k = 0, 1, 2, ..., N_s - 1$ be the DFT of $x'[n]$. The required number of zeros are padded at the end of the sequence $X'[k]$ to have the same length as the input vector $x[n]$. Thus, $X'[k]$ gives the SA DFT of $x[n]$.

Like other separable transforms SA DFT is also applicable to two dimensional matrices. Firstly, each column is processed using above mentioned 1D algorithm and secondly the same is applied to each row of the results. Given the 2D SA DFT representation for an image we extract the CFMT signature in the same way as described in Section 8.3.1 and finally obtain the SA-CFMT.

8.4 Experimental Results

We now describe the evaluation metric used to asses the performance of the proposed CFMT signature. Then, we proceed to present experimental results on duplicate detection for both whole and segmented image. Time performance is also discussed.

8.4.1 *Performance evaluation*

Fig. 8.4   Original image, log-polar transformed image and reconstructed image (from left to right) using only ~ 50 % of the total A.C. energy. Overall shape remains unchanged in the reconstructed image.

Precision-recall value has been used to measure the performance of our signature. Let $A(H, \Gamma)$ be the set of H retrievals based on the smallest distances from the query image, Γ, in the signature space and $C(\Gamma)$ be the set of D images in the database relevant to the query Γ. Then, precision P is defined by the number of images retrieved relevant to query image divided by the set of retrievals, H.

$$P(H, \Gamma) \stackrel{\text{def}}{=} \frac{|A(H, \Gamma) \bigcap C(\Gamma)|}{H}$$

Recall which is defined as

$$R(H, \Gamma) \stackrel{\text{def}}{=} \frac{|A(H, \Gamma) \bigcap C(\Gamma)|}{D}$$

is the proportion of relevant images retrieved from $C(\Gamma)$. A precision-recall curve is usually obtained by averaging precision and recall values over a large number of queries Γ to obtain a good estimate.

8.4.2 *Results on web image database*

In our implementation of AFMT, the image is first mapped to a log-polar domain and a 2D FFT is then computed on that domain. A 71×71 grid has been found to be adequate for the log-polar mapping. We extract all Fourier Mellin (FM) coefficients lying within a fixed radius, the *target radius*, from the center. We choose the *target radius* in such a way so that the energy of the AFM coefficients within it corresponds to 50% of the total AFM coefficients energy. Within the *target radius* (which in our implementation is 8 pixels) there are 96 independent AFM coefficients. The AFM coefficients are normalized by the central FM harmonic to get rid of the $\alpha^{-\sigma}$ term (see Eq. 8.4). Figure 8.4 shows the original image and the reconstructed image using the AFM coefficients which correspond to 50% of the total A.C energy.

A set of 100 random images are chosen as queries and for each of the query images 15 duplicates are generated by performing the operations described in Table 8.1.

Varying sizes of CFMT signature include: 4, 6, 8 and 12 dimensions with one byte per dimension. To give an idea of how much the signatures varies among duplicate images, the 4 dimensional CFMT representations for the images shown in Figure 8.1 are reported in Table 8.1.

Figure 8.5 shows the retrieval results for various sizes of CFMT signatures. Note that for the 12 dimensional CFMT signature for H=15 (at the knee point) the corresponding precision and recall are $P = 0.82, C = 0.81$. In Figure 8.6, a

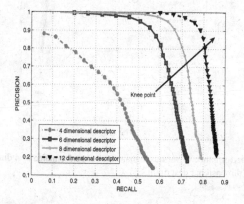

Fig. 8.5 Precision Recall curve on close to a 10 million image database averaged on 100 queries, each with 15 duplicates.

comparative study is obtained to show the scalability of CFMT signatures as the size of the database increases starting from 1 million up to 9 millions. It is clear from the figure that the 12 dimensional descriptor scales quite well with the size of the database.

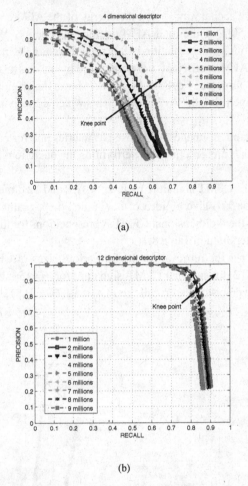

Fig. 8.6   Scalability performance of various signatures: (a) performance of 4 dimensional descriptor; (b) performance of 12 dimensional descriptor.

8.4.3   *Time performance*

We investigated different approaches to improve the run time performance of our system. A naive sequential search over the 10 million image database takes approximately 3 seconds for retrieving the 20 nearest neighbors. A k-d tree indexing data structure is also implemented. The k-d tree index structure built on a 12 dimensional feature space takes only about 0.03 seconds to retrieve the 20 nearest neighbors. It takes about 3 minutes to build this data structure and requires 1.5 GB of main memory to keep the data structure. Note that the entire k-d tree needs to be kept in memory during the query-retrieval time. Such high memory requirement might be crucial. In fact, if we increase our database size by 50% the k-d tree structure would require more than 2 GB of main memory. This motivated us to investigate clustering based methods for approximate nearest neighbor search and retrieval. The performance of the simple K-means clustering is summarized in Table 8.2. For the 10 million images with 64 clusters one can get about 65.6% accurate results with the search time of about 1.8 seconds. These clustering results are preliminary and suggest a trade off between accuracy and computations.

Table 8.2 Speed and accuracy using sequential search and K-means clustering.

#clusters	none	32	64
# points	11033927	1085509	583381
search (sec)	3.014	2.841	1.826
accuracy	82%	77.9%	65.6%

8.4.4 *Results on MM270K image database*

Preliminary results have also been obtained for region and similar scene retrieval on a smaller dataset. The MM270K database used in these experiments can be downloaded from `http://www.cs.cmu.edu/~yke/retrieval`.

Similar Scene Retrieval. In this case, the duplicates correspond to images of the same scene acquired under different imaging conditions. For example, these images are captured at different time, from different view point and may have occluded regions. See Figure 8.7 for some examples. The CFMT descriptor in its current form is not translation invariant and needs further modifications to address this issue. One simple solution is to construct the CFMT descriptor on top of the Fourier Transform of the image. Performance can be further improved by increasing the dimensionality of the descriptor. The precision recall curve obtained for the whole MM270K dataset is depicted in Figure 8.8 for the case of 12 dimensional and 36 dimensional modified descriptor. In this graph, the results are averaged over 14 queries with each having 4 similar scenes in the database. As can be seen from the graph, these preliminary results are quite promising.

Arbitrarily shaped region retrieval. The GPAC[Sumengen and Manjunath (2006)] segmentation method was used to automatically compute the foreground and background segmentation from the MM270K database for this experiment. We constructed 40 query examples, each having 12 duplicates. These duplicates correspond to the modifications (b)-(m) in Figure 8.1. GPAC segmentation was applied to the MM270K database, to the originals and its duplicates. Some results are shown in Figure 8.9. There was no manual parameter tuning on these

Fig. 8.7   Tested scene changes in the similar scene retrieval experiments. Similar images are taken with: slightly different view points, camera setting, occlusions, rotation and photometric changes.

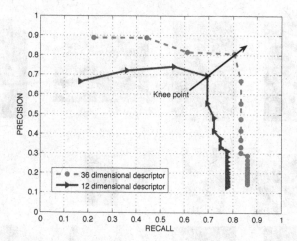

Fig. 8.8   Precision Recall curve on MM270K averaged on 14 queries, each with 4 similar scenes.

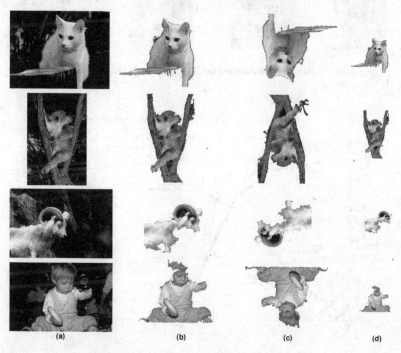

Fig. 8.9   (a) original images; (b)-(d) segmentation results on: original images, 180° rotated version of the original images, 25% scaled version of the original images.

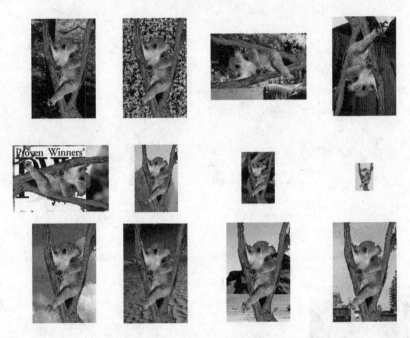

Fig. 8.10   Backgrounds used for testing CFMT and SA-CFMT in MM270K.

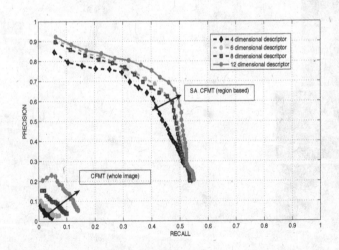

Fig. 8.11   Precision Recall curve on MM270K averaged on 40 queries, each with 12 duplicates.

results. The SA-CFMT descriptors was then computed on these segmented region as discussed in Section 8.3.2. We also computed the CFMT for the whole image with different kind of backgrounds as shown in Figure 8.10. Figure 8.11 shows the precision recall curve for MM270K database with CFMT (whole image) compared to GPAC plus SA-CFMT (region based). Note that a precision of 61% is achieved with a recall rate of 60% at the knee point for $H = 12$ for GPAC plus SA-CFMT and very low precision values are obtained by using only CFMT on the whole image for any size of signature.

8.5 Conclusion and Future Work

In this chapter we have presented a scalable duplicate detection method. The scalability of the 12 dimensional CFMT signature has been demonstrated for a web image database containing about 10 million images. We have provided detailed experimental results demonstrating the accuracy and efficiency of the proposed approach. On the 10 million image database we get about 82% accuracy with a search time of about 30 msec on a standard desktop. Preliminary results for arbitrarily shaped similar region retrieval as well as similar scene detection are very promising.

Acknowledgments

We would like to thank Anindya Sarkar for proofreading the manuscript. This project was supported by NSF grant #ITR-0331697.

Bibliography

Casasent, D. and Psaltis, D. (1976). Scale invariant optical transform, *Opt.Eng.* **15**, 3, pp. 258–261.

Casellas, V., Kimmel, R. and Sapiro, G. (1997). Geodesic active contours, *International Journal of Computer Vision* **22**, 1, pp. 61–79.

Chan, T. F. and Vese, L. A. (2001). Active contours without edges, *IEEE Transactions on Image Processing* **10**, 2, pp. 266–277.

Chang, E., Wang, J., Li, C. and Wiederhold, G. (1998). RIME: A replicated image detector for the world-wide web, in *SPIE Multimedia Storage and Archiving Systems*.

Derrode, S. and Ghorbel, F. (2001). Robust and effi cient Fourier-Mellin transform approximations for gray-level image reconstruction and complete invariant description, *Computer Vision and Image Understanding: CVIU* **83**, 1, pp. 57–78.

Fridrich, J., Soukal, D. and Lukas, J. (2003). Detection of copy-move forgery in digital images, in *Digital Forensic Research Workshop*.

Ghorbel, F. (1994). A complete invariant description for gray-level images by the harmonic analysis approach, in *Pattern Recognition Letters*, Vol. 15, pp. 1043–1051.

Gonzales, R. C. and Woods, R. E. (1992). *Digital Image Processing*.

Gotze, N., Drue, S. and Hartmann, G. (2000). Invariant object recognition with discriminant features based on local fast-fourier mellin transform, in *International Conference on Pattern Recognition*, Vol. 1.

Jolliffe, I. T. (2002). *Principal Component Analysis*.

Ke, Y. and Suthankar, R. (2004). Effi cient near duplicate detection and sub image retrieval, in *ACM Multimedia*.

Lin, C. Y., Yu, M., Bloom, J. A., Cox, I. J., Miller, M. L. and Lui, Y. M. (2001). Rotation scale and translation resilient watermarking for images, *IEEE Transaction on Image Processing* **10**, pp. 767–782.

Lu, C. S., Hsu, C. Y., Sun, S. W. and Chang, P. C. (2004). Robust mesh-based hashing for copy detection and tracing of images, in *ICME*, Vol. 1, pp. 731–734.

Luo, J. and Nascimento, M. (2003). Content based sub-image retrieval via hierarchical tree matching, in *ACM Workshop on Multimedia Databases*.

Maret, Y., Dufaux, F. and Ebrahimi, T. (2005). Image replica detection based on support vector classifi er, in *Optical Information System III, SPIE*, Vol. 5909, pp. 173–181.

Meng, Y., Chang, E. and Li, B. (2003). Enhancing dpf for near-replica image recognition, in *IEEE Computer Vision and Pattern Recognition*.

Raman, S. and Desai, U. (1995). 2-d object recognition using Fourier Mellin transform and a MLPnetwork, in *IEEE International Conference on Neural Networks 1995 Proceedings*, Vol. 4, pp. 2154–2156.

Roy, S. and Chang, E. C. (2005). A unifi ed framework for resolving ambiguity in copy detection, in *ACM Multimedia*, pp. 648–655.

Sebe, N., Lew, M. S. and Huijsmans, D. P. (1999). Multi-scale sub-image search, in *ACM Multimedia (2)*, pp. 79–82.

Stasinski, R. and Konrad, J. (1999). A new class of fast shape-adaptive orthogonal transforms and their application to region-based image compression, *IEEE Trans. Circuits Syst. Video Technol.* **9**, pp. 16–34.

Sumengen, B. and Manjunath, B. S. (2006). Graph partitioning active contours (GPAC) for image segmentation, *IEEE Transactions on Pattern Analysis and Machine Intelligence (PAMI)* **28**, 4, pp. 509–521.

Venkatesan, R., S. M. Koon, M. H. J. and Moulin, P. (2000). Robust image hashing, in *Int. Conf. Image Processing*, Vol. 3, pp. 664–666.

Wang, B., Li, Z., Li, M. and Ma, W. Y. (2006). Large-scale duplicate detection for web image search, in *ICME*, pp. 353–356.

Zhang, D. and Chang, S. F. (2004). Detecting image near-duplicate by stochastic attributed relational graph matching with learning, in *MULTIMEDIA '04: Proceedings of the 12th annual ACM international conference on Multimedia*, pp. 877–884.

Zheng, D. and Zhao, J. (2003). LPM-based RST invariant digital image watermarking, in *Electrical and Computer Engineering, 2003. IEEE CCECE 2003. Canadian Conference on*, Vol. 3, pp. 1951–1954.

Chapter 9

Unsupervised Context-Sensitive Change Detection Techniques Based on Self-Organizing Feature Map Neural Network

Swarnajyoti Patra, Susmita Ghosh and Ashish Ghosh* [1]

*Department of Computer Science and Engineering
Jadavpur University, Kolkata 700032, India*

**Machine Intelligence Unit and Center for Soft Computing Research
Indian statistical Institute, 203 B.T. Road, Kolkata 700108, India*

In this article unsupervised context-sensitive techniques for change detection in multitemporal remote sensing images have been proposed. Two different architecture of Self-Organizing Feature Map Neural Network are used to discriminates the changed and unchanged regions of the difference image. In both the networks, the number of neurons in the input layer is equal to the number of features of the input patterns. Depending on the number of neurons in the output layer the network is categorized as one-dimensional or two-dimensional. In one-dimensional network, the number of neuron in output layer is two, one represents the changed class and the other represents the unchanged class. In two-dimensional network, each spatial position of the input image corresponds to a neuron in the output layer and the network is updated depending on some threshold value. When the network converges, status of output neurons depict a change detection map. Two different criteria are suggested to select suitable thresholds. Both the proposed change detection techniques are distribution free. Experimental results are carried out on two multispectral and multitemporal remote sensing images to assess the effectiveness of the proposed approaches.

[1]Corresponding author. E-mail: ash@isical.ac.in

9.1   Introduction

In remote sensing applications, change detection is the process of identifying differences in the state of an object or phenomenon by analyzing a pair of images acquired on the same geographical area at different times[Singh (1989)]. Such a problem plays an important role in many different domains, like studies on land-use/land-cover dynamics[Cihelar *et al.* (1992)], monitoring shifting cultivations[Bruzzone and Serpico (1997)], burned area assessment[Bruzzone and Prieto (2000)], analysis of deforestation processes[Hame *et al.* (1998)], identification of vegetation changes[Chavez *et al.* (1994)], monitoring of urban growth[Merril and Jiajun (1998)] *etc.* Since all these applications usually require an analysis of large areas, development of completely automatic change detection techniques became of high relevance in order to reduce the effort required by manual image analysis.

In the literature[Bruzzone and Serpico (1997)]-[Bazi *et al.* (2005)] several supervised and unsupervised techniques for detecting changes in remote-sensing images have been proposed. The supervised methods require the availability of a "ground truth" from which a training set, containing information about the spectral signatures of the changes that occurred in the considered area between the two dates, is generated. The statistics of the classes can be more easily estimated, given the a priori information. Moreover, it is also possible to estimate the kind of changes that occurred. In contrast, unsupervised approaches perform change detection without using any additional information, besides the raw images considered. The difficulty with collecting ground truth information regularly in time makes it mandatory to develop unsupervised change detection methods to support the analysis of temporal sequences of remote-sensing images. Unsupervised change detection problem can be defined as a classification problem where a "changed" class and "unchanged" class have to be distinguished, given the input images.

In the literature, the most widely used unsupervised change detection techniques follow three sequential steps[Singh (1989)]: i) pre-processing, ii) image comparison, and iii) image analysis. During the pre-processing step two raw images are taken as input and are made compatible using operations like co-registration, radiometric and geometric corrections, and noise reduction[Richards and Jia (2006)]. In the next step, two pre-processed images are compared pixel by pixel to generate a third image, called the difference image, where differences between the two acquisitions (images) are highlighted. Different mathematical operations can be used to perform image comparison. The most widely used operator is difference. The difference can be applied to i) a single spectral band (Univariate Image Differencing)[Singh (1989)], ii) multiple spectral bands

(Change Vector Analysis)[Singh (1989); Bruzzone and Prieto (2000)], iii) vegetation indices (Vegetation Index Differencing)[Singh (1989); Townshend and Justice (1995)] or to other linear (e.g., Tasselled Cap Transformation[Fung (1990)]) or non liner combinations of spectral bands. Among these, the most popular technique, called Change Vector Analysis (CVA), generates the difference image considering several spectral channels at each date. For each pair of corresponding pixels, the "spectral change vector" is computed as the difference in the feature vectors at the two time stamps. The pixel values in the difference image are then associated with the magnitudes of the spectral change vectors. Once image comparison is performed, the image analysis (change detection) process can be carried out by adopting either context-insensitive or context-sensitive procedures. The most widely used context-insensitive analysis techniques are based on histogram thresholding[Bruzzone and Prieto (2000); Melgani *et al.* (2002)]. Thresholding procedures do not take into account the spatial correlation between neighboring pixels in the decision process. To overcome this limitation, different context-sensitive change detection procedures have been proposed in the literature[Bruzzone and Prieto (2000); Kasetkasem and Varshney (2002); Bruzzone and Prieto (2002); Ghosh *et al.* (2007a); Bazi *et al.* (2005)]. Among these, most of the approaches are based on Markov Random Fields (MRF) which require the selection of a proper model for the statistical distributions of changed and unchanged pixels. The EM algorithm[Dempster *et al.* (1977)] has been employed for estimation of these distributions under different assumptions for class distributions, e.g., Gaussian[Bruzzone and Prieto (2000)], generalized Gaussian[Bazi *et al.* (2005)] and mixture of Gaussians[Bruzzone and Prieto (2002)].

In order to overcome the limitations imposed by the need of selecting a statistical model for "change" and "unchange" class distributions, in this chapter we propose two unsupervised, distribution free and context-sensitive change detection techniques based on one-dimensional and two-dimensional Self-Organizing Feature Map (SOFM) neural network[Patra *et al.* (2006, 2007)]. Both the networks have two layers, input and output. Also the number of neurons in the input layer is equal to the dimension of the input patterns. The input patterns are generated considering each pixel in the difference image along with its neighboring pixels, in order to take into account the spatial contextual information from the neighborhood. In one-dimensional SOFM (1D-SOFM), the number of neurons in output layer is two. During learning process, 1D-SOFM learns the weights of the network in such a way that the pixels in the difference image belonging to the changed region is automatically mapped to one output neuron; and the pixels which belong to unchanged region are mapped to another neuron. In two-dimensional SOFM (2D-SOFM), each neuron in the output layer corresponds to a pixel in the difference image. The network is updated (until convergence) to generate a change detection map for a particular (assumed) threshold. Different change detection maps are generated by varying the threshold. To select an appropriate threshold, automatically, a correlation based and an energy based criteria are proposed. The major advantages of the proposed technique are i) it is distribution free ii) it is completely unsupervised (it does not require manual setting of any input parameter).

In order to assess the effectiveness of the proposed techniques, we considered two multitemporal data sets corresponding to the geographical areas in Mexico and the Island of Sardinia, Italy, and compared the results provided by the proposed technique with those obtained by a reference method published in the literature[Bruzzone and Prieto (2000)].

This chapter is organized into six Sections. Section13.2 provides a brief description of Kohonen's self-organizing feature map neural network. Section13.3 describes the proposed change detection techniques based on 1D-SOFM and 2D-SOFM. The data sets used in the experiments are described in Section13.4. Experimental results are discussed in Section13.5. Finally, in Section9.6, conclusions are drawn.

9.2   Kohonen's Model of Self-Organizing Feature Map

Kohonen's Self-Organizing Feature Map network[Kohonen (1982, 1997)] consists of an input and an output layer. Each neuron in the output layer is connected to all the neurons in the input layer i.e., the y-dimensional input signal $U = [u_1, u_2, ..., u_y]$ can be passed to all the output neurons. Let the synaptic weight vector of an output neuron j be denoted by $W_j = [w_{j1}, w_{j2}, ..., w_{jy}]^T$, $j = 1, 2, ...M$, where M is the total number of neurons in the output layer and w_{jk} is the weight of the jth unit for the kth component of the input. If the synaptic weight vector W_i of output neuron i is best matched with input vector U, then $\sum_{k=1}^{y} w_{ik}.u_k$ will be maximum among $\sum_{k=1}^{y} w_{jk}.u_k$, $\forall j$. The neuron i is then called the *wining neuron* for the input vector U. The *wining neuron* is located at the center of a topological neighborhood of cooperating units. Let $h_i(itr)$ denote the topological neighborhood of *wining neuron* i at epoch number itr. There are several ways to define a topological neighborhood[Lo *et al.* (1993)] such as Gaussian, rectangular. The size of the topological neighborhood shrinks with increase in itr. Fig. 9.1 shows how the size of the topological neighborhood of the *wining neuron* i decreases with itr (in case of rectangular topological neighborhood). For the ith unit and all its neighbors (within a specified radius defined by $h_i(itr)$) the following weight updating rule is applied

$$W_i(itr + 1) = W_i(itr) + \eta(itr)h_i(itr)(U - W_i(itr)).\qquad (9.1)$$

Here, η $(0 < \eta < 1)$ is the learning rate that determines how rapidly the system adjusts over itr. The learning rate parameter η also decreases as itr increases. The term $h_i(.)$ ensures updating the synaptic weights of the neurons inside the topological neighborhood of *wining neuron i* only. The above updating procedure moves the weight vector towards the input vector. So repeated presentation of training patterns tries to make the synaptic weight vectors tend to follow the distribution of the input vectors.

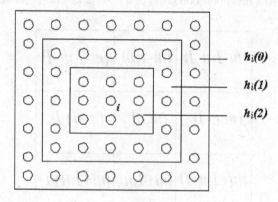

Fig. 9.1   Rectangular topological neighborhood of neuron i over itr

9.3   Proposed Change Detection Techniques

In this section we will describe two unsupervised techniques; one is based on one-dimensional self-organizing feature map neural network and the other is based on two-dimensional self-organizing feature map neural network. As both the networks work on the same input domain, the number of neurons in the input layer are the same and equal to the dimension of the input patterns. A details description of the generation of input patterns is given below.

Let us consider two co-registered and radiometrically corrected multispectral images X_1 and X_2 of size $p \times q$, acquired over the same area at different times T_1 and T_2, and let $D = \{l_{mn}, 1 \le m \le p, 1 \le n \le q\}$ be the difference image obtained by applying the CVA technique on X_1 and X_2. In order to use a

SOFM network for solving the change detection problems by exploiting both image radiometric properties and spatial-contextual information, the input patterns are generated corresponding to each pixel in the difference image D, considering its spatial neighborhood systems N of order d. For a given spatial position (m, n), $N^d(m, n)$ will be as follows: $N^d(m, n) = \{(m, n) + (i, j), (i, j) \in N^d\}$. In greater detail, if the input patterns take 1st order neighborhood information (N^1), then the input pattern U_{mn} corresponding to the spatial position (m, n) is generated by considering the grey value of the pixel at position (m, n) and its four nearest neighboring pixels i.e., $N^1 = \{(\pm 1, 0), (0, \pm 1)\}$. Similarly, with the 2nd order neighborhood (N^2), a pixel at position (m, n) considers its eight nearest neighboring pixels i.e., $N^2 = \{(\pm 1, 0), (0, \pm 1), (1, \pm 1), (-1, \pm 1)\}$. Fig. 9.2 depicts a 2nd order neighborhood (N^2) of a pixel at position (m, n).

(m-1,n-1)	*(m-1,n)*	*(m-1,n+1)*
(m,n-1)	*(m,n)*	*(m,n+1)*
(m+1,n-1)	*(m+1,n)*	*(m+1,n+1)*

Fig. 9.2 N^2 neighborhood of pixel (m, n)

9.3.1   *Change detection based on 1D-SOFM*

As in the present context there are only two regions (changed and unchanged), we propose to represent each data cluster with a single output neuron rather than a larger feature map. So, the output layer contains only two units; one is used to map the input patterns into "changed class" (cluster) and the other to "unchanged class" (cluster). Fig. 9.3 depicts a fully connected one-dimensional SOFM network with two output and nine input neurons. Let us describe the learning algorithm of this network in Table 9.1.

The above algorithm partitions the weight space $\Re^9$ into two regions such that all points within the same region have a single weight vector W_i $(i = 1, 2)$ as

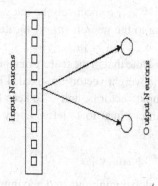

Fig. 9.3   One-dimensional SOFM network architecture

Table 9.1   Learning algorithm of the proposed network

Step 1: Initialize weights W_i $(i = 1, 2)$ of the network randomly and set $itr = 0$.
Step 2: Initialize the learning rate parameter $\eta(itr)$.
Step 3: Select an input vector U_{mn}.
Step 4: Find out the winning neuron and set $h_i(itr) = 1$ if i is the winning neuron else $h_i(itr) = 0$.
Step 5: Update the weights of the network using Eq. (9.1)
Step 6: Perform Steps 3-5 for all training patterns, completing one epoch.
Step 7: $itr = itr + 1$.
Step 8: If no noticeable changes in the feature map are observed or the number of epoches exceeds some
predefined number, then goto Step 10.
Step 9: Decrease the value of $\eta(itr)$ and goto Step 3.
Step 10: Stop.

their nearest neighbor. So this weight vectors represents the centroid of the clusters. The borders of these regions are hyperplane that are orthogonal to connecting weight vectors. Since SOFM maintains topological order, all the similar input data points are at a minimum distance from the same weight vector and are, therefore, mapped onto the same output neuron. So the network automatically generates the change detection map by mapping changed data patterns onto one neuron and the unchanged data patterns onto another.

9.3.2   *Change detection based on 2D-SOFM*

In this study we used a SOFM network where the number of neurons in the output layer is equal to the number of pixels in the difference image D and the number of neurons in the input layer is equal to the dimension of the input patterns. Let U_{mn} and W_{mn}, respectively be the y-dimensional input and weight vectors corresponding to the neuron (m, n) located at m^{th} row and n^{th} column of the output layer, i.e., $U_{mn} = [u_{mn,1}, u_{mn,2}, ..., u_{mn,y}]$ and $W_{mn} = [w_{mn,1}, w_{mn,2}, ..., w_{mn,y}]^T$. Note that in the feature mapping algorithm, the maximum lengths of the input and weight vectors are fixed. Let the maximum length for each component of the input vector be unity. To keep the value of each component of the input less than or equal to 1, let us apply a mapping function f where

$$f : [c_{min}, c_{max}] \rightarrow [0, 1].$$

Here c_{min} and c_{max} are the global minimum and maximum component (feature) values present in the input vectors. The initial component of the weight vectors are chosen randomly in [0,1].

9.3.2.1   *Learning the weights*

U_{mn} and W_{mn} be the input and weight vectors of the output neuron (m, n), respectively. Their dot product $x(m, n)$ are

$$x(m, n) = U_{mn}.W_{mn} = \sum_{k=1}^{y} u_{mn,k}.w_{mn,k}. \qquad (9.2)$$

Now only those neurons for which $x(m, n) \geq t$ (here t is assumed to be a predefined threshold) are allowed to modify (update) their weights along with their neighbors (specified by $h_{mn}(.)$). Consideration of a set of neighbors enables one to grow the region by including those which might have been dropped out because of the initial randomness of weights (i.e., if the assigned weights are such that $x(m, n) \geq t$ for a few (m, n), then the weights of these neurons and their neighboring neurons will also be updated and subsequently categorized into changed region, if they originally belong to changed region). The threshold t is varied from 0 to 1. To keep the value of dot product $x(m, n)$ for all (m, n) in $[0, 1]$, we normalize each components of the weight vector W_{mn} of neuron (m, n) such that $\sum_{k=1}^{y} w_{mn,k} = 1$ (here all components of the input and weight vectors are nonnegative). The kth component of the weight vector W_{mn} is normalized as follows:

$$w_{mn,k} = \frac{w_{mn,k}}{\sum_{k=1}^{y} w_{mn,k}}. \qquad (9.3)$$

The weight updating procedure is performed using Eq. (9.1). The value of learning rate parameter $\eta(itr)$ and the size of the topological neighborhood $h_{mn}(itr)$

decreases over itr. To check the convergence, total output $O(itr)$ for each epoch number itr is computed as follows

$$O(itr) = \sum_{x(m,n) \geq t} x(m,n). \tag{9.4}$$

The updating of the weights continue until $|O(itr) - O(itr-1)| < \delta$, where δ is a preassigned small positive quantity. After the network is converged, the pixel at spatial position (m,n) in D is assigned to *changed region* if $x(m,n) \geq t$, else to *unchanged region*. The network converges for any value of t (proof is available in[Ghosh and Pal (1992)]). The above mentioned learning algorithm is described in Table 9.2.

Table 9.2   Learning algorithm of the presented network

Step 1: Initialize $\boldsymbol{W}_{mn}$ randomly (in [0,1]) for each output neuron (m,n).
Step 2: Set $itr = 0$. Initialize $\eta(itr)$ and $h_{mn}(itr)$.
Step 3: Set $O(itr) = 0$.
Step 4: Select an input vector $\boldsymbol{U}_{mn}$ and corresponding normalize weight vector $\boldsymbol{W}_{mn}$.
Step 5: Compute their dot product $x(m,n)$ using Eq. (9.2).
Step 6: If $x(m,n) \geq t$ then update the weight vector $\boldsymbol{W}_{mn}$ along with the weight vectors of the neighboring
neurons of the $(m,n)th$ neuron using Eq. (9.1) and set $O(itr) = O(itr) + x(m,n)$.
Step 7: Repeat Steps 4-6 for all input patterns, completing one epoch.
Step 8: If $(\mid O(itr) - O(itr-1) \mid < \delta)$ then goto Step 11.
Step 9: $itr = itr + 1$.
Step 10: Decrease the value of $\eta(itr)$ and $h_{mn}(itr)$ and goto Step 3.
Step 11: Stop.

Note that, unlike the conventional SOFM, in the present network [Ghosh and Pal (1992)] instead of giving the same input to all output neurons and finding out the *wining neuron*, here different input is given to different output neurons and weight updating is performed based on the considered threshold t.

9.3.2.2 *Proposed threshold selection techniques*

As stated in the above algorithm, the updating of weights depends on the threshold value t. Initially for a particular threshold t, the network is updated till convergence. After convergence, if $x(m,n) \geq t$, then make the output value V_{mn} of neuron (m,n) 1, else make it -1. Thus in the output layer the neurons are divided into two groups G_u (represents *unchanged regions*) and G_c (represents *changed regions*) and a change detection map corresponding to threshold t is generated. By varying t (threshold values are varied by an amount $1/L$, where L is the maximum gray value of D), different change detection maps are generated. To select a threshold t_1 near the minimum error threshold t_0 (corresponding change detection results provide minimum error), we propose two different criteria as described below.

Correlation Maximization Criterion: In this case the correlation coefficient[Ross (1987)] between the input sequence (difference image) and the output sequence (change detection map generated assuming threshold t) is maximized to select the near optimal threshold t_1. As the threshold t is varied, the change detection map also varies, thereby the value of the correlation coefficient is changed. When the threshold corresponds to the boundary between changed and unchanged pixels, the correlation coefficient becomes maximum. Let Y and Z be two random variables that correspond to the input and output sequences, respectively. The correlation coefficient between Y and Z for threshold t (denoted as, $R_{Y,Z}(t)$) is defined as

$$R_{Y,Z}(t) = \frac{cov(Y,Z)}{\sigma_Y.\sigma_Z}.$$

Here $cov(Y,Z)$ is the covariance of Y and Z; σ_Y and σ_Z are the standard deviations of Y and Z, respectively. As l_{mn} and V_{mn} are the values of the difference image and output image (assuming threshold t) at the spatial position (m,n), respectively, the above formula may be rewritten as

$$R_{Y,Z}(t) = \frac{\sum\limits_{m,n} l_{mn}.V_{mn} - \dfrac{1}{p \times q} \sum\limits_{m,n} l_{mn}.\sum\limits_{m,n} V_{mn}}{\sqrt{\sum\limits_{m,n} l_{mn}^2 - \dfrac{1}{p \times q} \left(\sum\limits_{m,n} l_{mn}\right)^2} \sqrt{\sum\limits_{m,n} V_{mn}^2 - \dfrac{1}{p \times q} \left(\sum\limits_{m,n} V_{mn}\right)^2}}.$$

We compute the correlation coefficient assuming different threshold and t_1 is assumed to be a near optimal threshold, if the correlation coefficient $R_{Y,Z}(t_1)$ is maximum. Considering this automatically derived threshold t_1, we update the weights of the network and when the network converges the output layer implicitly generates a change detection map.

Energy Based Criterion: In this case, a near optimal threshold is found out by analyzing the overall status of the change detection maps obtained with different thresholds. To describe the overall status of the change detection map generated by any threshold t, we used the following expression of energy[Ghosh *et al.* (1992)]:

$$E(t) = -\sum_{m=1}^{p}\sum_{n=1}^{q}\left(\sum_{(i,j)\in N_{mn}^2} V_{mn}.V_{ij}\right) - \sum_{m=1}^{p}\sum_{n=1}^{q}V_{mn}^2. \qquad (9.5)$$

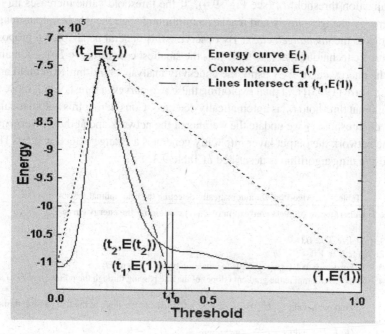

Fig. 9.4   Behavior of energy value with threshold. Threshold t_1 is detected by the proposed approach (t_0 is the optimal).

The energy expression defined in Eq. (9.5) has two parts. In terms of images, the first part can be seen as the impact of the gray values of the neighboring pixels on the energy function; whereas the second part can be attributed to the gray value of the pixel under consideration. As in the present context, the value of $V_{mn} = \pm 1$, $\forall(m,n)$, the above expression takes the minimum value when the generated change detection map totally belongs to either *unchanged regions* ($V_{mn} = -1, \forall(m,n)$) or *changed regions* ($V_{mn} = +1, \forall(m,n)$). It takes the maximum value when the number of *unchanged and changed regions* are very high. In the proposed procedure, we first compute the energy (at convergence) of each change detection map generated by different thresholds and plot these status values with the corresponding threshold value (see Fig. 9.4). By analyzing the behavior of this graph, one can see that initially the value of $E(t)$ increases with t (as the number of changed and unchanged regions increases). After a certain threshold value, $E(t)$ decreases (as some unchanged regions are merged together). After that the energy does not change significantly with change in threshold, i.e., *changed and unchanged regions* are not significantly altered. We expect that this stable behavior of the energy function $E(t)$ is reached around optimal initialization threshold t_0 (see Fig. 9.4). If the threshold value increases more, the energy changes slowly and reaches a minimum when the whole output image belongs to the *unchanged class*. By observing this general behavior, we propose a heuristic technique that first generates the smallest convex curve $E_1(.)$ containing the energy curve $E(.)$ using the concavity analysis algorithm[Rosenfeld and De La Torre (1983)] and then exploiting these two curves, a threshold t_1, close to the optimal threshold t_0, is automatically detected. Considering this automatically derived threshold t_1 we update the weights of the network and at the convergence of the network the output layer implicitly generates a change detection map. The corresponding algorithm is described in Table 9.3.

Table 9.3   Algorithm for automatically detecting the near optimal threshold t_1

Phase 1: Generate the smallest convex curve $E_1(.)$ containing the energy curve $E(.)$
Step 1: Initialize $k = 0.0$.
Step 2: While $k \neq 1.0$
Step 3:   For $i = k$ to 1.0 step $\frac{1}{L}$ (L is the maximum gray value of D)
Step 4:   Compute the gradient (slope) of the line passing through the points $(k, E(k))$ and $(i, E(i))$.
Step 5:   Find out a point $(j, E(j))$, $k < j \leq 1.0$, such that the slope of the line passing through the points $(k, E(k))$ and $(j, E(j))$ is maximum.
Step 6:   Join the two points $(k, E(k))$ and $(j, E(j))$ by a straight line (this line is a part of the convex curve $E_1(.)$).
Step 7:   Reset $k = j$.
Step 8: End While
Phase 2: Derive the initialization threshold value t_1
Step 9:   Find the point $(t_z, E(t_z))$ on the energy curve where energy value is maximum (see Fig. 9.4).
Step 10: Select t_2, so that $\{E_1(t_2) - E(t_2)\} = \max_i \{E_1(i) - E(i)\}$, $t_z \leq i \leq 1.0$.
Step 11: Select the threshold t_1, at the intersection between the straight line connecting $(t_z, E(t_z))$ and $(t_2, E(t_2))$ and the straight line parallel to the abscissa and passing through the minimum energy value $E(1)$ (see Fig. 9.4).
Step 12: Stop.

9.4   Description of the Data Sets

In order to carry out an experimental analysis aimed at assessing the effectiveness of the proposed approach, we considered two multitemporal data sets corresponding to geographical areas of Mexico and Island of Sardinia, Italy. A detailed description of each data set is given below.

9.4.1   *Data set related to Mexico area*

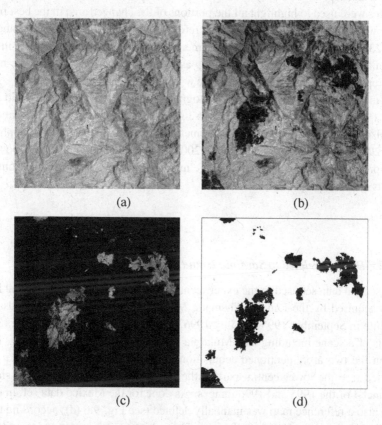

(a)   (b)

(c)   (d)

Fig. 9.5   Image of Mexico area. (a) Band 4 of the Landsat ETM+ image acquired in April 2000, (b) band 4 of the Landsat ETM+ image acquired in May 2002, (c) corresponding difference image generated by CVA technique, and (d) reference map of the changed area.

The first data set used in the experiment is made up of two multispectral images acquired by the Landsat Enhanced Thematic Mapper Plus (ETM+) sensor of the Landsat-7 satellite in an area of Mexico on 18th April 2000 and 20th May 2002. From the entire available Landsat scene, a section of 512×512 pixels has been selected as test site. Between the two aforementioned acquisition dates a fire destroyed a large portion of the vegetation in the considered region. Figs. 9.5 (a) and (b) show channel 4 of the 2000 and 2002 images, respectively. In order to be able to make a quantitative evaluation of the effectiveness of the proposed approach, a reference map was manually defined (see Fig. 9.5 (d)) according to a detailed visual analysis of both the available multitemporal images and the difference image (see Fig. 9.5 (c)). Different color composites of the above mentioned images were used to highlight all the portions of the changed area in the best possible way. This procedure resulted in a reference map containing 25599 changed and 236545 unchanged pixels. Experiments were carried out to produce, in an automatic way, a change detection map as similar as possible to reference map that represents the best result obtainable with a time consuming procedure.

Analysis of the behavior of the histograms' of multitemporal images did not reveal any significant difference due to light and atmospheric conditions at the acquisition dates. Therefore, no radiometric correction algorithm was applied. The 2002 image was registered on the 2000 one using 12 ground control points. The procedure led to a residual average misregistration error on ground control points of about 0.3 pixels.

9.4.2 *Data set related to Sardinia Island, Italy*

The second data set used in the experiment is composed of two multispectral images acquired by the Landsat Thematic Mapper (TM) sensor of the Landsat-5 satellite in September 1995 and July 1996. The test site is a section of 412×300 pixels of a scene including lake Mulargia on the Island of Sardinia (Italy). Between the two aforementioned acquisition dates the water level in the lake increased (see the lower central part of the image). Figs. 9.6 (a) and (b) show channel 4 of the 1995 and 1996 images. As done for the Mexico data set, in this case also a reference map was manually defined (see Fig. 9.6 (d)) according to a detailed visual analysis of both the available multitemporal images and the difference image (see Fig. 9.6 (c)). At the end, 7480 changed and 116120 unchanged pixels were identified. As histograms did not show any significant difference, no radiometric correction algorithms were applied to the multitemporal images. The images were co-registered with 12 ground control points resulting in an average residual misregistration error of about 0.2 pixels on the ground control points.

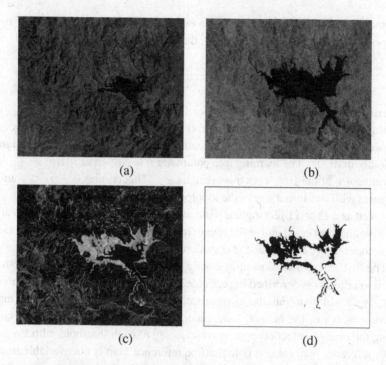

(a)   (b)

(c)   (d)

Fig. 9.6 Image of Sardinia island, Italy. (a) Band 4 of the Landsat TM image acquired in September 1995, (b) band 4 of the Landsat TM image acquired in July 1996, (c) difference image generated by CVA technique using bands 1, 2, 4, & 5; and (d) reference map of the changed area.

9.5 Experimental Results

9.5.1 *Description of experiments*

1D-SOFM: In this study, the input vector U_{mn} (for each pixel $(m, n) \in D$) contain nine components considering the gray value of the pixel (m, n) and the gray values of its eight neighboring pixels (here N^2 neighbor is considered). There is no need to scaling the components of the input vectors. We initialize the value of parameters η as 0.1 and performed $itr = 1000$ epoches to complete self organization process. We have used $\eta(itr) = 0.1 \times \exp\left(-\frac{itr}{200}\right)$, for decreasing the value of η in each epoch[Haykin (2003)]. Experimentally it is found that after an adequate number of training steps the weight vectors converge to their limiting values.

2D-SOFM: As described in 1D-SOFM, also in this experiment, the input vector U_{mn} contain nine components considering the gray value of the pixel (m, n)

and the gray values of its eight neighboring pixels. To map the value of each component of the input vectors in $[0 \; 1]$, the following formula is used:

$$\frac{u_{mn,k} - c_{min}}{c_{max} - c_{min}}$$

where $u_{mn,k}$ is the kth component value of input vector U_{mn} and c_{min}, c_{max} are the global minimum and maximum component values present in the input vectors. The weight vector is also having nine components. Initial weights are assigned randomly in $[0 \; 1]$. The learning rate parameter η is chosen as $\eta(itr) = \frac{1}{itr}$ i.e., the value of η at the itr^{th} epoch is taken as $\frac{1}{itr}$. This ensures $0 < \eta < 1$ and it decreases with itr. Initial size of the topological neighborhood $h_{mn}(itr), \forall(m,n)$ was taken as a 11×11 rectangular window, and gradually reduced to 3×3 after 5 epochs and kept constant for the remaining epochs (until converges). The value of the convergence parameter δ is considered as 0.01.

The first experiment aims at assessing the validity of the proposed threshold selection criteria (as described in section 9.3.2.2). To this end, the optimal threshold t_0 is chosen by a trial-and-error procedure where the change detection maps (at convergence of the network) are generated by varying threshold t and computing the change detection error corresponding to each threshold with the help of the reference map (please note that the reference map is not available in real situation). The threshold t_0 corresponds to the minimum change detection error. The change detection results obtained considering the threshold detected by the proposed criteria were compared with the change detection results produced by assuming optimal threshold t_0.

In order to establish the effectiveness of the proposed 2D-SOFM based technique, the second experiment compares the results (change detection maps) provided by our method with a context-insensitive Manual Trial and Error Thresholding (MTET) technique[Bazi *et al.* (2005)] and a context-sensitive technique presented in[Bruzzone and Prieto (2000)] based on the combined use of the EM algorithm and Markov Random Fields (we refer to it as EM+MRF technique). The obtained results are also compared with the results produce by the proposed 1D-SOFM based technique. The MTET technique generates a minimum error change detection map under the hypothesis of spatial independence among pixels by finding a minimum error decision threshold for the difference image. The minimum error decision threshold is obtained by computing change detection errors (with the help of the reference map) for all values of the decision threshold. Note that, this minimum error context-insensitive threshold is different from the context-sensitive optimal threshold t_0 as obtained in the first experiment. Comparisons were carried out in terms of both overall change detection error and number of false alarms (i.e., unchanged pixels identified as changed ones) and missed alarms (i.e., changed pixels categorized as unchanged ones).

9.5.2   Results on Mexico data

In order to determine the most effective spectral bands for detecting the burned areas in the considered data set we performed some trials. On the basis of the results of these trials, we found that band 4 is very effective to locate the burned area. Hence we generated the difference image by considering only spectral band 4.

To assess the validity of the threshold selection criteria, in the first experiment a comparison was carried out between the optimal threshold t_0 and the threshold t_1 detected by the proposed 2D-SOFM based technique using correlation criterion and energy criterion. Figs. 9.7 (a) and (b) show the variation of correlation coefficient and energy value, respectively with threshold. From Fig. 9.7, it is seen that the correlation criterion automatically selects a threshold t_1 which is on the right side of t_0 and the energy based criterion selects a threshold t_1 which is on the left side of t_0. But both the thresholds are near to the optimal one. Table 9.4 shows the change detection results produced by the proposed technique assuming optimal threshold t_0 and automatically detected thresholds t_1. As the correlation based criterion selects higher threshold value (with $t_1 = 0.232$), it generates higher missed alarms and lower false alarms as compared to energy based one (with $t_1 = 0.183$). Since correlation based criterion is able to detect a threshold t_1 which is closer to the optimal threshold t_0 (with $t_0 = 0.216$), the overall error produced by this criterion (3217 pixels) is close to the optimal one (2979 pixels).

Table 9.4   Change detection results obtained by the proposed 2D-SOFM based technique considering the optimal threshold t_0 and the automatically detected thresholds t_1 using correlation and energy criteria (Band 4, Mexico data set).

Techniques used	Detected thresholds	Missed alarms	False alarms	Overall error
2D-SOFM (Optimal)	0.216 (t_0)	1406	1573	2979
2D-SOFM (Correlation)	0.232 (t_1)	2039	1178	3217
2D-SOFM (Energy)	0.183 (t_1)	583	2929	3512

The change detection results produced by the proposed context-sensitive 2D-SOFM based approach are compared with those obtained by the context-insensitive MTET, context-sensitive EM+MRF (see[Bruzzone and Prieto (2000)]) and 1D-SOFM based techniques. The results are put in Table9.5. It is seen from the table that the overall error obtained by the proposed method (using two thresh-

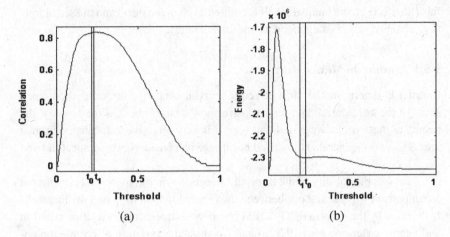

Fig. 9.7   Variation of (a) correlation coeffi cient, and (b) energy value with threshold. Detected threshold t_1 is close to the optimal threshold t_0 (Band 4, Mexico data).

old selection criteria) is much smaller than the overall error incurred by MTET technique. Concerning the error typology, the proposed technique based on correlation criterion and energy criterion resulted in 3217 and 3512 pixels as overall error respectively, whereas the MTET involved 4591 pixels. Table9.5 presents the best change detection result obtained by the context-sensitive EM+MRF technique, when the parameter β of MRF[Bruzzone and Prieto (2000)] was set to 1.5 (this value was defined manually and corresponds to the minimum possible error). The overall error obtained by the proposed technique based on correlation criterion is similar to the existing EM+MRF technique; whereas the technique based on energy criterion produces slightly poor results as compared to the existing EM+MRF technique. Note that the proposed 2D-SOFM based technique does not require the optimization of the parameter β, thus resulting in a more practical tool for application.

From Table 9.5 we can say that the 1D-SOFM based technique produced satisfactory result. The overall error obtained by this technique is much less than the overall error produced by MTET technique, similar to the EM+MRF technique and better than the proposed 2D-SOFM based technique (with energy criterion). But the technique produced higher miss alarms which is not expected. For a better understanding of the behavior of the different methods the change detection maps produced by them are depicted in Fig. 9.8. A visual comparison pointed out that both the proposed SOFM based approaches exploit the spatio-context information for reducing the noise present in the maps.

Table 9.5 Overall error, false alarms, and missed alarms resulting from the proposed context-sensitive 1D-SOFM based technique and 2D-SOFM based technique using correlation and energy criteria. The table also gives the errors associated with the context-insensitive MTET and context-sensitive EM+MRF techniques (Band 4, Mexico data).

Techniques used	Missed alarms	False alarms	Overall error
1D-SOFM	2440	834	3274
2D-SOFM (Correlation)	2039	1178	3217
2D-SOFM (Energy)	583	2929	3512
MTET	2404	2187	4591
EM+MRF ($\beta = 1.5$)	946	2257	3203

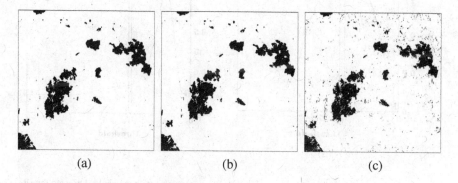

(a)   (b)   (c)

Fig. 9.8   Change detection map obtained for Mexico data by (a) the proposed 1D-SOFM based technique; (b) the proposed 2D-SOFM based technique with correlation criterion; and (c) the context-insensitive MTET technique.

9.5.3   Results on Sardinia Island data

We applied the CVA technique on spectral bands 1, 2, 4, and 5 of the two multi-spectral images to generate the difference image, as preliminary experiments show that the above channels contain useful information of the changes in water level.

In the first experiment, the results obtained by the proposed 2D-SOFM based approach with the automatically detected threshold t_1 using correlation criterion and energy criterion were compared with the results produced by considering the optimal threshold t_0. Figs. 9.9 (a) and (b) show the variation of correlation coefficient and energy value with threshold. From an analysis of Fig. 9.9 one can deduce that the proposed technique, based on both the correlation and energy criteria, select the thresholds which are on the left side of the optimal threshold t_0;

but both the thresholds are near the optimal one. Table 9.6 shows the change detection results produced by the proposed technique for the optimal threshold t_0 and automatically detected thresholds t_1. As the threshold ($t_1 = 0.356$) detected by the energy based criterion is higher than the threshold ($t_1 = 0.337$) detected by correlation based criterion, the energy based technique generated higher missed alarms and lower false alarms. As the energy based criterion detected a threshold t_1 which is more close to the optimal threshold ($t_0 = 0.368$), the overall error (1664 pixels) produced is more close to the optimal one (1648 pixels).

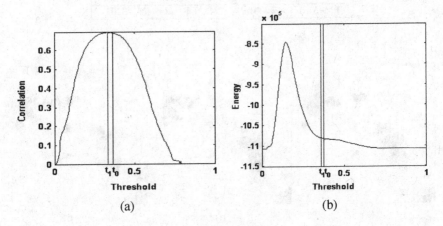

(a)   (b)

Fig. 9.9   Variation of the (a) correlation coefficient; (b) energy value with threshold. Detected threshold t_1 is close to the optimal threshold t_0 (Sardinia Island data).

Table 9.6   Change detection results obtained by the proposed 2D-SOFM based technique considering the optimal threshold t_0 and the automatically detected threshold t_1 using correlation and energy criteria (Sardinia Island data).

Techniques used	Detected thresholds	Missed alarms	False alarms	Overall error
2D-SOFM (Optimal)	$0.368(t_0)$	1090	558	1648
2D-SOFM (Correlation)	$0.337(t_1)$	721	1164	1885
2D-SOFM (Energy)	$0.356(t_1)$	935	729	1664

Concerning the second experiment, the change detection results produced by the proposed 2D-SOFM based approach were compared with the change detection results obtained by the MTET, EM+MRF and 1D-SOFM based techniques. Table 9.7 shows the change detection results obtained by applying different techniques. By analyzing those results, one can deduce that the overall change detection error obtained by the proposed technique using both the criteria are less than the overall error incurred by the MTET technique. For example, the overall error obtained by the proposed technique using correlation criterion and energy criterion are 1885 pixels and 1664 pixels, respectively; whereas the overall error yielded by the MTET technique is 1890 pixels. Table 9.7 presents the best change detection result obtained by the context-sensitive EM+MRF technique, when the parameter β of MRF[Bruzzone and Prieto (2000)] is set to 2.2. Although the overall error obtained by the proposed technique based on correlation criterion is slightly higher than the existing EM+MRF technique, the proposed technique based on energy criterion generated lower overall error.

Table 9.7 also shows the change detection results produced by 1D-SOFM based technique. The technique produced the worst result compared to the other three techniques. Due to the simple architecture adopted by the proposed technique it may fail to produce good change detection results. Fig. 9.10 shows the change detection maps produced by both the proposed SOFM based technique and MTET technique. A visual comparison pointed out that the proposed approaches exploited the spatio-contextual information and showed improved performance.

Table 9.7   Overall error, false alarms, and missed alarms resulting from the proposed context-sensitive 1D-SOFM based technique and 2D-SOFM based technique using correlation and energy criteria. The table also gives the errors associated with the context-insensitive MTET and context-sensitive EM+MRF techniques (Sardinia Island data).

Techniques used	Missed alarms	False alarms	Overall error
1D-SOFM	664	1725	2389
2D-SOFM (Correlation)	721	1164	1885
2D-SOFM (Energy)	935	729	1664
MTET	1015	875	1890
EM+MRF ($\beta = 2.2$)	592	1108	1700

9.6   Discussion and Conclusion

In this chapter unsupervised context-sensitive techniques for change detection in multitemporal remote sensing images have been proposed. The technique discriminates the changed and unchanged regions in the difference image by using two different architectures of self-organizing feature map neural networks. In both the networks, the number of input neurons is equal to the dimension of the input patterns and depending on the number of neurons in the output layer the network

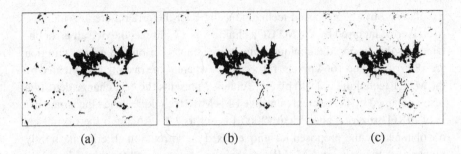

(a)   (b)   (c)

Fig. 9.10   Change detection map obtained for the data set related to the Island of Sardinia, Italy by (a) the proposed 1D-SOFM based technique; (b) the proposed 2D-SOFM based technique with energy criterion; and (c) the context-insensitive MTET technique.

is called one-dimensional and two-dimensional SOFM. In 1D-SOFM, the number of neurons in the output layer is two, one represents the changed regions and the other represents the unchanged regions. Whereas in 2D-SOFM, the number of neurons in the output layer are equal to the number of pixels in the difference image i.e., each spatial position of the input image corresponds to a neuron in the output layer. Depending on a particular threshold value each neuron in the output layer is assigned either changed regions or unchanged regions. Two different criteria are proposed to select a near optimal threshold.

Both the proposed SOFM based techniques show the following advantages with respect to the context-sensitive change detection method based on the EM+MRF[Bruzzone and Prieto (2000)]: i) they are distribution free, i.e., they do not require any explicit assumption on the statistical model of the distributions of classes of changed and unchanged pixels, ii) the proposed techniques do not require the manual setting of regularization parameter β (the EM+MRF technique requires the definition of the regularization parameter β that tunes the effect of the spatial-context information in the energy function to be optimized). The main disadvantage of the proposed 1D-SOFM based method is: the change detection result depends on the parameter η (learning rate). Further study needs to be done in finding out an optimum value of η automatically. Although the 2D-SOFM based technique itself used the learning rate parameter η and topological neighborhood information $h_{mn}(.)$, but there is no need to set them manually. The change detection map produced by the network (when converged) does not strictly depend on the setting of these parameters. So the proposed 2D-SOFM based technique is completely automatic in nature which is the major advantage of it. The time requirement of this technique is little more. It is worth noting that for the considered kind of application it is not fundamental to produce results in real time.

Experimental results obtained on different real multitemporal data sets confirm the effectiveness of the proposed 2D-SOFM based approach, which significantly outperforms the standard optimal manual context-insensitive technique and provides an overall change detection error comparable to the one achieved with the context-sensitive EM+MRF technique. Whereas, the 1D-SOFM based technique produced acceptable result for Mexico data set, but for Sardinia Island data set it failed to produce good result. This may have happened due to the simple network architecture used.

Acknowledgements

Authors would like to thank the Department of Science and Technology, Government of India and University of Trento, Italy, the sponsors of the ITPAR program and Prof. L. Bruzzone, the Italian collaborator of this project, for providing the data.

Bibliography

Bazi, Y., Bruzzone, L. and Melgani, F. (2005). An unsupervised approach based on the generalized Gaussian model to automatic change detection in multitemporal SAR images, *IEEE Trans. Geosci. Remote Sensing* **43**, 4, pp. 874–887.

Bruzzone, L. and Prieto, D. F. (2000). Automatic analysis of the difference image for unsupervised change detection, *IEEE Trans. Geosci. Remote Sensing* **38**, 3, pp. 1171–1182.

Bruzzone, L. and Prieto, D. F. (2002). An adaptive semiparametric and context-based approach to unsupervised change detection in multitemporal remote-sensing images, *IEEE Trans. Image Processing* **11**, 4, pp. 452–466.

Bruzzone, L. and Serpico, S. B. (1997). An iterative technique for the detection of landcover transitions in multitemporal remote-sensing images, *IEEE Trans. Geosci. Remote Sensing* **35**, 4, pp. 858–867.

Canty, M. J. (2006). *Image Analysis, Classification and Change Detection in Remote Sensing* (CRC Press, Taylor & Francis).

Chavez, P. S., Jr. and MacKinnon, D. J. (1994). Automatic detection of vegetation changes in the southwestern United States using remotely sensed images, *Photogram. Eng. Remote Sensing* **60**, 5, pp. 1285–1294.

Cihelar, J., Pultz, T. J. and Gray, A. L. (1992). Change detection with synthetic aperture radar, *Int. J. Remote Sensing* **13**, 3, pp. 401–414.

Dempster, A. P., Laird, N. M. and Rubin, D. B. (1977). Maximum likelihood from incomplete data via the EM algorithm, *J. R. Stat. Soc.* **39**, 1, pp. 1–38.

Fung, T. (1990). An assessment of TM imagery for land-cover change detection, *IEEE Trans. Geosci. Remote Sensing* **28**, 4, pp. 681–684.

Ghosh, A., Pal, N. R. and Pal, S. K. (1992). Object background classification using Hopfield type neural network, *Int. J. of Pattern Recognition and Artificial Intelligence* **6**, 5, pp. 989–1008.

Ghosh, A. and Pal, S. K. (1992). Neural network, self-organization and object extraction, *Pattern Recognition Letters* **13**, pp. 387–397.

Ghosh, S., Bruzzone, L., Patra, S., Bovolo, F. and Ghosh, A. (2007a). A context-sensitive technique for unsupervised change detection based on Hopfi eld-type neural networks, *IEEE Trans. Geosci. Remote Sensing* **45**, 3, pp. 778–789.

Ghosh, S., Patra, S. and Ghosh, A. (2007b). A neural approach to unsupervised change detection of remote-sensing images, in B. Prasad and S. R. M. Prasanna (eds.), *Speech, Audio, Image and Biomedical Signal Processing using Neural Networks* (Springer-Verleg, Germany).

Gopal, S. and Woodcock, C. (1996). Remote sensing of forest change using artifi cial neural networks, *IEEE Trans. Geosci. Remote Sensing* **34**, 2, pp. 398–404.

Hame, T., Heiler, I. and Miguel-Ayanz, J. S. (1998). An unsupervised change detection and recognition system for forestry, *Int. J. Remote Sensing* **19**, 6, pp. 1079–1099.

Haykin, S. (2003). *Neural Networks: A Comprehensive Foundation* (Pearson Education, Fourth Indian Reprint).

Kasetkasem, T. and Varshney, P. K. (2002). An image change detection algorithm based on Markov random fi eld models, *IEEE Trans. Geosci. Remote Sensing* **40**, 8, pp. 1815–1823.

Kohonen, T. (1982). Self-organized formation of topologically correct feature maps, *Biol. Cybernetics* **43**, pp. 59–69.

Kohonen, T. (1997). *Self-Organizing Maps* (2nd edn. Springer-Verlag, Berlin).

Lo, Z.-P., Yu, Y. and B.Bavarian (1993). Analysis of the convergence properties of topology preserving neural networks, *IEEE Trans. Neural Networks* **4**, pp. 207–220.

Melgani, F., Moser, G. and Serpico, S. B. (2002). Unsupervised change-detection methods for remote-sensing data, *Opt. Engineering* **41**, pp. 3288–3297.

Merril, K. R. and Jiajun, L. (1998). A comparison of four algorithms for change detection in an urban environment, *Remote Sens. Environ.* **63**, 2, pp. 95–100.

Patra, S., Ghosh, S. and Ghosh, A. (2006). Unsupervised change detection in remote-sensing images using one-dimensional self-organizing feature map neural network, in *9th Int. Conf. on Information Technology (ICIT-2006), Bhubaneswar, India* (IEEE Computer Society Press), pp. 141–142.

Patra, S., Ghosh, S. and Ghosh, A. (2007). Unsupervised change detection in remote-sensing images using modifi ed self-organizing feature map neural network, in *Int. Conf. on Computing: Theory and Applications (ICCTA-2007), Kolkata, India* (IEEE Computer Society Press), pp. 716–720.

Richards, J. A. and Jia, X. (2006). *Remote Sensing Digital Image Analysis* (4th ed. Berlin: Springer-Verlag).

Rosenfeld, A. and De La Torre, P. (1983). Histogram concavity analysis as an aid in threshold selection, *IEEE Trans. Syst., Man, Cybern.*, **SMC-13**, 3, pp. 231–235.

Ross, S. M. (1987). *Introduction to Probability and Statistics for Engineers and Scientists* (Wiley, New York).

Singh, A. (1989). Digital change detection techniques using remotely sensed data, *Int. J. Remote Sensing* **10**, 6, pp. 989–1003.

Townshend, J. R. G. and Justice, C. O. (1995). Spatial variability of images and the monitoring of changes in the normalized difference vegetation index, *Int. J. Remote Sensing* **16**, 12, pp. 2187–2195.

Chapter 10

Recent Advances in Video Compression: What's Next?

L. Liu, F. Zhu, M. Bosch, and E. J. Delp

Video and Image Processing Lab (VIPER)
School of Electrical and Computer Engineering
Purdue University
West Lafayette, Indiana USA [1]

In the last two decades, there have been significant advances in video coding. Since the early 1990s, a series of video coding standards have been developed to satisfy the growing requirements of video applications. Among these, H.264/MPEG-4 AVC is the most recent standard achieving high compression efficiency. The video compression research community has also continued working on new advances that go beyond traditional video coding architectures. In this paper, we give an overview of some recent advances in video coding and their potential applications. We discuss the most recent video coding standard and work in distributed coding, texture-based methods, scalable coding, and multi-view video coding.

10.1 Introduction and Overview of Video Coding Standards

Digital video is everywhere today with applications that include high definition television, video delivered and captured on mobile telephones and handheld devices (such as iPods), and video conferencing. The problem is that digital video has huge storage and transmission bandwidth requirements. Even with the rapid increase in processor speeds, disc storage capacity and broadband network techniques, a concise representation of the video signal is required. Video compres-

[1]This work was partially supported by grants from the Indiana 21st Century Research and Technology Fund and by Nokia. Address all correspondence to E. J. Delp, E-mail: ace@ecn.purdue.edu.

sion algorithms are used to reduce the data rate of the video signal while maintaining video quality [Schafer and Sikora (1995); Ebrahimi and Kunt (1998)]. A typical video coding system consists of an encoder and a decoder, which is referred to as a *codec* [Sullivan and Wiegend (2005)]. To ensure the inter-operability between different platforms and applications, standards have been developed for video compression.

Since the early 1990s, a series of video coding standards have been developed to satisfy the growing requirements of applications. Two groups actively involve in the standardization activities: the Video Coding Experts Group (VCEG) and the Moving Picture Experts Group (MPEG). VCEG is working under the direction of the ITU Telecommunication Standardization Sector (ITU-T), which is formerly known as International Telegraph and Telephone Consultative Committee (CCITT). This group works on the standard with the names "H.26x." MPEG does standardization work under ISO/IEC and labeled its standards as "MPEG-x" [Chiariglione (1997, 1998); Schafer and Sikora (1995)].

H.120 was the first international video coding standard [H12 (1988)]. H.120 was approved by ITU-T (when it was known as CCITT) in 1984 and revised in 1988. The next standard, H. 261 [Liou (1991); Carr (1990); h26 (1993)], was approved in 1991 mainly for video-conferencing systems and video-phone services using the Integrated Services Digital Network (ISDN). The H. 261 standard has two main modes: the INTRA and INTER modes. The INTRA mode is basically the same as JPEG [Pennebaker and Mitchell (1993)] where a DCT-based block transform is employed. For the INTER mode, motion estimation (ME) and motion compensation (MC) were first utilized. MPEG-1 [Mitchell *et al.* (1996); LeGall (1991); MPE (1993)] was developed in the early 1990s and approved in 1993 by ISO/IEC. Compared to H.261, it added bi-directionally predicted frames (B frame) and half-pixel motion search. MPEG-2, also known as H.262 [Haskell *et al.* (1997); MPE (1994)], was developed as a joint effort between VCEG and MPEG. MPEG-2/H.262 aims to serve a variety of applications, such as DVD video and digital television broadcasting. H.263 [h26 (1998)], and its extensions[Cote *et al.* (1998)], known as H.263+ and H.263++, share many similarities with H. 261 but having more coding options. It is widely used for video streaming applications ad video conferencing. With the new options, H.263 can achieve the same video quality as H.261 at half the data rate or lower. Meanwhile, ISO/IEC developed a new video coding standard, known as MPEG-4 [Schafer and Sikora (1995); MPE (1999)]. It has proven success in three fields: digital television, interactive graphics applications, and multimedia distribution over the networks. MPEG-4 enables object-based video coding by coding the contents independently. MPEG-4 also provides tools for animation, scalability, and error resilience.

Based on the previous hybrid coding video standards the latest standard, known as H.264/MPEG-4 AVC [jvt (2003); Wiegand *et al.* (2003)], is a hybrid video coding system using block-based transform coding and motion estimation. The new standard incorporates a collection of state-of-the-art video coding techniques. Various motion-prediction block types and multiple reference frames are described in the standard. One novel feature that is available in H.264/MPEG-4 AVC is in-the-loop deblocking filtering that can increase the video quality at lower data rates. Context-adaptive binary arithmetic coding (CABAC) can be used with high coding efficiency and coding complexity. The new features can reduce the data rate by up to 50% with similar perceptual quality when compared to H.263 and MPEG-4 [Sullivan and Wiegend (2005)]. The enhanced performance of H.264/MPEG-4 AVC presents a promising future for new video applications.

With the success of the various video coding standards based on hybrid motion compensated methods, the research community has been investigating new approaches that can address next-generation video services [Sullivan *et al.* (2006); Sikora (2005)]. The new functionalities of these approaches provide higher robustness, interactivity and scalability with lower complexity. This paper describes some of these recent advances in video coding. Distributed video coding is a new approach discussed in Section 10.2 that reduces the complexity of the encoder and has potential applications in video surveillance and error resilience. In Section 10.3 we describe the use of spatial and temporal models for texture-based video coding which improves the coding efficiency. Scalable video coding provides flexible adaptation to network conditions. We describe the main issues related to scalable coding in Section 10.4. In Section 10.5 we will examine multi-view and 3D video compression techniques.

10.2 Distributed Video Coding

In conventional video source coding, the encoder uses extra information, statistical or syntactic, to encode the source. Spatial and temporal correlations are exploited at the encoder and thus leads to an encoder structure with high complexity. The extra information is known as "side information." Side information may be supplied to the encoder, or estimated by the encoder. A classical example of side information in conventional video coding is the motion compensated reference frame characterized by motion vectors. Hence, the side information is known to both the encoder and the decoder for conventional video coding. In contrast, low complexity video encoding may require that the side information be known only to the decoder. Therefore, how one obtains the side information at the decoder, instead of at the encoder, is the most essential problem to be addressed for low complexity encoding.

A new approach to video coding, known as distributed coding or Wyner-Ziv coding [Girod *et al.* (2005)], was proposed recently. The ideal situation for Wyner-Ziv video coding is to achieve a coding efficiency the same as that of conventional source coding. In distributed video coding, source statistics are exploited only at the decoder so that it is feasible to design a simplified encoder [Girod *et al.* (2005)]. By exploiting the source statistics only at the decoder, the Wyner-Ziv video coder can allow the motion search to be shifted to the decoder, where more computational resources are available. The structure is very attractive for applications where the encoder needs to be simple to conserve memory and energy resources such as video surveillance and mobile applications [Girod *et al.* (2005)].

Two theoretical results presented in the 1970s [Slepian and Wolf (1973); Wyner and Ziv (1976)] play key roles in the foundations of distributed source coding. The Slepian and Wolf theorem [Slepian and Wolf (1973)] proved that a lossless encoding scheme without side information at the encoder may perform as well as an encoding scheme with side information at the encoder. Consider two correlated information sources X and Y, the minimum lossless rate needed to transmit them is their joint entropy $H(X, Y)$ if they are encoded jointly. If the sources are encoded separately and joint decoding is allowed, Slepian and Wolf [Slepian and Wolf (1973)] proved a similar result by a random coding argument:

$$R_X \geq H(X|Y), R_Y \geq H(Y|X), R_X + R_Y \geq H(X, Y) \qquad (10.1)$$

Here R_X and R_Y denote the rate to encode X and Y respectively, $H(X|Y)$ and $H(Y|X)$ denote the conditional entropy. We denote Y as the side information needed to encode X and vice versa. Wyner and Ziv [Wyner and Ziv (1976)] extended the result to establish rate-distortion bounds for lossy compression. Wyner and Ziv showed that

$$R^*(d) \geq R_{X|Y}(d) \qquad (10.2)$$

where $R^*(d)$ denotes the rate distortion function when side information Y is only available at the decoder and $R_{X|Y}(d)$ denotes the rate distortion function when side information Y is available at both the encoder and the decoder. There is rate loss when the side information is only available at the decoder. However, the Wyner-Ziv theorem showed that in certain cases the equality can be achieved. Not much progress on constructive Slepian-Wolf schemes has been achieved beyond the connection with error-correcting channel codes [Verdu (1998)] in the past twenty-five years. This is mainly due to the inability of finding a channel code efficient enough to approach the performance claimed in [Slepian and Wolf (1973)] and [Wyner and Ziv (1976)].

10.2.1 *Wyner-Ziv video coding*

These theoretic results were revisited in the late 1990s and many designs for Wyner-Ziv video coding have emerged. A Wyner-Ziv video codec generally formulates the video coding problem as an error correction or noise reduction problem where these methods are used to construct missing (noisy) information in the compressed video sequence. Hence existing channel coding methods are used in the these coders. For example, PRISM [Puri and Ramchandran (2003)] uses trellis codes to transmit the coset of the quantization lattice. Wyner-Ziv video coding using punctured turbo codes is also widely used[Girod *et al.* (2005)]. Several papers exploit the relationship between the side information and the original source [Trapanese *et al.* (2005)] [Westerlaken *et al.* (2005)]. A nested lattice quantizer with an LDPC Slepian-Wolf coder [Liveris *et al.* (2002)] has also been presented. In more practical Wyner-Ziv codecs, conventional motion search methods can be used at the decoder to extract side information. This substantially increases the decoding complexity. A new method for constructing side estimates based on universal prediction [Li *et al.* (2006)] was proposed. This method estimates the side information based on observations of past reconstructed video data and makes it possible to design both the encoder and the decoder with low complexity.

A Wyner-Ziv video methid using LDPC codes [Liu and Delp (2005)] is shown in Fig. 10.1. The input video sequence is divided into two groups which are coded by different methods. Half of the frames are coded using the H.264 intraframe encoder, which are denoted as key frames. Between two key frames, a frame is independently encoded as a Wyner-Ziv frame (WZ frame). As shown in Fig. 10.1, the Wyner-Ziv frame is coded using the integer transform proposed in H.264 [Wiegand *et al.* (2003)]. The transform coefficients are coded bitplane by bitplane. The most significant bitplane is first coded by the LDPC encoder, followed by the other bitplanes with less significance. Only the parity bits from the LDPC encoder are sent to the decoder. The decoder can request more parity bits until the bitplane is correctly decoded. To reconstruct the Wyner-Ziv frames, the decoder first derives the side information, which is an initial estimate, or noisy version of the current frame. The incoming parity bits help to reduce the noise and reconstruct the current Wyner-Ziv frame based on the initial estimate. A simple and widely used way to derive the side information is to either extrapolate or interpolate the information from the previously decoded frames. The advantage of frame extrapolation is that the frames can be decoded in sequential order, and hence every frame (except the first few frames) can be coded as Wyner-Ziv frames. However, the quality of the side estimation from the extrapolation process may be unsatisfactory [Aaron *et al.* (2003)]. This has led to research on more sophisticated extrapolation techniques to improve the side estimation. Many Wyner-Ziv coding methods also resort to the use of frame interpolation, which generally produces higher quality side estimates. The problem with interpolation is that it requires some frames, after the current frame in the sequence order, be decoded before the current frame.

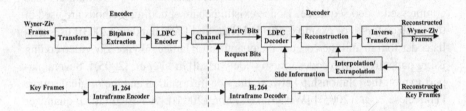

Fig. 10.1 A Wyner-Ziv video coding structure.

10.2.2 *Rate distortion analysis*

In [Li *et al.* (2007); Li (2005)] we presented a model to examine Wyner-Ziv video coding performance. The model uses the signal power spectrum and Fourier analysis tools presented in [Prades-Nebot *et al.* (2006); Cook *et al.* (2006); Liu *et al.* (2005)]. Wyner-Ziv video coding is compared with two conventional motion compensated video coding methods, i.e., DPCM-frame video coding and INTER-frame video coding. DPCM-frame coding subtracts the previous reconstructed frame from the current frame and codes the difference. INTER-frame coding performs motion search at the encoder and codes the residual frame. The rate difference between the three coding methods are:

$$\Delta R_{DPCM,WZ} = \frac{1}{8\pi^2} \int_{-\pi}^{\pi} \int_{-\pi}^{\pi} \log_2 \frac{1 - e^{-\frac{1}{2}\omega^T \omega \sigma_{MV}^2}}{1 - e^{-\frac{1}{2}\omega^T \omega (1-\rho^2)\sigma_{MV}^2}} d\omega \quad (10.3)$$

$$\Delta R_{DPCM,INTER} = \frac{1}{8\pi^2} \int_{-\pi}^{\pi} \int_{-\pi}^{\pi} \log_2 \frac{1 - e^{-\frac{1}{2}\omega^T \omega \sigma_{MV}^2}}{1 - e^{-\frac{1}{2}\omega^T \omega (1-\rho^2)\sigma_{\Delta_\beta}^2}} d\omega \quad (10.4)$$

where σ_{MV}^2 denotes the variance of the motion vector, ρ denotes the correlation between the true motion vector and the motion vector obtained by the side estimator, $\sigma_{\Delta_\beta}^2$ denotes the variance of the motion vector error. The rate savings between DPCM-frame coding and Wyner-Ziv coding is more significant when the motion vector variance σ_{MV}^2 is small. This makes sense since for smaller motion vector variance, the side estimator has a better chance of estimating a motion vector closer to the true motion vector. Wyner-Ziv coding can achieve a gain up to 6 dB (for small motion vector variance) or 1-2 dB (for normal to large motion vector variance) above DPCM-frame video coding. However, INTER-frame coding outperforms Wyner-Ziv video coding by 6 dB or so.

We also studied side estimators using two motion search methods, sub-pixel motion search and multi-reference motion search [Li *et al.* (2007); Li (2005)]. In conventional motion compensated video coding, the accuracy of the motion search has a great influence on the coding efficiency. However, Wyner-Ziv coding is not as sensitive to the accuracy of the motion search. For small σ_{MV}^2, motion search using integer pixel accuracy falls behind methods using quarter pixel accuracy by less than 0.4 dB. The coding difference with larger σ_{MV}^2 is even smaller. In this case, using 2 : 1 subsampling does not affect the coding efficiency significantly.

The rate difference between N references and one reference is:

$$\Delta R_{N,1} = \frac{1}{8\pi^2} \int_{-\pi}^{\pi} \int_{-\pi}^{\pi} log_2 I_{MR}(\omega, N) d\omega \tag{10.5}$$

and

$$I_{MR}(\omega, N) = \frac{\frac{N+1}{N} - 2e^{-\frac{1}{2}\omega^T \omega \sigma_{\Delta a}^2} + \frac{N-1}{N}e^{-(1-\rho_\Delta \omega^T \omega \sigma_{\Delta a}^2)}}{2 - 2e^{-\frac{1}{2}\omega^T \omega \sigma_{\Delta a}^2}} \tag{10.6}$$

where ρ_Δ is the correlation between two motion vector errors; we consider the case $\rho_\Delta = 0$. $\sigma_{\Delta a}^2$ denotes the actual variance of the motion vector error, which is due to the motion search pixel inaccuracy and the imperfect correlation between current motion vectors and previous motion vectors. The analysis of the rate difference using N references compared to one reference shows that multi-reference motion search can effectively improve the rate distortion performance of Wyner-Ziv coding. Our experimental results confirm the above theoretical analysis. The performance of current Wyner-Ziv video coding schemes still fall behind state-of-the-art video codecs. A better motion estimator at the decoder is essential to improve the performance.

10.2.3   *Backward channel aware Wyner-Ziv video coding*

The Wyner-Ziv video coding system described in Section 10.2.1 uses INTRA frame as the key frames, which is lower than the INTER frames in coding efficiency as discussed in Section 10.2.2. To improve the coding efficiency of the key frames, backward channel aware motion estimation (BCAME) was proposed in [Liu *et al.* (2006)] to code the key frames. The block diagram of backward channel aware Wyner-Ziv video coding is shown in Fig. 10.2. The basic idea of BCAME is to perform motion estimation at the decoder and send the motion information back to the encoder through a backward channel. We refer to these backward predictively coded frames as BP frames. Using the received motion vectors, a BCAME encoder can generate motion compensated frames. The residue between the original frame and motion compensated reference frame is transformed and entropy coded in the same way as H.264 Intra/Inter encoder. Since these motion vectors are also needed in the generation of side information for Wyner-Ziv frame, the increase in decoder complexity is marginal.

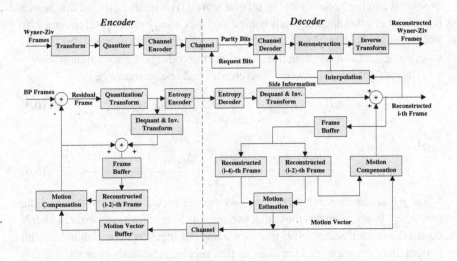

Fig. 10.2   Backward Channel Aware Wyner-Ziv video coding.

Depending on which of the previous decoded frames is used as the source (or the reference) at the decoder, we can have at least two sets of motion vectors for the BP frames. Mode I uses the forward motion vector between the two previously decoded frames as the prediction for the motion vector for the current frame. Mode II uses the backward motion vector. The two sets of motion vectors are sent back to the encoder. At the encoder, a mode decision can be made to choose the best motion vector, this is Mode III. Compared to the intra coded frames, BP frames with Mode I can significantly improve the coding efficiency with minimal usage of the backward channel. Mode III can further improve the performance with the use of more backward bandwidth. Compared to the inter coded frames, BP frames moves the computational-complexity task of motion estimation to the decoder, which results in reduction of complexity at the encoder.

We also consider the scenario when the backward channel is subjected to erasure errors or delays. In this case, the motion vector is not updated and the encoder continues to use the motion vectors of the previous frame. The decoder reconstructs the frame with the residual data and the current motion vector. Thus the reconstructed frames at the encoder and the decoder lose synchronization, which causes the drift problem and can propagate to the rest of the sequence. To address this problem, a two-stage procedure is proposed. A synchronization marker is used to provide a periodic synchronization check. The encoder then codes the key frames adaptively based on the decision of the synchronization detector. When desynchronization is detected, the encoder ignores the motion data and codes the key frames as an INTRA frame. After synchronization is reestablished, the encoder resumes coding the key frames as BP frames.

We presented a model to examine the complexity-rate-distortion performance of BCAWZ analytically in [Liu *et al.* (2007)]. Suppose we derive N motion vectors at the decoder. We can either send all N motion vectors to the encoder for the mode decision or send only the average of the N motion vectors. In the first situation, the complexity of the encoder is higher and the rate distortion performance is better. When the derived motion vectors are close to the true motion vector and the variance of the error motion vector is small, the second method can achieve similar performance as the first method.

10.3 Texture-Based Video Coding

Due to the growing interest in developing novel techniques for increasing the coding efficiency of video compression methods, one way to realize such goal beyond the data rates achievable by modern codecs, such as H.264/MPEG-4 AVC, is to not encode all the pixels in the sequence. Particularly, those pixels belonging to areas with large amount of detail that are costly to encode. In 1959, Schreiber and colleagues proposed a coding method he called, Synthetic Highs, which introduced the concept of dividing an image into textures and edges [Schreiber *et al.* (1959)]. Two different approaches were then described to encode each type of structure in the image. This approach, used in image coding, was later extended by using a model of the Human Visual System and a statistical model of the texture pixels in a frame [Kunt *et al.* (1985); Delp *et al.* (1979)]. The goal is to determine where "insignificant" texture regions in the frame are located and then use a texture model for the pixels in that region. By "insignificant" pixels we mean regions in the frame that the observer will not notice what has been changed. The encoder then fits the model to the image and transmits the model parameters to the decoder as side information which uses the model to reconstruct the pixels. An example of this approach is shown in Fig. 10.3 where the black area in the frame on the

Fig. 10.3   General approach: Texture and motion models used to construct a frame.

right is not transmitted but reconstructed by the decoder from a texture region in a previous frame shown on the left.

In general, "insignificant" or detail-irrelevant regions are highly texturized regions that are displayed with restricted spatial accuracy. Many "insignificant" textures regions are costly to code when using the mean square error (MSE) criterion as the coding distortion measure. Based on our experiments, we conclude that MSE is not an adequate distortion measure for efficient coding of detail-irrelevant textures since MSE-accurate regeneration of these regions are not required. Instead, global similarity measures, e.g MPEG-7 descriptors [MPE (2001)], or other texture analysis tools, described in later sections, are more suitable for assessing the distortion of such textures. The problem with using this approach in video is that if each frame is encoded separately the areas that have been reconstructed with the texture models will be obvious when the video is displayed. This then requires that the texture to be modeled both spatially and temporally [Peh and Cheong (2002)]. An example of such approach is described in [Ndjiki-Nya *et al*. (2004)], where a coder was designed using the fact that textures such as grass, water, sand, and flowers can be synthesized with acceptable perceptual quality instead of coding them. Since the latter has a higher data rate in order to represent the details in the textures which are not visually important, the proposed approach can be used to increase the overall coding efficiency. The issues then are the trade-offs between data rate, modeling efficiency, and image quality.

A general scheme for video coding using texture analysis and synthesis is illustrated in Fig. 10.4. The texture analyzer identifies homogeneous regions in a frame and labels them as textures. To ensure the temporal consistency of the identified textures throughout the video sequence, global motion models are used to warp texture regions from frame-to-frame. A set of parameters for each texture region is sent to the texture synthesizer at the decoder as side information.

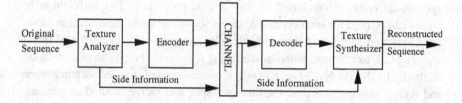

Fig. 10.4   Texture coding system overview.

The output of the texture analyzer is passed to a conventional video codec, e.g. H.264/MPEG-4 AVC, with synthesizable regions labeled as skip macroblocks. At the decoder, frames are partially reconstructed except for the synthesizable parts which are inserted later by the texture synthesizer using the texture side information [Zhu *et al.* (2007)].

10.3.1   *Spatial texture models*

The first step in implementing the system described in Fig.   10.4 is to extract regions in a frame that corresponds to the same texture. Texture segmentation is often a two step process in which features are first extracted, followed by a segmentation step which is a "grouping" operation of the homogeneous regions based on the feature properties and a grouping metric [Elfadel and Picard (1994); Comer and Delp (1999)]. Texture techniques can be categorized into statistical or feature-based methods, model-based methods, transform or spatial-frequency methods and structural methods [Haralick (1979)].

In our work, we have examined spatial texture models that are based on simple features, such as color and edge. The color feature we examined is a color histogram defined in the Hue-Saturation-Value color space with fixed color space quantization. We used the Kirsch edge operator as our edge detector [Zhu *et al.* (2007)]. We have also studied statistical and transform models, including gray level co-occurrence matrix and Gabor multi-bank filters.

We are currently exploring a new issue in texture analysis which is its extension to the temporal domain, known as dynamic textures. Many real-world textures are dynamic textures whose analysis should be based on both dynamic and static features. As a result, we transfer co-occurrence information from the spatial domain to the temporal domain [Bouthemy and Fablet (1998)] and extract motion features. From the temporal co-occurrence matrices, we extract motion features forming the input for the segmentation process.

Once we obtained the texture features, segmentation is used to divide the image into different regions based on their texture properties. Two different techniques can be used for such operation: direct segmentation or classification methods. Split and Merge and deterministic relaxation are some examples of direct segmentation techniques; whereas clustering techniques belong to classification methods. In [Ndjiki-Nya *et al.* (2004)], a combination of quadtree segmentation and region growing was described using a split and merge method to generate coarse masks for the spatial texture regions[Smith and Chang (1994)]. K-means clustering is a non-hierarchical method based on the square-root error criterion. The objective is to obtain a partition which minimizes the sum of the distances between each pattern and its cluster center.

10.3.2   *Temporal qnalysis*

The spatial texture models described in the previous sections operate on each frame of a given sequence independently of the other frames of the same sequence. This yields inconsistency in the segmentation across the sequence and can be very noticeable when the video is viewed. One can address this problem by using spatial-temporal texture models [Peh and Cheong (2002)] or using something similar to motion compensation for the texture models in each frame [Ndjiki-Nya *et al.* (2004)]. We explored low complexity approaches to spatial temporal models with a consistency check using the the motion model described below [Zhu *et al.* (2007)].

A video sequence is first divided into groups of frames (GoF). Each GoF consists of two reference frames (first and last frame) and several middle frames. For every texture region in the middle frames we look for similar textures in both reference frames. The texture regions are warped from frame-to-frame using a motion model to provide temporal consistency in the segmentation. The modified planar perspective motion model used to compensate the global motion is described as:

$$x' = (a_1 + a_3 x + a_4 y)/(1 + a_7 x + a_8 y)$$
$$y' = (a_2 + a_5 x + a_6 y)/(1 + a_7 x + a_8 y) \tag{10.7}$$

where (x, y) is the location of the pixel in the current frame and (x', y') is the corresponding mapped coordinates. The motion parameters $(a_0, a_1, \ldots, a_8)$ are estimated using a simplified implementation of a robust M-estimator for global motion estimation [Smolic and Ohm (2000)].

At the decoder, reference frames and non-synthesizable parts of other frames are conventionally decoded. The remaining parts labeled as synthesizable regions are skipped by the encoder and their values remain blank. The texture synthesizer is then used to reconstruct the corresponding missing pixels. Given the motion parameter set and the control parameter that indicated which frame is used as the reference frame, the texture regions can be reconstructed by warping the texture from the reference frame towards each synthesizable texture region identified by the texture analyzer.

The spatial-temporal models we described above were integrated into the H.264/MPEG-4 AVC JM 11.0 reference software and were tested using CIF sequences. The results look very promising and we were able to shown that this approach reduced the data rate by as much as 25%. For a complete description of our methods and the performance of this system see [Zhu *et al.* (2007)].

10.3.3 *A new perspective on texture-based video coding*

Taking into consideration the motion properties of a video sequence, we can also use the idea behind the texture-based video coding to not encode regions in a frame containing certain motion properties that are difficult to differentiate by the Human Visual System. The idea lies in the ability of the visual system to give priority to track fast motion objects even when the background is also moving. Therefore, we propose a method consisting of not encoding areas in a video frame that are secondary based on the human eye tracking properties in order to further increase the coding efficiency. In Fig. 10.5, the general scheme for video coding using motion analysis and synthesis is illustrated. We separate each frame into fast motion objects, noticeable but not fast motion objects, and non-noticeable motion objects. Due to the fact that fast motion objects are highly sensitive to reconstruction processes, they are directly passed into the H.264 encoder in order to avoid temporal artifacts in the reconstructed sequence.

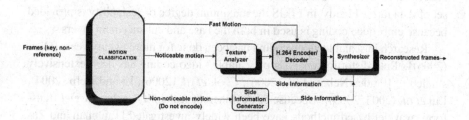

Fig. 10.5   Motion-based coding system.

As far as noticeable motion objects are concerned, they are analyzed by the texture-based methods to further identify homogeneous and/or textured areas to be skipped. Finally, all non-noticeable motion parts are not passed into the encoder and were reconstructed using the side information only. Currently, we are studying the foreground/background extraction problem to distinguish between noticeable and non-noticeable motion objects. In this approach, it is assumed that for non-noticeable regions, *i.e.* background areas, the viewer perceives the semantic meaning of the displayed background rather than the specific details therein. Thus, we synthesize all those background parts that the motion classification block labels as non-noticeable parts and replace them by the background of the key frame using the perspective model 10.7, in order to fit the key frame background properly into the current frame. Our initial implementation indicates promising results in terms of data rate savings. Again, the issues in this approach are the trade-offs between coding and modeling efficiency versus image quality.

10.4   Scalable Video Coding

Scalable video coding provides flexible adaptation to heterogeneous network conditions. The source sequence is encoded once and the bitstream can be decoded partially or completely to achieve a target performance [Ohm (2005)]. There are various types of scalability modes that have been studied: these include temporal, spatial, rate, and SNR scalability. Several scalable video coding schemes have been proposed such as Layered Scalable (LS) methods, Fine-Grained Scalable (FGS) methods and an extension termed Fully Fine-Grained Scalable (FFGS) [Cook *et al.* (2006)]. In LS codecs, the bitstream is divided into a base layer, that provides a minimum level of quality, and one or more enhancement layers. FGS codecs (e.g. MPEG-4 FGS) allow decoding of the bit stream for a very large set of data rates. Finally, in FFGS the maximum degree of scalability is provided because embedded coding is used in both the base and enhancement layers.

Research in scalable video coding has been done for more twenty years [Ohm (2005)]. Rate distortion analysis of scalable video coding has been extensively studied in [Prades-Nebot *et al.* (2006); Cook *et al.* (2006); Li and Delp (2004); Liu *et al.* (2003, 2005)]. Because of the inherent scalability in the wavelet transform, wavelet based methods have been widely investigated [Taubman and Zakhor (1994); Mehrseresht and D.Taubman (2006)]. A fully rate scalable video codec, known as SAMCoW (Scalable Adaptive Motion Compensated Wavelet), was proposed in [Shen and Delp (1999)]. A 3-D wavelet transform with MCTF (Motion Compensated Temporal Filtering) [Ohm (2005)] has been proposed. 3-D methods have been shown to preform well with excellent scalability features [Mehrseresht and D.Taubman (2006)]. The scalable extension of H.264/MPEG-4

AVC [Schwarz *et al*. (2006)] is a current standardization effort that will support temporal, spatial, and SNR scalability.

10.4.1 *Temporal scalability*

Temporal scalability allows decoding at several frame rates from the same compressed bitstream [Conklin and Hemami (1999)]. As shown in Fig. 10.6 temporal scalable video coding can be generated by a hierarchical structure. The first row index $T_i(i = 0, 1, 2, 3)$ represents the index of the layers, where T_0 is the base layer. The second row index denotes the coding order where the frames of the lower layer are coded before the neighboring frames with higher layers. The hierarchical structure shows an improved coding efficiency especially with cascading quantization parameters. The base layer is encoded with highest fidelity with a lower quality coded enhancement layers. Even though the enhancement layers are generally coded as B frames, they can be coded as P frames to reduce the delay with a small cost in the coding efficiency.

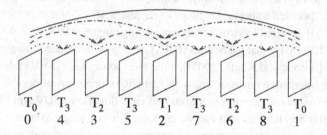

$$
\begin{array}{ccccccccc}
T_0 & T_3 & T_2 & T_3 & T_1 & T_3 & T_2 & T_3 & T_0 \\
0 & 4 & 3 & 5 & 2 & 7 & 6 & 8 & 1
\end{array}
$$

Fig. 10.6   Hierarchical structure of temporal scalability.

10.4.2 *Spatial scalability*

Spatial scalability allows the bitstream to be decoded at different spatial resolutions. In spatial scalability, each layer corresponds to a specific resolution. Spatial scalable video coding exploits the inter-layer correlation to achieve higher coding efficiency than simulcast coding. The inter-layer prediction can use the information from the lower layers as a reference. This ensures that a set of layers can be decoded independently of all higher layers. The inter-layer correlation can be exploited in several ways [Reichel *et al*. (2006)]. For example, inter-layer intra texture prediction uses the interpolation of the lower layer as the prediction of the current macroblock and can increase the compression efficiency.

10.4.3 *SNR and rate scalability*

In SNR and rate scalability the bitstream cna be decoded at different visual quality (SNR) or different rates. Two concepts are used in the design of these methods: coarse-granular scalability (CGS) and fine-granular scalability (FGS). In CGS, scalability is achieved by using the same inter-layer prediction techniques as described in Section 10.4.2 without the interpolation/upsampling. It can be regarded as an extreme case of spatial scalability that has the identical frame resolution through the layers. CGS is characterized by its simplicity in design and a low decoder complexity. FGS coding allows the truncating and decoding of a bitstream at any point in the decoding process with bit-plane coding. Progressive refinement (PR) slices are used in FGS to achieve scalability over a wide range of rate-distortion values.

10.5 Multi-View Coding

3D video (3DV) is an extension of two-dimensional video with depth information. MPEG has specified a special language to represent 3D graphic data [Smolic and Kauff (2005)], referred to virtual reality modeling language (VRML). A language known as, BInary Format for Scenes (BIFS), was later introduced as an extension of VRML [Smolic and Kauff (2005)]. Free viewpoint video (FVV) provides the viewers an interactive environment with realistic impressions of depth. Viewers are allowed to choose the view positions and view directions. 3DV and FVV have many similar applications and can be combined into a single system. Applications for 3DV span entertainment, education, sightseeing, surveillance, archive and broadcasting [mpe (2005)]. Generally multi-view video sequences are captured simultaneously by multiple cameras. Fig. 10.7 shows an example provided by HHI [Mller *et al.* (2006)]. The complete test sequences consist of eight video sequences captured by eight cameras with 20 cm spacing using 1D/parallel projection. Fig. 10.7 shows the first frames of three sequences taken by Camera 0, 2 and 4.

3DV and FVV representations require the transmission of a huge amount of data. Multi-view video coding (MVC) addresses the problem of jointly compressing multiple video sequences. Besides the spatial and temporal correlations in a single-view video sequence, multi-view video coding also exploits the inter-view correlations between the adjacent views. As shown in Fig. 10.7, the adjacent sequences have a high statistical dependency. Even though temporal prediction modes are used, inter-view prediction is more suitable for low frame rates and high motion sequences [Mller *et al.* (2006)]. After the call for proposals by MPEG,

Fig. 10.7   *Uli* sequences (Cameras $0, 2, 4$).

many MVC techniques have been proposed. A multi-view video coding scheme based on H.264/MPEG -4 AVC has been presented in [Mller *et al.* (2006)]. The bitstream is designed to be compliant with the H.264/MPEG-4 AVC standard. It was chosen as the reference solution in MPEG and used for the Joint Multiview Video Model (JMVM) software [Vetro *et al.* (2006)]. An inter-view direct mode was proposed in [Guo *et al.* (2006a)] to save bits in coding of the motion vectors. A view synthesis method is discussed in [Martinian *et al.* (2006)] to produce a virtual synthesis view by using a depth map. A novel scalable wavelet based MVC framework is introduced in [Garbas *et al.* (2006)]. Based on the idea of distributed video coding as discussed in Section 10.2, a distributed multi-view video coding framework is proposed in [Guo *et al.* (2006b)] to reduce the encoder complexity and inter-camera communication.

Joint Multiview Video Model (JMVM) [Vetro *et al.* (2006)] is reference software developed by the Joint Video Team (JVT). JMVM adopted the coding method presented in [Mller *et al.* (2006)]. The method is based on H.264/MPEG-4 AVC with a hierarchical B frame structure as shown in Fig. 10.8. The horizontal index T_i denotes the temporal index and the vertical index C_i denotes the index of the camera. The N video sequences from the N cameras are rearranged to form a single source signal. The spatial, temporal, and inter-view redundancies are removed to generate a standard-compliant compressed bitstream. At the decoder, the single bitstream is decoded and split to N reconstructed sequences. For each separate view, a hierarchical B frame structure as described in Section 10.4.1 is used. Inter-view prediction is exploited for every 2nd view, such as the view taken by the C_1 camera. Each group of picture (GOP) contains N times the length of the GOP for every view. For the *Uli* sequences the length of the GOP for every view is eight with eight views, which results in a total GOP size of $8 \times 8 = 64$ frames. The order of coding is arranged to minimize the memory requirements. However, the decoding of a higher layer frame still requires several reference frames. For example, the decoding of B_3 frame at (C_0, T_1) needs four references, namely, the frames at (C_0, T_0), (C_0, T_8), (C_0, T_4), and (C_0, T_2). The decoding of B_4 frame at (C_1, T_1) needs fourteen references decoded beforehand. From the experimental results, the scheme demonstrates high coding efficiency with a reasonable encoder complexity and memory requirements.

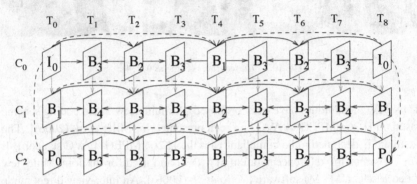

Fig. 10.8   Inter-view/temporal prediction structure.

10.6   Conclusion

In this paper, we presented an overview of the state of video coding. It is too early to say "video coding is dead" [Sullivan *et al.* (2006)]. In fact we believe this will never be true. Novel techniques provide interesting possibilities for improving coding efficiency and introducing new functionalities. There are still a lot of interesting areas for exploration!

Bibliography

(1988). Codec for videoconferencing using primary digital group transmission, ITU-T Recommendation H.120 Version 2.
(1993). Coding of moving pictures and associated audio for digital storage media at up to about 1.5 mbits/s - part 2: Video, ISO/IEC 11172-2 (MPEG-1).
(1993). Video codec for audiovisual services at $p \times 64$ kbits/s, ITU-T Recommendation H.261 Version 2.
(1994). Generic coding of moving pictures and associated audio information - part 2: Video, ITU-T Recommendation H.262 and ISO/IEC 13818-2 (MPEG-2).
(1998). Video coding for low bit rate communications, ITU-T Recommendation H.263 Version 2.
(1999). Coding of audiovisual objects - part 2: Visual, ISO/IEC 14496-2 (MPEG-4).

(2001). Text of iso/iec 159383/fdis information technology - multimedia content description interface - part 3 visual, .

(2003). Draft ITU-T recommendation and final draft international standard of joint video specification (ITU-T Rec. H.264/ISO/IEC 14 496-10 AVC), Joint Video Team (JVT) of ISO/IEC MPEG and ITU-T VCEG, JVT-G050.

(2005). Introduction to multi-view video coding, ISO/IEC JTC 1/SC 29/WG 11, Doc N7328.

Aaron, A., Setton, E. and Girod, B. (2003). Towards practical Wyner-Ziv coding of video, in *Proceeding of IEEE International Conference on Image Processing, ICIP-2003* (Barcelona, Spain), pp. 869–872.

Bouthemy, P. and Fablet, R. (1998). Motion characterization from temporal cooccurrence of local motion-based measures for video indexing, in *Proc. of 14th Int. Conf. on Pattern Recognition, ICPR'98* (Brisbane).

Carr, M. D. (1990). New video coding standard for the 1990s, *Electronics and Communications Engineering Journal* , pp. 119–124.

Chiariglione, L. (1997). MPEG and multimedia communications, *IEEE Transactions on Circuits and Systems for Video Technology* **7**, 1, pp. 5–18.

Chiariglione, L. (1998). Impact of MPEG standards on multimedia industry, *Proceedings of the IEEE* **86**, 1, pp. 1222–1227.

Comer, M. L. and Delp, E. J. (1999). Segmentation of textured images using a multiresolution Gaussian autoregressive model, *IEEE Transactions on Image Processing* **8**, 3, pp. 408–420.

Conklin, G. J. and Hemami, S. S. (1999). A comparison of temporal scalability techniques, *IEEE Transactions on Circuits and Systems for Video Technology* **9**, 6, pp. 909–919.

Cook, G., Prades-Nebot, J., Liu, Y. and Delp, E. (2006). Rate-distortion analysis of motion-compensated rate scalable video, *IEEE Transactions on Image Processing* **15**, 8, pp. 2170–2190.

Cote, G., Erol, B., Gallant, M. and Kossentini, F. (1998). H.263+: video coding at low bit rates, *IEEE Transactions on Circuits and Systems for Video Technology* **8**, 7, pp. 849–866.

Delp, E. J., Kashyap, R. L. and Mitchell, O. (1979). Image data compression using autoregressive time series models, *Pattern Recognition* **11**, pp. 313–323.

Ebrahimi, T. and Kunt, M. (1998). Visual data compression for multimedia applications, *Proceedings of the IEEE* **86**, 6, pp. 1109–1125.

Elfadel, I. and Picard, R. (1994). Gibbs random fields, cooccurrences, and texture modeling, *IEEE Transactions on Pattern Analysis and Machine Intelligence* **16**, 1, pp. 24–37.

Garbas, J., Fecker, U., Trger, T. and Kaup, A. (2006). 4D scalable multi-view video coding using disparity compensated view filtering and motion compensated temporal filtering, in *Proceedings of the IEEE International Workshop on Multimedia Signal Processing (MMSP)* (Victoria, Canada).

Girod, B., Aaron, A., Rane, S. and Rebollo-Monedero, D. (2005). Distributed video coding, *Proceedings of the IEEE* **93**, 1, pp. 71–83.

Guo, X., Lu, Y., Wu, F. and Gao, W. (2006a). Inter-view direct mode for multiview video coding, *IEEE Transactions on Circuits and Systems for Video Technology* **16**, 12, pp. 1527–1532.

Guo, X., Lu, Y., Wu, F., Gao, W. and Li, S. (2006b). Distributed multi-view video coding, in *Proceedings of the SPIE International Conference on Visual Communications and Image Processing* (San Jose, California).

Haralick, R. M. (1979). Statistical and structural approaches to texture, *Proceedings of the IEEE* **67**, 5, pp. 786–804.

Haskell, B. G., Puri, A. and Netravali, A. (1997). *Digital Video: An Introduction to MPEG-2* (Kluwer, Boston).

Kunt, M., Ikonomopoulos, A. and Kocher, M. (1985). Second-generation image-coding techniques, *Proceedings of the IEEE* **73**, 4, pp. 549–574.

LeGall, D. J. (1991). MPEG: A video compression standard for multimedia applications, *Communications of the ACM* **34**, 4, pp. 46–58.

Li, Z. (2005). *New Methods for Motion Estimation With Applications to Low Complexity Video Compression*, Ph.D. Thesis, School of Electrical and Computer Engineering, Purdue University, West Lafayette, IN.

Li, Z. and Delp, E. J. (2004). Channel-aware rate-distortion optimized leaky motion prediction, in *Proceedings of the IEEE International Conference on Image Processing* (Singapore), pp. 2079– 2082.

Li, Z., Liu, L. and Delp, E. J. (2006). Wyner-Ziv video coding with universal prediction, *IEEE Transactions on Circuits and Systems for Video Technology* **16**, 11, pp. 1430–1436.

Li, Z., Liu, L. and Delp, E. J. (2007). Rate distortion analysis of motion side estimation in Wyner-Ziv video coding, *IEEE Transactions on Image Processing* **16**, pp. 98–113.

Liou, M. (1991). Overview of the px64 kbit/s video coding standard, *Communications of the ACM* **34**, 4, pp. 59–63.

Liu, L. and Delp, E. J. (2005). Wyner-Ziv video coding using LDPC codes, in *Proceedings of the IEEE 7th Nordic Signal Processing Symposium (NORSIG 2006)* (Reykjavik, Iceland).

Liu, L., Li, Z. and Delp, E. J. (2006). Backward channel aware Wyner-Ziv video coding, in *Proceedings of the IEEE International Conference on Image Processing* (Atlanta, Georgia).

Liu, L., Li, Z. and Delp, E. J. (2007). Complexity-constrained rated-distortion optimization for Wyner-Ziv video coding, in *Proceedings of the Visual Communications and Image Processing Conference* (San Jose, California).

Liu, Y., Li, Z., Salama, P. and Delp, E. J. (2003). A discussion of leaky prediction based scalable coding, in *Proceedings of IEEE International Conference on Multimedia and Expo (ICME)*, Vol. 2 (Baltimore, Maryland), pp. 565–568.

Liu, Y., Salama, P., Li, Z. and Delp, E. (2005). An enhancement of leaky prediction layered video coding, *IEEE Transactions on Circuits and Systems for Video Technology* **15**, 11, pp. 1317–1331.

Liveris, A. D., Xiong, Z. and Georghiades, C. N. (2002). Compression of binary sources with side information at the decoder using LDPC codes, *IEEE Communications Letters* **6**, 10, pp. 440–442.

Martinian, E., Behrens, A., Xin, J. and Vetro, A. (2006). View synthesis for multiview video compression, in *Proceedings of Picture Coding Symposium (PCS)* (Beijing, China).

Mehrseresht, N. and D.Taubman (2006). An efficient content-adaptive motion-compensated 3-d dwt with enhanced spatial and temporal scalability, *IEEE Transactions on Image Processing* **15**, 6, pp. 1397–1412.

Mitchell, J. L., Pennebaker, W. B., Fogg, C. E. and LeGall, D. J. (1996). *MPEG Video Compression Standard* (Kluwer, Boston).

Mller, K., Merkle, P., Schwarz, H., Hinz, T., Smolic, A. and Wiegand, T. (2006). Multiview video coding based on H.264/AVC using hierarchical B-frames, in *Proceedings of Picture Coding Symposium (PCS)* (Beijing, China).

Ndjiki-Nya, P., Stuber, C. and Wiegand, T. (2004). Improved video coding through texture analysis and synthesis, in *Proceedings of the 5th International Workshop on Image Analysis for Multimedia Interactive Services* (Lisboa, Portugal).

Ohm, J.-R. (2005). Advances in scalable video coding, *Proceedings of the IEEE* **93**, 1, pp. 42–56.

Peh, C.-H. and Cheong, L.-F. (2002). Synergizing spatial and temporal texture, *IEEE Transactions on Image Processing* **11**, 10, pp. 1179–1191.

Pennebaker, W. B. and Mitchell, J. L. (1993). *JPEG: Still Image Data Compression Standard* (Van Nostrand Reinhold, New York).

Prades-Nebot, J., Cook, G. W. and Delp, E. J. (2006). An analysis of the effi ciency of different SNR-scalable strategies for video coders, *IEEE Transactions on Image Processing* **15**, 4, pp. 848–864.

Puri, R. and Ramchandran, K. (2003). Prism: An uplink-friendly multimedia coding paradigm, in *Proceedings of the IEEE International Conference on Acoustics, Speech, and Signal Processing*, Vol. 4 (Hongkong, China).

Reichel, J., Schwarz, H. and Wien, M. (2006). Joint scalable video model JSVM-7, JVT-T202.

Schafer, R. and Sikora, T. (1995). Digital video coding standards and their role in video communications, *Proceedings of the IEEE* **83**, 6, pp. 907–924.

Schreiber, W. F., Knapp, C. F. and Kay, N. D. (1959). Synthetic highs, an experimental tv bandwidth reduction system, *Journal of Society of Motion Picture and Television Engineers* **68**, pp. 525–537.

Schwarz, H., Marpe, D. and Wiegand, T. (2006). Overview of the scalable H.264/MPEG4-AVC extension, in *Proceedings of the IEEE International Conference on Image Processing* (Atlanta, Georgia).

Shen, K. and Delp, E. J. (1999). Wavelet based rate scalable video compression, *IEEE Transactions on Circuits and Systems for Video Technology* **9**, 1, pp. 109–122.

Sikora, T. (2005). Trends and perspectives in image and video coding, *Proceedings of the IEEE* **93**, 1, pp. 6–17.

Slepian, D. and Wolf, J. (1973). Noiseless coding of correlated information sources, *IEEE Transactions on Information Theory* **19**, 4, pp. 471–480.

Smith, J. R. and Chang, S.-F. (1994). Quad-tree segmentation for texture-based image query, in *Proceedings of the second ACM international conference on Multimedia* (San Francisco, CA.).

Smolic, A. and Kauff, P. (2005). Interactive 3-D video representation and coding technologies, *Proceedings of the IEEE* **93**, 1, pp. 98–110.

Smolic, A. and Ohm, J. (2000). Robust global motion estimation using a simplifi ed m-estimator approach, in *Proceedings of the IEEE International Conference on Image Processing* (Vancouver, Canada).

Sullivan, G. J., Ohm, J.-R., Ortega, A., Delp, E. J., Vetro, A. and Barni, M. (2006). DSP Forum - future of video coding and transmission, *IEEE Signal Processing Magazine* **23**, 6, pp. 76–82.

Sullivan, G. J. and Wiegend, T. (2005). Video compression: From concepts to the H.264/AVC standard, *Proceedings of the IEEE* **93**, 1, pp. 18–31.

Taubman, D. and Zakhor, A. (1994). Multirate 3-d subband coding of video, *IEEE Transactions on Image Processing* **3**, 5, pp. 572–588.

Trapanese, A., Tagliasacchi, M., Tubaro, S., Ascenso, J., Brites, C. and Pereira, F. (2005). Improved correlation noise statistics modeling in frame-based pixel domain wyner-ziv video coding, in *International Workshop on Very Low Bitrate Video Coding* (Sardinia, Italy).

Verdu, S. (1998). Fifty years of Shannon Theory, *IEEE Transactions on Information Theory* **IT-44**, 6, pp. 2057–2078.

Vetro, A., Su, Y., Kimata, H. and Smolic, A. (2006). Joint multiview video model (JMVM) 2.0, JVT-U207.

Westerlaken, R., Gunnewiek, R. K. and Lagendijk, R. (2005). The role of the virtual channel in distributed source coding of video, in *Proceedings of the IEEE International Conference on Image Processing* (Genova, Italy), pp. 581 – 584.

Wiegand, T., Sullivan, G. J., Bjntegaard, G. and Luthra, A. (2003). Overview of the H.264/AVC video coding standard, *IEEE Transactions on Circuits and Systems for Video Technology* **13**, 7, pp. 560–576.

Wyner, A. D. and Ziv, J. (1976). The rate-distortion function for source coding with side information at the decoder, *IEEE Transactions on Information Theory* **22**, 1, pp. 1–10.

Zhu, F., Ng, K. K., Abdollahian, G. and Delp, E. J. (2007). Spatial and temporal models for texture-based video coding, in *Proceedings of the Visual Communications and Image Processing Conference* (San Jose).

Chapter 11

Hardware Architecture for Ridge Extraction in Fingerprints: A Combinatorial Approach

A. Bishnu[1,1], P. Bhowmick[2], J. Dey[3], B. B. Bhattacharya[4]
M. K. Kundu[4], C. A. Murthy[4] and T. Acharya[5]

[1] *Department of Computer Science and Engineering*
Indian Institute of Technology, Kharagpur - 721302, India.

[2] *Department of Computer Science and Technology*
Bengal Engineering and Science University, Howrah - 711103, India.

[3] *IXIA, Block GP, Sector-5, Salt Lake City, Kolkata - 700091, India.*

[4] *Indian Statistical Institute, 203 B. T. Road, Kolkata - 700108, India.*

[5] *Avisere Inc., Chandler, AZ-85226, USA.*

Automatic Fingerprint Identification Systems (AFIS) have various applications in biometric authentication, forensic decision, and in many other areas. Most of the fingerprint matching techniques require extraction of ridge lines and/or minutiae for processing. Minutiae are the terminations and bifurcations of the ridge lines in a fingerprint image. Detection of ridge lines from a noisy gray-scale fingerprint image is a challenging task. In this work, a novel combinatorial approach is proposed for designing a hardware architecture aimed at classifying each pixel into one of the three classes (crest, valley, and slope), based on its gray-scale topographical relationship with its neighbors. A two-pass algorithm is developed

[1]This work is an embodiment of a preliminary version presented in the 3rd *Indian Conf. on Computer Vision, Graphics and Image Processing*, held at Ahmedabad, India, 2002; and of two US Patents, viz. "Architecture for Processing Fingerprint Images", US Patent 6,795,592, Sep. 21, 2004; and "Method and Apparatus for Providing a Binary Fingerprint Image", US Patent 7,136,515, Nov. 14, 2006. This work was funded in part by a grant from Intel Corp., USA.
[1]Author for correspondence, e-mail: arijit.bishnu@iitkgp.ac.in

for the pixel classification scheme. The ridge lines are then detected as formed by the thinned version of the crest pixels. The algorithm is robust, performs very well in the presence of noise, and has minimal dependence on thresholding. It has been tested on several benchmark fingerprint images and is observed to produce good results both in terms of quality of solutions and CPU time. A simple pipelined design is proposed for its hardware implementation. The design does not need any floating point operation, and hence, can be used to build a fast coprocessor for online fingerprint analysis.

11.1 Introduction

Automatic fingerprint identification systems (AFIS) are often used for personal identification. Fingerprints of each person have distinctive properties that persist over time. These properties make fingerprints highly suitable for biometric authentication purposes. AFISs are usually based on minutiae matching [Maltoni *et al.* (2003); Farina *et al.* (1999); Jain *et al.* (1997); Kovács-Vajna (2000)]. Minutiae, or Galton's characteristics, are local discontinuities in terms of ridge endings and bifurcations of ridge flow patterns that constitute a fingerprint. These two types of minutiae have been considered by the Federal Bureau of Investigation for identification purposes [Wegstein (1982)]. AFIS based on minutiae matching involves several stages (see Fig. 11.1(a) for an illustration): (i) fingerprint image acquisition; (ii) preprocessing of the fingerprint image; (iii) feature extraction (e.g., minutiae) from the image; (iv) matching of fingerprint images for identification. Depending on the fingerprint matching application at hand, a fingerprint recognition system is either a *verification system* or an *identification system* [Maltoni *et al.* (2003)]. A verification system either rejects or accepts the submitted claim of identity. On the other hand, in an identification system, the subject's identity is established (or rejected, if the subject is not enrolled in the system database), without the subject having to claim an identity. It is well known that the performance of fingerprint identification and verification depends heavily on the preprocessing phase [Chang and Fan (2001)]. For the AFIS to perform better in terms of correct verification and identification within acceptable time, the preprocessing phase has a contradictory objective in providing better performance in lesser time. The step of feature extraction (in terms of minutiae or other features), and the final verification or identification depends heavily on a correct and reliable preprocessing. A detailed and insightful discussion on all these steps can be found in the literature [Jain *et al.* (1997); Maltoni *et al.* (2003)].

Deriving a one-pixel thick binary image from the original gray level image

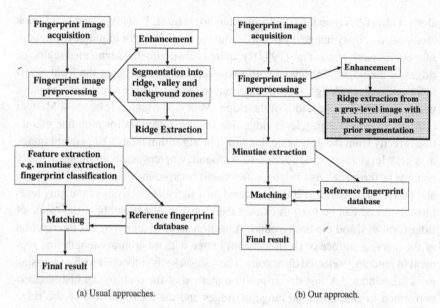

(a) Usual approaches.   (b) Our approach.

Fig. 11.1 Two flowcharts showing the different phases in fingerprint analysis taken by (a) usual approaches and (b) our method. In (b) the highlighted module shows the area of our work.

is a difficult task, as noise and different levels of contrast in the image may produce false minutiae or hide real minutiae. A robust ridge detection procedure for minutiae extraction should not miss any ridge. False ridges leading to spurs and bridges [Farina *et al.* (1999)] may be taken care of by a preprocessing stage prior to minutiae extraction. Thus, a complete ridge finding algorithm for a gray-level fingerprint image is of utmost importance for any AFIS. Usually, ridge extraction in a gray-scale fingerprint image is preceded by a segmentation procedure as shown in the flowchart of Figure 11.1(a).

During the segmentation procedure, a fingerprint image is classified into ridge and valley (ravine) regions for the actual ridge extraction. The work by Jain et al. [Jain *et al.* (1997)] introduced a segmentation algorithm based on the local certainty level of estimated orientation field of the fingerprint image in order to locate the region of interest. Mehtre and Chatterjee [Mehtre and Chatterjee (1989)] described a method of segmenting a fingerprint image into ridge zones and background based on some statistics of local orientations of ridges of the original image. A gray-scale variance method is used in the image blocks having uniform gray-level, where the directional method of segmentation fails.

Once the regions in a gray-level fingerprint image are marked as ridges, pixels on the ridges can be found by detecting the local maxima of the gray values along a direction normal to the local ridge orientation. Usually, a one-pixel thick skeletonized binary image is obtained from the ridge lines for minutiae extraction. Jain et al.'s work [Jain *et al.* (1997)] requires convolving the segmented region of ridges in the fingerprint image with two masks for accentuating the local maximum gray values along a direction normal to the local ridge direction. The mask width is adapted to the width of the ridge. Maio and Maltoni [Maio and Maltoni (1997)] developed a gray level ridge line tracing algorithm for minutiae extraction directly from the gray scale domain. The algorithm treats a fingerprint image as a gray level zone of ridges and background, whereas, such an image actually consists of three regions - ridges, valleys, and background. The method of Chang and Fan [Chang and Fan (2001)] is based on a statistical analysis of the gray level histogram and can be used to extract the global information about the range of ridges, valleys, and the background. A section set is obtained by the intersection of the discrete surface of the fingerprint image with an arbitrary length line segment in randomly selected directions. The section set is smoothed with a Gaussian masking window. A fast decomposition method of the multimodal histogram is performed to determine the range of ridges and the local maxima of the ridge regions are found to determine the exact ridges.

   In this work, we propose an algorithm for ridge extraction in a fingerprint image after enhancing it by applying an earlier algorithm [Inc. (1985)]. Our algorithm treats the image as is, i.e., with background, and performs ridge extraction without any segmentation of ridge and background zones as opposed to other algorithms [Jain *et al.* (1997); Maio and Maltoni (1997)]. We have developed our ridge finding algorithm as a solution to the problem stated as a future research goal by Chang and Fan [Chang and Fan (2001)]. The proposed algorithm can be directly used prior to invoking the minutiae extraction procedure from a 1-pixel thick binary image due to Farina et al. [Farina *et al.* (1999)]. The role of our algorithm is depicted in Figure 11.1(b). The problem of ridge extraction from a gray-level fingerprint image is treated as a twofold process: a new combinatorial pixel classification scheme for ridge extraction followed by binary thinning of the ridges. Ridges or crests (henceforth the term ridge or crest will be used interchangeably) are extracted from a fingerprint image by classifying each pixel combinatorially. A two-pass algorithm is developed to classify a pixel into three classes, namely crest (CR), valley (VA), or slope (SL). The proposed crest finding algorithm is based on the use of a Look-Up-Table (LUT). The crest pixels necessarily trace out the ridge lines in the image. Any standard binary thinning algorithm [Rosenfeld and Kak (1982)] can then be applied on the crest pixels as object, and the rest as background, to extract the one-pixel thick ridge lines. A preprocessing algorithm usually consumes almost 90-95% of the total time required for fingerprint identification and verification [Blue *et al.* (1994)]. Since ridge extraction is complex and time consuming, an online AFIS requires an efficient hardware engine to accomplish this task. The proposed ridge extraction algorithm is combinatorial in nature and embodies an inherent modularity and parallelism. Exploiting these features, we describe a simple hardware design using basic logic modules like D flip-flop, comparators, adders for the first pass of the algorithm. The second pass involves only integer addition and comparison. Finally, any standard binary thinning algorithm [Rosenfeld and Kak (1982); Shih *et al.* (1995)] can be employed on the crest pixels as object, and the rest as background, to extract one-pixel thick ridge lines. The design does not need any floating point operation, and hence, can be used to build a fast coprocessor for online fingerprint analysis.

11.2   Proposed Method

11.2.1   *Theme*

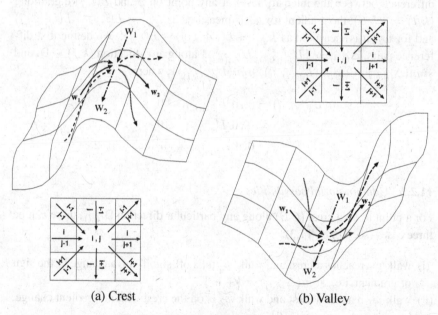

(a) Crest (b) Valley

Fig. 11.2   Intensity profiles of crest and valley.

In order to find crests in discrete points and implement it on-chip, we develop a new algorithm using a Look-Up-Table (LUT). Let I be an $N \times M$ gray-scale image with g gray levels. Let $L(i, j)$ be the gray level of the $(i, j)^{th}$ pixel P of I. Denote the boundary pixels B of P as $\{p_{i-1,j}, p_{i+1,j}, p_{i-1,j-1}, p_{i+1,j+1}, p_{i,j-1}, p_{i,j+1}, p_{i+1,j-1}, p_{i-1,j+1}\}$ respectively with corresponding directions $\{$N, S, NW, SE, W, E, SW, NE$\}$ as shown in Figure 11.2. Fix the direction of the straight line walk from each point in B to another point in B through P. It is obvious that 4 such directions are possible (see Figure 11.2). The directions D, are $(k, l) \in \{(N, S), (NW, SE), (W, E), (SW, NE)\}$, where (k, l) is a fixed direction of walk from k to l. We define two types of elementary walks, w_1 and w_2. A movement from any point in B to P is defined as w_1; w_2 is defined as a movement from P to any point in B. It is obvious that a walk along any of the directions of D consists of a walk w_1 followed by a walk w_2 in the same direction. (e.g., a walk along (N, S) consists of a walk w_1 from $p_{i-1,j}$ to P followed by a walk w_2 from P to $p_{i+1,j}$). The sign of the gradient changes for walks w_1 and w_2 if there is a crest (valley) (See Figure 11.2) in a particular direction. The gradient along w_1 is measured as the difference between $L(i, j)$ and the intensity level at any point on B, where w_1 starts. Similarly, the gradient along w_2 is the difference between the intensity level at any point on B and $L(i, j)$ e.g., along $(k, l) = (N, S)$, the gradient for w_1 is measured as $L'_{w_1} = L(i, j) - L(i - 1, j)$ and for w_2, it is measured as $L'_{w_2} = L(i + 1, j) - L(i, j)$. We define first difference pairs, $\Delta_{(k,l)} = \{L'_{w_1,(k,l)}, L'_{w_2,(k,l)}\}$ along any direction $(k, l) \in$ D; and $sign(\Delta_{(k,l)}) = \{sign(L'_{w_1,(k,l)}), sign(L'_{w_2,(k,l)})\}$, where,

$$sign(L'_{w_x,(k,l)}) = +, \text{if } L'_{w_x,(k,l)} > 0,$$
$$= -, \text{if } L'_{w_x,(k,l)} < 0,$$
$$= 0, \text{if } L'_{w_x,(k,l)} = 0, \text{for } x = 1, 2$$

11.2.2 *Combinatorial possibilities*

For a point to be a crest (CR) along any particular direction $D_{(k,l)}$, there can be three cases (see Figure 11.3):

(i) walk w_1 reaches a crest and walk w_2 falls off signifying a change in the sign of gradient, i.e., $sign(\Delta_{(k,l)}) = \{+, -\}$,

(ii) walk w_1 reaches a crest and walk w_2 is on the crest with no gradient change, i.e., $sign(\Delta_{(k,l)}) = \{+, 0\}$,

(iii) walk w_1 is on the crest with no gradient change, and walk w_2 falls off the crest, i.e., $sign(\Delta_{(k,l)}) = \{0, -\}$.

Similarly for a valley (VA), the three cases are (see Figure 11.3):

CASE	a	b	GRAY LEVELS	CLASS OF P
1	+	+	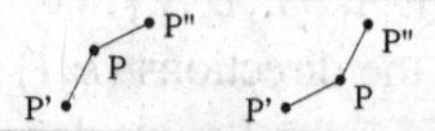	PL
2	+	-	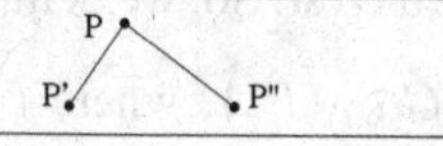	CR
3	+	0	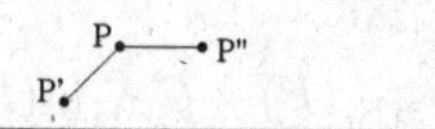	CR
4	-	+	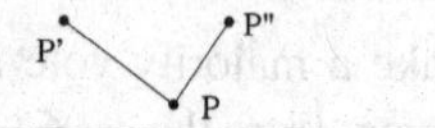	VA
5	-	-	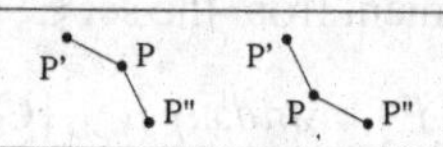	PL
6	-	0	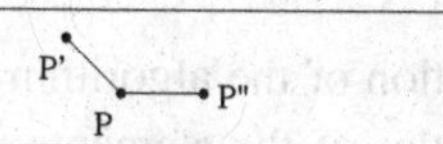	VA
7	0	+	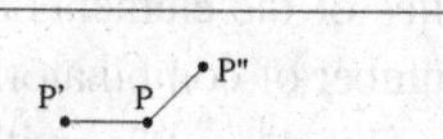	VA
8	0	-	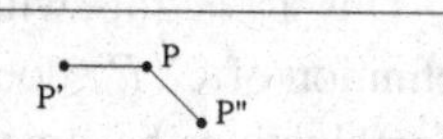	CR
9	0	0	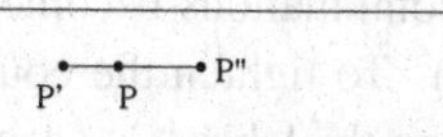	UN

Fig. 11.3 Relative position of P w.r.t. P' and P''.

(i) walk w_1 reaches a valley and walk w_2 rises from the point signifying a change in the sign of gradient, i.e., $sign(\Delta_{(k,l)}) = \{-,+\}$,

(ii) walk w_1 reaches a valley and walk w_2 is on the valley with no gradient change, i.e., $sign(\Delta_{(k,l)}) = \{-,0\}$,

(iii) walk w_1 is on the valley with no gradient change, and walk w_2 rises from the valley, i.e., $sign(\Delta_{(k,l)}) = \{0,+\}$.

For a pixel P which is on the slope of the intensity landscape, we call P to be a slope (SL) point. Obviously there would be no change in the sign of gradients (see Figure 11.3):

(i) $sign(\Delta_{(k,l)}) = \{+,+\}$,

(ii) $sign(\Delta_{(k,l)}) = \{-,-\}$.

Note that considering the pairs from the set $\{+,-,0\}$, we have $3^2 = 9$ cases of which 8 (3 cases of CR, 3 cases of VA and 2 cases of SL) have been taken care of, and in the last case, i.e., where $sign(\Delta_{(k,l)}) = \{0,0\}$, we label P as undecidable (UN).

So, along any direction $(k, l) \in$ D, we can label P from any one of the elements of set $C = \{CR, VA, SL, UN\}$, i.e. $C_{(k,l)}(P) = CR/VA/SL/UN$. Note that if along most of the directions $(k, l) \in$ D, P is a crest, then there is a high probability of P to be a crest. So, we define the label of $C(P)$ as:

$$C(P) = f_{(k,l) \in D}\{C_{(k,l)}(P)\}, \text{ where } f \text{ is a function as follows:}$$

$$f : C_{(N,S)}(P) \times C_{(NW,SE)}(P) \times C_{(W,E)}(P) \times C_{(SW,NE)}(P) \rightarrow C(P)$$

As an example, we can take a majority vote among the different directions to finally assign P to any element from the set C, i.e.,

$$C(P) = max_{(k,l) \in D}\{C_{(k,l)}(P)\}.$$

For hardware implementation of the algorithm, we need to consider the number of combinatorial possibilities of the elements of C along directions $(k, l) \in$ D. The upper bound on the number of combinatorial possibilities of the elements of C along directions $(k, l) \in$ D is $4^4 = 256$, with 4 possibilities along each of the 4 directions. Since the definition of $C(P)$ does not take into account the effect of directionality, several combinations become identical (e.g., 2 CRs along *any* 2 directions are the same). To tighten the count, we define $x_i, (i \in C)$, as the number of directions having the label 'i'. Clearly, x_i can take integral values in $[0, 4]$. Further, the total number of directions is bounded by 4. Thus, $\sum_{i \in C} x_i = x_{CR} + x_{VA} + x_{SL} + x_{UN} = 4$. Finding the number of possible integral solutions of the above equation is equivalent to finding the coefficient of x^4 in the *generating function* [Roberts (1984)] $(x^0 + x^1 + x^2 + x^3 + x^4)^4$

$$\text{i.e., the coefficient of } x^4 \text{ in } (1 + x + x^2 + x^3 + x^4)^4$$

$$= \text{the coefficient of } x^4 \text{ in } (1 - x)^{-4}(1 - x^5)^4 = 35.$$

Fact 1: The number of combinatorial possibilities, thus determined, depends on the cardinality of the set D $((k, l) \in$ D) of directions and not on the set B of boundary pixels. Generalizing, if n directions are chosen, and along each direction the number of possibilities is 4, then the number of combinatorial possibilities is the coefficient of x^n in $(1 - x)^{-4}(1 - x^{n+1})^4 = (n+1)(n+2)(n+3)/6$. Thus, the size of the Look-Up-Table (LUT) is $(n + 1)(n + 2)(n + 3)/6 = O(n^3)$. In our case, the LUT will therefore, have 35 rows (see Table 11.1). $\qquad \square$

11.2.3 *Implementation details*

The discrete surface $z = L(i, j)$ corresponding to a part of such an image I is shown in Figure 11.4(a). The pixels with gray-levels close to g (or 1) are bright

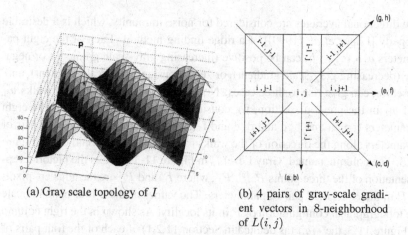

(a) Gray scale topology of I

(b) 4 pairs of gray-scale gradient vectors in 8-neighborhood of $L(i, j)$

Fig. 11.4   Magnified view of a part of the gray scale topology with the gradient vectors.

(or dark). The fingerprint ridge lines (appearing bright in image I) correspond to surface ridges or crests, and the space between the ridge lines (appearing dark in I) correspond to the ravines or valleys. The relative gray-scale topographical configuration of L in its locality can be viewed from four possible directions as shown in Figure 11.4(b). To calculate the first difference pairs along the walks w_1 and w_2 defined in Section 11.2.1, we take directional averages along the directions $(k, l) \in D$ for calculating L'_{w_1} and L'_{w_2}. The calculation of L'_{w_1} and L'_{w_2} at P using directional averages for a 5×5 neighborhood along a direction (NW, SE) is as follows:

$$L'_{w_1,(NW,SE)} = L(i, j) - (L(i - 1, j - 1) + L(i - 2, j - 2))/2,$$
$$L'_{w_2,(NW,SE)} = (L(i + 1, j + 1) + L(i + 2, j + 2))/2 - L(i, j).$$

Consider a neighborhood of P as defined above and using directional averages, the first difference pairs are:

$$\Delta_{(N,S)} = (a, b) : a = L(i, j) - (L(i - 1, j) + L(i - 2, j))/2,$$
$$b = (L(i + 1, j) + L(i + 2, j))/2 - L(i, j),$$
$$\Delta_{(NW,SE)} = (c, d) : c = L(i, j) - (L(i - 1, j - 1) + L(i - 2, j - 2))/2,$$
$$d = (L(i + 1, j + 1) + L(i + 2, j + 2))/2 - L(i, j),$$
$$\Delta_{(W,E)} = (e, f) : e = L(i, j) - (L(i, j - 1) + L(i, j - 2))/2,$$
$$f = (L(i, j + 1) + L(i, j + 2))/2 - L(i, j),$$
$$\Delta_{(SW,NE)} = (g, h) : g = L(i, j) - (L(i + 1, j - 1) + L(i + 2, j - 2))/2,$$
$$h = (L(i - 1, j + 1) + L(i - 2, j + 2))/2 - L(i, j).$$

$$(11.1)$$

The directional averages are considered for noise immunity, which is a desirable property [López *et al.* (1999)] of a ridge finding method. Each of the eight parameters $a, b, c, \ldots, h$, can be positive (increasing gray-scale gradient), or negative (decreasing gray-scale gradient), or zero (constant gray-scale gradient), and, therefore, can give rise to three cases. Now, based on the definition of walks w_1 and w_2 in the previous section, we consider the pairwise property of the eight parameters (i.e. a and b, c and d, e and f, g and h) and, therefore, each pair of parameters along the direction of the walks can have 9 cases as laid out in Figure 11.3. The column, named 'Gray Levels', in Figure 11.3 exhibits the pictorial representation of the three points P, P', P'', where P' and P'' are the adjacent pixels of P in the concerned pair of parameters. The values of these four pairs indicate the topographical configuration of P in its locality. As shown in the right column of Figure 11.3, the *sign* (as defined in Section 11.2.1) of each of the four pairs of parameters $((a, b), (c, d), (e, f), (g, h))$ is used to assign one out of the following four classes to the respective pixel P:

CR: P is a crest pixel if either the gray-value of P is higher than the gray-values of both P' and P'' (see case 2 in Figure 11.3), or, the gray-value of P is same as that of one of P' and P'' but higher than that of the other (see cases 3 and 8 in Figure 11.3).

VA: P is a valley pixel if either the gray-value of P is lower than the gray-values of both P' and P'' (see case 4 in Figure 11.3), or, the gray-value of P is same as that of one of P' and P'' but lower than that of the other (see cases 6 and 7 in Figure 11.3).

SL: P is a slope pixel if the gray-value of P lies strictly within the gray-values of P' and P'' (see cases 1 and 5 in Figure 11.3).

UN: P is an undecidable pixel if the gray-values of P, P' and P'' are same (see case 9 in Figure 11.3).

Thus, each pixel P is assigned to any one of the four preliminary classes along a single direction. After the preliminary classification pass, P can be either strongly classified or weakly classified as discussed next.

11.2.4 *Classification of a pixel*

11.2.4.1 *Preliminary classification*

Let C_{ab}, C_{cd}, C_{ef} and C_{gh} denote the four classes preliminarily assigned to P by the four pair of parameters $(sign(a, b), sign(c, d), sign(e, f), sign(g, h))$. Note that each of these four classes is one of the four possible preliminary classes (CR,

Table 11.1   Classification of a pixel.

No. of cases	No. of classes in preliminary set				Preliminary Class
	CR	VA	SL	UN	
1	0	0	0	4	XX
2	0	0	1	3	XX
3	0	0	2	2	XX
4	0	0	3	1	SL
5	0	0	4	0	SL
6	0	1	0	3	XX
7	0	1	1	2	XX
8	0	1	2	1	XX
9	0	1	3	0	VS
10	0	2	0	2	VA
11	0	2	1	1	VA
12	0	2	2	0	VS
13	0	3	0	1	VA
14	0	3	1	0	VA
15	0	4	0	0	VA
16	1	0	0	3	XX
17	1	0	1	2	XX
18	1	0	2	1	CS
19	1	0	3	0	CS
20	1	1	0	2	CV
21	1	1	1	1	CV
22	1	1	2	0	CV
23	1	2	0	1	CV
24	1	2	1	0	CV
25	1	3	0	0	VA
26	2	0	0	2	CR
27	2	0	1	1	CR
28	2	0	2	0	CR
29	2	1	0	1	CR
30	2	1	1	0	CR
31	2	2	0	0	CV
32	3	0	0	1	CR
33	3	0	1	0	CR
34	3	1	0	0	CR
35	4	0	0	0	CR

VA, SL and UN). We implement the Look-Up-Table given in Table 11.1 with a bias towards crest (CR). This stems from the particular application to fingerprint images because the minutiae may be defined as the discontinuities on the crest lines. The cases that cannot be topographically resolved to any of the classes in C, are kept for further processing. We define four intermediate classes CV, CS, VS and XX into which the unresolvable pixels are classified for further processing. P is classified to one of the classes among CR, VA, SL, CV(can be crest or valley), CS(crest or slope), VS(valley or slope), XX(crest or valley or slope) depending on the following exhaustive 35 cases as deduced in Section 11.2.2 (see Table 11.1) :

CR : (a): if 3 or 4 classes among C_{ab}, C_{cd}, C_{ef} and C_{gh} are equal to CR;
     (b): if 2 classes are CR and at most 1 of the other 2 classes is VA;
VA : (a): if 3 or 4 classes are VA;
     (b): if 2 classes are VA and not any one class is CR;
SL : (a): if 4 classes are SL;
     (b): if 3 classes are SL and 1 is UN;
CV : the pixel may be a crest or valley, if the number of CRs and VAs are non-

zero and the difference between the number of CRs and VAs is at most one.

CS : the pixel may be a crest or slope, if there is one CR and SL is in majority;

VS : the pixel may be a valley or slope, if there are one or two VA and the rest SL;

XX : the pixel may be a crest or valley or slope in all other cases.

It may be observed that even if along any direction at least one CR is present, the possibility of that pixel to be labeled CR is not ruled out; it may be labeled as either CV, CS or XX, thus keeping the option of CR at the next stage of classification.

11.2.4.2   *Final classification*

In Table 11.1, the classes CR, VA and SL denote the final classes. However, the criteria of being strongly classified, is not satisfied by some of the cases in Table 11.1 which are the ambiguous classes CV, VS, CS and XX. These pixels are finally classified in the second pass by inspecting the presence of the unambiguous classes in its neighborhood. This method can be viewed as the multilocal approach suggested by Lopez et al. [López *et al.* (1999)]. For the ambiguously classified pixels P belonging to CV, CS, VS or XX, we define a neighborhood R(P) whose size is determined by some criteria (as stated next). In R(P), we find the average value of the pixels belonging to the unambiguous classes (CR, VA and SL). Let in R(P), the average gray value of the pixels belonging to CR be $Ave(CR)$. Similarly, $Ave(VA)$ and $Ave(SL)$ be the average gray values of pixels classified as valley and slope respectively. For any pixel $P \in CV$, we classify it to either crest or valley based on the closeness of the gray value $L(i,j)$ of P to $Ave(CR)$ or $Ave(VA)$ i.e. if $|L(i,j) - Ave(CR)| \leq |L(i,j) - Ave(VA)|$, assign P to CR, else assign it to VA. Similarly, assign CS to CR or SL; and VS to VA or SL. The pixel $P \in XX$ is assigned to either CR, VA or SL, for which its gray-value difference is minimum.

Determination of R(P):

R(P) is a square region of size $w \times w$ centered at P. We estimate w from the domain knowledge of fingerprints. We know the approximate range of the number of ridges in a typical fingerprint. Let the number of ridges be approximately k. The size of the fingerprint image is $N \times M$. Let l be the width of the ridges in terms of pixels. So, the image dimension can be estimated in terms of k, l and the inter-ridge distance λ. Therefore, the approximate inter-ridge distance λ can be

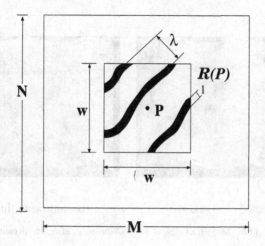

Fig. 11.5   Determination of R(P)

estimated roughly as (see Figure 11.5)

$$(\lambda + l)k = \sqrt{N^2 + M^2}$$
$$\text{or } \lambda = \frac{\sqrt{N^2 + M^2}}{k} - l$$

The size of R(P) should be such that it includes at least some of the crest lines. To include, say, r crest lines, w should be equal to $(r\lambda)/\sqrt{2}$.

11.2.5   *Thinning*

After the final classification, the image contains 2- or 3- pixels thick crest lines, valley lines, and the rest slope regions, (see Figure 11.6(a)). The valley and slope pixels are treated as background and the crest pixels are treated as foreground object. The resulting image is a binary image with only crests as objects. Any of the standard thinning techniques, widely reported in literature [Rosenfeld and Kak (1982); Shih *et al.* (1995)], can now be used on the binary image to obtain one-pixel thick crest lines (see Figure 11.6(b)). Figures 11.6(a) and (b) are perspective projections of a part of the original pixel matrix.

11.2.6   *Algorithm*

We now present the complete algorithm for detecting a crest, valley, or slope in a gray-level fingerprint image.

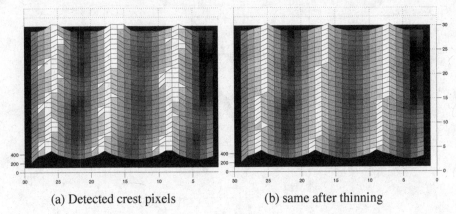

(a) Detected crest pixels   (b) same after thinning

Fig. 11.6   Magnified view of a part of the image after classification.

Algorithm Crest_Detect

Input: A Gray level fingerprint image I of size $N \times M$
Output: Identification of crest/valley

/* First Pass of Classification */
1. **for** (all pixels in the image)
2.   Calculate a, b, c, d, e, f, g, h following equation 11.1;
3.   Calculate $sign(a, b)$, $sign(c, d)$, $sign(e, f)$ and $sign(g, h)$ and classify P
    along each of the directions to $CR/VA/SL/UN$;
4.   Use Look-Up-Table (LUT) given in Table 11.1 to classify P
5.   **if** $(P \in \{CV, CS, VS \text{ or } XX\})$ **then**
6.   Put the pixel location and gray value of P in a list L;
    endif
  endfor
/* Second Pass of Classification */
7. **while** (L is not empty) **do**
8.   Consider R(P) for each P in L;
9.   Find $Ave(CR)$, $Ave(VA)$ and $Ave(SL)$ in R(P);
10.   **if** $(P \in CV)$ **then**
        if $(|L(i, j) - Ave(CR)| \leq |L(i, j) - Ave(VA)|)$ **then**
          Classify P to CR; **else** Classify P to VA;
        endif
    endif
11.   **else if** $(P \in CS)$ **then**
        if $(|L(i, j) - Ave(CR)| \leq |L(i, j) - Ave(SL)|)$ **then**
          Classify P to CR; **else** Classify P to SL;
        endif
    endif
12.   **else if** $(P \in VS)$ **then**

```
            if (|L(i, j) − Ave(V A)| ≤ |L(i, j) − Ave(SL)|) then
                Classify P to V A; else Classify P to SL;
            endif
        endif
13.     else if (P ∈ XX) then
            if (|L(i, j) − Ave(CR)| ≤ |L(i, j) − Ave(V A)| and
            |L(i, j) − Ave(CR)| ≤ |L(i, j) − Ave(SL)|) then
                Classify P to CR;
            else if (|L(i, j) − Ave(V A)| ≤ |L(i, j) − Ave(SL)| then
                Classify P to V A;
            else Classify P to SL;
            endif
        endif
    endwhile
```

It is simple to analyse that the space and the worst case time complexity is $O(N \times M)$, i.e., $O(N^2)$ when $M \approx N$.

11.3   Evaluation and Results

11.3.1   *Evaluation criteria for ridge/valley finding algorithms*

López et al. [López *et al.* (1999)] devised a set of desirable properties for clean and robust extraction of ridges. These are:

P1. Irrelevant ridges should not be detected.

P2. Salient ridges should always be detected.

P3. Ridges extracted from a continuous object must be continuous.

P4. A creaseness measure should have a similar value along the crease and a much higher value than the region around it.

P5. Small perturbations of the image should not alter greatly the shape or the location of the ridges.

P6. Ridges should run as closely as possible through the center of anisotropic regions.

For a fingerprint image, any minutiae extraction method involves a lot of preprocessing even on the one-pixel thick binary image [Farina *et al.* (1999)]. Further, retention of crest lines is more important. Crest lines should not be missed; if irrelevant ridges in noisy zones (see Figure 11.7) or in form of spurs (see Figure 11.8) and bridges (see Figure 11.9) occur, they are taken care of during minutiae extraction. Hence, property P2 is more important to our case than P1. Property P4

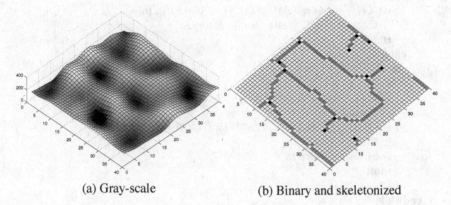

(a) Gray-scale   (b) Binary and skeletonized

Fig. 11.7   Gray-scale topography of a noisy zone and its corresponding skeletonized binary structure found out by our algorithm followed by thinning.

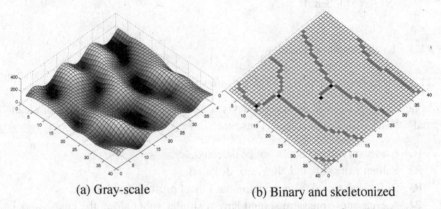

(a) Gray-scale   (b) Binary and skeletonized

Fig. 11.8   Magnified view of spur in a fingerprint image found out by our algorithm followed by thinning.

does not hold as our method is a classification scheme and not a creaseness measure. Properties P3, P5 and P6 are qualitative in nature and cannot be quantified. Experimental results are now reported below.

11.3.2   *Results*

We have used the fingerprint images from (i) NIST Special Database 4[Watson and Wilson (1992)], (ii) NIST Special Database 14[Candela *et al.* (1995)], (iii) Database B1 of FVC2000[FVC 2000 (2000)], and (iv) Database B2 of

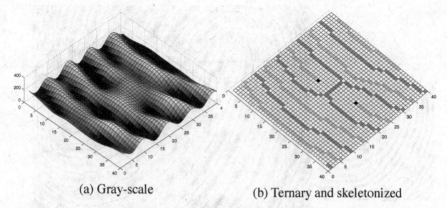

(a) Gray-scale   (b) Ternary and skeletonized

Fig. 11.9   Magnified view of bridge in a fingerprint image found out by our algorithm followed by thinning.

FVC2000[FVC 2000 (2000)]. The images of (i) and (ii) are of size 480×512. The images of (iii) are of size 300×300 and (iv) are of size 364×256. All the images are of 500 dpi resolution. The proposed algorithm was implemented in C on a Sun_Ultra 5_10, Sparc, 333 MHz, the OS is SunOS Release 5.7 Generic in a multi-user environment. The images were first enhanced by an algorithm that is also used by PCASYS [Candela *et al.* (1995)], the much widely used package. It involves cutting out subregions of the images, taking their FFT, and suppression of a band of low and high frequency components followed by some non-linear operations in the frequency domain, and transforming it back to the spatial domain. This algorithm was also used by Kovács-Vajna [Kovács-Vajna (2000)]. We have also used this enhancement algorithm in our work owing to its simplicity and

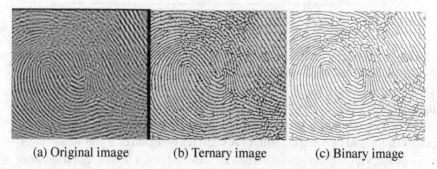

(a) Original image   (b) Ternary image   (c) Binary image

Fig. 11.10   An image sample from NIST 14 sdb showing the stages of classification.

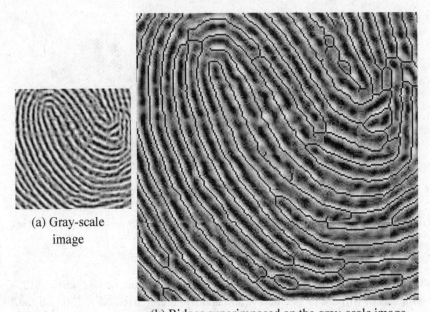

(a) Gray-scale
image

(b) Ridges superimposed on the gray-scale image

Fig. 11.11 Detected ridge pixels on a region of a gray-scale fingerprint image.

Table 11.2   Comparative results

Finger print Data-base	Image size	Time for enhan-cement (in secs.)	% of pixels classified as crest		Time for ridge class. (in secs.)		% of crest pixels after thinning		Time for thinning (in secs.)	
			Mean	Var.	Mean	Var.	Mean	Var.	Mean	Var.
NIST sdb-4	480× 512	1.25	23.72	5.08	2.55	0.08	7.58	0.06	0.84	0.01
NIST sdb-14	480× 512	1.25	22.98	1.3449	2.60	0.01	7.44	0.10	0.93	0.08
FVC2000 db-1	300× 300	1.24	19.19	1.67	0.87	0.06	6.63	0.62	0.27	0.00
FVC2000 db-2	364× 256	1.28	18.87	0.61	0.92	0.00	6.40	0.20	0.31	0.00

elegance. Thereafter, our ridge finding algorithm described here was run on the images followed by a thinning algorithm to obtain the 1-pixel thick ridges. The Table 11.2 shows the image sizes, the time taken by the enhancement algorithm, the mean and variance of the number of pixels classified as crest after ridge classification and thinning and the mean and variance of the time taken by the ridge classification and thinning algorithm. A small noisy region of a gray-scale fingerprint image with 500 dpi resolution and the detected crests in that region is shown in Figure 11.7. Figures 11.8 and 11.9 show small regions with detected crests

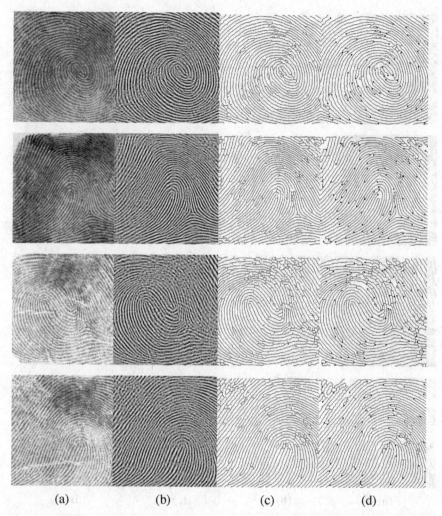

Fig. 11.12   Results on four sample images. Top two rows: NIST-4 database; bottom two rows: NIST-14 database.

forming spurs and bridges respectively. Figure 11.10(a) shows a sample image from NIST 14 sdb. Figure 11.10(b) shows the ternary image showing detected crests, valleys and slope pixels and Figure 11.10(c) shows the 1-pixel thick ridge image. Figure 11.11(a) shows a part of an image and (b) shows a magnified view of the ridges superimposed on the original image showing how the ridges run close to the centre of the crest region, thus satisfying property P6 devised by López et

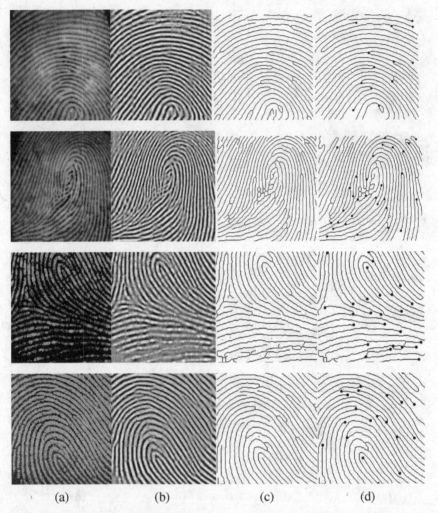

Fig. 11.13   Results on four other sample images. Top two rows: FVC2000 DB1 database; bottom two rows: FVC2000 DB2 database.

al. [López *et al.* (1999)] as mentioned in the previous subsection. Figures 11.12-11.13(a), (b), (c) and (d) show respectively the original image, enhanced image, 1-pixel thick ridge extracted image and the detected minutiae. The minutiae were detected by a simple, modified version of the algorithm due to Farina et al. [Farina *et al.* (1999)], thus showing that the output of our algorithm can act as an input to the Farina et al.'s algorithm.

11.4 Parallel Algorithm and Hardware Architecture

11.4.1 *Parallel algorithm*

We describe below a parallel algorithm for classifying each pixel in the image to any of the seven classes $\{CR, VA, SL, CV, CS, VS, XX\} \in C$.

Algorithm Classify_Parallel
Input: A gray level fingerprint image I of size $N \times M$.
Output: A classified image into seven classes.

1. **for** ($j \leftarrow$ column number 1 to M) **do** in **parallel**
2.   Calculate directional averages;
3.   Calculate $a, \ldots, h$ for each pixel in the jth column;
4.   Pair up corr. first difference pairs $(a, b), (c, d),$
    (e, f) and (g, h);
5.   Find the number of CR, VA, SL and UN
    along each of the directions;
6.   Use *look-up-table* (LUT) given in Table 11.1 to find
    the element in C to which the pixel belongs;
   endfor

11.4.2 *Hardware architecture*

We now describe a hardware architecture for implementation of the first pass of the pixel classification scheme proposed in Section 11.2.3. The first pass of the algorithm over the image-pixel matrix resolves pixels to any of the following seven classes namely CR, VA, SL, CV, VS, CS and XX as shown in Table 11.1.

The algorithm discussed in the earlier section, being highly modular, has an inherent parallelism in it. We exploit these properties to design a pipeline architecture for implementing the first pass of classification including directional averaging. At each clock pulse, a column of the pixel matrix is fed into the pipeline. The simple directional averaging requires holding back data in columns that were fed in the previous clocks. The circuit elements Ave_d for calculating first difference pairs are shown in Figure 11.14. It adds two 8-bit numbers, representing the gray values of the pixels, and uses a serial shift left register (SLR) to multiply the pixel value at $L(i, j)$ by two. This is done to avoid the floating point operation needed according to the equation 11.1. The size of the registers should be equal to 9 bits to accommodate the sum of two 8-bit numbers and the left shifted value in the SLR. Table 11.3 shows the input lines and corresponding clock pulses at which the respective pixel values are available for calculating the first differences a, b, c, d, e, f, g and h for the pixel at location (i, j). The column indices

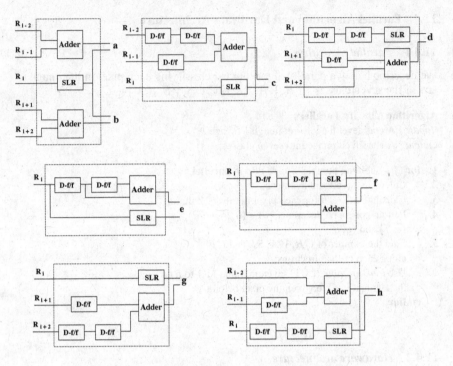

Fig. 11.14   Circuits for computing the first difference pairs.

of the pixels match with the clocks at which they are available. As an example, $c = L(i,j) - (L(i-1,j-1) + L(i-2,j-2))/2$, is calculated as follows. The pixels corresponding to $L(i-2,j-2)$ and $L(i-1,j-1)$ are available on the input lines R_{i-2} and R_{i-1} at the clocks $j-2$ and $j-1$ respectively. To hold them back, we use a bank of D flip-flops. Obviously, line R_{i-2} is to be retained for two clock pulses, and line R_{i-1} should be held for one clock pulse. The outputs from the D flip-flops corresponding to lines R_{i-2} and R_{i-1} are fed to the circuit block Ave_d (see Figure 11.15) for computing the directional average. The pixel corresponding to $L(i,j)$, available on the line R_i at clock t_j is multiplied by two using a serial shift left register during which the addition of the values at the other two input lines take place. The circuits given in Figure 11.14 show separately the computation of all first difference pairs. To combine the first difference pairs and calculate $sign(a,b)$, $sign(c,d)$, $sign(e,f)$ and $sign(g,h)$, comparator circuits [Mano (1992)] are used(see Figure 11.15). It may be noted that, a, b, c, e and g are available at the comparator input after the t_j^{th} clock pulse, while d, f and h are available at the comparator input after the $(t_j + 2)^{th}$ clock pulse. Thus, the

Table 11.3 Availabilty of pixels at different clock pulses

	Pixels needed	Input line at which it is available	Time at which it is available	Pixels needed	Input lines at which they are available	Time at which they are available
a	(i,j)	R_i	t_j	$(i-1,j)$, $(i-2,j)$	R_{i-1}, R_{i-2}	t_j
b	(i,j)	R_i	t_j	$(i+1,j)$, $(i+2,j)$	R_{i+1}, R_{i+2}	t_j
c	(i,j)	R_i	t_j	$(i-1,j-1)$, $(i-2,j-2)$	R_{i-1}, R_{i-2}	t_j-1, t_j-2
d	(i,j)	R_i	t_j	$(i+1,j+1)$, $(i+2,j+2)$	R_{i+1}, R_{i+2}	t_j+1, t_j+2
e	(i,j)	R_i	t_j	$(i,j-1)$, $(i,j-2)$	R_i	t_j-1, t_j-2
f	(i,j)	R_i	t_j	$(i,j+1)$, $(i,j+2)$	R_i	t_j+1, t_j+2
g	(i,j)	R_i	t_j	$(i+1,j-1)$, $(i+2,j-2)$	R_{i+1}, R_{i+2}	t_j-1, t_j-2
h	(i,j)	R_i	t_j	$(i-1,j+1)$, $(i-2,j+2)$	R_{i-1}, R_{i-2}	t_j+1, t_j+2

outputs of the comparator circuits are to be held for two clock pulses for further processing.

The comparator block C_j (see Figure 11.15) has five 8-bit magnitude comparators, one each for a, b, c, e and g. After the clock pulse t_j, C_j calculates *signs* of a, b, c, e and g for the pixel at location (i,j) of the image pixel matrix. The comparator block C_{j+2} (see Figure 11.15) has three 8-bit magnitude comparators, one each for d, h and f. The block C_{j+2} calculates *signs* of d, h and f for the pixel at location (i,j) after the $(t_j+2)^{th}$ clock pulse. After clock pulse (t_j+2), C_j calculates *signs* of a, b, c, e and g corresponding to the pixel at location $(i, j+2)$ of the pixel matrix; C_{j+2} calculates *signs* of d, h and f corresponding to the pixel at location (i,j). The *signs* of h, d and f are available two clock pulses after *signs* of a, b, c, e and g are available. So, the outputs from C_j are held for two clock pulses by the two banks of D flip-flops, called D_4 (see Figure 11.15). The bus-width of the outputs from the comparators C_j and C_{j+2} is 3, since the outputs of the magnitude comparator can be either $+$, or $-$, or 0.

The outputs from the comparators are fed into four combinational circuits, P_1, P_2, P_3, and P_4 that generate $sign(a,b)$, $sign(c,d)$, $sign(e,f)$ and $sign(g,h)$ respectively. The circuit diagram of $P_i, i = 1, 2, 3, 4$ is shown in Figure 11.16.

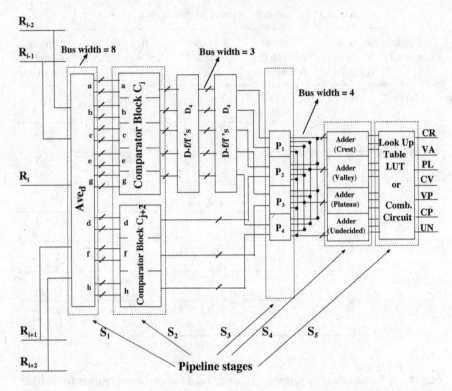

Fig. 11.15 A sample circuit for the first pass classification of a row R_i; pipeline latches are not explicitly shown.

The combinational circuits $P_i, i = 1 \ldots 4$ implement the table given in Figure 11.3. Along any of the directions $(a, b), (c, d), (e, f)$ or (g, h), we can have either a crest, or valley, or slope, or undecided. Thus, out of the four output lines (each line being 1 bit wide) from each of P_1, P_2, P_3 and P_4, only one line can go high indicating the presence of crest or valley or slope or undecided pixel.

Next, four adders are required. The CR, VA, SL, and UN (all 1-bit) output lines shown in Figure 11.15 are fed respectively to Crest-adder, Valley-adder, Slope-adder and Undecided-adder. As we have four directions, the maximum number of occurrences of any of crest, valley, slope or undecided can be four. Therefore, in an adder, we require three bits to represent the sum. As we have four adders, the bus-width for the *look-up-table LUT* is twelve. The outputs from the adders are fed into the LUT implementing the classification scheme of Table 11.1. The LUT outputs any one of the seven classes (CR, VA, SL, CV, CS, VS or XX) and the corresponding output line is enabled. The LUT (Figure 11.15)

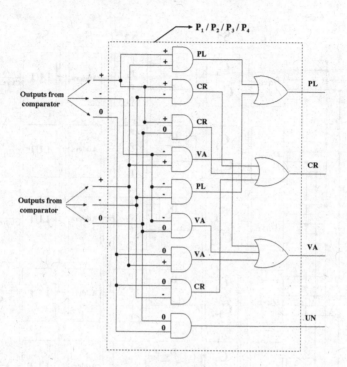

Fig. 11.16 Circuit for each P_i, $i = 1, 2, 3, 4$.

decodes the 12-bit input to one of the 35 entries in it. Thus, a location of the LUT is addressed, and any one of the corresponding seven lines is enabled. The maximum count of any one of CR, VA, SL, or UN may be 4, requiring 3 bits each. As there are seven intermediate classes, we require 3 bits to represent them. So, to store the *look-up-table* we require $35 \times (3 \times 4 + 3) = 525$ bits.

To summarise, the computation of the first pass of classification resembles a linear pipeline [Hwang and Briggs (1985)] with five stages, namely S_1, S_2, S_3, S_4 and S_5 as shown in Figure 11.15. An entire column of the pixel matrix is fed into the pipeline at the same time. Stage S_1 computes the directional average. Stage S_2 consists of magnitude comparators. The two banks of flip-flops, shown as D_4 in Figure 11.15, are used to insert the required delay. Stage S_3 is used to form the pairing of the *sign*s of the first difference pairs; the outputs are added in the stage S_4. A LUT is used in stage S_5 to decode the input to any one of the outputs, namely CR, VA, SL, CV, CS, VS, or XX. Figure 11.17 shows a schematic circuit diagram for classifying an image having 8 rows.

After the first pass, each of the $N \times M$ pixels is classified into one of the seven classes. The second pass can be easily implemented as another stage of the

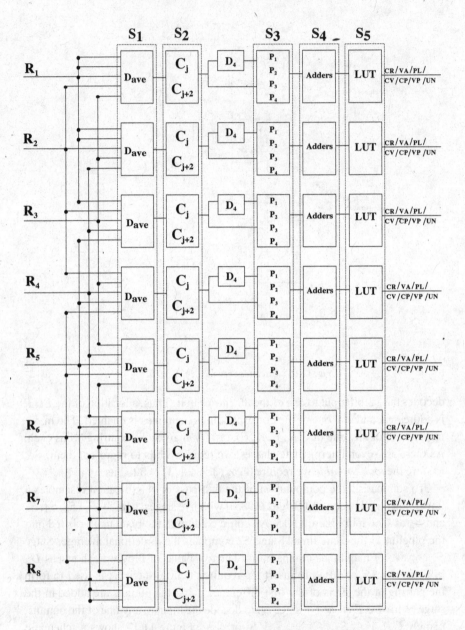

Fig. 11.17   A schematic circuit for classifying pixels in an image having 8 rows.

pipeline. The stage involves addition of pixels in a square region R(P) (discussed in Section 11.2.4.2). That can be easily done by summing along vertical and horizontal directions. This would involve some vertical and horizontal movement of the data in the pixel matrix. This added result is to be compared with the value of the pixel at the centre of the square region R(P).

11.4.3 *Time complexity*

The number of stages in the linear pipeline is five. The clock period of the linear pipeline is determined by the longest pipeline stage. Here, stage S_1 is the longest one requiring 9 clock cycles (8 clock cycles for addition followed by a single clock for serial shift right register). Now, the number of steps in the linear pipeline is $M + 5$. Thus, the number of clock cycles required to perform the classification is $9(M + 5) = 9M + 45$, i.e., $O(M) \approx O(N)$. The number of circuit elements required is clearly $O(N)$. The time complexity of the first pass of the sequential classification algorithm is $O(N^2)$. Using $O(N)$ processing elements, the first pass of the classification can be performed in $O(N)$ parallel time of execution. Thus, the speed-up achieved is $O(N)$.

11.4.4 *Circuit cost*

The components used to implement the architecture in hardware for processing of each row of an $N \times M$ image are given below. The requirements for each stage S_i are shown separately:

S_1 : (a) 3 banks of D flip-flops each having 8 flip-flops, requiring a total of 24 flip-flops. Each line R_i requires at most 3 flip-flops (see Figure 11.14).
    (b) 8 pieces of 9-bit adder and 8 pieces of 9-bit shift register.
S_2 : 8 pieces of 8-bit magnitude comparator.
S_3 : 36 2-input AND gates (9 each for P_1, P_2, P_3 and P_4) and 12 3-input OR gates (3 each for P_1, P_2, P_3 and P_4).
S_4 : 4 pieces of 3-bit adder.
S_5 : *Look-up-table, LUT* implemented with ROM of 525 bits $\approx$ 33 16-bit words.

Apart from these, for each row, we require two delay stages for synchronization. The bus width at this particular stage is three. Since each line requires 3 flip-flops, the total number of D flip-flops required for five lines and two stages, is 30. The latches required for synchronizing pipeline stages have not been shown in Figure 11.15 or taken into consideration for circuit cost computation.

11.5   Discussions and Conclusions

In this work, we have enumerated the exhaustive combinatorial possibilities that a particular pixel can have in a digital image landscape in terms of the first difference pairs. Based on the possibilities, the pixels are classified into three different classes using a two-pass algorithm. The combinatorial possibilities stored as a LUT provide us an efficient tool for hardware implementation of the first pass of the classification scheme on-chip. The proposed hardware design does not need any floating point operation, and hence, can be used to build a fast coprocessor for online fingerprint analysis. The construction of the LUT is based on some empirical observations, and relevant experiments have been performed on the NIST sdb4 and NIST sdb14 and FVC2000 databases. The proposed method provides a very convenient technique for extracting ridge lines from a fingerprint image. The performance of our algorithm for extraction of the ridges from noisy zones is also an added benefit. The implementation of our algorithm for ridge extraction was used as an input module of the works [Bhowmick *et al.* (2005)] successfully. A better design of the LUT including magnitudes in addition to signs needs further investigation. The generating function has to be suitably tailored for calculating the combinatorial possibilities accordingly.

Bibliography

Bhowmick, P., Bishnu, A., Bhattacharya, B. B., Kundu, M. K., Murthy, C. A. and Acharya, T. (2005). Determination of minutiae scores for fi ngerprint image applications, *Intl. J. Image and Graphics* **5**, 3, pp. 1–35.

Blue, J. L., Candela, G. T., Grother, P. J., Chellappa, R., Wilson, C. L. and Blue, J. D. (1994). Evaluation of pattern classifi ers for fi ngerprint and ocr application, *Pattern Recognition* **27**, 4, pp. 485–501.

Candela, G. T., Grother, P. J., Watson, C. I., Wilkinson, R. A. and Wilson, C. L. (1995). *PCASYS — A Pattern-Level Classification Automation System for Fingerprints*, NI-STIR 5647 (National Institute of Standards and Technology).

Chang, J. H. and Fan, K. C. (2001). Fingerprint ridge allocation in direct gray-scale domain, *Pattern Recognition* **34**, 10, pp. 1907–1925.

Farina, A., Kov´acs-Vajna, Z. M. and Leone, A. (1999). Fingerprint minutiae extraction from skeletonized binary images, *Pattern Recognition* **32**, pp. 877–889.

FVC 2000 (2000). Fingerprint Verifi cation Competition, 2000, http://bias.csr.unibo.it/fvc2000/download.asp.

Hwang, K. and Briggs, F. A. (1985). *Computer Architecture and Parallel Processing* (McGraw-Hill International Edition, Singapore).

Inc., D. P. (1985). Automated classifi cation system reader project (acs), Technical Report.

Jain, A. K., Hong, L., Pankanti, S. and Bolle, R. (1997). An identity-authentication system using fi ngerprints, *Proc. of IEEE* **85**, 9, pp. 1365–1388.

Kov´acs-Vajna, Z. M. (2000). A fi ngerprint verifi cation system based on triangular matching and dynamic time warping, *IEEE Trans. PAMI* **22**, 11, pp. 1266–1276.

L´opez, A. M., Lumbreras, F., Serrat, J. and Villanueva, J. J. (1999). Evaluation of methods for ridge and valley detection, *IEEE Trans. PAMI* **21**, 4, pp. 327–335.

Maio, D. and Maltoni, D. (1997). Direct gray-scale minutiae detection in fi ngerprints, *IEEE Trans. PAMI* **19**, pp. 27–39.

Maltoni, D., Maio, D., Jain, A. K. and Prabhakar, S. (2003). *Handbook of Fingerprint Recognition* (Springer-Verlag, New York).

Mano, M. N. (1992). *Computer System Architectures* (Prentice Hall India Ltd., New Delhi).

Mehtre, B. M. and Chatterjee, B. (1989). Segmentation of fi ngerprint images – A composite method, *Pattern Recognition* **22**, pp. 381–385.

Roberts, F. S. (1984). *Applied Combinatorics* (Prentice Hall Inc., Englewood Cliffs, NJ).

Rosenfeld, A. and Kak, A. C. (1982). *Digital Picture Processing* (Academic Press Inc., New York).

Shih, F. Y., King, C. T. and Pu, C. C. (1995). Pipeline architectures for recursive morphological operations, *IEEE Trans. Image Processing* **4**, 1, pp. 11–18.

Watson, C. I. and Wilson, C. L. (1992). *Fingerprint Database, Special Database 4, FPDB* (National Institute of Standards and Technology).

Wegstein, J. H. (1982). *An Automated Fingerprint Identification System* (US Government Publication, Washington).

Chapter 12

Rough-Fuzzy Hybridization for Protein Sequence Analysis

Pradipta Maji and Sankar K. Pal

Machine Intelligence Unit, Indian Statistical Institute, Kolkata
{pmaji,sankar}@isical.ac.in

In most pattern recognition algorithms, amino acids cannot be used directly as inputs since they are nonnumerical variables. They, therefore, need encoding prior to input. In this regard, bio-basis function maps a nonnumerical sequence space to a numerical feature space. It is designed using an amino acid mutation matrix. One of the important issues for the bio-basis function is how to select a minimum set of bio-bases with maximum information. In this chapter, we describe an algorithm, termed as rough-fuzzy c-medoids algorithm, to select most informative bio-bases. It comprises a judicious integration of the principles of rough sets, fuzzy sets, c-medoids algorithm, and amino acid mutation matrix. While the membership function of fuzzy sets enables efficient handling of overlapping partitions, the concept of lower and upper bounds of rough sets deals with uncertainty, vagueness, and incompleteness in class definition. The concept of crisp lower bound and fuzzy boundary of a class, introduced in rough-fuzzy c-medoids, enables efficient selection of a minimum set of most informative bio-bases. Some indices are introduced for evaluating quantitatively the quality of selected bio-bases. The effectiveness of the algorithm, along with a comparison with other algorithms, has been demonstrated on different types of protein data sets.

12.1 Introduction

Recent advancement and wide use of high throughput technology for biological research are producing enormous size of biological data. Data mining techniques and machine learning methods provide useful tools for analyzing these biological data. The successful analysis of biological sequences relies on the efficient coding of the biological information contained in sequences/subsequences. For example, to recognize functional sites within a biological sequence, the subsequences obtained through moving a fixed length sliding window are generally analyzed. The problem with using most pattern recognition algorithms to analyze these biological subsequences is that they cannot recognize nonnumerical features such as the biochemical codes of amino acids. Investigating a proper encoding process prior to modeling the amino acids is then critical.

The most commonly used method for coding a subsequence is distributed encoding, which encodes each of 20 amino acids using a 20-bit binary vector [Qian and Sejnowski (1988)]. However, in this method the input space is expanded unnecessarily. Also, this method may not be able to encode biological content in sequences efficiently. On the other hand, different distances for different amino acid pairs have been defined by various mutation matrices, and validated [Dayhoff *et al.* (1978); Henikoff and Henikoff (1992); Johnson and Overington (1993)]. But, they cannot be used directly for encoding an amino acid to a unique numerical value.

In this background, Yang et al. [Thomson *et al.* (2003); Berry *et al.* (2004); Yang and Thomson (2005)] proposed the concept of bio-basis function for analyzing biological sequences. It uses a kernel function to transform biological sequences to feature vectors directly. Bio-bases consist of sections of biological sequence that code for a feature of interest in the study, and are responsible for the transformation of biological data to high dimensional feature space. Transformation of input data to high dimensional feature space is performed based on the similarity of an input sequence to a bio-basis with reference to a biological similarity matrix. Thus, the biological content in the sequences can be maximally utilized for accurate modeling. The use of similarity matrices to map features allows the bio-basis function to analyze biological sequences without the need for encoding.

The most important issue for bio-basis function is how to select a minimum set of bio-bases with maximum information. Berry et al. [Berry *et al.* (2004)] used genetic algorithms for bio-bases selection considering Fisher ratio as the fitness function. Yang et al. [Yang and Thomson (2005)] proposed a method to select bio-bases using mutual information. In principle, the bio-bases in nonnumerical sequence space should be such that the degree of resemblance between pairs of bio-bases would be as minimum as possible. Each of them would then represent a unique feature in numerical feature space. As this is a feature selection problem, clustering method can be used which partitions the given biological sequences into subgroups around each bio-basis, each of which should be as homogeneous/informative as possible. However, the methods proposed in [Berry *et al.* (2004); Yang and Thomson (2005)] have not adequately addressed this problem. Also, it has not been paid much attention earlier.

In biological sequences, the only available information is the numerical values that represent the degrees to which pairs of sequences in the data set are related. Algorithms that generate partitions of that type of relational data are usually referred to as relational or pair-wise clustering algorithms. An well-known relational clustering algorithm is c-medoids due to Kaufman and Rousseeuw [Kaufman and Rousseeuw (1990)]. The c-medoids algorithm is applicable to situations where the objects to be clustered cannot be represented by numerical features, rather, only represented with similarities/dissimilarities between pairs of objects. So, the relational clustering algorithms can be used to cluster biological subsequences if one can come up with a similarity measure to quantify the degree of resemblance between pairs of subsequences. The pair-wise similarities are usually stored in the form of a matrix called the similarity matrix.

One of the main problems in biological subsequence analysis is uncertainty. Some of the sources of this uncertainty include incompleteness and vagueness in class definitions. In this background, the possibility concept introduced by the fuzzy sets theory [Zadeh (1965)] and rough sets theory [Pawlak (1991)] have gained popularity in modeling and propagating uncertainty. Both fuzzy sets and rough sets provide a mathematical framework to capture uncertainties associated with the data [Dubois and H.Prade (1990); Banerjee *et al.* (1998); Pal *et al.* (2003); Skowron *et al.* (2005)]. Two of the early rough clustering algorithms are those due to Hirano and Tsumoto [Hirano and Tsumoto (2003)] and De [De (2004)]. Other notable algorithms include rough c-means [Lingras and West (2004)], rough self organizing map [Pal *et al.* (2004)], rough support vector clustering [Asharaf *et al.* (2005)], etc. In [Pal and Mitra (2002)], the indiscernibility relation of rough sets has been used to initialize the expectation maximization algorithm. Most notable fuzzy relational algorithm is fuzzy c-medoids due to Krishnapuram et al. [Krishnapuram *et al.* (2001)]. Recently, combining rough sets and fuzzy sets, Mitra et al. proposed rough-fuzzy collaborative clustering [Mitra *et al.* (2006)].

In this chapter, we described an algorithm, termed as rough-fuzzy c-medoids algorithm [Maji and Pal (2007)], based on rough sets and fuzzy sets to select most informative bio-bases. While the membership function of fuzzy sets enables efficient handling of overlapping partitions, the concept of lower and upper approximations of rough sets deals with uncertainty, vagueness, and incompleteness in class definition. Each partition is represented by a medoid (bio-basis), a crisp lower approximation, and a fuzzy boundary. The lower approximation influences the fuzziness of the final partition. The medoid (bio-basis) depends on the weighting average of the crisp lower approximation and fuzzy boundary. The concept of "degree of resemblance", based on non-gapped pair-wise homology alignment score, circumvents the initialization and local minima problems of c-medoids, and enables efficient selection of a minimum set of most informative bio-bases. Some quantitative measures are introduced based on mutual information and non-gapped pair-wise homology alignment scores to evaluate the quality of selected bio-bases. The effectiveness of the algorithm, along with a comparison with hard c-medoids [Kaufman and Rousseeuw (1990)], rough c-medoids, fuzzy c-medoids [Krishnapuram *et al.* (2001)], Berry's method [Berry *et al.* (2004)], and Yang's method [Yang and Thomson (2005)], has been demonstrated on different protein data sets.

The structure of the rest of this chapter is as follows. Section 12.2 briefly introduces necessary notions of bio-basis function, rough sets, and fuzzy sets. In Section 12.3, a new c-medoids algorithm is described based on rough sets and fuzzy sets for bio-bases selection. Some quantitative measures are described in Section 12.4 to select most informative bio-bases. A few case studies and a comparison with other methods are described in Section 12.5. Concluding remarks are given in Section 12.6.

12.2   Bio-Basis Function, Rough Set, and Fuzzy Set

In this section, the basic notions in the theories of bio-basis function, rough sets, and fuzzy sets are reported.

12.2.1   *Bio-basis function*

The most successful method of sequence analysis is homology alignment [Altschul *et al.* (1990, 1994)]. In this method, the function of a sequence is annotated through aligning a novel sequence with known sequences. If the homology alignment between a novel sequence and a known sequence gives a very high similarity score, the novel sequence is believed to have the same or similar function as the known sequence. In homology alignment, an amino acid mutation matrix is commonly used. Each mutation matrix has 20 columns and 20 rows. A value at nth row and mth column is a probability or a likelihood value that the nth amino acid mutates to the mth amino acid after a particular evolutionary time [Henikoff and Henikoff (1992); Johnson and Overington (1993)].

However, the principle of homology alignment cannot be used directly for subsequence analysis. Because, a subsequence may not contain enough information for conventional homology alignment. A high homology alignment score between a novel subsequence and a known subsequence cannot assert that two subsequences have the same function. However, it can be assumed that they may have the same function statistically.

The design of bio-basis function is based on the principle of conventional homology alignment used in biology. Using a table look-up technique, a homology alignment score as a similarity value can be obtained for a pair of subsequences. The non-gapped homology alignment method is used to calculate this similarity value, where no deletion or insertion is used to align two subsequences. The definition of bio-basis function is as follows [Thomson *et al.* (2003); Yang and Thomson (2005)]:

$$f(x_j, v_i) = \exp\left\{\gamma \frac{h(x_j, v_i) - h(v_i, v_i)}{h(v_i, v_i)}\right\} \tag{12.1}$$

where $h(x_j, v_i)$ is the non-gapped pair-wise homology alignment score between a subsequence x_j and a bio-basis v_i calculated using an amino acid mutation matrix [Henikoff and Henikoff (1992); Johnson and Overington (1993)], $h(v_i, v_i)$ denotes the maximum homology alignment score of the ith bio-basis v_i, and γ is a constant. Let $\mathbb{A}$ be the set of 20 amino acids, $X = \{x_1, \cdots, x_j, \cdots, x_n\}$ be the set of n subsequences with m residues, and $V = \{v_1, \cdots, v_i, \cdots, v_c\} \subset X$ be the set of c bio-bases such that $v_{ik}, x_{jk} \in \mathbb{A}, \forall_{i=1}^c, \forall_{j=1}^n, \forall_{k=1}^m$. The non-gapped pair-wise homology alignment score between x_j and v_i is then defined as

$$h(x_j, v_i) = \sum_{k=1}^m M(x_{jk}, v_{ik}) \tag{12.2}$$

where $M(x_{jk}, v_{ik})$ can be obtained from an amino acid mutation matrix through a table look-up method. The function value is high if two subsequences are similar or close to each other, and one for two identical subsequences. The value is small if two subsequences are distinct.

The bio-basis function transforms various homology alignment scores to a real number as a similarity within the interval $[0, 1]$. Each bio-basis is a feature dimension in a numerical feature space. It needs a subsequence as a support. A collection of c bio-bases formulates a numerical feature space $\mathbb{R}^c$. After the mapping using bio-bases, a nonnumerical subsequence space $\mathbb{A}^m$ will be mapped to a c-dimensional numerical feature space $\mathbb{R}^c$, i.e., $\mathbb{A}^m \to \mathbb{R}^c$.

The most important assumption about bio-basis function is that the distribution of the amino acids in sequences depends on the specificity of the sequences. If the distribution of amino acids is in random, the selection of bio-basis will be very difficult. Fortunately, the biological experiments have shown that the distribution of amino acids at the specific subsites in sequences does depend on the specificity of the sequences.

12.2.2 *Rough sets*

The theory of rough sets begins with the notion of an approximation space, which is a pair $< U, R >$, where U be a non-empty set (the universe of discourse) and R an equivalence relation on U, i.e., R is reflexive, symmetric, and transitive. The relation R decomposes the set U into disjoint classes in such a way that two elements x and y are in the same class iff $(x, y) \in R$. Let denote by U/R the quotient set of U by the relation R, and

$$U/R = \{X_1, \cdots, X_i, \cdots, X_p\}$$

where X_i is an equivalence class of R, $i = 1, 2, \cdots, p$. If two elements x, y in U belong to the same equivalence class $X_i \in U/R$, we say that x and y are indistinguishable. The equivalence classes of R and the empty set $\emptyset$ are the elementary sets in the approximation space $< U, R >$. Given an arbitrary set $X \in 2^U$, in general it may not be possible to describe X precisely in $< U, R >$. One may characterize X by a pair of lower and upper approximations defined as [Pawlak (1991)]:

$$\underline{R}(X) = \bigcup_{X_i \subseteq X} X_i; \quad \overline{R}(X) = \bigcup_{X_i \cap X \neq \emptyset} X_i$$

That is, the lower approximation $\underline{R}(X)$ is the union of all the elementary sets which are subsets of X, and the upper approximation $\overline{R}(X)$ is the union of all the elementary sets which have a non-empty intersection with X. The interval $[\underline{R}(X), \overline{R}(X)]$ is the representation of an ordinary set X in the approximation space $< U, R >$ or simply called the rough set of X. The lower (resp., upper) approximation $\underline{R}(X)$ (resp., $\overline{R}(X)$) is interpreted as the collection of those elements of U that definitely (resp., possibly) belong to X. Further,

- a set $X \in 2^U$ is said to be definable (or exact) in $< U, R >$ iff $\underline{R}(X) = \overline{R}(X)$;
- for any $X, Y \in 2^U$, X is said to be roughly included in Y, denoted by $X \tilde{\subset} Y$, iff $\underline{R}(X) \subseteq \underline{R}(Y)$ and $\overline{R}(X) \subseteq \overline{R}(Y)$;
- X and Y is said to be roughly equal, denoted by $X \simeq_R Y$, in $< U, R >$ iff $\underline{R}(X) = \underline{R}(Y)$ and $\overline{R}(X) = \overline{R}(Y)$.

In [Pawlak (1991)], Pawlak discusses two numerical characterizations of imprecision of a subset X in the approximation space $< U, R >$: accuracy and roughness. Accuracy of X, denoted by $\alpha_R(X)$, is the ratio of the number of objects in its lower approximation to that in its upper approximation; namely

$$\alpha_R(X) = \frac{|\underline{R}(X)|}{|\overline{R}(X)|}$$

The roughness of X, denoted by $\rho_R(X)$, is defined by subtracting the accuracy from 1:

$$\rho_R(X) = 1 - \alpha_R(X) = 1 - \frac{|\underline{R}(X)|}{|\overline{R}(X)|}$$

Note that the lower the roughness of a subset, the better is its approximation. Further, the following observations are easily obtained:

(1) As $\underline{R}(X) \subseteq X \subseteq \overline{R}(X), 0 \leq \rho_R(X) \leq 1$.
(2) By convention, when $X = \emptyset$, $\underline{R}(X) = \overline{R}(X) = \emptyset$ and $\rho_R(X) = 0$.
(3) $\rho_R(X) = 0$ if and only if X is definable in $< U, R >$.

12.2.3 *Fuzzy set*

Let U be a finite and non-empty set called universe. A fuzzy set F of U is a mapping from U into the unit interval $[0, 1]$:

$$\mu_F : U \to [0, 1]$$

where for each $x \in U$ we call $\mu_F(x)$ the membership degree of x in F. Practically, we may consider U as a set of objects of concern, and a crisp subset of U represents a non-vague concept imposed on objects in U. Then a fuzzy set F of U is thought of as a mathematical representation of a vague concept described linguistically. The support of fuzzy set F is the crisp set that contains all the elements of U that have a non-zero membership value in F [Zadeh (1965)].

A function mapping all the elements in a crisp set into real numbers in $[0, 1]$ is called a membership function. The larger value of the membership function represents the higher degree of the membership. It means how closely an element resembles an ideal element. Membership functions can represent the uncertainty using some particular functions. These functions transform the linguistic variables into numerical calculations by setting some parameters. The fuzzy decisions can then be made.

12.3 Rough-Fuzzy C-Medoids Algorithm

In this section, we first describe two existing relational clustering algorithms - hard c-medoids [Kaufman and Rousseeuw (1990)] and fuzzy c-medoids [Krishnapuram *et al.* (2001)], for selection of bio-bases. Next, we describe two relational algorithms - rough c-medoids and rough-fuzzy c-medoids, incorporating the concept of lower and upper approximations of rough sets into hard c-medoids and fuzzy c-medoids respectively. Some quantitative measures are introduced to select minimum set of most informative bio-bases.

12.3.1   Hard C-medoids

The hard c-medoids algorithm [Kaufman and Rousseeuw (1990)] uses the most centrally located object in a cluster, which is termed as the medoid. A medoid is essentially an existing data from the cluster, which is closest to the mean of the cluster.

The objective of the hard c-medoids algorithm for selection of bio-bases is to assign n subsequences to c clusters. Each of the clusters β_i is represented by a bio-basis v_i, which is the medoid for that cluster. The process begins by randomly choosing c subsequences as the bio-bases. The subsequences are assigned to one of the c clusters based on the maximum value of the non-gapped pair-wise homology alignment score $h(x_j, v_i)$ between the subsequence x_j and the bio-basis v_i. After the assignment of all the subsequences to various clusters, the new bio-bases are calculated as follows:

$$v_i = x_q \tag{12.3}$$

where q is given by

$$q = \arg\max \{h(x_k, x_j)\}; \; x_j \in \beta_i; \; x_k \in \beta_i$$

and $h(x_k, x_j)$ can be calculated as per Equation 12.2. The basic steps are outlined as follows:

(1) Arbitrarily choose c subsequences as the initial bio-bases $v_i, i = 1, 2, \cdots, c$.
(2) Assign each remaining subsequences to the cluster for the closest bio-basis.
(3) Compute the new bio-basis as per Equation 12.3.
(4) Repeat steps 2 and 3 until no more new assignments can be made.

12.3.2   Fuzzy C-medoids

This provides a fuzzification of the hard c-medoids algorithm [Krishnapuram *et al.* (2001)]. For bio-bases selection, it maximizes

$$J = \sum_{j=1}^{n} \sum_{i=1}^{c} (\mu_{ij})^{\acute{m}} \{h(x_j, v_i)\} \tag{12.4}$$

where $1 \le \acute{m} < \infty$ is the fuzzifier, $\mu_{ij} \in [0, 1]$ is the fuzzy membership of the subsequence x_j in cluster β_i, such that

$$\mu_{ij} = \sum_{l=1}^{c} \left\{ \frac{h(x_j, v_i)}{h(x_j, v_l)} \right\}^{\frac{1}{\acute{m}-1}} \tag{12.5}$$

subject to

$$\sum_{i=1}^{c} \mu_{ij} = 1, \forall j, \text{ and } 0 < \sum_{j=1}^{n} \mu_{ij} < n, \forall i.$$

The new bio-bases are calculated as:

$$v_i = x_q \qquad (12.6)$$

where q is given by

$$q = \arg \max \sum_{k=1}^{n} (\mu_{ik})^{\acute{m}} \{h(x_k, x_j)\}; \; 1 \le j \le n.$$

The algorithm proceeds as follows:

(1) Assign initial bio-bases $v_i, i = 1, 2, \cdots, c$. Choose values for fuzzifier $\acute{m}$ and threshold ϵ_1. Set iteration counter $t = 1$.
(2) Compute membership μ_{ij} by Equation 12.5 for c clusters and n subsequences.
(3) Update bio-basis v_i by Equation 12.6.
(4) Repeat steps 2 to 4, by incrementing t, until $|\mu_{ij}(t) - \mu_{ij}(t-1)| > \epsilon_1$.

12.3.3 *Rough C-medoids*

Let $\underline{A}(\beta_i)$ and $\overline{A}(\beta_i)$ be the lower and upper approximations of cluster β_i, and $B(\beta_i) = \overline{A}(\beta_i) - \underline{A}(\beta_i)$ denotes the boundary region of cluster β_i (Fig. 12.1). In rough c-medoids algorithm, the concept of c-medoids algorithm is extended by viewing each cluster β_i as an interval or rough set. However, it is possible to define a pair of lower and upper bounds $[\underline{A}(\beta_i), \overline{A}(\beta_i)]$ or a rough set for every set $\beta_i \subseteq U$, U be the set of objects of concern [Pawlak (1991)]. The family of upper and lower bounds are required to follow some of the basic rough set properties such as:

(1) an object x_j can be part of at most one lower bound;
(2) $x_j \in \underline{A}(\beta_i) \Rightarrow x_j \in \overline{A}(\beta_i)$; and
(3) an object x_j is not part of any lower bound $\Rightarrow x_j$ belongs to two or more upper bounds.

Incorporating rough sets into c-medoids algorithm, we describe rough c-medoids for generating bio-bases. It adds the concept of lower and upper bounds of rough sets into hard c-medoids algorithm. It classifies the subsequence space into two parts - lower approximation and boundary region. The bio-basis (medoid) is calculated based on the weighting average of the lower bound and boundary region. All the subsequences in lower approximation take the same weight w while

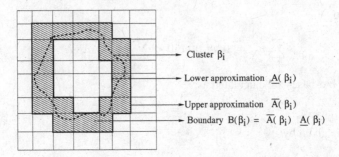

Fig. 12.1   Rough c-medoids: cluster β_i is represented by lower and upper bounds $[\underline{A}(\beta_i), \overline{A}(\beta_i)]$.

all the subsequences in boundary take another weighting index $\tilde{w}$ uniformly. Calculation of the bio-bases is modified to include the effects of lower as well as upper bounds. The modified bio-bases calculation for rough c-medoids is given by:

$$v_i = x_q \qquad (12.7)$$

where q is given by

$$q = \arg\max \begin{cases} w \times \mathcal{A} + \tilde{w} \times \mathcal{B} & \text{if } \underline{A}(\beta_i) \neq \emptyset, B(\beta_i) \neq \emptyset \\ \mathcal{A} & \text{if } \underline{A}(\beta_i) \neq \emptyset, B(\beta_i) = \emptyset \\ \mathcal{B} & \text{if } \underline{A}(\beta_i) = \emptyset, B(\beta_i) \neq \emptyset \end{cases}$$

$$\mathcal{A} = \sum_{x_k \in \underline{A}(\beta_i)} h(x_k, x_j); \quad \mathcal{B} = \sum_{x_k \in B(\beta_i)} h(x_k, x_j)$$

The parameters w and $\tilde{w}$ ($= 1 - w$) correspond to the relative importance of lower bound and boundary region. Since the subsequences lying in lower approximation definitely belong to a cluster, they are assigned a higher weight w compared to $\tilde{w}$ of the subsequences lying in boundary region. That is, $0 < \tilde{w} < w < 1$. The main steps of rough c-medoids algorithm are as follows:

(1) Assign initial bio-bases $v_i, i = 1, 2, \cdots, c$. Choose value for threshold ϵ_2.
(2) For each subsequence x_j, calculate homology alignment score $h(x_j, v_i)$ between itself and the bio-basis v_i of cluster β_i.
(3) If $h(x_j, v_i)$ is maximum for $1 \leq i \leq c$ and $h(x_j, v_i) - h(x_j, v_k) \leq \epsilon_2$, then $x_j \in \overline{A}(\beta_i)$ and $x_j \in \overline{A}(\beta_k)$. Furthermore, x_j is not part of any lower bound.
(4) Otherwise, $x_j \in \underline{A}(\beta_i)$ such that $h(x_j, v_i)$ is the maximum for $1 \leq i \leq c$. In addition, by properties of rough sets, $x_j \in \overline{A}(\beta_i)$.
(5) Compute new bio-basis as per Equation 12.7.
(6) Repeat steps 2 to 5 until no more new assignments can be made.

12.3.4 *Rough-fuzzy C-medoids*

Incorporating both fuzzy sets and rough sets, next we describe another version of c-medoids algorithm, termed as rough-fuzzy c-medoids [Maji and Pal (2007)]. The rough-fuzzy c-medoids algorithm adds the concept of fuzzy membership of fuzzy sets, and lower and upper approximations of rough sets into c-medoids algorithm. While the lower and upper bounds of rough sets deal with uncertainty, vagueness, and incompleteness in class definition, the membership of fuzzy sets enables efficient handling of overlapping partitions.

In fuzzy c-medoids, the bio-basis (medoid) depends on the fuzzy membership values of different subsequences. Whereas in rough-fuzzy c-medoids, after computing the memberships for c clusters and n subsequences, the membership values of each subsequence are sorted and the difference of two highest memberships is compared with a threshold value ϵ_2. Let μ_{ij} and μ_{kj} be the highest and second highest memberships of subsequence x_j. If $(\mu_{ij} - \mu_{kj}) > \epsilon_2$, then $x_j \in \underline{A}(\beta_i)$ as well as $x_j \in \overline{A}(\beta_i)$ and $x_j \notin \underline{A}(\beta_k)$, otherwise $x_j \in B(\beta_i)$ and $x_j \in B(\beta_k)$. That is, the algorithm first separates the "core" and overlapping portions of each cluster β_i based on the threshold value ϵ_2. The "core" portion of the cluster β_i is represented by its lower approximation $\underline{A}(\beta_i)$, while the boundary region $B(\beta_i)$ represents the overlapping portion. In effect, it minimizes the vagueness and incompleteness in cluster definition.

According to the definitions of lower approximations and boundary of rough sets, if a subsequence $x_j \in \underline{A}(\beta_i)$, then $x_j \notin \underline{A}(\beta_k), \forall k \neq i$, and $x_j \notin B(\beta_i), \forall i$. That is, the subsequence x_j is contained in β_i definitely. Thus, the weights of the subsequences in lower approximation of a cluster should be independent of other bio-bases and clusters, and should not be coupled with their similarity with respect to other bio-bases. Also, the subsequences in lower approximation of a cluster should have similar influence on the corresponding bio-basis and cluster. Whereas, if $x_j \in B(\beta_i)$, then the subsequence x_j possibly belongs to β_i and potentially belongs to another cluster. Hence, the subsequences in boundary regions should have different influence on the bio-bases and clusters.

So, in rough-fuzzy c-medoids, after assigning each subsequence in lower approximations and boundary regions of different clusters based on ϵ_2, the memberships μ_{ij} of the subsequences are modified. The membership values of the subsequences in lower approximation are set to 1, while those in boundary regions are remain unchanged. In other word, the new c-medoids first partitions the data into two classes - lower approximation and boundary. The concept of fuzzy memberships is applied only to the subsequences of boundary region, which enables the algorithm to handle overlapping clusters. Thus, in rough-fuzzy c-medoids, each cluster is represented by a bio-basis (medoid), a crisp lower approximation, and a fuzzy boundary (Fig. 12.2). The lower approximation influences the fuzziness of final partition. The fuzzy c-medoids can be reduced from rough-fuzzy c-medoids when $\underline{A}(\beta_i) = \emptyset, \forall i$. Thus, the algorithm is the generalization of existing fuzzy c-medoids algorithm.

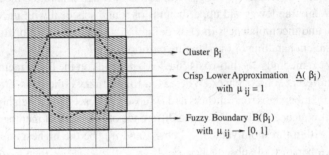

Fig. 12.2   Rough-fuzzy c-medoids: cluster β_i is represented by crisp lower bound and fuzzy boundary.

The new bio-bases are calculated based on the weighting average of the crisp lower approximation and fuzzy boundary. Computation of the bio-bases is modified to include the effects of both fuzzy membership and lower and upper bounds. Since the subsequences lying in lower approximation definitely belong to a cluster, they are assigned a higher weight compared to that of the subsequences lying in boundary region. The modified bio-bases calculation for rough-fuzzy c-medoids is therefore given by:

$$v_i = x_q \tag{12.8}$$

where q is given by

$$q = \arg\max \begin{cases} w \times \mathcal{A} + \tilde{w} \times \mathcal{B} & \text{if } \underline{A}(\beta_i) \neq \emptyset, B(\beta_i) \neq \emptyset \\ \mathcal{A} & \text{if } \underline{A}(\beta_i) \neq \emptyset, B(\beta_i) = \emptyset \\ \mathcal{B} & \text{if } \underline{A}(\beta_i) = \emptyset, B(\beta_i) \neq \emptyset \end{cases}$$

$$\mathcal{A} = \sum_{x_k \in \underline{A}(\beta_i)} h(x_k, x_j); \quad \mathcal{B} = \sum_{x_k \in B(\beta_i)} (\mu_{ik})^{\tilde{m}} h(x_k, x_j)$$

The main steps of this algorithm proceeds as follows:

(1) Assign initial bio-bases $v_i, i = 1, 2, \cdots, c$. Choose values for fuzzifier $\tilde{m}$ and thresholds ϵ_1 and ϵ_2. Set iteration counter $t = 1$.
(2) Compute membership μ_{ij} by Equation 12.5 for c clusters and n subsequences.
(3) If μ_{ij} is maximum for $1 \leq i \leq c$ and $(\mu_{ij} - \mu_{kj}) \leq \epsilon_2$, then $x_j \in \overline{A}(\beta_i)$ and $x_j \in \overline{A}(\beta_k)$. Furthermore, x_j is not part of any lower bound.

(4) Otherwise, $x_j \in \underline{A}(\beta_i)$ such that μ_{ij} is the maximum for $1 \leq i \leq c$. In addition, by properties of rough sets, $x_j \in \overline{A}(\beta_i)$.

(5) Compute new bio-basis as per Equation 12.8.

(6) Repeat steps 2 to 6, by incrementing t, until $|\mu_{ij}(t) - \mu_{ij}(t-1)| > \epsilon_1$.

12.3.5 *Selection of initial bio-basis*

A limitation of the c-medoids algorithm is that it can only achieve a local optimum solution that depends on the initial choice of the bio-bases. Consequently, computing resources may be wasted in that some initial bio-bases get stuck in regions of the input space with a scarcity of data points and may therefore never have the chance to move to new locations where they are needed. To overcome this limitation of the c-medoids algorithm, next we describe a method to select initial bio-bases, which is based on a similarity measure using amino acid mutation matrix. It enables the algorithm to converge to an optimum or near optimum solutions (bio-bases).

Prior to describe the method for selecting initial bio-bases, next we provide a quantitative measure to evaluate the similarity between two subsequences in terms of non-gapped pair-wise homology alignment score.

- Degree of resemblance (DOR): The DOR between two subsequences x_i and x_j is defined as

$$\mathrm{DOR}(x_j, x_i) = \frac{h(x_j, x_i)}{h(x_i, x_i)} \tag{12.9}$$

It is the ratio between the non-gapped pair-wise homology alignment scores of two input subsequences x_i and x_j based on an amino acid mutation matrix to the maximum homology alignment score of the subsequence x_i. It is used to quantify the similarity in terms of homology alignment score between pairs of subsequences. If functions of two subsequences are different, the DOR between them is small. A high value of $\mathrm{DOR}(x_i, x_j)$ between two subsequences x_i and x_j asserts that they may have the same function statistically. If two subsequences are same, the DOR between them is maximum, - that is, $\mathrm{DOR}(x_i, x_i) = 1$. Thus, $0 < \mathrm{DOR}(x_i, x_j) \leq 1$. Also, $\mathrm{DOR}(x_i, x_j) \neq \mathrm{DOR}(x_j, x_i)$.

Based on the concept of DOR, next we describe the method for selecting initial bio-bases. The main steps of this method proceeds as follows.

(1) For each subsequence x_i, calculate $\mathrm{DOR}(x_j, x_i)$ between itself and the subsequence $x_j, \forall_{j=1}^{n}$.

(2) Calculate similarity score between subsequences x_i and x_j

$$S(x_j, x_i) = \begin{cases} 1 \text{ if DOR}(x_j, x_i) > \epsilon_3 \\ 0 \text{ Otherwise} \end{cases}$$

(3) For each x_i, calculate total number of similar subsequences of x_i as

$$N(x_i) = \sum_{j=1}^{n} S(x_j, x_i)$$

(4) Sort n subsequences according to their values of $N(x_i)$ such that $N(x_1) > N(x_2) > \cdots > N(x_n)$.

(5) If $N(x_i) > N(x_j)$ and $\text{DOR}(x_j, x_i) > \epsilon_3$, then x_j cannot be considered as a bio-basis, resulting in a reduced set of subsequences to be considered for initial bio-bases.

(6) Let there be $\acute{n}$ subsequences in the reduced set having $N(x_i)$ values such that $N(x_1) > N(x_2) > \cdots > N(x_{\acute{n}})$. A heuristic threshold function can be defined as [Banerjee *et al.* (1998)]

$$\text{Tr} = \frac{R}{\epsilon_4}; \text{ where } R = \sum_{i=1}^{\acute{n}} \frac{1}{N(x_i) - N(x_{i+1})}$$

where ϵ_4 is a constant (= 0.5, say), so that all subsequences in reduced set having $N(x_i)$ value higher than it are regarded as the initial bio-bases.

The value of Tr is high if most of the $N(x_i)$'s are large and close to each other. The above condition occurs when a small number of large clusters are present. On the other hand, if the $N(x_i)$'s have wide variation among them, then the number of clusters with smaller size increases. Accordingly, Tr attains a lower value automatically.

Note that the main motive of introducing this threshold function lies in reducing the number of bio-bases. We attempt to eliminate noisy bio-bases (subsequence representatives having lower values of $N(x_i)$) from the whole subsequences. The whole approach is, therefore, data dependent.

12.4   Quantitative Measure

In this section we describe some quantitative indices to evaluate the quality of selected bio-bases incorporating the concepts of non-gapped pair-wise homology alignment scores and mutual information.

12.4.1 *Using homology alignment score*

Based on the non-gapped pair-wise homology alignment scores, next we introduce two indices - β index and γ index for evaluating quantitatively the quality of selected bio-bases.

- β Index: It is defined as

$$\beta = \frac{1}{c} \sum_{i=1}^{c} \frac{1}{n_i} \sum_{x_j \in \beta_i} \frac{h(x_j, v_i)}{h(v_i, v_i)} \quad (12.10)$$

$$\text{i.e., } \beta = \frac{1}{c} \sum_{i=1}^{c} \frac{1}{n_i} \sum_{x_j \in \beta_i} \text{DOR}(x_j, v_i)$$

where n_i is the number of subsequences in the ith cluster β_i and $h(x_j, v_i)$ is the non-gapped pair-wise homology alignment scores, obtained using an amino acid mutation matrix, between subsequence x_j and bio-basis v_i. The β index is the average normalized homology alignment scores of input subsequences with respect to their corresponding bio-bases. A good clustering procedure for bio-bases selection should make all input subsequences as similar to their bio-bases as possible. The β index increases with increase in homology alignment scores within a cluster. Therefore, for a given data set and c value, the higher the homology alignment scores within the clusters, the higher would be the β value. The value of β also increases with c. In an extreme case when the number of clusters is maximum, i.e., $c = n$, the total number of subsequences in the data set, we have $\beta = 1$. Thus, $0 < \beta \leq 1$.

- γ Index: It can be defined as

$$\gamma = \max_{i,j} \frac{1}{2} \left\{ \frac{h(v_j, v_i)}{h(v_i, v_i)} + \frac{h(v_i, v_j)}{h(v_j, v_j)} \right\} \quad (12.11)$$

$$\text{i.e., } \gamma = \max_{i,j} \frac{1}{2} \left\{ \text{DOR}(v_j, v_i) + \text{DOR}(v_i, v_j) \right\}$$

$0 < \gamma < 1$. The γ index calculates the maximum normalized homology alignment score between bio-bases. A good clustering procedure for bio-bases selection should make the homology alignment score between all bio-bases as low as possible. The γ index minimizes the between-cluster homology alignment score.

12.4.2 *Using mutual information*

Using the concept of mutual information, one can measure the within-cluster and between-cluster shared information. In principle, mutual information is regarded as a nonlinear correlation function and can be used to measure the mutual relation between a bio-basis and the subsequences as well as the mutual relation between each pair of bio-bases. It is used to quantify the information shared by two objects. If two independent objects do not share much information, the mutual information value between them is small. While two highly nonlinearly correlated objects will demonstrate a high mutual information value. In the present case, the objects can be the bio-bases and the subsequences.

Based on the mutual information, the β index would be as follows.

$$\overline{\beta} = \frac{1}{c} \sum_{i=1}^{c} \frac{1}{n_i} \sum_{x_j \in \beta_i} \frac{\mathrm{MI}(x_j, v_i)}{\mathrm{MI}(v_i, v_i)} \tag{12.12}$$

$\mathrm{MI}(x_i, x_j)$ is the mutual information between subsequences x_i and x_j. The mutual information $\mathrm{MI}(x_i, x_j)$ is defined as

$$\mathrm{MI}(x_i, x_j) = \mathrm{H}(x_i) + \mathrm{H}(x_j) - \mathrm{H}(x_i, x_j) \tag{12.13}$$

with $\mathrm{H}(x_i)$ and $\mathrm{H}(x_j)$ being the entropy of subsequences x_i and x_j respectively, and $\mathrm{H}(x_i, x_j)$ their joint entropy. $\mathrm{H}(x_i)$ and $\mathrm{H}(x_i, x_j)$ are defined as

$$\mathrm{H}(x_i) = -\mathrm{p}(x_i)\ln\mathrm{p}(x_i) \tag{12.14}$$

$$\mathrm{H}(x_i, x_j) = -\mathrm{p}(x_i, x_j)\ln\mathrm{p}(x_i, x_j) \tag{12.15}$$

$\mathrm{p}(x_i)$ and $\mathrm{p}(x_i, x_j)$ are the a priori probability of x_i and joint probability of x_i and x_j respectively. The $\overline{\beta}$ index is the average normalized mutual information of input subsequences with respect to their corresponding bio-bases. A bio-bases selection procedure should make the shared information between all input subsequences and their bio-bases as high as possible. The $\overline{\beta}$ index increases with increase in mutual information within a cluster. Therefore, for a given data set and c value, the higher the mutual information within the clusters, the higher would be the $\overline{\beta}$ value. The value of $\overline{\beta}$ also increases with c. When $c = n, \overline{\beta} = 1$. Thus, $0 < \overline{\beta} \leq 1$.

Similarly, γ index would be

$$\overline{\gamma} = \max_{i,j} \frac{1}{2} \left\{ \frac{\mathrm{MI}(v_i, v_j)}{\mathrm{MI}(v_i, v_i)} + \frac{\mathrm{MI}(v_i, v_j)}{\mathrm{MI}(v_j, v_j)} \right\} \tag{12.16}$$

The $\overline{\gamma}$ index calculates the maximum normalized mutual information between bio-bases. A good clustering procedure for bio-bases selection should make the shared information between all bio-bases as low as possible. The $\overline{\gamma}$ index minimizes the between-cluster mutual information.

12.5 Experimental Results

The performance of rough-fuzzy c-medoids (RFCMdd) is compared extensively with that of various other related ones. These involve different combinations of the individual components of the hybrid scheme as well as other related schemes. The algorithms compared are (i) hard c-medoids (HCMdd) [Kaufman and Rousseeuw (1990)], (ii) rough c-medoids (RCMdd), (iii) fuzzy c-medoids (FCMdd) [Krishnapuram *et al.* (2001)], (iv) method proposed by Yang et al. [Yang and Thomson (2005)] using mutual information (MI), and (v) method proposed by Berry et al. [Berry *et al.* (2004)] using genetic algorithms and Fisher ratio (GAFR). All the experiments are implemented in C language and run in LINUX environment having machine configuration Pentium IV, 3.2 GHz, 1 MB cache, and 1 GB RAM.

12.5.1 *Description of data set*

To analyze the performance of new method, we have used real data sets of five whole HIV (human immunodeficiency virus) protein sequences, Cai-Chou HIV data set [Cai and Chou (1998)], and caspase cleavage protein sequences. The initial bio-bases for different c-medoids algorithms, which represent crude clusters in the nonnumerical sequence space, have been generated by the methodology described in Section 12.3.5. The Dayhoff amino acid mutation matrix [Dayhoff *et al.* (1978); Henikoff and Henikoff (1992); Johnson and Overington (1993)] is used to calculate the non-gapped pair-wise homology alignment score between two subsequences.

12.5.1.1 *Five whole HIV protein sequences*

HIV protease belongs to the family of aspartyl proteases, which have been well-characterized as proteolytic enzymes. The catalytic component is composed of carboxyl groups from two aspartyl residues located in both NH_2- and COOH-terminal halves of the enzyme molecule in HIV protease [Pearl and Taylor (1987)]. They are strongly substrate-selective and cleavage-specific demonstrating their capability of cleaving large, virus-specific polypeptides called polyproteins between a specific pair of amino acids. Miller et al. showed that the cleavage sites in HIV polyprotein can extend to an octapeptide region [Miller *et al.* (1989)]. The amino acid residues within this octapeptide region are represented by P_4-P_3-P_2-P_1-$P_{1'}$-$P_{2'}$-$P_{3'}$-$P_{4'}$, where P_4-P_3-P_2-P_1 is the NH_2-terminal half and $P_{1'}$-$P_{2'}$-$P_{3'}$-$P_{4'}$ the COOH-terminal half. Their counterparts in the HIV protease are represented by S_4-S_3-S_2-S_1-$S_{1'}$-$S_{2'}$-$S_{3'}$-$S_{4'}$ [Chou (1993)]. The HIV protease cleavage site is exactly between P_1 and $P_{1'}$.

Table 12.1   Five whole HIV protein sequences from NCBI.

Accession No	Length	Cleavage Sites at P_1
AAC82593	500	132(MA/CA), 363(CA/p2), 377(p2/NC), 432(NC/p1), 448(p1/p6)
AAG42635	498	132(MA/CA), 363(CA/p2), 376(p2/NC), 430(NC/p1), 446(p1/p6)
AAO40777	500	132(MA/CA), 363(CA/p2), 377(p2/NC), 432(NC/p1), 448(p1/p6)
NP_057849	1435	488(TF/PR), 587(PR/RT), 1027(RT/RH), 1147(RH/IN)
NP_057850	500	132(MA/CA), 363(CA/p2), 377(p2/NC), 432(NC/p1), 448(p1/p6)

The five whole HIV protein sequences have been downloaded from NCBI (the National Center for Biotechnology Information, http://www.ncbi.nlm.nih.gov). The accession numbers are AAC82593, AAG42635, AAO40777, NP_057849, and NP_057850. Details of these five sequences are included in Table 12.1. Note that MA, CA, NC, TF, PR, RT, RH, and IN are matrix protein, capsid protein, nucleocapsid core protein, transframe peptide, protease, reverse transcriptase, RNAse, and integrase, respectively. They are all cleavage products of HIV protease. p1, p2, and p6 are also cleavage products [Chou (1996)]. For instance, 132 (MA/CA) means that the cleavage site is between the residues 132 (P_1) and 133 ($P_{1'}$) and the cleavage split the polyprotein producing two functional proteins, the matrix protein and the capsid protein. The subsequences from each of five whole protein sequences are obtained through moving a sliding window with 8 residues. Once a subsequence is produced, it is considered as functional if there is a cleavage site between P_1-$P_{1'}$, otherwise it is labeled as non-functional. The total number of subsequences with 8 residues in AAC82593, AAG42635, AAO40777, NP_057849, and NP_057850 are 493, 491, 493, 1428, and 493 respectively.

12.5.1.2   *Cai-Chou HIV data set*

In [Cai and Chou (1998)], Cai and Chou have described a benchmark data set of HIV. It consists of 114 positive oligopeptides and 248 negative oligopeptides, in total 362 subsequences with 8 residues. The data set has been collected from University of Exeter, United Kingdom.

12.5.1.3 *Caspase cleavage data set*

The programmed cell death, also known as apoptosis, is a gene-directed mechanism, which serves to regulate and control both cell death and tissue homeostasis during the development and the maturation of cells. The importance of apoptosis study is that many diseases such as cancer, ischemic damage, etc., result from apoptosis malfunction. A family of cysteine proteases called caspases, that are expressed initially in the cell as proenzymes, is the key to apoptosis [Rohn *et al*. (2004)]. As caspase cleavage is the key to programmed cell death, the study of caspase inhibitors could represent effective drugs against some disease where blocking apoptosis is desirable. Without a careful study of caspase cleavage specificity effective drug design could be difficult.

Table 12.2   Thirteen Caspase cleavage proteins from NCBI.

Proteins	Gene	Length	Cleavage sites
O00273	DFFA	331	117(C3), 224(C3)
Q07817	BCL2L1	233	61(C1)
P11862	GAS2	314	279(C1)
P08592	APP	770	672(C6)
P05067	APP	770	672(C6), 739(C3/C6/C8/C9)
Q9JJV8	BCL2	236	64(C3 and C9)
P10415	BCL2	239	34(C3)
O43903	GAS2	313	278(C)
Q12772	SREBF2	1141	468(C3 and C7)
Q13546	RIPK1	671	324(C8)
Q08378	GOLGA3	1498	59(C2), 139(C3), 311(C7)
O60216	RAD21	631	279(C3/C7)
O95155	UBE4B	1302	109(C3/C7), 123(C6)

The 13 protein sequences containing various experimentally determined caspase cleavage sites have been downloaded from NCBI (http://www.ncbi.nih.gov). Table 12.2 represents the information of these sequences. Ci depicts the ith caspase. The total number of non-cleaved subsequences is about 8340, while the number of cleaved subsequences is only 18. In total, there are 8358 subsequences with 8 residues.

12.5.2 *Example*

Consider the data set NP_057849 with sequence length 1435. The number of subsequences obtained through moving a sliding window with 8 residues is 1428. The parameters generated in the DOR based initialization method for bio-bases selection are shown next only for NP_057849 data, as an example. The values of input parameters used are also presented here.

Sequence length = 1435
Number of subsequences $n = 1428$
Value of $\epsilon_3 = 0.75$
Number of subsequences in reduced set $\acute{n} = 223$
Value of $\epsilon_4 = 0.5$; Value of Tr = 35.32
Number of bio-bases $c = 36$

Value of fuzzifier $\acute{m} = 2.0$
Values of $w = 0.7$ and $\tilde{w} = 0.3$
Parameters: $\epsilon_1 = 0.001$ and $\epsilon_2 = 0.2$

Quantitative Measures:
HCMdd: $\beta = 0.643, \gamma = 0.751, \overline{\beta} = 0.807, \overline{\gamma} = 1.000$
RCMdd: $\beta = 0.651, \gamma = 0.751, \overline{\beta} = 0.822, \overline{\gamma} = 1.000$
FCMdd: $\beta = 0.767, \gamma = 0.701, \overline{\beta} = 0.823, \overline{\gamma} = 0.956$
RFCMdd: $\beta = 0.836, \gamma = 0.681, \overline{\beta} = 0.866, \overline{\gamma} = 0.913$

The similarity score of each subsequence in original set and reduced set are shown in Fig. 12.3. The initial bio-bases for c-medoids algorithms have been obtained from reduced set using the threshold value of Tr. The initial bio-bases with similarity scores are also shown in Fig. 12.3. Each c-medoids algorithm has been evolved using these initial bio-bases. The performance obtained by the c-medoids algorithms are shown above.

12.5.3 *Performance analysis*

The experimental results on the data sets, reported in Section 12.5.1, are presented in Tables 12.3-12.9. Subsequent discussions analyze the results presented in these tables with respect to $\beta, \gamma, \overline{\beta}, \overline{\gamma}$, and execution time.

12.5.3.1 *Optimum value of parameter ϵ_3*

Table 12.3 reports the values of β, γ, $\overline{\beta}$, and $\overline{\gamma}$ of different algorithms for the data set NP_057849. Results are presented for different values of ϵ_3. Fig. 12.4 shows the similarity scores of initial bio-bases as a function of ϵ_3. The parameters generated from the data set NP_057849 are shown in Table 12.3. The value of c is computed using the method described in Section 12.3.5. It may be noted that the optimal choice of c is a function of the value ϵ_3. From Fig. 12.4, it is seen that as the value of ϵ_3 increases, the initial bio-bases, which represent the crude clusters, are becoming more prominent. The best result is achieved at $\epsilon_3 = 0.75$. The subsequences selected as initial bio-bases at $\epsilon_3 = 0.75$ have higher values of $N(x_i)$. For the purpose of comparison, c bio-bases are generated using the methods proposed by Berry et al. (GAFR) and Yang et al. (MI).

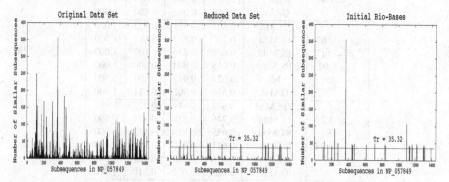

Fig. 12.3 Similarity scores of subsequences of HIV protein NP_057849 considering $\epsilon_3 = 0.75$ and $\epsilon_4 = 0.50$.

It is seen from the results of Table 12.3 that the RFCMdd achieves consistently better performance than other algorithms with respect to the values of $\beta, \gamma, \overline{\beta}$, and $\overline{\gamma}$ for different values of ϵ_3. Also, the results reported in Table 12.3 establish the fact that as the value of ϵ_3 increases, the performance of RFCMdd also increases. The best performance with respect to the values of $\beta, \gamma, \overline{\beta}$, and $\overline{\gamma}$, is achieved with $\epsilon_3 = 0.75$. At $\epsilon_3 = 0.75$, the values of $N(x_i)$ for most of the subsequences in reduced data set are large and close to each other. So, the threshold Tr attains a higher value compared to that of other values of ϵ_3. In effect, the subsequences selected as initial bio-bases with $\epsilon_3 = 0.75$, have higher values of $N(x_i)$. Hence, the quality of generated clusters using different c-medoids algorithms is better compared to other values of ϵ_3.

12.5.3.2 *Random versus DOR based initialization*

Tables 12.4 and 12.5 provide comparative results of different c-medoids algorithms with random initialization of bio-bases and the DOR based initialization method described in Section 12.3.5 considering $\epsilon_3 = 0.75$. The DOR based initialization is found to improve the performance in terms of $\beta, \gamma, \overline{\beta}$, and $\overline{\gamma}$ as well as reduce the time requirement of all c-medoids algorithms. It is also observed that HCMdd with DOR based initialization performs similar to RFCMdd with random

Table 12.3   Performance of different algorithms on NP_057849.

Parameters	Algorithms	β	γ	$\bar{\beta}$	$\bar{\gamma}$
$\epsilon_3 = 0.60$ $\acute{n} = 15$ Tr = 4.05 $c = 13$	RFCMdd	0.736	0.914	0.817	1.000
	FCMdd	0.719	0.914	0.805	1.000
	RCMdd	0.612	0.938	0.805	1.000
	HCMdd	0.607	0.938	0.801	1.000
	MI	0.611	0.944	0.813	1.000
	GAFR	0.609	0.962	0.804	1.000
$\epsilon_3 = 0.65$ $\acute{n} = 34$ Tr = 6.02 $c = 26$	RFCMdd	0.801	0.821	0.822	1.000
	FCMdd	0.746	0.837	0.811	1.000
	RCMdd	0.632	0.836	0.807	1.000
	HCMdd	0.618	0.844	0.800	1.000
	MI	0.624	0.913	0.801	1.000
	GAFR	0.616	0.902	0.811	1.000
$\epsilon_3 = 0.70$ $\acute{n} = 84$ Tr = 16.58 $c = 27$	RFCMdd	0.801	0.819	0.822	0.982
	FCMdd	0.746	0.828	0.811	0.996
	RCMdd	0.635	0.829	0.812	1.000
	HCMdd	0.621	0.827	0.803	1.000
	MI	0.625	0.913	0.801	1.000
	GAFR	0.618	0.902	0.810	1.000
$\epsilon_3 = 0.75$ $\acute{n} = 223$ Tr = 35.32 $c = 36$	RFCMdd	0.836	0.681	0.866	0.913
	FCMdd	0.767	0.701	0.823	0.956
	RCMdd	0.651	0.751	0.822	1.000
	HCMdd	0.643	0.751	0.807	1.000
	MI	0.637	0.854	0.802	1.000
	GAFR	0.646	0.872	0.811	1.000
$\epsilon_3 = 0.80$ $\acute{n} = 594$ Tr = 28.05 $c = 6$	RFCMdd	0.682	0.937	0.809	1.000
	FCMdd	0.667	0.941	0.805	1.000
	RCMdd	0.604	0.941	0.805	1.000
	HCMdd	0.605	0.938	0.807	1.000
	MI	0.611	0.938	0.811	1.000
	GAFR	0.608	0.957	0.803	1.000

initialization, although it is expected that RFCMdd is superior to HCMdd in partitioning subsequences. While in random initialization, the c-medoids algorithms get stuck in local optimums, the DOR based scheme enables the algorithms to converge to an optimum or near optimum solutions. In effect, the execution time required for different c-medoids is lesser in DOR based initialization compared to random initialization.

12.5.3.3   *Optimum values of parameters $\acute{m}$, w, and ϵ_2*

The fuzzifier $\acute{m}$ has an influence on the clustering performance of both RFCMdd and FCMdd. Similarly, the performance of RFCMdd and RCMdd depends on the parameter w and the threshold ϵ_2. Tables 12.6-12.8 report the performance of different c-medoids algorithms for different values of $\acute{m}$, w and ϵ_2 respectively.

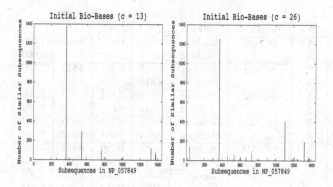

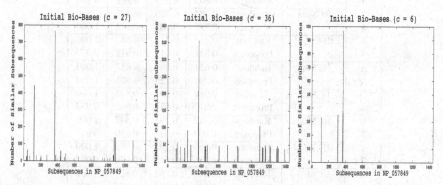

Fig. 12.4 Similarity scores of initial bio-bases of HIV protein NP_057849 for different values of ϵ_3 considering $\epsilon_4 = 0.50$. (a) $\epsilon_3 = 0.60$ and Tr = 4.05; (b) $\epsilon_3 = 0.65$ and Tr = 6.02; (c) $\epsilon_3 = 0.70$ and Tr = 16.58; (d) $\epsilon_3 = 0.75$ and Tr = 35.32; (e) $\epsilon_3 = 0.80$ and Tr = 28.05.

The results and subsequent discussions are presented in these tables with respect to $\beta, \gamma, \overline{\beta}$, and $\overline{\gamma}$.

The fuzzifier $\acute{m}$ controls the extent of membership sharing between fuzzy clusters. From Table 12.6, it is seen that as the value of $\acute{m}$ increases, the values of β and $\overline{\beta}$ increase, while γ and $\overline{\gamma}$ decrease. The RFCMdd and FCMdd achieve their best performance with $\acute{m} = 2.0$ for HIV protein NP_057849, $\acute{m} = 1.9$ and 2.0 for Cai-Chou HIV data set, and $\acute{m} = 2.0$ for caspase cleavage protein sequences respectively. But, for $\acute{m} > 2.0$, the performance of both algorithms decreases with the increase in $\acute{m}$. That is, the best performance of RFCMdd and FCMdd is achieved when the fuzzy membership value of a subsequence in a cluster is equal to its normalized homology alignment score with respect to all the bio-bases.

The parameter w has an influence on the performance of RFCMdd and RCMdd. Since the subsequences lying in lower approximation definitely belong to a cluster, they are assigned a higher weight w compared to $\tilde{w}$ of the sub-

Table 12.4 Performance of different c-medoids algorithms.

Data	Algorithms	Bio-bases	β	γ	$\bar{\beta}$	$\bar{\gamma}$
A	HCMdd	Random	0.615	0.817	0.809	1.000
A		Proposed	0.719	0.702	0.852	1.000
C	FCMdd	Random	0.655	0.791	0.821	1.000
8		Proposed	0.814	0.680	0.901	0.956
2	RCMdd	Random	0.674	0.813	0.825	1.000
5		Proposed	0.815	0.677	0.872	0.983
9	RFCMdd	Random	0.713	0.728	0.847	0.987
3		Proposed	0.874	0.633	0.913	0.916
A	HCMdd	Random	0.657	0.799	0.803	1.000
A		Proposed	0.714	0.664	0.853	1.000
G	FCMdd	Random	0.698	0.706	0.818	1.000
4		Proposed	0.807	0.674	0.892	0.924
2	RCMdd	Random	0.685	0.709	0.812	1.000
6		Proposed	0.768	0.681	0.882	1.000
3	RFCMdd	Random	0.717	0.719	0.847	1.000
5		Proposed	0.831	0.611	0.912	0.957
A	HCMdd	Random	0.651	0.864	0.837	1.000
A		Proposed	0.794	0.723	0.881	1.000
O	FCMdd	Random	0.718	0.804	0.842	1.000
4		Proposed	0.817	0.634	0.912	0.977
0	RCMdd	Random	0.717	0.791	0.847	1.000
7		Proposed	0.809	0.633	0.879	0.977
7	RFCMdd	Random	0.759	0.793	0.890	1.000
7		Proposed	0.856	0.613	0.930	0.947
N	HCMdd	Random	0.601	0.882	0.801	1.000
P		Proposed	0.643	0.751	0.807	1.000
0	FCMdd	Random	0.606	0.802	0.811	1.000
5		Proposed	0.767	0.701	0.823	0.956
7	RCMdd	Random	0.600	0.811	0.801	1.000
8		Proposed	0.651	0.751	0.822	1.000
4	RFCMdd	Random	0.698	0.798	0.804	1.000
9		Proposed	0.836	0.681	0.866	0.913
N	HCMdd	Random	0.611	0.913	0.792	1.000
P		Proposed	0.714	0.719	0.801	1.000
0	FCMdd	Random	0.648	0.881	0.796	1.000
5		Proposed	0.784	0.692	0.886	0.983
7	RCMdd	Random	0.639	0.895	0.794	1.000
8		Proposed	0.758	0.702	0.826	0.993
5	RFCMdd	Random	0.702	0.824	0.803	1.000
0		Proposed	0.851	0.629	0.911	0.928

sequences lying in boundary regions. Hence, for both RFCMdd and RCMdd, $0 < \tilde{w} < w < 1$. Table 12.7 presents the performance of RFCMdd and RCMdd for different values w considering $\acute{m} = 2.0$ and $\epsilon_2 = 0.20$. When the subsequences of both lower approximation and boundary region are assigned approximately equal weights, the performance of RFCMdd and RCMdd is significantly

Table 12.5 Execution Time (milli sec) of Different c-Medoids Algorithms.

Methods	Bio-bases	AAC8 2593	AAG4 2635	AAO4 0777	NP_05 7849	NP_05 7850
RFCMdd	Random	10326	17553	16218	316764	18038
	Proposed	8981	12510	13698	251058	11749
FCMdd	Random	7349	16342	11079	293264	13217
	Proposed	5898	11998	9131	240834	9174
RCMdd	Random	6108	13816	8053	268199	10318
	Proposed	5691	8015	5880	160563	5895
HCMdd	Random	2359	2574	2418	8728	2164
	Proposed	535	534	532	4397	529

poorer than HCMdd. As the value of w increases, the values of β and $\overline{\beta}$ increase, while γ and $\overline{\gamma}$ decrease. The best performance of both algorithms is achieved with $w = 0.70$. The performance significantly reduces with $w \simeq 1.00$. In this case, since the clusters cannot see the subsequences of boundary regions, the mobility of the clusters and the bio-bases reduces. As a result, some bio-bases get stuck in local optimum. On the other hand, when the value of $w = 0.70$, the subsequences of lower approximations are assigned a higher weight compared to that of boundary regions as well as the clusters and the bio-bases have a greater degree of freedom to move. In effect, the quality of generated clusters is better compared to other values of w.

The performance of RFCMdd and RCMdd also depends on the value of ϵ_2, which determines the class labels of all the subsequences. In other word, the RFCMdd and RCMdd partition the data set of a cluster into two classes - lower approximation and boundary, based on the value of ϵ_2. Table 12.8 presents the comparative performance of RFCMdd and RCMdd for different values of ϵ_2 considering $\acute{m} = 2.0$ and $w = 0.70$. For $\epsilon_2 = 0.0$, all the subsequences will be in lower approximations of different clusters and $B(\beta_i) = \emptyset, \forall i$. In effect, both RFCMdd and RCMdd reduce to conventional HCMdd. On the other hand, for $\epsilon_2 = 1.0$, $\underline{A}(\beta_i) = \emptyset, \forall i$ and all the subsequences will be in the boundary regions of different clusters. That is, the RFCMdd boils down to FCMdd. The best performance of RFCMdd and RCMdd with respect to β, $\overline{\beta}$, γ, and $\overline{\gamma}$ is achieved with $\epsilon_2 = 0.2$, which is approximately equal to the average difference of highest and second highest fuzzy membership values of all the subsequences. In practice, we find that both RFCMdd and RCMdd work well for $\epsilon_2 = \delta$, where

$$\delta = \frac{1}{n} \sum_{j=1}^{n} (\mu_{ij} - \mu_{kj}) \qquad (12.17)$$

n is the total number of subsequences, μ_{ij} and μ_{kj} are the highest and second highest fuzzy membership values of the subsequence x_j. The values of δ for HIV protein NP_057849, Cai-Chou HIV data set, and caspase cleavage proteins are 0.197, 0.201, and 0.198 respectively.

12.5.3.4 *Comparative performance of different algorithms*

Finally, Table 12.9 provides the comparative results of different algorithms for the protein sequences reported in Section 12.5.1. It is seen that the RFCMdd with DOR based initialization produces bio-bases having the highest β and $\overline{\beta}$ values and lowest γ and $\overline{\gamma}$ values for all the cases. Table 12.9 also provides execution time (in milli sec.) of different algorithms for all protein data sets. The execution time required for RFCMdd is comparable to MI and GAFR. For the HCMdd, although the execution time is less, the performance is significantly poorer than that of RCMdd, FCMdd, and RFCMdd.

Following conclusions can be drawn from the results reported in Tables 12.3-12.9:

(1) It is observed that RFCMdd is superior to HCMdd both with random and DOR based initialization. However, HCMdd requires considerably less time compared to RFCMdd. But, the performance of HCMdd is significantly poorer than RFCMdd. The performance of FCMdd and RCMdd are intermediate between RFCMdd and HCMdd.

(2) The DOR based initialization is found to improve the values of β, γ, $\overline{\beta}$, and $\overline{\gamma}$ as well as reduce the time requirement substantially for all c-medoids algorithms.

(3) Use of rough sets and fuzzy sets adds a small computational load to the HCMdd algorithm; however the corresponding integrated methods (FCMdd, RCMdd, and RFCMdd) show a definite increase in β and $\overline{\beta}$ values and decrease in γ and $\overline{\gamma}$ values.

(4) Integration of three components - rough sets, fuzzy sets, and c-medoids, in the RFCMdd algorithm produces minimum set of most informative bio-bases in the least computation time compared to MI and GAFR.

(5) It is observed that the RFCMdd algorithm requires significantly less time compared to MI and GAFR having comparable performance. Reduction in time is achieved due to DOR based initialization. The DOR based initialization reduces the convergence time of the RFCMdd algorithm considerably compared to random initialization.

The best performance of the RFCMdd algorithm in terms of β, γ, $\overline{\beta}$, and $\overline{\gamma}$ is achieved due to the following three reasons:

(1) the DOR based initialization of bio-bases enables the algorithm to converge to an optimum or near optimum solutions;

Table 12.6   Performance of RFCMdd and FCMdd for different values of fuzzifier $\acute{m}$.

Value of $\acute{m}$	Algorithms	HIV Protein NP_057849				Cai-Chou HIV Data Set				Caspase Cleavage Proteins			
		β	γ	β	$\bar{\gamma}$	β	γ	β	$\bar{\gamma}$	β	γ	β	$\bar{\gamma}$
1.5	RFCMdd	0.759	0.744	0.832	0.997	0.755	0.714	0.867	0.992	0.748	0.662	0.882	0.989
	FCMdd	0.699	0.733	0.811	1.000	0.732	0.753	0.824	1.000	0.734	0.678	0.871	1.000
1.6	RFCMdd	0.762	0.717	0.839	0.966	0.781	0.692	0.878	0.979	0.773	0.658	0.899	0.985
	FCMdd	0.716	0.726	0.814	1.000	0.739	0.749	0.833	0.994	0.761	0.677	0.882	1.000
1.7	RFCMdd	0.799	0.702	0.843	0.956	0.794	0.677	0.895	0.950	0.785	0.647	0.907	0.977
	FCMdd	0.725	0.746	0.817	1.000	0.750	0.728	0.868	0.973	0.772	0.671	0.883	0.978
1.8	RFCMdd	0.814	0.695	0.852	0.947	0.818	0.639	0.907	0.932	0.803	0.628	0.923	0.972
	FCMdd	0.738	0.729	0.818	0.985	0.764	0.695	0.890	0.954	0.795	0.671	0.890	0.978
1.9	RFCMdd	0.831	0.681	0.858	0.913	0.829	0.618	0.911	0.927	0.814	0.611	0.937	0.965
	FCMdd	0.755	0.702	0.821	0.972	0.809	0.656	0.903	0.941	0.808	0.668	0.898	0.962
2.0	RFCMdd	0.836	0.681	0.866	0.913	0.829	0.618	0.911	0.927	0.839	0.608	0.942	0.944
	FCMdd	0.767	0.701	0.823	0.956	0.809	0.656	0.903	0.941	0.816	0.662	0.901	0.953
2.1	RFCMdd	0.835	0.684	0.861	0.927	0.811	0.622	0.908	0.945	0.826	0.617	0.935	0.949
	FCMdd	0.754	0.701	0.820	0.956	0.802	0.671	0.901	0.948	0.801	0.665	0.899	0.973
2.2	RFCMdd	0.817	0.699	0.847	0.931	0.802	0.640	0.903	0.958	0.817	0.639	0.928	0.954
	FCMdd	0.751	0.722	0.813	0.978	0.767	0.692	0.892	0.977	0.798	0.665	0.895	0.973
2.3	RFCMdd	0.816	0.712	0.847	0.959	0.791	0.658	0.882	0.961	0.801	0.641	0.901	0.961
	FCMdd	0.734	0.759	0.809	0.991	0.760	0.703	0.877	0.982	0.784	0.668	0.886	0.979
2.4	RFCMdd	0.802	0.712	0.835	0.959	0.774	0.699	0.878	0.967	0.792	0.642	0.894	0.961
	FCMdd	0.712	0.771	0.808	1.000	0.752	0.726	0.876	0.983	0.763	0.672	0.885	0.981
2.5	RFCMdd	0.795	0.751	0.829	0.984	0.767	0.711	0.863	0.967	0.785	0.657	0.887	0.979
	FCMdd	0.701	0.771	0.801	1.000	0.751	0.744	0.854	0.989	0.755	0.673	0.874	0.996

Table 12.7   Performance of RFCMdd and RCMdd for different values of parameter w ($= 1 - \bar{w}$).

Value of w	Algorithms	HIV Protein NP_057849			Cai-Chou HIV Data Set			Caspase Cleavage Proteins			
		β	γ	$\bar{\gamma}$	β	γ	$\bar{\gamma}$	β	γ	β	$\bar{\gamma}$
0.51	RFCMdd	0.632	0.941	1.000	0.684	0.827	1.000	0.683	0.714	0.808	1.000
	RCMdd	0.604	0.952	1.000	0.649	0.856	1.000	0.668	0.733	0.781	1.000
0.55	RFCMdd	0.637	0.839	1.000	0.739	0.743	1.000	0.727	0.688	0.833	1.000
	RCMdd	0.604	0.844	1.000	0.718	0.807	1.000	0.714	0.709	0.803	1.000
0.60	RFCMdd	0.648	0.750	0.983	0.788	0.708	0.991	0.779	0.649	0.883	0.983
	RCMdd	0.617	0.766	1.000	0.731	0.733	1.000	0.762	0.697	0.837	1.000
0.65	RFCMdd	0.817	0.708	0.934	0.811	0.633	0.958	0.821	0.622	0.927	0.957
	RCMdd	0.644	0.761	1.000	0.763	0.694	0.998	0.774	0.680	0.852	1.000
0.70	RFCMdd	0.836	0.681	0.913	0.829	0.618	0.927	0.839	0.608	0.942	0.944
	RCMdd	0.651	0.751	1.000	0.771	0.677	0.993	0.782	0.673	0.887	1.000
0.75	RFCMdd	0.819	0.713	0.940	0.807	0.627	0.951	0.838	0.611	0.939	0.953
	RCMdd	0.647	0.758	1.000	0.764	0.698	1.000	0.771	0.684	0.858	1.000
0.80	RFCMdd	0.766	0.784	0.992	0.793	0.651	0.978	0.817	0.622	0.914	0.964
	RCMdd	0.645	0.821	1.000	0.753	0.704	1.000	0.753	0.702	0.851	1.000
0.85	RFCMdd	0.713	0.839	1.000	0.781	0.692	0.991	0.804	0.647	0.887	1.000
	RCMdd	0.642	0.861	1.000	0.747	0.718	1.000	0.736	0.719	0.843	1.000
0.90	RFCMdd	0.648	0.841	1.000	0.748	0.711	1.000	0.761	0.682	0.825	1.000
	RCMdd	0.641	0.862	1.000	0.736	0.727	1.000	0.708	0.732	0.816	1.000
0.95	RFCMdd	0.639	0.862	1.000	0.702	0.774	1.000	0.728	0.711	0.814	1.000
	RCMdd	0.635	0.865	1.000	0.698	0.781	1.000	0.681	0.753	0.803	1.000
0.99	RFCMdd	0.602	0.968	1.000	0.671	0.813	1.000	0.675	0.762	0.798	1.000
	RCMdd	0.601	0.968	1.000	0.671	0.813	1.000	0.674	0.762	0.794	1.000

Table 12.8   Performance of RFCMdd and RCMdd for different values of parameter ϵ_2.

Value of ϵ_2	Algorithms	HIV Protein NP_057849				Cai-Chou HIV Data Set				Caspase Cleavage Proteins			
		β	γ	β	$\bar{\gamma}$	β	γ	β	$\bar{\gamma}$	β	γ	β	$\bar{\gamma}$
0.00	RFCMdd	0.643	0.751	0.807	1.000	0.713	0.782	0.817	1.000	0.707	0.698	0.862	1.000
	RCMdd	0.643	0.751	0.807	1.000	0.713	0.782	0.817	1.000	0.707	0.698	0.862	1.000
0.05	RFCMdd	0.704	0.723	0.812	1.000	0.753	0.707	0.868	1.000	0.766	0.683	0.881	1.000
	RCMdd	0.644	0.751	0.810	1.000	0.716	0.754	0.839	1.000	0.723	0.687	0.863	1.000
0.10	RFCMdd	0.793	0.709	0.837	0.981	0.794	0.683	0.882	0.991	0.801	0.641	0.907	0.995
	RCMdd	0.647	0.751	0.814	1.000	0.738	0.726	0.841	1.000	0.738	0.681	0.872	1.000
0.15	RFCMdd	0.811	0.702	0.855	0.946	0.806	0.629	0.902	0.964	0.819	0.622	0.928	0.973
	RCMdd	0.651	0.751	0.819	1.000	0.744	0.694	0.856	1.000	0.764	0.678	0.879	1.000
0.20	RFCMdd	0.836	0.681	0.866	0.913	0.829	0.618	0.911	0.927	0.839	0.608	0.942	0.944
	RCMdd	0.651	0.751	0.822	1.000	0.771	0.677	0.897	0.993	0.782	0.673	0.887	1.000
0.25	RFCMdd	0.836	0.707	0.852	0.936	0.811	0.638	0.907	0.952	0.814	0.631	0.932	0.980
	RCMdd	0.651	0.792	0.819	1.000	0.759	0.698	0.881	1.000	0.767	0.692	0.855	1.000
0.30	RFCMdd	0.817	0.718	0.844	0.990	0.805	0.681	0.894	0.988	0.791	0.667	0.908	0.995
	RCMdd	0.648	0.828	0.801	1.000	0.738	0.731	0.878	1.000	0.741	0.723	0.839	1.000
0.35	RFCMdd	0.801	0.739	0.831	1.000	0.784	0.704	0.875	1.000	0.772	0.671	0.881	1.000
	RCMdd	0.631	0.857	0.779	1.000	0.706	0.757	0.849	1.000	0.728	0.756	0.814	1.000
0.40	RFCMdd	0.792	0.784	0.804	1.000	0.757	0.762	0.872	1.000	0.759	0.699	0.863	1.000
	RCMdd	0.629	0.914	0.758	1.000	0.681	0.796	0.826	1.000	0.719	0.779	0.794	1.000
0.45	RFCMdd	0.716	0.833	0.796	1.000	0.732	0.783	0.850	1.000	0.706	0.737	0.827	1.000
	RCMdd	0.617	0.957	0.792	1.000	0.667	0.817	0.803	1.000	0.678	0.793	0.779	1.000
0.50	RFCMdd	0.708	0.864	0.781	1.000	0.713	0.805	0.813	1.000	0.684	0.798	0.769	1.000
	RCMdd	0.617	0.962	0.781	1.000	0.659	0.836	0.793	1.000	0.659	0.822	0.746	1.000

Table 12.9   Comparative performance of different methods.

Data Set	Algorithms	β	γ	$\overline{\beta}$	$\overline{\gamma}$	Time
AAC8 2593	RFCMdd	0.847	0.633	0.913	0.916	8981
	FCMdd	0.814	0.680	0.901	0.956	5898
	RCMdd	0.815	0.677	0.872	0.983	5691
	HCMdd	0.719	0.702	0.852	1.000	535
	MI	0.764	0.788	0.906	0.977	8617
	GAFR	0.736	0.814	0.826	1.000	12213
AAG4 2635	RFCMdd	0.831	0.611	0.912	0.957	12510
	FCMdd	0.807	0.674	0.892	0.924	11998
	RCMdd	0.768	0.681	0.882	1.000	8015
	HCMdd	0.714	0.664	0.853	1.000	534
	MI	0.732	0.637	0.829	0.989	13082
	GAFR	0.707	0.713	0.801	1.000	12694
AAO4 0777	RFCMdd	0.856	0.613	0.930	0.947	13698
	FCMdd	0.817	0.634	0.912	0.977	9131
	RCMdd	0.809	0.633	0.879	0.977	5880
	HCMdd	0.794	0.723	0.881	1.000	532
	MI	0.801	0.827	0.890	0.982	12974
	GAFR	0.773	0.912	0.863	1.000	11729
NP_05 7849	RFCMdd	0.836	0.681	0.866	0.913	251058
	FCMdd	0.767	0.701	0.823	0.956	240834
	RCMdd	0.651	0.751	0.822	1.000	160563
	HCMdd	0.643	0.751	0.807	1.000	4397
	MI	0.637	0.854	0.802	1.000	250138
	GAFR	0.646	0.872	0.811	1.000	291413
NP_05 7850	RFCMdd	0.851	0.629	0.911	0.928	11749
	FCMdd	0.784	0.692	0.886	0.983	9174
	RCMdd	0.758	0.702	0.826	0.993	5895
	HCMdd	0.714	0.719	0.801	1.000	529
	MI	0.736	0.829	0.833	1.000	9827
	GAFR	0.741	0.914	0.809	1.000	10873
Cai-Chou HIV Data	RFCMdd	0.829	0.618	0.911	0.927	6217
	FCMdd	0.809	0.656	0.903	0.941	4083
	RCMdd	0.771	0.677	0.897	0.993	3869
	HCMdd	0.713	0.782	0.817	1.000	718
	MI	0.764	0.774	0.890	1.000	6125
	GAFR	0.719	0.794	0.811	1.000	7016
Caspase Cleavage	RFCMdd	0.839	0.608	0.942	0.944	513704
	FCMdd	0.816	0.662	0.901	0.953	510961
	RCMdd	0.782	0.673	0.887	1.000	473380
	HCMdd	0.707	0.698	0.862	1.000	8326
	MI	0.732	0.728	0.869	1.000	511628
	GAFR	0.713	0.715	0.821	1.000	536571

(2) membership function of fuzzy sets handles efficiently overlapping partitions; and

(3) the concept of lower and upper bounds of rough sets deals with uncertainty, vagueness, and incompleteness in class definition.

In effect, the minimum set of bio-bases having maximum information are obtained using RFCMdd algorithm.

12.6 Conclusion

The contribution of the chapter is three fold, namely,

(1) the development of a methodology integrating the merits of rough sets, fuzzy sets, c-medoids algorithm, and amino acid mutation matrix for bio-bases selection;
(2) defining new measures based on mutual information and non-gapped pairwise homology alignment score to evaluate the quality of selected bio-bases; and
(3) demonstrating the effectiveness of the RFCMdd algorithm, along with a comparison with other algorithms, on different types of protein data sets.

The concept of "degree of resemblance" is found to be successful in effectively circumventing the initialization and local minima problems of iterative refinement clustering algorithms like c-medoids. In addition, this concept enables efficient selection of a minimum set of most informative bio-bases compared to existing methods. Although the methodology of integrating rough sets, fuzzy sets, and c-medoids algorithm has been efficiently demonstrated for biological sequence analysis, the concept can be applied to other relational unsupervised classification problems.

Bibliography

Altschul, S. F., Boguski, M. S., Gish, W. and Wootton, J. C. (1994). Issues in Searching Molecular Sequence Databases, *Nature Genet.* **6**, pp. 119–129.

Altschul, S. F., Gish, W., Miller, W., Myers, E. and Lipman, D. J. (1990). Basic Local Alignment Search Tool, *J. Molec. Biol.* **215**, pp. 403–410.

Asharaf, S., Shevade, S. K. and Murty, M. N. (2005). Rough Support Vector Clustering, *Pattern Recognition* **38**, pp. 1779–1783.

Banerjee, M., Mitra, S. and Pal, S. K. (1998). Rough Fuzzy MLP: Knowledge Encoding and Classification, *IEEE Transactions on Neural Networks* **9**, 6, pp. 1203–1216.

Berry, E. A., Dalby, A. R. and Yang, Z. R. (2004). Reduced Bio-Basis Function Neural Network for Identification of Protein Phosphorylation Sites: Comparison with Pattern Recognition Algorithms, *Computational Biology and Chemistry* **28**, pp. 75–85.

Cai, Y. D. and Chou, K. C. (1998). Artificial Neural Network Model for Predicting HIV Protease Cleavage Sites in Protein, *Advances in Engineering Software* **29**, 2, pp. 119–128.

Chou, K. C. (1993). A Vectorised Sequence-Coupling Model for Predicting HIV Protease Cleavage Sites in Proteins, *J. Biol. Chem.* **268**, pp. 16938–16948.

Chou, K. C. (1996). Prediction of Human Immunodeficiency Virus Protease Cleavage Sites in Proteins, *Anal. Biochem.* **233**, pp. 1–14.

Dayhoff, M. O., Schwartz, R. M. and Orcutt, B. C. (1978). A Model of Evolutionary Change in Proteins. Matrices for Detecting Distant Relationships, *Atlas of Protein Sequence and Structure* **5**, pp. 345–358.

De, S. K. (2004). A Rough Set Theoretic Approach to Clustering, *Fundamenta Informaticae* **62**, 3-4, pp. 409–417.

Dubois, D. and H.Prade (1990). Rough Fuzzy Sets and Fuzzy Rough Sets, *International Journal of General Systems* **17**, pp. 191–209.

Henikoff, S. and Henikoff, J. G. (1992). Amino Acid Substitution Matrices from Protein Blocks, *PNSA* **89**, pp. 10915–10919.

Hirano, S. and Tsumoto, S. (2003). An Indiscernibility-Based Clustering Method with Iterative Refinement of Equivalence Relations: Rough Clustering, *Journal of Advanced Computational Intelligence and Intelligent Informatics* **7**, 2, pp. 169–177.

Johnson, M. S. and Overington, J. P. (1993). A Structural Basis for Sequence Comparisons: An Evaluation of Scoring Methodologies, *J. Molec. Biol.* **233**, pp. 716–738.

Kaufman, L. and Rousseeuw, P. J. (1990). *Finding Groups in Data, An Itroduction to Cluster Analysis* (JohnWiley & Sons, Brussels, Belgium).

Krishnapuram, R., Joshi, A., Nasraoui, O. and Yi, L. (2001). Low Complexity Fuzzy Relational Clustering Algorithms for Web Mining, *IEEE Transactions on Fuzzy System* **9**, pp. 595–607.

Lingras, P. and West, C. (2004). Interval Set Clustering of Web Users with Rough K-means, *Journal of Intelligent Information Systems* **23**, 1, pp. 5–16.

Maji, P. and Pal, S. K. (2007). Rough-Fuzzy C-Medoids Algorithm and Selection of Bio-Basis for Amino Acid Sequence Analysis, *IEEE Transactions on Knowledge and Data Engineering* **19**, 6, pp. 859–872.

Miller, M., Schneider, J., Sathayanarayana, B. K., Toth, M. V., Marshall, G. R., Clawson, L., Selk, L., Kent, S. B. H. and Wlodawer, A. (1989). Structure of Complex of Synthetic HIV-1 Protease with Substrate-Based Inhibitor at 2.3 Resolution, *Science* **246**, pp. 1149–1152.

Mitra, S., Banka, H. and Pedrycz, W. (2006). Rough-Fuzzy Collaborative Clustering, *IEEE Transactions on Systems, Man, and Cybernetics, Part B: Cybernetics* **36**, 4, pp. 795–805.

Pal, S. K., Gupta, B. D. and Mitra, P. (2004). Rough Self Organizing Map, *Applied Intelligence* **21**, 3, pp. 289–299.

Pal, S. K. and Mitra, P. (2002). Multispectral Image Segmentation Using the Rough Set-Initialized-EM Algorithm, *IEEE Transactions on Geoscience and Remote Sensing* **40**, 11, pp. 2495–2501.

Pal, S. K., Mitra, S. and Mitra, P. (2003). Rough-Fuzzy MLP: Modular Evolution, Rule Generation, and Evaluation, *IEEE Transactions on Knowledge and Data Engineering* **15**, 1, pp. 14–25.

Pawlak, Z. (1991). *Rough Sets, Theoretical Aspects of Resoning About Data* (Dordrecht, The Netherlands: Kluwer).

Pearl, L. H. and Taylor, W. R. (1987). A Structural Model for the Retroviral Proteases, *Nature* **329**, pp. 351–354.

Qian, N. and Sejnowski, T. J. (1988). Predicting the Secondary Structure of Globular Proteins Using Neural Network Models, *J. Molec. Biol.* **202**, pp. 865–884.

Rohn, T. T., Cusack, S. M., Kessinger, S. R. and Oxford, J. T. (2004). Caspase Activaion Independent of Cell Death is Required for Proper Cell Dispersal and Correct Morphology in PC12 Cells, *Experimental Cell Research* **293**, pp. 215–225.

Skowron, A., Swiniarski, R. W. and Synak, P. (2005). Approximation Spaces and Information Granulation, *Transactions on Rough Sets* **3**, pp. 175–189.

Thomson, R., Hodgman, C., Yang, Z. R. and Doyle, A. K. (2003). Characterising Proteolytic Cleavage Site Activity Using Bio-Basis Function Neural Network, *Bioinformatics* **19**, pp. 1741–1747.

Yang, Z. R. and Thomson, R. (2005). Bio-Basis Function Neural Network for Prediction of Protease Cleavage Sites in Proteins, *IEEE Transactions on Neural Networks* **16**, 1, pp. 263–274.

Zadeh, L. A. (1965). Fuzzy Sets, *Information and Control* **8**, pp. 338–353.

Chapter 13

Knowledge Reuse in the Design of Models of Computational Intelligence

Witold Pedrycz

Department of Electrical and Computer Engineering, University of Alberta,
Edmonton, Canada and Systems Research Institute Polish Academy of Sciences,
Warsaw, Poland
pedrycz@ee.ualberta.ca

In this study, we discuss the concept of knowledge reuse in Computational Intelligence (CI) by showing how the CI constructs could be formed by reconciling data and a suite of existing models. As the models are reflective of the available knowledge being formed on a basis of existing data, their use is effectively a sound mechanism of knowledge reuse. We introduce a certain performance index whose minimization helps establish the most effective level of knowledge reuse (viz. a level of reliance on the existing models). Fuzzy rule-based systems are used as a comprehensive example which illustrates the algorithmic details of the proposed approach. Furthermore we show, by making use of the principle of justifiable granularity, how the parameters of the rules can be represented in the form of information granules, and triangular fuzzy numbers in particular.

13.1 Introduction

System modeling realized in the setting of Computational Intelligence has brought a vast array of new approaches and algorithmic enhancements. The methodology of CI which is strongly established through the unified and highly collaborative use of its underlying information technologies of fuzzy sets (and granular computing, in general), neural networks and evolutionary optimization has offered a new avenue of analysis and synthesis (design) of intelligent systems. In the context of the design of intelligent systems we are usually faced with various sources of data in terms of their quality, granularity and origin. We may encounter large quantities of numeric data coming from noisy sensors, linguistic findings conveyed by rules and associations and perceptions offered by human observers. Given the enormous diversity of the sources of data and knowledge the ensuing quality of data deserves careful attention. Knowledge reuse and knowledge sharing have been playing a vital role in knowledge management which has become amplified over the time once we encounter information systems of increasing complexity and of a distributed nature.

In spite of the evident diversity of available models of CI, all of them exploit the existing data in order to establish a structure of the respective model and estimate its parameters. This general observation equally well applies to regression models, neural networks, cognitive maps, rule-based systems, fuzzy systems [Campello and Amaral (2006); Cao *et al.* (1997); Casillas *et al.* (2003); Cordón *et al.* (2003); Fasol and J̈orgl (1980); Gaweda and Zurada (2003); Janikow (1998); Mencar *et al.* (2006); Mitra and Hayashi (2000); Molina *et al.* (2006); Pedrycz and Gomide (2007); Serra and Bottura (2007); Tekegi and Sugeno (1985); Yen *et al.* (1998)]. With regard to the way in which the data are used, we encounter several fundamental problems that require careful attention. Generalization capabilities of the models rely in a direct manner on the characteristics of data (in particular their representative capabilities with respect to the problem at hand) and the nature of the model itself. The characteristics of data deserve particular attention in case we encounter small data sets which could be also biased by some noise. The models developed on a basis of the limited and noisy data set typically exhibit low prediction capabilities. A certain alleviation of the problem of this nature could be realized by contemplating reliance on other sources of knowledge about the system to be modeled where they might have been acquired in the past. They are not necessarily data themselves (whose accessibility could be limited to various reasons) but could be available as knowledge conveyed by the models. In the anticipated modeling scenario, it becomes advantageous not only consider currently available data but also actively exploit previously obtained findings. Such observations bring us to the following formulation of the problem:

Given some experimental and limited data of a certain quality, construct a model which is consistent with the findings (models) produced for some previously available data. Owing to the existing requirements such as privacy or security of data as well as some other technical limitations, in the construction of the model an access to these previous data is not available however we can take advantage of the already acquired knowledge available in the form of the model.

Considering the need to achieve a certain desired consistency of the proposed model with the previous findings, we refer to the development of such models as experience-consistent modeling. Thus the resulting models are constructs which directly reuse accumulated knowledge. In this sense, the study can be positioned at the junction of the CI and knowledge reuse.

In the experience-consistent models we may encounter a number of essential limitations which imply a way in which the underlying processing can be realized. For instance, it is common that the currently available data are quite limited in terms of its size (which implies a limited evidence of the data set) while the previously available data sets could be substantially larger meaning that relying on the models formed in the past could be beneficial for the development of the current model.

In what follows, we adhere to the following scheme and notation. A currently available data set using which we construct the model is denoted by D. It consists of the pairs of data $(\mathbf{x}_k, y_k)$, k=1, 2, ..., N. The previously collected data sets are denoted by $D_1, D_2, \ldots, D_P$. An interaction between the data sites (and ensuing local constructs) is visualized in Figure 13.1. Note that any possible interaction between the models occurs at the level of knowledge links (that are clearly distinguished from the data links as shown in the figure).

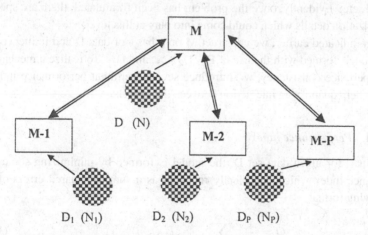

Fig. 13.1 Two types of links (data and knowledge links) between D and Di's realized indirectly through passing the parameters of the models available at $D_1, D_2, \ldots, D_P$.

The study is organized as follows. We start with a general problem formulation (Section 13.2). Here we formulate a suitable performance index and discuss a way of expressing a level of knowledge reuse and elaborate on a way of its optimization. Further refinement of the process of knowledge reuse is presented as well; we show that the relevance of various sources of knowledge could be quantified vis--vis the locally available data which are directly used in the formation of the model. Fuzzy rule-based models are discussed in the setting of experience-consistent design. The reuse of knowledge requires a coordination of the components of the models, which calls for a certain scheme of alignment of information granules (presented in Section13.4). The principle of justifiable granularity presented in Section13.5 becomes instrumental in the overall characterization of the rule-based fuzzy model; here we show that conclusions of the rules can be represented in the form of information granules subsequently leading to the notion of fuzzy regression and fuzzy regression models.

13.2   Problem Formulation

The model to be developed is generally described by $M(\mathbf{x}; \mathbf{a})$ where $\mathbf{a}$ denotes a vector of parameters and $\mathbf{x}$ stands for the input variables. As emphasized, as we strive for the generality of our investigations, the model "M" could be viewed as any CI construct, say a fuzzy rule-based model, neural network, regression model, etc. Evidently, once the problem has been formulated, there are specific optimization details which could come into play at this level.

As indicated earlier, we construct M on a basis of data D and influenced by the models formed with the use of $D_1, D_2, \ldots,$ and D_P. To realize a mechanism of experience consistency, we introduce several pertinent performance indexes which help quantify an interaction between the models.

13.2.1   *Performance index*

As usual, for given data set D, the model is formed by minimizing some performance index which is typically regarded as a sum of squared errors of the following format

$$Q = \frac{1}{N} \sum_{\substack{x_k \in D \\ y_k \in D}} \| M(\mathbf{x}_k, \mathbf{a}) - \mathrm{y}_k \|^2 \qquad (13.1)$$

With each data site (data set) $D_1, D_2, \ldots. D_p$ we associate its local model $M_i i(\mathbf{x}, \mathbf{a}[ii])$ described by its vector of its parameters $\mathbf{a}[ii]$, ii=1,2,...P. To arrive at a transparent notation, the indexes shown in squared brackets refer to the specific data set. The crux of the consistency-driven modeling is to form the model on a basis of D while making the model follow close the individual models formed for the respective D_i's. Using the following performance index we strike a balance between the model formed exclusively on a basis of data D and the consistency of the model with the results produced by the models formed on a basis of some other data sites D_i's

$$V = \frac{1}{N} \sum_{\substack{x_k \in D \\ y_k \in D}} \| M(\mathbf{x}_k, \mathbf{a}) - y_k \|^2 + \alpha \sum_{j=1}^{P} \sum_{\substack{x_k \in D \\ y_k \in D}} \| M(\mathbf{x}_k, \mathbf{a}) - M_{ii}(\mathbf{x}_k, \mathbf{a}[j]) \|^2 z$$

(13.2)

The minimization of V for some predefined value of a leads to the optimal collection of the parameters of the model. Denote the vector of these parameters by $\mathbf{a}_{opt}$. An overall balance captured by (2) is achieved for a certain value of a. Here a general tendency becomes clearly visible: higher values of a stress higher relevance of other models and their more profound impact on the constructed model. The essence of the minimized performance index is schematically illustrated in Figure13.2(a). Observe that the assessment of consistency is realized by making use of the data set D. First, the model is constructed on the basis of D. Second, the consistency is expressed on a basis of differences between the constructed model and those models coming from D_is where the differences are assessed with the use of data D. There is yet another interesting view at the format of the minimized performance index. The second component in V plays a role that is similar to that of a regularization term (which might be referred to as knowledge-based regularization) being typically used in estimation problems. Note however that its origin here is substantially different from the one encountered in the literature. In other words, we consider other data (and models) rather than focusing on the complexity of the model quantified in terms of its parameters and their number.

For given value of a, the details of the minimization of V depend on the nature of the model. In some cases, one could develop an analytical expression leading to the global minimum of V. More often we have to resort ourselves to some learning scheme.

13.2.2 *Optimization of the level of knowledge reuse*

While the meaning of the performance index (2) is straightforward, a choice of a specific numeric value of a requires attention. The general tendency is obvious: higher values of a stress the relevance of knowledge reuse. The value of α being equal to zero brings us back to the design of the model in which we exclusively

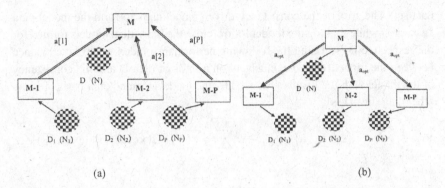

(a)   (b)

Fig. 13.2   Minimization of the performance index V - a schematic view at the construction of the model (a) and a way of the maximization of consistency of the model across all data sets (b).

rely on locally available data and ignore whatever knowledge could be taken into consideration. To optimize the level of contribution coming from the data sets, we may adhere to the following evaluation process which consists of two fundamental components. The quality of the optimal model is evaluated with respect to data D. The same optimized model is transferred to each D_i (viz. the parameters of the model are made available at D_i) and its quality is evaluated there. We combine the results (viz. the corresponding squared errors) by adding their normalized values. Given these observations, the index quantifying a global behavior of the optimal model arises in the following form

$$VV = \frac{1}{N} \sum_{\substack{x_k \in D \\ y_k \in D}} \| M(\mathbf{x}_k, \mathbf{a}_{\mathrm{opt}}) - \mathrm{y}_k \|^2 + \sum_{j=1}^{P} \frac{1}{N} \sum_{\substack{x_k \in D_j \\ y_k \in D_j}} \| M(\mathbf{x}_k, \mathbf{a}_{\mathrm{opt}}) - \mathrm{y}_k \|^2$$

(13.3)

Apparently the expression of VV is a function of and the optimized level of consistency is that for which VV attaints its minimal value, namely

$$\alpha_{opt} = \arg Min_{\alpha} VV(\alpha)$$

(13.4)

A schematic view of computing realized with the aid of (3) is presented in Figure13.2(b). The optimization process is useful not only to determine the minimum of VV but also to reveal its character of VV regarded as a function α. Some illustrative example plots of the relationship are shown in Figure13.3. The intensity of knowledge reuse could depend on numerous factors including the models themselves and the quality of the individual data sets.

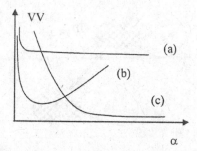

Fig. 13.3　Plots of example relationships of VV regarded as a function : (a) limited need of knowledge reuse with the value of a close to zero, (b) existence of clearly delineated level of knowledge reuse which manifests as a minimum of VV, and (c) monotonic behavior of VV pointing at high values of with the monotonically decreasing values of VV. In this case some saturation effect takes place: higher values of do not change the values of VV.

13.2.3　*Refinement of knowledge reuse*

The optimization scheme (2) along with its evaluation mechanisms governed by (3) can be generalized by admitting various levels of impact each data D_i could have in the process of achieving consistency. We introduce some positive weights (weight factors) $w_i, i = 1, 3, \ldots p$ which are used in the slightly augmented performance index

$$V = \frac{1}{N} \sum_{\substack{x_k \in D \\ y_k \in D}} \| M(\mathbf{x}_k, \mathbf{a}) - y_k \|^2 + \alpha \sum_{j=1}^{P} w_j \sum_{\substack{x_k \in D \\ y_k \in D}} \| M(\mathbf{x}_k, \mathbf{a}) - M_j(\mathbf{x}_k, \mathbf{a}[j]) \|^2$$

$$(13.5)$$

Lower values of w_i indicate lower influence of the model formed on a basis of data D_i when constructing the model for data D. The role of such weights is particularly apparent when dealing with data D_i which are in some temporal or spatial relationships with respect to D. In these circumstances, the values of the weights are reflective of how far (in terms of time or distance) the sources of the individual data are positioned vis-a-vis D. For instance, if D_j denotes a collection of data gathered some time ago in comparison to the currently collected data D_i, then it is intuitively clear that the weight w_j is lower than w_i.

While both the temporal as well as spatial distribution of data sets are well justified and intuitively appealing, we can arrive at specific numeric values of the weights by computing the performance of the model for data D and D_{ii}. More specifically, see Figure13.4, we determine the following expressions

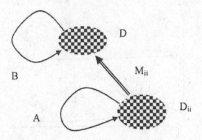

Fig. 13.4 Computing the weight $w_i i$ through assessing the performance of the model $M_i i$ formed for $D_i i$ and afterwards assessed on data sets D and $D_i i$.

$$A = \frac{1}{N_{ii}} \sum_{\substack{x_k \in D \\ y_k \in D}} \| M_{ii}(\mathbf{x}_k, \mathbf{a}[ii]) - y_k \|^2 \qquad (13.6)$$

and

$$B = \frac{1}{N} \sum_{\substack{x_k \in D \\ y_k \in D}} \| M_{ii}(\mathbf{x}_k, \mathbf{a}) - y_k \|^2 \qquad (13.7)$$

If we have the inequality $A \leq B$ (and this relationship typically holds), the value of w_{ii} is determined as

$$w_{ii} = 1 - \frac{|B - A|}{B}, B \neq 0 \qquad (13.8)$$

As we stressed, the scheme discussed above is general in the sense that no assumption has been made as to the structure of the models. Interestingly, the mechanism of experience consistency is equally applicable to neural networks, nonlinear regression models and fuzzy models, just to provide some examples. Furthermore when running the experience consistency development, we may encounter a variety of models involved in this process, $M_1, M_2, \ldots, M_P$.

13.3 Fuzzy Rule-based Models and Their Experience-consistent Design

Fuzzy rule-based models are interesting examples of fuzzy models assuming a predominant position in fuzzy modeling, see Takagi and Sugeno [Tekegi and Sugeno (1985)]. For this category of models we develop the detailed schemes of knowledge reuse. The underlying architectural details of the rule-based model are outlined as follows. For each data site D and $D_i i$, we consider the rules with local regression models assuming the form

Data D

$$\text{-if } \mathbf{x} \text{ is } B_i \text{ then } y = \mathbf{a}_i^T \mathbf{x} \tag{13.9}$$

where $\mathbf{x} \in \mathbf{R}^{n+1}$ and Bi are information granules- fuzzy sets, cf. [Zadeh (1997)], defined in the n-dimensional input space, i=1, 2, ..., c. The local regression model standing in the i-th rule is a linear regression function described by a certain vector of parameters $\mathbf{a}_i$. More specifically, the n-dimensional vector of the original input variables is augmented by a constant input so we have $\mathbf{x} = [x_1 x_2 \ldots x_n \ 1]^T$ and $\mathbf{a} = .[a_1 a_2 \ldots a_n a_0]^T$ where a_0 stands for a bias term that translates the location of the original hyperplane.

The same number of rules (c) is encountered at all other data sites, $D_1, D_2, \ldots, D_P$. The format of the rules is also the same as for D, for the ii-th data sited $D_i i$ we obtain

$$\text{-if } \mathbf{x} \text{ is } B_i[ii] \text{ then } y = \mathbf{a}_i[ii]^T \mathbf{x} \tag{13.10}$$

As before the fuzzy sets in the condition part of the i-th rule are denoted by $B_i[ii]$ while the parameters of the local model are denoted by $\mathbf{a}_i[ii]$. Following the accepted notation, let us recall that the index in the square brackets refers to the specific data site, that is D_{ii} for $\mathbf{a}_i[ii]$. The rule-based system is denoted by FM when it concerns D and FM[j] for D_j.

Alluding to the format of the data at D, it comes in the form of input - output pairs (x_k, y_k), k=1, 2, ..., N which are used to carry out learning in a supervised mode. The previously collected data sets denoted by $D_1, D_2, \ldots, D_P$ consists of $N_1, N_2,$ and N_P data points.

Given the architecture of the rule-based system, it is well known that we encounter here two fundamental design phases, that is (a) a formation of the fuzzy sets standing in the conditions of the rules and (b) the estimation of the corresponding conclusion parts. There are numerous ways of carrying out this construction. Typically, when it comes to the condition parts of the rules, the essence of the design is to granulate data by forming a collection of fuzzy sets. The common technique relates to fuzzy clustering when the condition part of the rule involves a fuzzy set defined in $\mathbf{R}_n$ or a Cartesian product of fuzzy sets defined in $\mathbf{R}$. These fuzzy sets are fully characterized by the prototypes we constructed during data clustering. The conclusion part where we encounter local regression models is formed by estimating the parameters $\mathbf{a}_i$. Such an estimation process is standard to a high extent as it is nothing but a global minimization of the well-known squared error criterion. The fuzzy model for D_j can be represented in the form of the parameters $\{(\mathbf{v}_i[j], \mathbf{a}_i[j])\}$, $i = 1, 2, \ldots, c$ and these parameters are sufficient to communicate the model when reusing available knowledge.

The organization of the consistency-driven knowledge reuse relies on the reconciliation of the conclusion parts of the rules. We assume that the condition parts, viz. fuzzy sets are developed independently from each other. In other words, we cluster data in the input space of $D, D_1, \ldots, D_P$ assuming the same number of clusters (c) which results in the same collection of rules. Then the mechanism of experience consistency is realized for the conclusions of the rules. Given the independence of the construction process of the clusters at the individual sites, before moving on with the quantification of the obtained consistency of the conclusion parts of the rules, it becomes necessary to align the information granules obtained at D and the individual data sites D_i.

The calculations of $FM[j](\mathbf{x}_k)$ for some $\mathbf{x}_k$ in D require some words of explanation. The model is communicated to D by transferring the prototypes of the clusters (fuzzy sets) and the coefficients of the linear models standing in the conclusions of the rules refer to Figure 13.5.

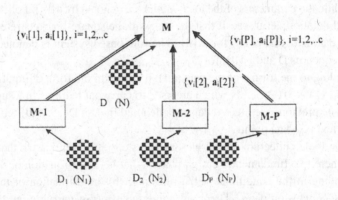

Fig. 13.5 Communication between D and D_j realized by transferring parameters of the rule-based model available at individual data sites D_j.

When used at D, the prototypes $\mathbf{v}_i[j]$, $i = 1, 2, \ldots, c$ give rise to an induced partition matrix in which the k-th column (for data $\mathbf{x}_k$) assumes the following membership values $w_i(\mathbf{x}_k)$ computed in the standard manner as already being encountered when running the FCM algorithm, that is

$$w_i(w_k)[j] = \frac{1}{\sum_{l=1}^{c} \left(\frac{\| x_k - v_j[j] \|}{\| x_k - v_l[j] \|} \right)^{\frac{2}{2-m}}} \tag{13.11}$$

The transferred parameters of the local models obtained at the j-th data site produce the output of the model FM[j]($\mathbf{x}_k$) obtained at D as a weighted sum of the form, refer to Takagi and Sugeno[Tekegi and Sugeno (1985)]

$$\text{FM}[j](\mathbf{x}_k) = \sum_{i=1}^{c} w_i(\mathbf{x}_k)[j] a_i^T[j] \mathbf{x}_k \tag{13.12}$$

where $\mathbf{x}_k \in D$.

The minimization of the performance index V for some predefined value of α leads to the optimal vectors of the parameters of the linear models a_i(opt), i=1, 2,..., c which is reflective of the process of satisfying the consistency constraints.

The estimation of the parameters $a_1, a_2, \ldots, a_c$ follows a standard least-square error minimization problem. We introduce here some auxiliary notation which leads to the more concise notation. The output of the model comes as a weighted sum of each of the local models

$$\hat{y}_k = \sum_{i=1}^{c} w_i(\mathbf{x}_k) a_i^T \mathbf{x}_k \tag{13.13}$$

To arrive at the optimal parameters of the local linear models, we introduce some notation which makes the formulation of the problem more concise and readable. First, each input data is weighted by the membership degree of the individual cluster thus yielding an (n+1) vector $\hat{\mathbf{x}}_{lk} = u_{lk} \mathbf{x}_k$ the above fuzzy model (12) can be written down in a matrix format as

$$\hat{y}_k = [\hat{\mathbf{x}}_{lk}^T \ \hat{\mathbf{x}}_{2k}^T \ldots \hat{\mathbf{x}}_{ck}^T] \begin{bmatrix} a_1 \\ a_2 \\ \\ a_c \end{bmatrix} \tag{13.14}$$

Here all parameters of the models are collected in the form of a single c(n+1)-dimensional vector such that

$$a = \begin{bmatrix} a_1 \\ a_2 \\ \\ a_c \end{bmatrix} \tag{13.15}$$

The input data transformed through the fuzzy sets (clusters) are organized in a single matrix $\hat{X}$ with N rows and c(n+1) columns. Furthermore collect all outputs in a single vector y with the entries

$$y = \begin{bmatrix} y_1 \\ y_2 \\ \vdots \\ y_n \end{bmatrix} \tag{13.16}$$

Let us consider the performance index in the following form

$$Q = \|\mathbf{y} - \hat{X}\mathbf{a}\|^2 + \alpha\|\mathbf{y}_1 - \hat{X}\mathbf{a}\|^2 + \alpha\|\mathbf{y}_2 - \hat{X}\mathbf{a}\|^2 + \ldots + \alpha\|\mathbf{y}_p - \hat{X}\mathbf{a}\|^2 \tag{13.17}$$

The vectors $\mathbf{y}_1, \mathbf{y}_2, \ldots, \mathbf{y}_P$ denote the outputs produced by the consecutive fuzzy models developed for $D_1, D_2, \ldots,$ and D_P. Taking the gradient of Q with respect to $\mathbf{a}$, we obtain

$$\begin{aligned}
\nabla_a Q = &-\hat{X}^T y - \hat{X}^T y + 2(\hat{X}^T \hat{X})\mathbf{a} - \alpha(\hat{X}^T y_1 + \hat{X}^T y_1) + 2\alpha(\hat{X}^T \hat{X})\mathbf{a} \\
&-\alpha(\hat{X}^T y_2 + \hat{X}^T y_2) + 2\alpha(\hat{X}^T \hat{X})\mathbf{a} \ldots - \alpha(\hat{X}^T y_p + \hat{X}^T y_p) \\
&+2\alpha(\hat{X}^T \hat{X})\mathbf{a}
\end{aligned} \tag{13.18}$$

By zeroing the gradient of Q, $\nabla_a Q = \mathbf{0}$, we arrive at the global minimum to the optimization problem

$$\begin{aligned}
\mathbf{a}_{opt} &= \tfrac{1}{\alpha P+1}(\hat{X}^T \hat{X})^{-1}\hat{X}^T(y + \alpha y_1 + \alpha y_2 + \ldots \alpha y_p) = \\
&= \tfrac{1}{\alpha P+1}\hat{X}^{\#}(y + \alpha y_1 + \alpha y_2 + \ldots + \alpha y_p)
\end{aligned} \tag{13.19}$$

where $\hat{X}^{\#}$ is the pseudoinverse of the data matrix. In what follows, we also introduce a computationally effective measure articulating a level of experience consistency obtained for D in the form of granular characterization of the parameters of local regression models. Before moving with the details, we elaborate on a way in which individual rules existing in the models formed for D and the data sites $D_1, D_2, \ldots, D_p$ are "synchronized" (aligned).

13.4   The Alignment of Information Granules

The rules forming each fuzzy model have been formed independently at each data site. If we intend to evaluate a level of consistency of the rules at D vis--vis the modeling evidence available at D_j, some alignment of the rules become essential. Such an alignment concerns a way of lining up the prototypes forming the condition part of the rules. We consider the models obtained at D and $D_j, j=1, 2, \ldots, P$ with their prototypes $\mathbf{v}_1, \mathbf{v}_2, \ldots, \mathbf{v}_c$ and $\mathbf{v}_1[j], \mathbf{v}_2[j], \ldots, \mathbf{v}_c[j]$. We say that the rule "i" at D and the rule "l" at D_j are aligned if the prototypes $\mathbf{v}_k$ and $\mathbf{v}_l[j]$ are the closest within the collections of the prototypes produced for D and D_j. The alignment process is realized by successively finding the pairs of the prototypes being characterized by the lowest mutual distance. Overall, the alignment process can be described in the following manner:

Form two sets of integers (indexes) $\mathbf{I}$ and $\mathbf{J}$, where $\mathbf{I} = \mathbf{J} = \{1, 2, \ldots, c\}$. Start with an empty list of alignments, $\mathbf{L} = \emptyset$.

Repeat

Find a pair of indexes i_0 and j_0 for which the distance attains minimum
$$(i_0, j_0) = \arg \min_{i,l} \ \|\mathbf{v}_i - \mathbf{v}_l(j)\|$$
The pair (i_0, j_0) is added to the list of alignments, $\mathbf{L} = \mathbf{L} \bigcup (i_0, j_0)$

Reduce the set of indexes I and J by removing the elements that were placed on the list of alignments, $\mathbf{I} = \mathbf{I} \setminus i_0$ and $\mathbf{J} = \mathbf{J} \setminus j_0$

until $\mathbf{I} = \emptyset$

Once the above loop has been completed, we end up with the list of alignment of the prototypes in the form of pairs $(i_1, j_1), (i_2, j_2), \ldots, (i_c, j_c)$

13.5 Granular Characterization of Experience-consistent Rule-based Models

Once the mechanism of experience consistency has been completed and the local models have been aligned (following the scheme provided in the previous section), we can now look at the characterization of the set of the related parameters of the local regression models. In essence, through the alignment of the prototypes ad D and D_j, we obtain the corresponding vectors of the parameters of the regression models of the conclusion parts. Denote these vectors corresponding to a certain rule by $\mathbf{a}, \mathbf{a}_j, \mathbf{a}_k, \ldots,$ and $\mathbf{a}_l$ altogether arriving at P+1 of them. If we now consider the j-th coordinate of all of them, we obtain the numeric values a_j, $a_{ij}, \ldots, a_{lj}$. The essence of their aggregation concerns their global representation completed in the form of a single fuzzy set. Its whose modal value is just a_j while the membership function is reflective of the numeric values of the corresponding parameters of the local models. The principle of justifiable granularity introduced by Pedrycz and Vukovich[Pedrycz and Vukovich (2002)] follows this observation. Let us consider a finite number of numeric values $\{a_j, a_{ij}, \ldots, a_{lj}\}$ refer to Figure13.6. We intend to span a unimodal fuzzy set A over data a_j in such a way that it represents these data to the highest possible extent. The form of the membership is also defined in advance. For instance, we could consider a certain type of membership functions, say triangular, Gaussian, parabolic, etc. Furthermore we consider that a modal value of A_j, that is a_j is given. Let us look at the values of a_{ji} that are lower than a_j, $a_{ji} ¡ a_j$. Denote this set by Ω, $\Omega =$

$\{a_{ji}|a_{ji} < a_j\}$.We use them to estimate the parameters of the left-hand side of the membership function. The determination of the right-hand side of the member-ship function is realized in an analogous manner by considering the set $\Omega+$ where $\Omega= \{a_{ji}|a_{ji} > a_j\}$.

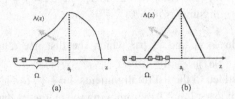

(a)   (b)

Fig. 13.6 Computing of a membership function of A realized on a basis of numeric evidence. Small dark boxes denote available experimental data. The same estimation procedure applies to the right-hand portion of the membership function of the fuzzy set (a) Construction of the triangular fuzzy set in which the linear segments are rotated around the modal value of the membership function (b).

There are two fundamental requirements guiding the design of this fuzzy set (Pedrycz and Vukovich[Pedrycz and Vukovich (2002)]), namely

(a) maximization the experimental evidence behind the fuzzy set; this implies that we tend to "cover" as many numeric data as possible, viz. the coverage has to be made as high as possible. Graphically, in the optimization of this re-quirement, we adjust the parameter(s) of the membership function that make it shrink or expand so that more data are embraced. Normally, the sum of the membership grades $\sum_{a_{ji}\in\Omega} A(a_{ji})$ where A is the increasing portion of the membership function to be optimized and a_{ji} is located to the left to the modal value (a_j) has to be maximized

(b) Simultaneously, we would like to make the fuzzy set as specific as possible so that is comes with some well defined semantics. This requirement is met by making the support of A as small as possible, that is $\min_a - a_j$ -a— where "a" is the lower end of the support.

To accommodate these two conflicting requirements, we have to combine (a) and (b) into a form of a single scalar index which in turn becomes maximized. A certain alternative is described as follows

$$\min_{a\neq a_j} = \frac{\sum_{a_{ji}\in\Omega} A_{ji}}{|a_j - a|} \qquad (13.20)$$

In particular, we can consider a linear form of the membership function. In this case the optimization can be visualized as a process of rotating the linear portion of the membership function; see Figure 13.6(b). The linearly decreasing portion of the membership function positioned at the right-hand side of the modal value (a_j) is optimized in the same manner. The result of the aggregation becomes a triangular fuzzy number of the j-th parameter of the local regression model. Denote it by $A_j = (a_{j-}, a_j, a_{j+})$ with the three parameters denoting the lower, modal, and upper bound of the fuzzy number. Applying the same procedure to all remaining parameters of the vector **a**, we produce the corresponding fuzzy numbers $A_1, A_2, \ldots, A_{j-1}, A_{j+1}, \ldots, A_n$, and A_0. Given them the rule in D reflects the nature of the incorporated evidence offered by the remaining models D_1, D_2, etc. If there is a fairly high level of consistency, this effect is manifested through a fairly "concentrated" fuzzy number. Increasing inconsistency results in a broader, less specific fuzzy number of the parameters. In summary, a certain fuzzy rule assumes the following format

$$\text{If } x \text{ is } B \text{ then } Y = A_0 \oplus A_1 \otimes x_1 \oplus A_2 \otimes x_2 \oplus \ldots \oplus A_n \otimes x_n \qquad (13.21)$$

The symbols $\oplus$ and $\otimes$ being used above underline the nonnumeric nature of the arguments standing in the model over which the multiplication and addition are carried out. For given numeric inputs $\mathbf{x} = [x_1, x_2, \ldots, x_n]^T$ the resulting output Y of this local regression model is again a triangular fuzzy number $Y = <w, y, z>$ where their parameters are computed as follows

Modal value $\quad y = a_0 + a_1 x_1 + a_2 x_2 + \ldots + a_n x_n$

Lower bound $w = a_0 + \min(a_1 - x_1, a_1 + x_1) + \min(a_2 - x_2, a_2 + x_2)$
$\qquad + \ldots + \min(a_n - x_n, a_n + x_n)$

Upper bound $z = a_0 + \max(a_1 - x_1, a_1 + x_1) + \max(a_2 - x_2, a_2 + x_2)$
$\qquad + \ldots + \max(a_n - x_n, a_n + x_n)$

$$(13.22)$$

The above process is of the formation of the fuzzy numbers of the local regression model of the rule is repeated for all rules. At the end we arrive at the rules of the form

$$\text{If } x \text{ is } B_1 \text{ then } Y = A_{10} \oplus A_{11} \otimes x_1 \oplus A_{12} \otimes x_2 \oplus \ldots A_{1n} \otimes x_n$$
$$\text{If } x \text{ is } B_2 \text{ then } Y = A_{20} \oplus A_{21} \otimes x_1 \oplus A_{22} \otimes x_2 \oplus \ldots A_{2n} \otimes x_n$$
$$\ldots \qquad\qquad (13.23)$$
$$\text{If } x \text{ is } B_c \text{ then } Y = A_{c0} \oplus A_{c1} \otimes x_1 \oplus A_{c2} \otimes x_2 \oplus \ldots A_{cn} \otimes x_n$$

Given this structure, the input vector **x** implies the output fuzzy set with the following membership function

$$Y = \sum_{i=1}^{c} w_i \mathbf{x} \otimes [A_{i0} \oplus (a_{i1} \otimes x_1) \oplus (a_{i2} \otimes x_2) \oplus \ldots \oplus (a_{in} \otimes x_n)] \qquad (13.24)$$

Owing to the fact of having fuzzy sets of the parameters of the regression model in the conclusion part of the rules, Y becomes a fuzzy number rather than a single numeric value.

13.6   Conclusions

In this study, we have raised an issue of knowledge reuse in the setting of constructs of Computational Intelligence. One could note that the knowledge-based component (viz. previously constructed models) can serve as a certain form of the regularization mechanism encountered quite often in various modeling platforms. The optimization procedure applied there helps us strike a sound balance between the data-driven and knowledge-driven evidence. We introduced a general scheme of optimization and showed an effective way of reusing knowledge. We demonstrated the details in relation to fuzzy rule-based models. Given the multiplicity of the sources of knowledge, it was shown that as result of this, the parameters of the local regression models standing in the conclusions of the rules can be described as fuzzy numbers. In this sense, the principle of justifiable granularity gives rise to so-called fuzzy linear regression models. It is important to note that the granularity of the fuzzy numbers of the parameters of the local regression models becomes helpful in the quantification of the reconciled differences between the sources of knowledge. The experience-based modeling could be realized when dealing with a variety of models available at each data site D_j and this facet of knowledge reuse underlines the generality of the assumed approach.

Acknowledgements

Support from the Natural Sciences and Engineering Research Council of Canada (NSERC) and Canada Research Chair (CRC) is gratefully acknowledged.

Bibliography

Campello, R. J .G. B. and Caradori do Amaral, W. (2006), Hierarchical fuzzy relational models: linguistic interpretation and universal approximation, *IEEE Trans. on Fuzzy Systems*, **14**, (3), pp. 446–453.

Cao, S. G., Rees, N. W. and Feng, G. (1997), Analysis and design for a class of complex control systems, *Part I and Part II, Automatica*, **33**, (6), pp. 1017–1028, and **33**, (6), pp. 1029–1039.

Casillas, J. et al. (eds.) (2003), *Interpretability Issues in Fuzzy Modeling*, Springer Verlag, Berlin.

Cord´on, O., Herrera, F. and Zwir, I. (2003), A hierarchical knowledge-based environment for linguistic modeling: models and iterative methodology, *Fuzzy Sets and Systems*, **138**, (2), pp. 307–341.

Fasol K. H., and Jörgl, H. P. (1980), Principles of model building and identifi cation, *Automatica*, **16**, (5), pp. 505–518.

Gaweda, A. and Zurada, J. (2003), Data-driven linguistic modeling using relational fuzzy rules, *IEEE Trans. Fuzzy Systems*, **11**, (1), pp. 121–134.

Janikow, C. (1998), Fuzzy decision trees: issues and methods, *IEEE Trans. Systems Man, Cybernetics-Part B*, **28**, (1), pp. 1–14.

Mencar, C. Castellano, G. and Fanelli, A. (2006), Interface optimality in fuzzy inference systems, *Int. Journal of Approximate Reasoning*, **41**, (2), pp. 128–145.

Mitra, S. and Hayashi, Y. (2000), Neuro-fuzzy rule generation: survey in soft computing framework, *IEEE Transaction on Neural Networks*, **11**, (3), pp. 748–768.

Molina, C., Rodrguez-Ariza, L., S´anchez , D. and Amparo Vila, M. (2006), A new fuzzy multidimensional model, *IEEE Trans. on Fuzzy Systems*, **14**, (6), pp. 897–912.

Pedrycz, W. and Vukovich, G. (2001), On elicitation of membership functions, *IEEE Trans. on Systems, Man, and Cybernetics, Part B*, **32**, pp. 761–767.

Pedrycz, W. (2005), *Knowledge-Based Clustering: From Data to Information Granules*, J. Wiley, Hoboken, NJ.

Pedrycz, W. and Gomide, F. (2007), *Fuzzy Systems Engineering*, J. Wiley, Hoboken, NJ.

Serra, G. and Boṭṭura, C. (2007), An IV-QR algorithm for neuro-fuzzy multivariable online identifi cation, *IEEE Trans. on Fuzzy Systems*, **15**, (2), pp. 200–210.

Takagi, T. and Sugeno, M. (1985), Fuzzy identifi cation of systems and its application to modelling and control, *IEEE Trans. on Systems, Man, and Cybernetics*, **15**, pp. 116–132.

Yen, J., Wang, L. and Gillespie, C. (1998), Improving the interpretability of TSK fuzzy models by combining global learning and local learning, *IEEE Trans. Fuzzy Systems*, **6**, (4), pp. 530–537.

Zadeh, L. A. (1997), Towards a theory of fuzzy information granulation and its centrality in human reasoning and fuzzy logic, *Fuzzy Sets and Systems*, **90**, pp. 111–117.

Index